Augmented Reality for Enhanced Learning Environments

Gerardo Reyes Ruiz
Universidad Autónoma del Estado de México, Mexico

Marisol Hernández Hernández
Universidad Autónoma del Estado de México, Mexico

A volume in the Advances in Computer and Electrical Engineering (ACEE) Book Series

IGI Global
DISSEMINATOR OF KNOWLEDGE

Published in the United States of America by
IGI Global
Information Science Reference (an imprint of IGI Global)
701 E. Chocolate Avenue
Hershey PA, USA 17033
Tel: 717-533-8845
Fax: 717-533-8661
E-mail: cust@igi-global.com
Web site: http://www.igi-global.com

Library of Congress Cataloging-in-Publication Data

Names: Reyes Ruiz, Gerardo, 1971- editor. | Hernandez Hernandez, Marisol, 1971- editor.
Title: Augmented reality for enhanced learning environments / Gerardo Reyes Ruiz and Marisol Hernandez Hernandez, editors.
Description: Hershey, PA : Information Science Reference, 2018. | Includes bibliographical references.
Identifiers: LCCN 2017037446| ISBN 9781522552437 (hardcover) | ISBN 9781522552444 (ebook)
Subjects: LCSH: Computer-assisted instruction. | Augmented reality. | Virtual reality in education.
Classification: LCC LB1044.87 .A94 2018 | DDC 371.33/468--dc23 LC record available at https://lccn.loc.gov/2017037446

This book is published in the IGI Global book series Advances in Computer and Electrical Engineering (ACEE) (ISSN: 2327-039X; eISSN: 2327-0403)

British Cataloguing in Publication Data
A Cataloguing in Publication record for this book is available from the British Library.

Advances in Computer and Electrical Engineering (ACEE) Book Series

ISSN:2327-039X
EISSN:2327-0403

Editor-in-Chief: Srikanta Patnaik, SOA University, India

MISSION

The fields of computer engineering and electrical engineering encompass a broad range of interdisciplinary topics allowing for expansive research developments across multiple fields. Research in these areas continues to develop and become increasingly important as computer and electrical systems have become an integral part of everyday life.

The **Advances in Computer and Electrical Engineering (ACEE) Book Series** aims to publish research on diverse topics pertaining to computer engineering and electrical engineering. **ACEE** encourages scholarly discourse on the latest applications, tools, and methodologies being implemented in the field for the design and development of computer and electrical systems.

COVERAGE

- VLSI Design
- Computer Architecture
- Optical Electronics
- Sensor Technologies
- Programming
- Computer science
- Circuit Analysis
- Qualitative Methods
- Computer Hardware
- Applied Electromagnetics

IGI Global is currently accepting manuscripts for publication within this series. To submit a proposal for a volume in this series, please contact our Acquisition Editors at Acquisitions@igi-global.com or visit: http://www.igi-global.com/publish/.

The Advances in Computer and Electrical Engineering (ACEE) Book Series (ISSN 2327-039X) is published by IGI Global, 701 E. Chocolate Avenue, Hershey, PA 17033-1240, USA, www.igi-global.com. This series is composed of titles available for purchase individually; each title is edited to be contextually exclusive from any other title within the series. For pricing and ordering information please visit http://www.igi-global.com/book-series/advances-computer-electrical-engineering/73675. Postmaster: Send all address changes to above address.

Titles in this Series

For a list of additional titles in this series, please visit:
https://www.igi-global.com/book-series/advances-computer-electrical-engineering/73675

Modeling and Simulations for Metamaterials Emerging Research and Opportunities
Ammar Armghan (Aljouf University, Saudi Arabia) Xinguang Hu (HuangShan University, China) and Muhammad Younus Javed (HITEC University, Paistan)
Engineering Science Reference • ©2018 • 171pp • H/C (ISBN: 9781522541806) • US $155.00

Electromagnetic Compatibility for Space Systems Design
Christos D. Nikolopoulos (National Technical University of Athens, Greece)
Engineering Science Reference • ©2018 • 346pp • H/C (ISBN: 9781522554158) • US $225.00

Soft-Computing-Based Nonlinear Control Systems Design
Uday Pratap Singh (Madhav Institute of Technology and Science, India) Akhilesh Tiwari (Madhav Institute of Technology and Science, India) and Rajeev Kumar Singh (Madhav Institute of Technology and Science, India)
Engineering Science Reference • ©2018 • 388pp • H/C (ISBN: 9781522535317) • US $245.00

EHT Transmission Performance Evaluation Emerging Research and Opportunities
K. Srinivas (Transmission Corporation of Andhra Pradesh Limited, India) and R.V.S. Satyanarayana (Sri Venkateswara University College of Engineering, India)
Engineering Science Reference • ©2018 • 160pp • H/C (ISBN: 9781522549413) • US $145.00

Fuzzy Logic Dynamics and Machine Prediction for Failure Analysis
Tawanda Mushiri (University of Johannesburg, South Africa) and Charles Mbowhwa (University of Johannesburg, South Africa)
Engineering Science Reference • ©2018 • 301pp • H/C (ISBN: 9781522532446) • US $225.00

Creativity in Load-Balance Schemes for Multi/Many-Core Heterogeneous Graph Computing...
Alberto Garcia-Robledo (Center for Research and Advanced Studies of the National Polytechnic Institute (Cinvestav-Tamaulipas), Mexico) Arturo Diaz-Perez (Center for Research and Advanced Studies of the National Polytechnic Institute (Cinvestav-Tamaulipas), Mexico) and Guillermo Morales-Luna (Center for Research and Advanced Studies of the National Polytechnic Institute (Cinvestav-IPN), Mexico)
Engineering Science Reference • ©2018 • 217pp • H/C (ISBN: 9781522537991) • US $155.00

For an entire list of titles in this series, please visit:
https://www.igi-global.com/book-series/advances-computer-electrical-engineering/73675

IGI Global
DISSEMINATOR OF KNOWLEDGE

701 East Chocolate Avenue, Hershey, PA 17033, USA
Tel: 717-533-8845 x100 • Fax: 717-533-8661
E-Mail: cust@igi-global.com • www.igi-global.com

Table of Contents

Detailed Table of Contents

The purpose of this chapter is to investigate the potential of augmented reality as an educational resource. The use of augmented reality technologies and the integration of augmented reality into learning environments will also be investigated in light of current learning approaches. In total, 153 full-text, accessible international articles and conference proceedings published between 2007 and 2016 on augmented reality were found on the web under the category of educational research on the Web of Science's SSCI. These studies were evaluated in terms of purpose, target group, rationale, method, approach, augmented reality environment components, findings, and contributions to the field. This chapter will identify the tendencies toward the use of augmented reality in educational research, fields of research, and the use of augmented reality tools that are suitable for different age groups. The findings of this study can serve a guide for future studies in this field.

The technology has now ventured into multiple educational environments. The case of augmented reality has served to create new digital environments of search that help the location of any physical reference in a public library. In these educational spaces, it is important to have information resources that are innovative and, simultaneously, which motivate the users to enter them. For physical learning resources, these informative tools must provide a fast and efficient inquiry/location. Augmented reality helps this location by showing, through digital content, the three-dimensional space (3D) of that location, highlighting categories and classifications of physical references so that, in turn, the user able to visualize it, using a mobile device, and is therefore directed to the exact place of the location in a relatively short time. Thus, this study shows that the application of new technologies in a public library can make the user feel immersed in a new learning environment, which is transmitted through a digital environment through augmented reality.

Instructional and training approaches have evolved to become more inclusive of active learning activities that include diverse types of technologies such as augmented reality (AR). Although AR is not a novel concept, it has only recently gained more recognition as being an effective tool to use in formal learning contexts. Researchers who have focused on the use of AR in educational and organizational settings have found that it helps to enhance learners' levels of motivation and their attainment of content knowledge and critical thinking and problem-solving skills. AR tools are also considered to be beneficial since they provide users the opportunity to experience real-world events that they may not be able to experience due to cost constraints (e.g., travel) and lack of prior training (e.g., mechanical equipment).

Around the world a large number of undesirable events, commonly called accidents, occur every year. These events have implications such as injuries of all kinds, fatalities (in many cases tens, hundreds, and thousands), infrastructure losses, economic losses, and negative impacts on the environment. After a detailed analysis of most of these events and the reflection about them, two aspects are obvious: the first is that they all have multiple causal factors and the second is that most are avoidable. There are many reasons why they are not avoided, but the main reason is the inability of individuals and organizations to learn from mistakes.

Autism spectrum disorder (ASD) is an umbrella term used to group a range of brain development disorders. The learning profile of most people with ASD is mainly visual, and VR and AR technologies offer important advantages to provide a visually based mean for gaining access to educational contents. The prices of VR and AR glasses and helmets have fallen. Also, a number of tools that facilitate the development and publication of AR and VR contents have recently appeared. Therefore, a scenario of opportunity for new developments has appeared in this field. This chapter offers guidelines for developing AR and VR learning contents for people on the autism spectrum and analyses those guidelines from the perspective of two important case studies developed in previous years.

The following chapter will discuss the impact of technology use and mobile learning, specifically augmented reality (AR), in the process of learning a second or foreign language, namely English and Spanish. The chapter will begin with an overview of AR and then include a discussion of the theoretical framework, language learning contexts, as well as AR tools and applications in the process of second or foreign language learning. An overview of the benefits of AR in language learning will also be included, as well as an introduction to AR applications and specific AR systems, platforms, and case studies in language learning. The research will also provide a discussion of the challenges of using AR in language learning contexts, including specific attention to challenges with AR and learning, AR and language learning, and mobile learning as a whole. The chapter will conclude with final thoughts from the authors in terms of potential areas of AR development that are in need of further attention.

This work uses augmented reality (AR) as a supplementary tool in teacher's evaluation of low environmental impact 3D concepts in industrial design, which are part of contents in subjects taken by fifth semester undergraduate students of Industrial Design at the Autonomous University of the State of Mexico (UAEM), specifically in the Tool Design Workshop. Design criteria are presented and they will be used to evaluate 3D concepts through the use of AR. The project is developed in three stages: 1) presenting the 3D concept through AR scenarios in order to be evaluated, 2) visual evaluation with established technical criteria, and 3) evaluation feedback so as to improve the 3D concept. The aim is to reduce evaluation subjectivity in order to reduce production costs, waste generation, and energy use in producing mockups and models.

Foreword

Undoubtedly the use of technology in the learning and training of different skills is fundamental in our days. Immersed within it, is the augmented reality (RA) where, like many other technologies, it provides new and varied ways of generating, exploring, analyzing, constructing and processing different types of information. The RA has had an important growth in almost all the areas of the knowledge, jointly, its application has had good acceptance in productive areas as they are it: the services and the commerce mainly.

The construction of learning environments, based on augmented reality, helps in the process of transforming information into knowledge. Until relatively recently, the levels of use of augmented reality were relatively scarce. However, due to accelerated technological advances and equipment portability, in software and hardware mainly, processing capacities are already achievable for a large part of the population. In short, there are portable and powerful equipment that can process applications with this type of technology.

The present book finds out in different fields of knowledge how augmented reality can be integrated into learning environments in different training areas. The main objective of the different chapters that make up the book is to contribute to the compression and transformation of data into useful information for decision-making in various areas of science, technology and innovation.

In this sense, interesting applications are delineated through the book, for example; a couple of chapters address the problem in the teaching of languages and develop learning environments based on augmented reality proposing new ways in which students master a foreign language; likewise, a group of researchers propose a 3D modeling to evaluate environmental elements in industrial design; Another chapter addresses the approach of scenarios that cause an accident or incident using augmented reality in order to learn, correct and deal with future undesired events. The researchers who contributed in the book not only build solutions in traditional learning environments, but address in training of education to people with different abilities In this context, there are proposals within the research that address scenarios for teaching-learning of students with autism.

Likewise, this project is a reflection of the joint work of researchers and experts from different countries, motivated by the use and approach of augmented reality in the daily work of each one of them.

Alejandro Barragán

Preface

The technological development has shown multiple and rapid advances in the last decades. These advances have undoubtedly strengthened the learning-learning strategies and this progress has been overcome every day by more efficient technologies, whose mission is to help students and teachers in their educational process.

Educational technologies are embedded with various devices and means of communication, these technologies have been making use of the Internet, mobile devices, the cybernetic cloud and different technological objects to support in a more efficient way the task of learning. However, Augmented Reality (AR) has emerged, as a technology that also supports educational environments, but which, within its most salient features, is a very efficient alternative that supports abstract educational content to make it easier to understand by the students.

Over time, economic models based on the exploitation and export of natural resources, mostly non-renewable, have been gradually displaced by economic models based on education. Human capital, in an economy based increasingly on the level of knowledge, is the key element that allows the technological, economic and social development of a territory. Much of the human capital models emphasize the way in which education enriches an entire production process, so that it, in turn, benefits from the externalities that a society generates by having a higher level of education. Therefore, the level of knowledge is essential to allow the generation of innovation and its adoption by others.

The role of human capital and training in the so-called technology transfer is increasingly widely recognized. This means of technology transfer is presented in a variety of ways, including, among others, training specifically aimed at the management of technology transfer, the use of specialized consultants, the training of students (taking into account their international training), the exchange or transfer of specialized personnel and, of course, the informal relationships that exist between the different scientific levels.

The need to have better prepared human resources and innovative ideas, whether generated during their studies or not, motivates the research community to respond, even in a timely manner, to each of the problems generated, in turn, for those needs. In this context, it makes sense to create and provide a new form of learning for a specific group of students, in particular students of some degree. The transfer of knowledge has gradually evolved over time, and it is also logical that teaching (which is nothing more than the process of education) also does so. Thus, the new generations of students must be prepared for the challenges that the new technologies bring.

In an environment where some countries are emerging from recession at different speeds and some others remain in a gloomy economic environment, education plays a vital role in decreasing the negative impact of global economic problems. In this sense, new technologies favor education to generate human resources with a better educational quality. The subject regarding the transfer of technology and, simultaneously, knowledge has been the object of study of multiple research works. However, at the same time, multiple researches around the world have shown that aid to developing countries consisting only in the transfer of capital would not be sufficient if the country does not have an adequate level of human capital to derive all the possible benefit of that aid. Therefore, and through new technologies, it is essential to create a new horizon in science and technology in terms of favoring and / or strengthening the current learning system in all areas of knowledge.

Augmented Reality (AR) emerged in the year of 1996, when ARQuake was presented, the first outdoor game with mobile RA devices, developed by Bruce H. Thomas. Then, in 2008, the WIkitude tour and travel guide application was released, which was made using augmented reality by means of a digital compass, orientation and accelerometer sensors, maps, video and informative content from Wikipedia. In 2009, ARToolkit emerged, which is a platform totally oriented to generate RA. From these applications, the RA has been used as a basis for numerous projects in different areas, ranging from entertainment, industry, maintenance, music, medicine and education, among others. Moreover, very specific applications have been made as a harp that was designed for people with disabilities, which works through vibrations.

In the industry, through the development of manuals with RA, it has been shown that the performance of workers who use this type of manuals is modified in a palpable improvement compared to workers who use manuals made with paper. This result is mainly due to the behavioral, physiological and psychological data of the workers. Therefore, the use of RA in the orientation of the assembly of products has been widely recommended. In addition, this technique includes retrieval of information and real-time assembly and encourages the reduction of assembly error, all under the cognitive workload and high skill transfer to improve tasks. Intelligent Tutorial Systems (STI) have also been made, such as the "Intelligent Augmented Reality Training for Motherboard Assembly", which helps with training for manual assembly tasks.

In the educational field, with the AR, molecular structures, mathematics, architecture, astronomy and physical activities can be taught to children with disabilities. In medicine and education, specialized projects have been developed that show the RA as an efficient tool in the learning of medicine, such as the "An Interactive Augmented Reality System for Learning Anatomy Structure" that is composed of three activities ; the first is to show the parts of the anatomical structure of the human body, the second is that it allows the students to identify each anatomical part of the human body and the third allows to glimpse in depth the internal parts of the aforementioned anatomical structure.

The main audience of the present proposal are the teachers/professors and even researchers who want to adapt their knowledge to the new technologies in order to enrich the transfer of their knowledge to their respective students. Without a doubt, the process can not be immediate. However, what is desired with this work is to motivate both the teacher and all those students who are interested in the new learning environments through the RA.

The present work increases the characteristics exposed in the immediately previous text, since the proposals will serve to learn processes composed of three-dimensional elements, processes in which the students will learn activities that could hardly do it in a traditional way. Because the way of learning can include different senses such as sight, hearing, touch, this work proposes interactive platforms that contain elements related to these senses and with the purpose of making learning more complete, dynamic and interactive between the teacher and student. Therefore, the present work sets out as a general objective to show new learning platforms, through the RA, that serve to strengthen the knowledge assimilated by the students.

We believe that our book is innovative from the very moment of its approach, since today there are no works that have addressed the problem we have described. In addition, we are completely confident that our contribution will contribute to the generation of new projects and research. The challenges are many and very important, but we are aware that a contribution like ours would be of great importance to expand the current learning horizon and why not, to create new areas of knowledge or reinforce those that are not yet fully known in the international arena.

The creation of new learning platforms, through the RA, will allow students from any area of knowledge to obtain quality knowledge as well as a correct approach to new technologies for the timely execution and/or development of their activities. In order to acquire competences of know-how, students must learn to perform new procedures. Some of these procedures can be simulated with RA. Thus, various platforms with these qualities are a suitable means of training for each student to evaluate their own learning.

The main problem solved by this proposal is to contribute to the decrease of dropout and/or dropping out of school, since by making the dynamics of the classes more interesting and attractive, the student will not be absent from them. It is also important to mention that this work aims to motivate both the teacher and the student so that both generate better dynamics in the transfer of knowledge.

The multiple scenarios offered by the RA are extremely competent. They can also be adopted in various fields of knowledge. Moreover, there are applications that target the mass market for advertising, entertainment and education. However, this work is unique because there are currently no contributions of this nature. That is to say, we have not seen many works that seek to motivate both teachers and students through new learning environments, carried out through the RA. Consequently, from its precise approach, this contribution is different in relation to any that could exist in the educational market of the RA.

Surely the most interested in this book will be the teachers because they will have at their disposal innovative and innovative material for their classes. That is to say, with the RA the professors can carry out more innovative work dynamics and, surely, the new technologies would be a catalyst aspect so that the students learn in a more emotional way and, with this, develop more aptitudes and skills in the class. However, our proposal is not limited to being a didactic material or support material for teaching activities. This material is also aimed at students of the area with or without specific knowledge about the RA so that they feel motivated to develop new applications, processes or software that help and strengthen the transfer of knowledge in a classroom.

The potential readers will find in the book innovative proposals for class dynamics. The works that will integrate the book will be totally new ideas, since nowadays there are no books that integrate proposals of this nature. There are books that use the RA to show applications made with this new technology but there are no books that contain a whole process and / or procedure to perform an entire activity with the students. Undoubtedly, our proposal also aims to motivate researchers to use the RA in some process—or several—that is interesting for their research dynamics.

We are also convinced that creating and/or promoting new educational environments will improve the quality of teaching/learning. And not only of the students but also of the teachers who choose to introduce the augmented RA to their teaching activities. We are confident that the creation of a new learning platform, through the RA, will allow students from any area of knowledge to obtain quality knowledge as well as a correct approach to new technologies for the timely execution of their activities.

To acquire the know-how skills, students must learn to perform new and innovative procedures. These processes can be simulated with RA. A platform with these qualities is a means of training for each student to evaluate their own learning, before realizing it in real life. Therefore, this book sets out as a general objective to show new platforms that serve for the learning of some educational procedures.

In addition, in the aforementioned platforms, students will be able to train these educational processes and repeat them as many times as they wish since the respective system will provide metrics for evaluating the processes as well as feedback from the system. Each platform can be used as a coach before students perform those processes in real life. In turn, this platform would entail having a system that would be understood as a set of useful tools to apply them in the teaching-learning process with an integral approach that contains a simulator, a trainer, a visualizer and a learning evaluator. This platform would be a new way of learning and whose main advantage, among others, would be the accessibility to any student, since its price would be relatively low.

In addition to the above, each new learning platform describes, in turn, the design of a system such as the establishment of data structures, the general architecture of software and the representations of interfaces and algorithms. That is, the process that translates the requirements into software specifications. The objective of the design phase is to publicize the behavior of the proposed solution; this is conceived taking into account that the design is a pre-phase that starts the construction of programs and/or processes of activities that are usually carried out by users, which seek to improve by adding speed, efficiency, efficiency, savings and design visual. The first action, which starts with the design, is the determination of the architecture of the system, which is nothing more than the hierarchical structure of the modules of the program, which is focused on how to interact between its components and the structure of the data used by them.

Today, there are several architectural styles of software. However, due to the nature of the system that is intended to be built and the one that should be modeled is the "Service Oriented Architecture" (SOA), which is an architecture paradigm for designing and developing distributed systems and has been created to provide ease and flexibility of integration with legacy systems as well as direct alignment to business processes thus reducing implementation costs. Another advantage is that it implements the innovation of customer services and an agile adaptation to changes, including an early reaction to competitiveness.

The knowledge necessary to understand the proposals that will make up our book are not specialized. Therefore, we consider that our proposal has a greater scope, since by being oriented to students, professors, software developers, and even to researchers, then the potential market segment increases. This will undoubtedly allow a higher level of sales and a greater distribution of our work. We are convinced that the transfer of knowledge has changed over time and, therefore, proposals that use innovative ideas such as ours will be a clear reference for future contributions in this educational field.

Acknowledgment

The coordinators of this book Gerardo Reyes Ruiz and Marisol Hernández Hernández thank the support of CONACYT de México, through the project of Basic Science 254087, for the realization of their work.

Chapter 1
Augmented Reality:
Educational Resources

Mustafa Serkan Abdusselam
Giresun University, Turkey

Ebru Turan Güntepe
Giresun University, Turkey

ABSTRACT

The purpose of this chapter is to investigate the potential of augmented reality as an educational resource. The use of augmented reality technologies and the integration of augmented reality into learning environments will also be investigated in light of current learning approaches. In total, 153 full-text, accessible international articles and conference proceedings published between 2007 and 2016 on augmented reality were found on the web under the category of educational research on the Web of Science's SSCI. These studies were evaluated in terms of purpose, target group, rationale, method, approach, augmented reality environment components, findings, and contributions to the field. This chapter will identify the tendencies toward the use of augmented reality in educational research, fields of research, and the use of augmented reality tools that are suitable for different age groups. The findings of this study can serve a guide for future studies in this field.

INTRODUCTION

The habits and interests of students change each passing day due to rapid technological developments. Developments in technology and changing interests make it necessary to design educational environments based on current conditions. The attention of students and educators can be enhanced by augmented reality (AR). AR began to be

DOI: 10.4018/978-1-5225-5243-7.ch001

used in the twentieth century but became widespread in the twenty-first century. The areas where it is used are accelerating, especially in recent years, and it is envisaged to spread in this century. AR makes its users' world more understandable with digital information and provides interaction between technological tools and information.

New technologies have been developed to use data efficiently and in a favorable way with computers; these technologies have gained importance through developments in the last century and are being widely used. AR technology is one of these technologies is (Vallino, 1998). AR is a knowledge processing process that "augments" the individual's understanding by presenting computer-derived virtual data or visuals and the real environment images. AR also images the real world directly or indirectly through digital objects; following that, it develops and enriches the real world by adding perceptual digital-generated inputs such as audio, video, graphics, and GPS location information along with these digital objects. Thus, the perceived reality becomes, in a sense, enriched.

It can be argued that the AR-supported application environment provides more diversity and usage area in the current applications because it is based on the real world independently from time and place (Wang & Duston, 2007). This suggests AR might be of interest in the field of education as well as in many other fields. The use of an AR environment is inevitable, considering the advantages it provides (Krevelen & Poelman, 2010). This environment is preferred in education, especially because it interacts the reality with the virtual perfectly; it can create the virtual objects by interfaces, control it during the application, and combine the real and virtual environments (Billinghurst, 2002). Furthermore, AR is more successful than a normal desktop-based learning activity because it enhances students' interest in the lesson: the visualized 3D objects can attract students' attention more easily (Winn et al., 2002). One of the criteria that affect the success of augmented reality environments is how close the digital objects created by developers are to reality. Design success, calibration, and illumination are key elements in the real appearance of digital objects. Design success is related to understanding the purposes of virtual objects, why they are used, and what changes mean so that AR environment is achieved in the desired way (Wagner & Barakonyi, 2003; Winkler et al., 2002).

It has become inevitable for AR technology to take part in educational environments within the framework of the above-mentioned points, and the researchers' tendency to use these technologies in education environments has increased. In this regard, this investigation aims to reveal the current situation by examining the studies about AR in the field of education. Existing studies will be brought together systematically so that the researchers who wish to study in this field will be able to obtain in-depth information. This is significant for identification of existing deficiencies.

BACKGROUND

Students are surrounded by a great network of knowledge in today's world. Students' previous experiences, content knowledge, cognitive, and motivational individual differences influence their construction of knowledge (Alexander et al., 1998). The success of combining real and virtual environments and making virtual statements meaningful are significant in bringing the two environments together. This makes it easier to construct knowledge (Zagoranski & Digipak, 2003). AR environments contribute to education because they contribute to the development of students' psychomotor skills and activate more sense organs in learning by including more sensors (Hanson & Shelton, 2008). AR environments are not burdensome because virtual objects are transferred to the real environment (Woods et al., 2004): they help individuals increase their personal experience because they enable participants to become practitioners (Matsumoto, 2009; Müller et al., 2007; Müller & Ferreira, 2004).

Three-dimensional activities in the AR environment play a key role in enabling students to learn concepts such as position, angle, rotation, and turning. This appears to be an effective technology that helps students to embody concepts in their minds (Shelton & Hedley, 2002; 2004). AT technology offers advantages to students when it is adapted to the learning environment with the understanding that students themselves can perform learning activities or new activities. Students actively participate in their own learning in the AR-based learning environments because such environments provide students with the opportunities of scientific thinking, hypothesizing, and testing those hypothesizes (Winn, Windschitl, Fruland, & Lee, 2002).

Over the last two decades, the AR applications used in different areas of education have become widespread and enriched in terms of its content. Students can experience learning that is contextual and on-site to explore the real word data in the virtual environment and simulations.

- Students can gain new powerful ways to embody the abstract relationship and connection with the digital objects that are enriched with the data based on real world.
- Student can reach the location maps and the data about their environment thanks to the AR outdoor use. Similarly, it is possible to automatically reach the geographically coded data while organizing field observations and records.

It is necessary to revise the education system according to the current learning approaches to equip individuals with the necessary skills of the twenty-first-century societies based on scientific and technological developments. As an alternative to the traditional approaches, there is a need for the approaches that attract students' attention more and can create the desired effect on students. The old-fashioned teaching methods, the lack of the applications in which students are active, and the inability to actively use the up-to-date educational technologies in the classrooms are among the reasons behind this situation. In addition, the lack of context in education provided in the traditional environment does not reflect the nature of the learner and the real world, and the relationship between the learner and the real world.

The approaches such as game-based learning, project-based learning, challenge-based learning, inquiry-based learning, situated learning, collaboration-based learning, and problem-based learning are adopted in the published studies about AR. This chapter will touch upon the approaches that have the potential to become prominent in the AR field.

AR and Current Learning Approaches

Lave and Wenger (1991) pointed out that it is impossible to solve the problems encountered in the daily life within the scope of solely one discipline because they fall under the scope of more than one discipline. Therefore, there is a need to address interdisciplinary approaches based on current necessities (Bybee, 2010; Shirazi & Behzadan 2015) and the approaches that attach importance to context (Coştu, 2009; Crawford, 2001; Lave & Wenger, 1991) as a neutral consequence of the development and transformation. Through this, students will be able to apply their new knowledge using innovative technologies and transfer this knowledge to create new knowledge.

Interdisciplinary learning approaches that deal with the knowledge and skills that are generated through the combination of different context and disciplines such as Situated Learning and Science, Technology, Engineering, and Mathematics (STEM) Education (Coştu, 2009; Turna, Bolat, & Keskin, 2012) should be addressed to assist individuals to better understand the world and to find innovative solutions to the problems they encountered, as required by the nature of AR (Dönmez Usta, 2011).

Situated Learning

In traditional learning environments, knowledge is seen an abstract concept that is obtained outside the context, not as a part of the context. However, learning and thinking should be considered not only in the interpersonal processes but also in realistic situations. Lave and Wenger (1991) ascertain that because uncontextual education given in the traditional environment does not reflect the nature of the learner and the real world, and the relationship between the learner and the real world. Students cannot be thought of as an empty vase that can be filled with the knowledge by their teachers. On the contrary, students can learn in the community of practice in which they actively play a role, through the interactions with others who are the participants of the community like themselves. A community of practice is a community in which individuals with the same interest come together, share activities, help each other, and learn new information. Individuals, both teachers and students, try to understand the world by shaping the realistic context in which they exist. In brief, situated learning is achieved through the participation of the individuals in the community of the practice and through the interaction with each other.

Anchored Instruction developed by the Cognition and Technology Group at Vanderbilt, (CTGV) (1990, 1997) is an approach that is based on Situated Learning Theory and transports this theory to the classroom. In this approach, realistic stories in which meaningful problems and the information necessary to solve these problems are included are presented to students via video technology. The main purpose of this approach is to elicit the knowledge that is called inert knowledge and that individuals do not use during problem-solving; yet, remember when asked explicitly (CTGV, 1990, 1997). This approach provides students with different perspectives in the rich and complex problem-solving environments. This approach includes 7 design principles that can be present in various learning environments such as science, geography, language, and reading. In this approach, conducted in a form of case study, learning and teaching activities are designed within the frame of a complex problem situation and solving the subproblems required for students to solve the complex problem is achieved through providing them a way to discover these activities (CTGV,1990).

STEM Education

The STEM education approach, which is assumed to be one of the most important educational movements in the recent years, is a contemporary learning approach that approaches real-world problems in the learning environments by establishing connection among the disciplines of science, technology, engineering, and mathematics (Bybee, 2010). For many years, several countries have been conducting studies about the STEM educational approach (Scott, 2009). STEM and engineering education, which have gained great importance in recent years, are thought to play a significant role in producing solutions to real-life problems in the light of the scientific knowledge.

The old-fashioned and ineffective teaching methods and the lack of using educational technologies and hands-on activities are among the important reasons why students do not follow STEM disciplines (Chen & Soldner, 2014; Shirazi

& Behzadan 2015). STEM education prevents this situation by using different educational tools such as scaffolding, informal learning, and digital visualization (Yoon et al., 2011). Students in a riveting learning environment such as STEM education can try to better understand complex scientific concepts (Johnson et al., 2013). Moreover, collaborative studies can be supported thanks to an effective AR technology involving visualization tools (Dunston & Wang, 2005; Shirazi & Behzadan 2015). In addition, the use of AR can be proposed for STEM education with the help of various AR-based educational activities independent of teachers' prior knowledge about programming.

The use of AR has changed learning activities, to a great extent because of mobile and wearable devices. Thanks to the increasing processing power of these devices, it is possible to use AR inside or outside the classroom with increasing number of AR applications (Figueiredo, 2015). Considering the studies about the AR use in science education, the visualization tools are found to provide positive outcomes in terms of embodying abstract theories (Dori & Belcher, 2005; Sengupta & Wilensky, 2009; Yoon et al., 2011). In mathematics education, AR technologies may be a motivator for students because they can spend more time on problem-solving practice, and they are accessible by students and are easily used tools (Figueiredo, 2015).

AR Components

The components of an AR environment are presented in Figure 1. In the figure, these components are listed as application interface, application system, programming library, tracking methods, imaging equipment, application universe, and application environment.

Application Universe

This component consists of three main categories: head mounted, handheld, and spatial. Digital lenses and glasses are head-mounted devices; mobile devices and smartwatches are handhelds; tools that are directly related to the environment and indirectly related to individuals such as screens, and projectors in belong to the spatial category. However, the handheld category is often preferred in the application universe component of AR environment in terms of cost and usability.

Application Environment

This component consists of three main categories. An appropriate application environment should be selected according to the designed scenario. AR applications

Figure 1. AR Components (Developed, ᵝ Developing digital objects)*
Source (Karal & Abdusselam, 2015)

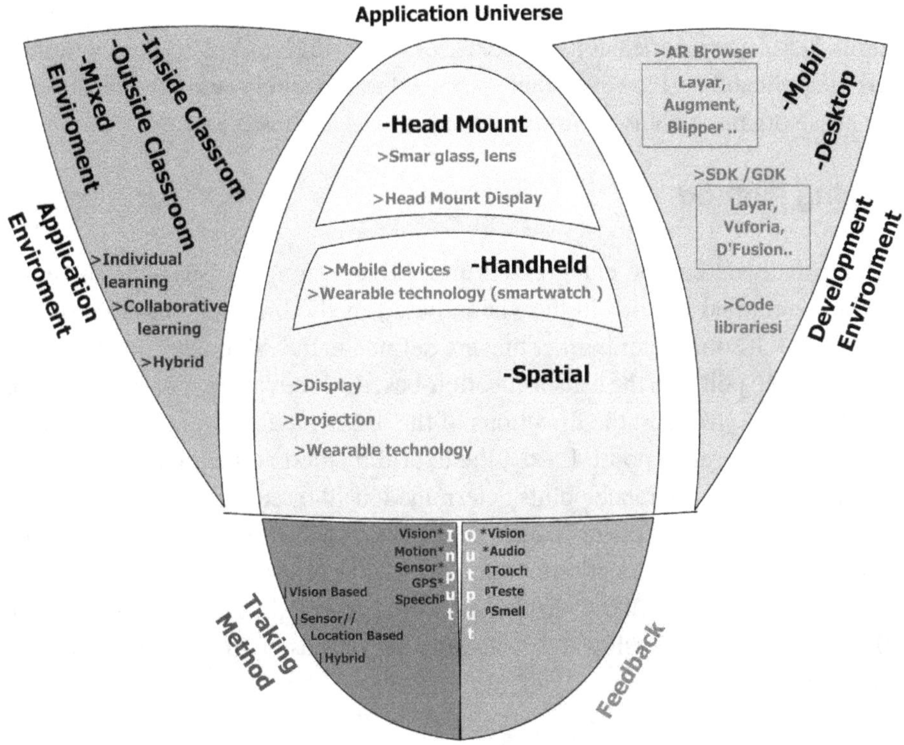

are mostly conducted in the classroom because educational activities are nowadays conducted in the classroom. However, it is thought that non-class activities will become widespread, and the mixed environments will come to the forefront day by day.

Development Environment

The software and interfaces that developers will use vary based on their programming skills. AR browsers that are not required any programming literacy can be used in Android and iOS platforms. Some of these browsers are BlippAR, Layar, Junaioi, and Augment. A developer with moderate programming skill can benefit from these environments by uploading a software developer kit (SDK) that can be integrated to the software development environments. A developer with high programming skill, on the other hand, can develop AR applications directly through libraries and code blocks.

Feedback

In today's applications, the focus is the representation of digital objects such as pictures, text, three-dimensional models, or video that appeal to the eyesight in terms of applicability. However, there is a need to separately study the feedback on other sense organs such as vibration, sound, smell, and taste.

Tracking Method

Tracking methods can be categorized under three groups: vision-based, sensor/location-based, and hybrid. In the vision-based method, the photograph, picture, tag, logo, 2D/3D objects or marker that are defined in the AR environment are used as the reference point. In the sensor/location-based AR environments, the data from GPS, RFID, or sensors in the directions of the user's navigation in the application is used as the reference point. Lastly, the hybrid method is the application of both these methods. The reference points determined in all three methods provide a way to locate the digital objects on which place, how, and with which angle and how to update the image and location in the real environment based on these reference points (Dunleavy et al., 2009). In the software presented in the AR field and the applications developed using this software, vision-based studies were the most often encountered.

FOCUS OF THE CHAPTER

Issues, Controversies, Problems

This study aims to determine the components of AR technology based on the educational studies conducted about AR between 2007 and 2016. The study was designed as a document analysis design, a qualitative research method. The study intended to determine the subdimensions of AR and the data was collected by a document analysis method. Content analysis was used to analyze and interpret the data. As from the analysis, the answers to the following questions were sought:

1. What are the purposes of AR for use in the educational studies?
2. What are the target groups in the studies?
3. What are the preferred research methods in the studies?
4. Which is the AR application environment that researchers prefer?
5. Which is the AR application universe that researchers prefer?
6. What are the researchers' preferences for the development of AR application?

7. What are the researchers' preferences for AR tracking methods and feedback?
8. In which fields of education are AR applications used?

Methodology

Document analysis design, a qualitative research method, was used in the study because it aimed to obtain in-depth information and explain the relationship among the obtained data. Document analysis is aimed at deeply examining a subject and making new inferences by analyzing the written documents (Patton, 2014). In addition, this study adopted document analysis design because it enables the researcher to collect data from persons who cannot otherwise be easily reached, have an opportunity to analyze the data for a long time, access a large sample, and pursue a qualified working process (Creswell, 2012).

The data in the documents that the researcher obtained have been checked previously; this makes it possible to have qualified data, and thus the validity and reliability of the study are enhanced. Because the document analysis method has features that make it possible to collect data over a long period of time, that ensure collecting qualified data (Bailey, 2008), and that access individual and authentic data, (Creswell, 2012), this method was adopted as a guide for this study.

There are various stages to follow when conducting document analysis. Basically, document analysis goes through five different stages: accessing the documents, confirming originality, understanding the documents, analyzing the data, and using the data (Bailey, 2008). These stages were followed in this study.

Accessing Documents

At the beginning of the document analysis, the researcher determines the types of documents to be analyzed and the methods used to obtain documents (Patton, 2014). In the present study, the related documents were obtained from the Web of Science database. To ensure that the documents are reliable and valid, the databases covering educational research, and studies in the field of education were preferred. In this way, the study aimed that the documents to be used in the document analysis were collected from correct and competent sources. The keywords used to browse the databases were determined after a consulting the opinions of a field expert and the evaluations of the researcher. In this study, a member of the faculty of education who had been conducting studies on AR for 8 years was preferred. Another influential component in the keyword selection process was considered for the previous studies. The keywords included in this study were discussed with the field experts, and they were used after the researcher evaluated them. While conducting an evaluation on the keywords, the researcher considered the relations of the preferred keywords with the research questions. Thereby, the aim was to ensure that the accessed documents were related to the research. Upon searching the keywords "educational research" and "Augmented Reality", applying the filters determined by the researcher, and evaluation of the abstracts and titles of each study, 153 articles were subjected to investigation.

Because it was found out that AR was first used in education around the early 2000s and with the developments in technology the studies of AR in the field of education became diversified between 2007 and 2016, this study focused on the AR studies published during the last ten years. Along with this, to ensure the reliability of the obtained documents, only international articles and conference proceedings were considered for the study.

In document analysis, the collected documents were investigated from the perspectives of purpose, target group, rationale, method, approach, augmented reality environment components, findings and contributions to the field; they were then compared using these aspects. At the end of the investigation, the obtained studies were not classified under themes. The data collected from the sample were subjected to content analysis, and new themes and codes were determined. In the analysis of the data, first, the sample was determined because of an investigation of the documents in terms of their titles, abstracts, and contents by the researcher. At the end of the sampling, the studies were analyzed from the perspectives of purpose, methodology, and findings. In the analysis stage, the sentences and words in the related sections of the studies were considered as the unit of analysis, and the data were analyzed through content analysis; as a result, themes and categories were determined. The components obtained upon the analysis of the studies were listed. Then, the list was subjected to content analysis and associated with the AR components.

RESULTS

The data were analyzed by content analysis. The subheadings for the determined research questions were examined in detail and presented in tables.

What Are the Purposes of AR Use in the Educational Studies?

Most of the studies indicated that AR applications are preferred in education to increase the academic success of its users. The purposes of AR use in the educational studies are listed in Table 1. 204 purposes were inferred from a total of 153 studies that were examined within the scope of this study; some studies indicated multiple purposes.

Table 1. The purposes of AR use in the educational environments

Purpose	f	%
Academic achievement	74	36
Developing the use of teaching system	53	26
Alternative learning	36	18
Gaining behavior/experience	16	8
Attitude	11	5
Motivation	7	3
AR satisfaction	4	2
The perspectives about AR	3	1
Total	**204**	**100**

Table 1 indicates that AR technology was used in the educational studies to increase academic achievement by 36%; to develop the use of the existing teaching system and support students' learning by 26%; to provide an alternative learning environment by 18%; to provide students gain behavior/experience by 8%, to determine attitudes by 5%, to examine motivation by 3%, and to determine the perspectives about AR by 1%.

What Are the Target Groups in the Studies?

The researchers used AR technologies for teachers and parents as well as for students. They also had the opportunity to apply simultaneously more than one group, such as both teachers and students. This indicates that the technology is used in every process of education. However, a more frequent preference for the technology was determined during K-12 and university education. The target groups determined in the studies are listed in Table 2.

As shown in Table 2, 85% of the AR applications in the educational studies were conducted with students, 37% with K-12, 28% with universities, 3% with teachers, and 1% parents.

What Are the Preferred Research Methods in the Studies?

The preferred research methods varied because some studies examine adopted different aims and thus different research questions. Case study, narrative method, phenomenology, design-based, and document analysis are examples of qualitative research, whereas experimental method, survey method, and metaanalysis are

Table 2. The target groups in the educational environment

Group	Area	f		%	
Student	K-12	58	133	37	85
	University	43		28	
	Lifelong	26		17	
	Preschool	6		4	
Teacher	4			3	
Parent	2			1	
Unspecified	17			11	
Total	156			100	

examples of quantitative research. It was observed that mixed methods are also used, as well as both these methods. The preferred research methods are listed in Table 3.

As seen in Table 3, 58% of the studies were designed as a qualitative study, 28% were designed as a quantitative study, and 13% were designed as a mixed method study.

Which Is the AR Application Environment That Researchers Prefer?

Learning occurs not only in the classroom but also outside classrooms and in the mixed environments. In these learning environments, some studies adopted individual and collaborative learning and some studies adopted a combination of individual and collaborative learning. Researchers included AR applications in different environments. The classroom environment was found to be more preferred as compared with other environments. The AR application environments that researchers prefer are listed in Table 4.

Preferences for application environment generally vary as inside classroom, outside classroom, and mixed. However, the application of each was diversified as individual, collaborative, and hybrid. Considering the in-class environments, 25%

Table 3. The preferred research methods

Method	f	%
Quantitative	88	58
Qualitative	45	29
Mixed	20	13
Total	**153**	**100**

Table 4. The AR application environments that researchers prefer

Application Environment	Usage	f	%
Inside classroom	Individual	39	25
	Collaborative	36	24
	Hybrid	8	5
Outside classroom	Individual	27	18
	Collaborative	20	13
	Hybrid	1	1
Mixed	Individual	5	3
	Hybrid	1	1
Unspecified	16		10
Total	**153**		**100**

were individual, 21% were collaborative, and 5% were hybrid. Considering the outside-class applications, 18% were individual, 13% were collaborative, and 1% were hybrid. Lastly, considering the mixed applications, 5% were individual and 1% were hybrid.

Which Is the AR Application Universe That Researchers Prefer?

The hardware that individuals use has diversified with the development of technology. The weight of hardware has been gradually lowered, and processors have become more powerful. The hardware has been enriched with different capabilities, and their use has become diversified thanks to these developments. In this sense, hardware has provided the ability to use more than one universe at the same time. Basically, these universes can be classified as handheld screens, head mount, spatial, or mixed. The AR application universes that researchers prefer are listed in Table 5.

Table 5. The AR application universes that researchers prefer

Universe	F	%
Handheld screens	66	43
Spatial	61	40
Head mount	14	9
Mixed	12	8
Total	**153**	**100**

As seen in Table 5, handheld screens, in general, are preferred by 43%, whereas space screens are preferred by 40%. Mixed universes are preferred by 8%, whereas the head mount universe accounts for 9%.

What Are the Researchers' Preferences for AR Application Development?

Developing an AR-based application is as complicated as it is simple. In this process, although there is a need for good programming skills to develop an AR application, applications can be developed with drag-and-drop only through AR browsers. The preferences for the development of AR application are listed in Table 6.

As seen in Table 6, the developers preferred software development kit (SDK) most, by 36%. AR applications were directly developed via coding knowledge by 18% and AR browsers were used by 14%. However, the researchers did not mention the development environment of the applications that are used or developed, at a rate of 33%.

What Are the Researchers' Preferences for AR Tracking Methods and Feedback?

AR tracking methods apply a rich range of hardware and techniques. However, in the AR environment, a reference point is required about in which place, how, and with which angle the digital object is visualized in the environment in which the individual lives. Basically, this reference point can be grouped in two ways. The first is to determine a reference point by analyzing an image, movement, and object in the environment in which the individual lives with the camera of the system used. The second is to determine a reference point in the system is used via sensors, without cameras. The first tracking methods are designated vision-based; the second is designated sensor/location-based. The preferences for AR tracking methods are listed in Table 7.

Table 6. The preferences for the development of AR application

Option	F	%
SDK	55	36
Coding	27	18
Browser	21	14
Unspecified	50	33
Total	**153**	**100**

Table 7. The preferences for AR tracking methods

Method	Content	f	%
Vision based	Marker	46	28
	2D objects	33	20
	Gesture-based	26	16
	3D objects	15	9
Sensor/Location based	Sensor	21	13
	GPS	16	10
	Haptic	4	2
Hybrid	6		4
Total	**167**		**100**

Table 7 indicates that considering the vision-based method, 28% of the preferences are a marker, 20% of them are 2D objects, 16% of them are gesture-based, and 9% of them are 3D objects. Considering the sensor/location-based method, 13% of the preferences are for sensors, 10% of them are for GPS, and 2% of them are for haptics, and hybrid methods constituted 4% of the total preferences.

The main purpose of using tracking methods is to determine when and how to provide feedback to the user. The success of feedback depends significantly on good tracking. In addition, achieving the aims that are set within the scope of the study depends on adequate feedback. The quality of feedback can affect learning in a positive way: the AR application has a lasting impact to the extent that feedback addresses as many sense organs as possible. For this reason, some researchers opted to use more than one type of feedback at the same time. The types of feedback used in AR environments are listed in Table 8.

As seen in Table 8, of the types of feedback, 62% are 3D images/models, 17% are 2D images, 10% are videos, 9% are pictures, and 2% are smell-sound.

Table 8. The types of feedback used in AR environments

Type	F	%
3D images/models	107	62
2D images	29	17
Video	18	10
Picture	15	9
Smell-Sound	3	2
Total	**172**	**100**

In Which Fields of Education Are AR Applications Used?

When the AR applications that have been developed in the field of education were examined within the scope of the study, it was determined that AR applications were developed in many fields—from science to social science. The frequencies of the studies about AR in the field of education are presented in Table 9.

As seen in Table 9, of the AR studies in the field of education, 29% were conducted in technology and science, 23% were conducted in technology and engineering. Notably, the studies about the AR-based learning environment constituted 14% of the studies. In other fields, fewer studies were conducted compared to this field.

DISCUSSION

The use of information technologies has brought about many changes in the types of learning and teaching (Figueiredo, 2015; Fernandes & Ferreira, 2012). One of these changes is the learning thanks to the interaction that is experienced through AR use (Johnson et al., 2012). In the studies examined for this analysis, AR technology appears to play a supporting role in students' learning processes and is particularly used in the context of understanding abstract situations. When the concepts that are abstract for the student are embodied through this technology, an increase in academic achievement will be possible by facilitating the learning process. Researchers have particularly attempted to develop alternative learning environments by supporting the existing teaching system with AR technology. These alternative learning environments are known to facilitate the learning process, increase motivation (Wang

Table 9. The frequencies of the studies about AR in the field of education (152)

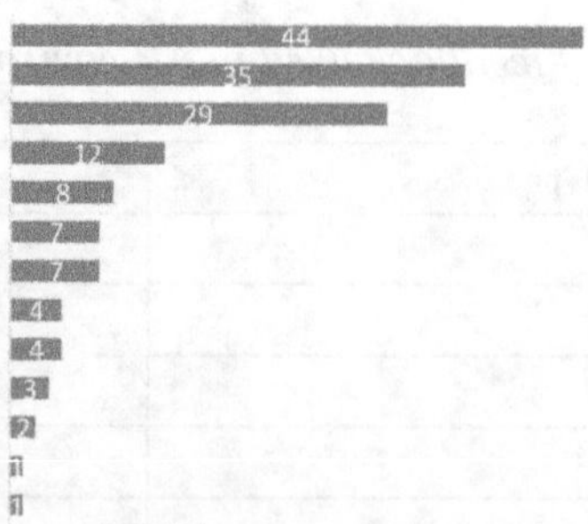

	f	%
TECHNOLOGY AND SCIENCE	44	28
TECHNOLOGY AND ENGINEERING	35	22
TECHNOLOGY AND LEARNING ENVIRONMENT	29	18
TECHNOLOGY AND LANGUAGE EDUCATION	12	7
TECHNOLOGY AND MATHEMATICS EDUCATION	8	5
TECHNOLOGY AND GEOGRAPHY	7	4
TECHNOLOGY AND HISTORY	7	4
TECHNOLOGY AND HEALTH	4	3
TECHNOLOGY AND MUSIC	4	3
TECHNOLOGY AND LIFELONG LEARNING	3	2
TECHNOLOGY AND PAINTING	2	1
TECHNOLOGY AND ART	1	1
TECHNOLOGY AND PRESCHOOL	1	1
Total	**152**	**100**

& Duston, 2007), and help to comprehend difficult concepts (Quarles et al., 2008). This situation might stem from the integration of three-dimensional realistic objects to the learning environment through AR technology. Similarly, the association of learning process with the daily life are known to facilitate learning. In this context, activities that establish the connection between technology and daily life become prominent in the educational applications of AR (Quarles et al., 2008). The fact that AR environments attract students' attention and allow them to monitor the learning process carefully enables them to benefit from these technologies outside the learning environment. These technologies create opportunities for students to explore the subjects that they are curious about in daily life outside of school (Lin et al., 2011).

In the studies examined, researchers primarily prefer qualitative studies to examine the developed environment adequately and obtain in-depth findings. Because AR technology is a developing field, directed researchers have been inspired to obtain more information. The fact that none of the research methods were predominantly preferred indicates how rich and fruitful this field is.

Researchers mostly preferred the classroom environment as the application environment. The reason behind this preference may stem from habit. However, AR technologies can be used outside classrooms due to the neutral consequence of its nature. Thus, learning can become more interesting by transferring it to the outside of classrooms within the bounds of these opportunities in the future. It is also predicted that AR technology will play a more significant role in the hybrid environments as the in-class and out-class uses become widespread. Individual learning has primarily become the focus in the in-class and out-class applications. However, it is predicted that collaborative learning also gains more importance as AR technology develops.

Most of the documented researchers preferred the handheld universe that the individuals are familiar with in the AR application universe or performed applications in the spatial universe. The head-mount universe was determined to be the least preferred one among the universes, due to the continued development of the hardware in this field.

Researchers frequently developed AR applications via SDK. This indicates that AR researchers develop AR applications based on their programming knowledge. The use of AR browsers that do not require programming knowledge was left behind using the SDK and code libraries. An AR browser that is easier and more accessible based on the needs of the developers in the AR field is thought to be needed.

Researchers preferred vision-based markers most among the tracking methods. The reason for this preference can be explained by the ease of application and the easy use in any time and place. Most of the feedback appealed to the eyesight, but, feedback will start appealing to other organs as the technology develops.

One of the criteria that affect the success of AR environments is how close the digital objects created by developers are to reality. Design success, calibration, and illumination are key elements in the real appearance of digital objects. Design success is related to understanding the purposes of virtual objects, why they are used, and what changes mean so that augmented reality environment is achieved in the desired way (Johnson et al., 2009; Wagner & Barakonyi, 2003; Winkler et al., 2002). Thanks to the designs that involve the mentioned elements, AR makes learning more effective (Zhou et al., 2008), attracts students' attention more because AR includes three-dimensional objects more concretely (Winn, Windscheid, Fruland and Lee, 2002). Besides, it was found out that AR motivates students (Yang, Chen, & Jeng, 2010), and encourages them to use their imagination and creativity (Klopfer & Sheldon, 2010). In addition, AR that makes it possible to represent the real world using virtual elements that provide opportunities to develop student-centered learning environments for different learning types (Abdüsselam, 2014).

The fact that the diverse opportunities that AR provides in the learning process involve more sense organs and that the interaction is diversified as touch-and-talk instead of click-and-type caused the AR applications to be classified differently according to their levels. Rice (2011) grouped AR into four different levels that are physical world hyperlinking, marker-based AR, markerless AR, and augmented vision; Billngurst, Kato & Poupyrev (2008) suggested a new approach to designing AR interfaces. However, AR should not be limited to only one area from a general point of view. Applications should focus on the features such as the internet, sensory organs, visuals, and interaction. AR application transforms from non-immersive to immersive by using all the features.

SOLUTIONS AND RECOMMENDATIONS

AR applications are implemented in the design processes of current technologies, but there can be occasional technical troubles, especially with hardware. The design and

Figure 2.

use of AR are known to be complicated. It is possible to eliminate this complexity by technological developments such as the development of mobile technologies and increased internet connection bandwidth, which will improve AR applications and make them accessible them to new users. Increasingly, AR applications will be supported by internet browsers that will add an AR function.

It is predicted that difficulties with the design and use of AR applications will decrease. These environments will become widespread with advances in mobile applications, hardware, and software, as well as the development of special add-ons that can operate with today's web browsers. Its use will become easier with the development of wearable computers, mobile devices, and uncomplicated AR software.

Learning is influenced positively when learners are given the opportunity to experience on-site learning in addition to the learning process using traditional methods. In this direction, it is possible to design more effective and efficient learning environments to increase the academic achievement that researchers often prefer by achieving more permanent learning with the teaching methods that enable students to actively participate in the process and by providing students with the opportunity to acquire in-class and out-of-class experiences.

The fact that researchers prefer AR applications in the fields of science and engineering is promising for the spread of the STEM education approach. The number of the studies about this issue is limited in the mathematics education among STEM disciplines. In this regard, the learning can be facilitated by incorporating mathematics-related applications into daily life with the equipment that individuals use, without the need for additional ones. It is thus possible to achieve deliberate and latent learning.

FUTURE RESEARCH DIRECTIONS

The rapid development of the technology in terms of hardware allows the development of chips that can be used with AR. The digital objects visualized in these environments will approach reality more closely and the components that appeal to the taste and small senses will continue to develop. With the developing components, learning environments will be enriched by developing learning objects that appeal to different sense organs using three-dimensional real objects without the need for programming knowledge. Learnings that are appropriate for the individual differences will be preferred, and the learning will be shaped within specific qualities.

Additionally, AR technologies are projected to play a more active role in the daily practices due to the development of wearable technologies and the head mount universe becomes widespread. Therefore, the use of this technology will be facilitated both inside and outside the classroom. Thanks to this hardware, it will be also possible to design a more ergonomic learning environment for the use of disabled persons. Thus, the possibility of receiving education of the disabled persons along with other persons will increase in light of the equality of opportunity in education perspective.

The use of AR will become widespread due to the continuous development of desktop, mobile, and web software, and new applications will be offered. The development of the generation called Web 4.0, artificial intelligence will especially be accelerated due to the advances in technologies such as cloud storage and AR. In this regard, it is important that AR become a field of interest for researchers and to increase the number of studies conducted in this field.

CONCLUSION

AR enhances the permanence of learning by embodying abstract concepts. Therefore, the AR environment is considered to provide students with an alternative learning environment, contribute to the students' achievement because it embodies abstract concepts. Furthermore, it is possible with AR applications to make the learning of boring or difficult topics more enjoyable, considering that students have negative attitudes about such topics. Similarly, it is possible with these applications to prevent students' misconceptions that occur because of teachers' incomplete or unclear drawings. Increasing students' academic achievement by overcoming the anxiety towards abstract concepts is dependent on demonstrating the activities in a realistic way and relating the examples used to the daily life. It can be said that the applications about how to use the knowledge gained helps to attract students' attention more and to enjoy learning. The fact that students find AR applications interesting particularly, citing examples about how to use the concept in the real life, and presenting a more visual environment by examing the environment and using AR in the 3D demonstrations are thought to influence students' learning in a positive way. Similarly, the AR applications that are designed with the collaboration of teachers and students influence students' latent learning in a positive way. In this regard, individual learning should be replaced with the hybrid applications in which both individual and collaborative environments are used, contrary to existing research.

REFERENCES

Akkoyunlu, B. (1996). The influence of computer literacy competencies and existing curriculum programs on student achievement and attitudes. *Hacettepe University Education Faculty Journal*, *12*(12), 127–134.

Alexander, P. A., Graham, S., & Harris, K. R. (1998). A perspective on strategy research: Progress and prospects. *Educational Psychology Review, 10*(2), 129–154. doi:10.1023/A:1022185502996

Bailey, K. (2008). *Methods of social research.* Simon and Schuster.

Billinghurst, M. (2002). Augmented reality in education. *New Horizons for Learning, 12.*

Billinghurst, M., Kato, H., & Poupyrev, I. (2008). Tangible augmented reality. In *Proceedings of the Conference and Exhibition on Computer Graphics & Interactive Techniques in Asia* (pp. 1-11). ACM.

Bybee, R. W. (2010). What is STEM education? *Science, 329*(5995), 996–996. doi:10.1126cience.1194998 PMID:20798284

Carter, R. (2013). *Defining characteristics of an integrated STEM curriculum in K-12 education* (PhD Thesis). University of Arkansas.

Chen, Z., & Soldner, M. (2014). *Stem Attrition: College Students' Paths into and out of Stem Fields.* U.S. Department of Education.

Cognition and Technology Group at Vanderbilt. (1990). Anchored instruction and its relationship to situated cognition. *Educational Researcher, 19*(6), 2–10. doi:10.3102/0013189X019006002

Cognition and Technology Group at Vanderbilt. (1997). *The jasper project: Lessons in curriculum, instruction, assessment, and professional development.* Mahwah, NJ: Lawrence Erlbaum Associates Publishers.

Coştu, S. (2009). *Teacher experiences from a learning environment based on contextual teaching and learning in mathematics teaching* (Unpublished Master Thesis). KTÜ, Institute of Science, Trabzon.

Creswell, J. W. (2012). *Qualitative Inquiry and Research Design: Choosing Among Five Approaches.* SAGE Publications.

Dönmez Usta, N. (2011). *Developing, implementing and evaluating cai materials related to? radioactivity? topic based on constructivist learning theory* (Unpublished Master Thesis). KTÜ, Institute of Educational Sciences, Trabzon.

Dori, Y., & Belcher, J. (2005). Learning electromagnetism with visualization and active learning. In J. Gilbert (Ed.), *Models and Modeling in Science Education* (Vol. 1, pp. 187–216). Dordrecht, The Netherlands: Springer. doi:10.1007/1-4020-3613-2_11

Dunston, P. S., & Wang, X. (2005). Mixed Reality-Based Visualization Interfaces for Architecture, Engineering, and Construction Industry. *Journal of Construction Engineering and Management*, *131*(12), 1301–1309. doi:10.1061/(ASCE)0733-9364(2005)131:12(1301)

Figueiredo, M. (2015). Teaching Mathematics with Augmented Reality. *Proceedings of 12th International Conference on Technology in Mathematics Teaching*, 183.

Hanson, K., & Shelton, B. E. (2008). Design and Development of Virtual Reality: Analysis of Challenges Faced by Educators. *Journal of Educational Technology & Society*, *11*(1), 118–131.

Johnson, L., Adams Becker, S., Estrada, V., & Martín, S. (2013). *Technology Outlook for STEM+ Education 2013-2018: An NMC Horizon Project Sector Analysis*. New Media Consortium.

Karal, H., & Abdüsselam, M. S. (2015). Augmented Reality. In B. Akkoyunlu, A. İşman, & H.F. Odabaşı (Eds.), Education technology readings 2015 (pp. 149-171). Ankara: Pegem Akademi.

Krevelen, D. W., & Poelman, F. (2010). A Survey of Augmented Reality Technologies, Applications and Limitations. *The International Journal of Virtual Reality*, *9*(2), 1–20.

Lave, J., & Wenger, E. (1991). *Situated learning: Legitimate peripheral participation*. Cambridge, MA: Cambridge University Press. doi:10.1017/CBO9780511815355

Matsumoto, Y., Sakamoto, K., Nomura, S., Hirotomi, T., Shiwaku, K., & Hirakawa, M. (2009). Activity Replay System of Life Review Therapy Using Mixed Reality Technology. *Proceedings of the International MultiConference of Engineers and Computer Scientists*, 1-6.

Müller, D., Bruns, F. W., Erbe, H. H., Robben, B., & Yoo, Y. H. (2007). Mixed Reality Learning Spaces for Collaborative Experimentation: A Challenge for Engineering Education and Training. *International Journal of Online Engineering*, *3*(4), 27–41.

Müller, D., & Ferreira, J. M. (2004, December). MERVEL: A Mixed Reality Learning Environment for Vocational Training Mechatronics. *Proceedings of International Conference on Technology-Enhanced Learning*.

Patton, M. Q. (2014). *Qualitative research and evaluation methods*. Ankara: Pegem Akademi.

Rice, R. (2011, Jan 20). *The Augmented Reality Hype Cycle*. Retrieved January 20, 2011, from url: http://www.sprxmobile.com/the-augmented-reality-hype-cycle

Scott, C. E. (2009). *A comparative case study of the characteristics of science, technology, engineering, and mathematics (STEM) focused high schools* (PhD Thesis). George Mason University.

Sengupta, P., & Wilensky, U. (2009). Learning electricity with NIELS: Thinking with electrons and thinking in levels. *International Journal of Computers for Mathematical Learning*, *14*(1), 21–50. doi:10.100710758-009-9144-z

Shelton, B. E., & Hedley, N. R. (2002). Using augmented reality for teaching earth-sun relationships to undergraduate geography students. Augmented Reality Toolkit. In *Proceedings of The First IEEE International Workshop* (pp. 8-21). IEEE. 10.1109/ART.2002.1106948

Shelton, B. E., & Hedley, N. R. (2004). Exploring a cognitive basis for learning spatial relationships with augmented reality. Technology, Instruction. *Cognition and Learning*, *1*(4), 323.

Shirazi, A., & Behzadan, A. H. (2015). Content Delivery Using Augmented Reality to Enhance Students' Performance in a Building Design and Assembly Project. *Advances in Engineering Education*, *4*(3), 1–24.

Turna, Ö., Bolat, M., & Keskin, S. (2012, June). Interdisciplinary Approach: Music, Physics, Mathematics Example. *Proceedings of X. National Science and Mathematics Education Congress.*

Vallino, J. R. (1998). *Interactive augmented reality* (Doctoral dissertation). University of Rochester.

Wagner, D., & Barakonyi, I. (2003, October). Augmented reality kanji learning. In *Proceedings of the 2nd IEEE/ACM International Symposium on Mixed and Augmented Reality* (p. 335). IEEE Computer Society. 10.1109/ISMAR.2003.1240747

Wang, X., & Dunston, P.S. (2007). Design, Strategies, and Issues Towards an Augmented Reality-Based Construction Training Platform. *Journal of information technology in construction (ITcon), 12*, 363-380.

Winkler, T., Herczeg, M., & Kritzenberger, H. (2002). Mixed reality environments as collaborative and constructive learning spaces for elementary school children. In *EdMedia: World Conference on Educational Media and Technology* (pp. 1034-1039). Association for the Advancement of Computing in Education (AACE).

Winn, W., Windschitl, M., Fruland, R., & Lee, Y. (2002). When does immersion in a virtual environment help students construct understanding. *Proceedings of International Conference of the Learning Sciences*, 497-503.

Woods, E., Billinghurst, M., Looser, J., Aldridge, G., Brown, D., Garrie, B., & Nelles, C. (2004, June). Augmenting the science centre and museum experience. *Proceedings of the 2nd international conference on Computer graphics and interactive techniques in Australasia and South East Asia*, 230-236. 10.1145/988834.988873

Yoon, S., Steinmeier, C., Wang, J., & Tucker, S. (2011). Learning science through knowledge-building and augmented reality in museums. In *Proceedings of CSCL2011* (*Vol. 1*, pp. 9-16). Academic Press.

Zagoranski, S., & Divjak, S. (2003). Use of augmented reality in education. *EUROCON Computer as a Tool The IEEE Region*, *8*(2), 339–342. doi:10.1109/EURCON.2003.1248213

KEY TERMS AND DEFINITIONS

Sensor: Is an electronic component which detect events or changes in its environment and send the information to other electronics, frequently a computer processor.

Wearable Technology: Is a smart electronic device with microcontrollers that can be worn on the body as implant or accessories.

Chapter 2
Augmented Reality as a Search System in Libraries

Gerardo Reyes Ruiz
Universidad Autónoma del Estado de México, Mexico

Marisol Hernández Hernández
Universidad Autónoma del Estado de México, Mexico

Samuel Olmos Peña
Universidad Autónoma del Estado de México, Mexico

ABSTRACT

The technology has now ventured into multiple educational environments. The case of augmented reality has served to create new digital environments of search that help the location of any physical reference in a public library. In these educational spaces, it is important to have information resources that are innovative and, simultaneously, which motivate the users to enter them. For physical learning resources, these informative tools must provide a fast and efficient inquiry/location. Augmented reality helps this location by showing, through digital content, the three-dimensional space (3D) of that location, highlighting categories and classifications of physical references so that, in turn, the user able to visualize it, using a mobile device, and is therefore directed to the exact place of the location in a relatively short time. Thus, this study shows that the application of new technologies in a public library can make the user feel immersed in a new learning environment, which is transmitted through a digital environment through augmented reality.

DOI: 10.4018/978-1-5225-5243-7.ch002

INTRODUCTION

Changes in technology are more than evident and there is no doubt that the dynamics between human beings and technology has been invested with the passing time. So much so that today human beings must assimilate quickly the so-called new technologies rather than they are adapted to the needs of human beings. In other words, the human being has become a co-dependent entity of new technologies, regardless of any technological innovation to meets their needs in specific. However, the benefits of technological advances are also more than evident. The life that we lived in the 21st century is, by far, easier life, for example, of 100 years ago. This is due, no doubt, strides with that have been advancing both the science and the technology.

In this sense, everyday life has also been transformed with the proliferation of new technologies. Just to mention two examples, there are now countless establishments that allow you to make purchases only using a telephone connected to the internet worldwide (Agrebi and Jallais, 2015; Reyes, Olmos and Hernández, 2016). Moreover, some of these establishments have the service of bringing such purchases to the door of the home (Bulearca and Tamarjan, 2010). Similarly, and also with a telephone connected to the internet, can be countless payments from the comfort of home (no doubt, the banking institutions have facilitated and promoted such changes in our lives).

Of course, learning (which is nothing more than the process of learning) in educational institutions has also changed and has had to adapt, little by little, these technological changes (Zhou, Duh and Billinghurst, 2008; Yu, Jin, Luo and Lai, 2010; Hugues, Fuchs and Nannipieri, 2011). It is currently difficult thinking that a young student does not have access to a smart phone, a tablet or any other mobile with internet access. The great diversity of these new technologies and their most affordable allow its approach to contemporary generations of students, including, and in some countries or regions, at an early age. The way to learn these new generations of students had to adapt to these changes in technology and the need to create new educational environments is now already a reality (Greenfield, 2009; Yang, 2011; Wu et al, 2013). In this sense, technological development has shown multiple advances as support for the strategies of learning-learning, this progress every day is exceeded by more efficient technologies and whose mission is to serve as support to students and teachers interested in the generation of a new educational process (Azuma et al, 2001; Tanner, Karas and Schofield, 2014).

Educational technologies are transmitted (embedded) through different devices and media, same that have earned the Internet, mobile devices, cyber cloud and various technological objects to create a more efficient way in the long road of learning (Bacca et al, 2014). For this context, Augmented Reality (AR) has emerged as a relatively young technology, which can generate new educational environments (Zendjebil et al, 2008; Ghasemil and Javidan, 2014; Martín Gutiérrez and Meneses Fernández, 2014), but that, within its most outstanding characteristics, can well serve as a support so abstract educational content are transmitted in a more understandable and interesting way for students (Kirner, Reis and Kirner, 2012; Schmitz, Specht and Klemke, 2012; Cuendet, Bonnard, Do-Lenh and Dillenbourg, 2013). Undoubtedly the AR complements other technologies but one aspect that is worth highlighting, is that expensive devices, not are required to implement an environment with AR since it enough to have a web cam and basics, such as a mouse and a keyboard.

Applications that use AR are more and more innovative, attractive and motivating for adoption (Alkhamisi and Monowar, 2013; Di Serio, Ibáñez and Kloos, 2013; Ibáñez, Di Serio, Villarán and Delgado Kloos, 2014; Riobó Iglesias et al, 2015; Techakosit and Wannapiroon, 2015; Estapa, A. and Nadolny, 2015). Today the AR is main topic in countless research papers and, what is most outstanding, their applications are multiplied in various real-life activities (Caudell and Mizell, 1992; Kaufmann, 2002; Shelton, and Hedley, 2002; Weidenhausen, Knoepfle and Stricker, 2003; Savioja et al, 2007; Leblanc et al, 2010; Perez-Lopez and Contero, 2013; Wang, Kim, Love and Kang, 2013; Kucuk, Yilmaz and Goktas, 2014; Yang and Liao, 2014; Riddle, Wasser and McCarthy, 2017). Libraries have always been the site ideal where it concentrates, first physically and in recent years in a digital, the largest number of academic references, even unique character (Chang et al, 2014). However, these niches of knowledge have also had to adapt to the new technologies change (Bishop, 2012; Chen and Tsai, 2012; Brinkman and Brinkman, 2013; Zak, 2014). Today you can visit countless libraries, museums, cities, monuments, etc. from a mobile device with connection to the internet (e.g. http://www.europeana.eu/portal/es). At the same time, the search for information in a library has also had important advances: has become a simple search on a computer using a mobile device, a Global Positioning System (GPS) to physically locate the publication that you want to see (Walsh, 2011; Choudari, 2013). In this sense, the search for information in a library has also been a theme where the AR has proved to be a tool that can well be used to make more attractive the visit of a person to a site of this nature. And although it is not central theme of this work also mention another aspect to consider is the speed for the transmission of data and storing them on a mobile device (Orlosky, Kiyokawa and Takemura, 2017).

While a library was created as an intimate place where a person is concentrated in a considerable number of books ordered for reading, currently the Royal Spanish Academy (http://www.rae.es) considered that a library is an institution, usually public, whose mission is to acquire, preserve, study and exhibit books and documents on an ongoing basis. Today young people have many tools that can be used for search of bibliographical references, even from the comfort of your home. This progress of generations contemporary of students to new technology, the vast majority of these technologies based search engines of data through the internet, have had a strong impact on libraries. That is to say, students visit fewer libraries, to carry out any consultation of bibliographical references and these niches of knowledge have become more architectural symbols and museums as places of bibliographic inquiries. It seems that libraries have become mystical places that serve today only to guide tours of elementary or preschool students. However, it seems ironic that new technologies, to be the main cause of that students already do not visit as often amount of libraries, themselves are which could rescue these niches of the knowledge of the potential and total abandonment. Without a doubt, the experience of visiting a library, by itself, is rewarding and motivator. However, this experience may lead to more interesting levels with the AR. From the very moment that the person enters a library experience can be innovative, since if deployed in places specific codes showing, via a mobile device, the reading of the AR will be then urging potential user that you enter and use services that offers a place of this nature. For its part, and recognizing that the main problem facing, and has faced, a library is the search for a physical reference by a person who does not have knowledge of how these references are catalogued. In this context, mobile devices, connected to the internet, again play a leading role so the user carry out the physical location of the reference that you want to check. As mentioned, the AR can provide guidance for take the user to the target reference and not precisely with GPS technology, but rather in a manner more interactive, attractive and innovative for the user.

The AR takes importance in the year of 1996, when occurs AR Quake (Thomas et al, 2002) the first game to air free with mobile devices AR, developed by Bruce H. Thomas. Then, in 2008 goes on sale application for travel guide cars Wikitude (https://www.wikitude.com), which was done by augmented reality through a digital compass, sensors for orientation and an accelerometer, maps, video and news content on Wikipedia. In 2009 emerges AR Toolkit (http://www.hitl.washington.edu/artoolkit/), which is a fully oriented platform to generate AR. From these applications, the AR has been used as the basis for numerous projects in different areas, ranging from entertainment, industry, maintenance, music, medicine, and education, to name just a few. Moreover, there have been very specific applications such as a harp, whose operation is carried out by means of vibrations, which designed for people with a disability.

For its part, the industry, through the development of manuals with AR, has shown that the performance of workers who use this type of manuals is modified in a palpable improvement in comparison with workers using manuals with paper (Shin and Dunston, 2008). This result is due, mainly, to behavioral data, physiological and psychological workers. Therefore, it has been recommended widely the use of AR in the orientation of the assembly of products (Caudell and Mizell, 1992). In addition, this technique includes the information retrieval and installation in real time and promotes the reduction of error in the assembly, all under the cognitive workload and the transfer of high skill to improve the tasks. They have also been Intelligent Tutorial Systems (ITS), as the "Intelligent Augmented Reality Training for Motherboard Assembly", which helps with the training for manual assembly tasks.

In the educational field, the AR can teach molecular structures, mathematics, architecture, astronomy, physical activities to children with some disabilities, to mention a few. In medicine and education, specialized projects have been developed that show AR as an efficient tool in the learning of medicine, such as the system "An Interactive Augmented Reality System for Learning Anatomy Structure" that is integrated of three activities; The first is to show the parts of the anatomical structure of the human body, the second facilitates the students to identify each anatomical part of the human body and the third allows a deep glimpse of the internal parts of the anatomical structure (Nicolson, Chalk, Robert, Funnell and Daniel, 2006; Temkin, Acosta, Malvankar and Vaidyanath, 2006). Thus, all these examples allow glimpse to the AR as an effective tool that encourages the creation of new educational environments that facilitate the learning process.

BACKGROUND

The internet, mobile devices and high speed for data transfer nowadays play a preponderant role to pass knowledge to new generations of users. This is because nowadays it is hard to imagine a young student that does not have access to a mobile phone with an internet connection and data transfer or either you don't have access to a library that has wireless internet access. In this context, a public, view library as a service provider, has to improve and adapt their services/processes most important demands, precisely, these new generations of users. These public institutions have to face the monetary cost to upgrade and modernize both its facilities and its services, which in many cases is not possible, because of budget constraints. This problem has been resolved, in a certain way, thanks to donations carried out by private individuals. However, these public institutions face a reality: doing more with less.

It is here, precisely where it takes sense to use new technologies that do not represent a considerable expense and that have also proved to be useful to transmit and generate new learning environments. Technology called Augmented Reality is accessible and, from a certain point, is not as expensive as you really think. In addition, it offers the great advantage that only with a mobile device, and assuming that the library offers free Wi-Fi, can offer very creative and motivating environments for users who want to plunge into the rough world of the new technologies. For this context, it is of utmost importance difference between Augmented Reality and

Virtual Reality (VR). The first is a technology through which the environment for real-world vision is precisely, augmented by items or objects generated/created, in the majority of cases, by a computer. The AR is generated through a mediated reality, where a vision of the real world is modified using a computer system, even moving way (Schall, 2008; Izkara, Perez, Basogain and Borro, 2009). On the contrary, the VR replaces real-world simulation (Milgram et al., 1995; Billinghurst, Kato and Poupyrev, 2001; Woodward et al, 2007; Schall, Mendez and Schmalstieg, 2008). In this way, and as says Milgram et al (1994), the AR is located between the virtual world and the real world such as defined in the Reality-Virtuality continuum.

Thus, the AR allows us to appreciate virtual images generated by a computer that overlaps, with much precision, real objects in real time (Shin and Dunston, 2008; Takacs et al, 2010). Then, AR well can be understood as a direct, or indirect, vision of the environment of the real world that is incremented/increases through real entries generated by a computer. A particular feature of the AR, is that the user interacts with the real world in a quite natural way. In this context, the main difference between the AR and the VR is that in the latter the user is entirely immersed in an artificial world, while in the first, a computer is used to add / enhance information to a segment of real-world objects. Therefore, in the AR computer is used to explore the information related to the real world and, simultaneously, the user interacts with the computer-generated virtual objects. In contrast, the user of VR is immersed, from the beginning, completely to an artificial world (Azuma, 1997; Nicolson et al, 2006).

The use of the AR implies a technological educational task that uses different scenarios of VR in order to simulate its operation, so that through various visual effects and multimedia, students may abstract their meaningful learning. As already mentioned previously, digital content for the AR uses (Vacchetti, Lepetit and Fua, 2004) 3D images and other multimedia files such as images in 2D (Liu, Tan and Chu, 2007), audio, animation and text resources that are used to model and build your simulation. This educational content is reflected in text, with different images, which show a variety of Visual effects through the AR, simulating their operation when they are displayed through the web or mobile device.

In this way, one can say that AR is a technology-oriented objects, that is to say, it is a completely visual tool that combines 3D virtual objects in two or three dimensions with an environment of real objects to this project the virtual objects in real time (Bowman, Kruijff, LaVoila and Poupyrev, 2005; Temkin, Acosta, Malvankar and Vaidyanath, 2006). AR technology has been chosen for this job because it has the following advantages: is able to expand the perception of the user towards the object and provide a new experience of the user in relation to the displayed 3D object. In addition, allows the user interaction, which cannot be done in the real world, and increases significantly the possibility of using a variety of tools (devices) according to the needs and availability of these devices (Mutiara, Hapsari and Handayani, 2014).

Moreover, the technology of AR can be used by students whose studies are related to the construction of compilers, search engines on web sites and the construction of computers. Also, these aspects can be studied by students of different educational programs such as engineering, computer engineering, computer systems, and engineering in electronic or electromechanical, and similar. Extensive study time could be reduced to move towards another type of learning, since the environment generated by the AR is situated in meaningful learning. In this way, we can say that this type of technology is a viable proposal, since they may well interact with other technologies that are of interest to students of other degrees. No doubt expected that with the passage of time the interaction of these new technologies will increase for the benefit of all types of students learning.

Multiple scenarios offered by the AR are extremely competent. They can also be adopted in various fields of knowledge. Moreover, there are applications that target the mass market for advertising, entertainment, and education. However, let's look at the issue of libraries, where the AR can be the catalyst to make these niches of knowledge more interesting a person's visit to their facilities. At this point, the following question takes sense: ¿What is the main need of who wants to meet someone in a library? Without a doubt, the answer is not unique and, much less, easy answer. We believe that one of the main needs that satisfies a library is responding in the way more quickly and efficiently, in search of any reference that is within their facilities, whether physical or digital. If the reference is scanned and does not take greater problem perform the search on a computer and the result is, without a doubt, immediate. Moreover, if such reference is then physical search can be done in a more attractive way for the user with the tool of AR. In this context, the present work increases the features exposed in the previous immediate text, since the proposed environment will serve to learn small processes of three-dimensional elements (processes in which students mainly learn activities that could hardly do it in a traditional way), through which those interested in visiting a library can do some reference search from a mobile device and with the tool of AR. Since the way of learning may include different senses such as sight, hearing, touch, this work proposes an interactive platform that contains items related to these senses and with the purpose of learning being full and, above all, attractive for anyone interested in visiting a library that provides an experience of this nature. In addition to the foregoing, this new learning environment describes the design of a system such as the establishment of data structures, the general architecture of the software and the representations 3D interfaces and algorithms. This process translates requirements into software specifications. The purpose of the design phase is to publicize the performance of the proposed solution; this is conceived taking into account that the design is a pre-fase which starts the construction of programs and/or processes of activities that are typically performed by users, which seek to improve is adding speed, efficiency, savings and visual design. The first action, beginning with design, is the determination of the system architecture, which is nothing more than the hierarchical structure of the program modules. Thus, this structure is focused to the way to interact between its components and the structure of the data used by these. In the subsequent sections we present the structure of the proposed design for a library in particular.

MAIN FOCUS OF THE CHAPTER

Issues, Controversies, Problems

In a so-called society of information and knowledge, the libraries are very important institutions in any school or even in any place, they can be the starting point for developing theories or to arouse the imagination of students is also an area of inquiry for troubleshooting or monitoring of history or geography. It would be very risky to nominate all areas of inquiry in order to motivate students to delve into the intellectual world.

A library is a collection of books regularly organized for use (Carreón, 2002), i.e., the libraries are a place where physically stores the information for obtaining and strengthening of knowledge and that is the inspiration by which libraries must provide users tools to facilitate the search for information in an educational space. Those tools translated into applications that must take into account the diversity of attendees who visit the library, with divergent thoughts and different queries. It should provide to them a search service easy, friendly and suitable to your various profiles, same that vary with age, grades, profession and changing topics of interest.

Services that give the library are essential to meet the needs of teachers regarding the use of the bibliographic material, e.g. the preparation of material for their kinds of teaching, the literature supporting their research or simply for those who want to discover new worlds or increase their general culture. To provide these services in libraries, there are several types on information systems for searches, the most common systems are those in which computer makes a filter using words that identify the bibliographical material, those lexicons can be title, author, topic or category of the book. When the system receives these words makes them items of search in the database, locates the book related to those fields and filters the result, showing the details of the material synthesized in attributes such as title, author, Publisher and classification. This serves locate it on the library shelves, a query of this type shown in Figure 1.

The figure shows a classification of the book that is composed of several characters that can symbolize the key location, classification number, the code of the author,

Figure 1. Search System in a Library

title, year of publication and issue number. Therefore, we can infer that the location key is which directed the reader toward shelves of the library. The detailed process gives good search results; however, there are still problems when the user wants to search the shelf where the book is located. To search for the book, they compares the classification with the results of the query displayed by the system, the system emits classifications that are difficult to read and understand quickly and the student who does not know where to go to locate those categorizations, since numbers are very small and therefore little visible and comprehensible for the user. For the development of the system, was taken as a precedent that the students of current generations were born in times where it is frequent the use of electronic tools that are easily accessible and that, accordingly, they have essential digital skills that encourage them to use information and communication technologies constantly. From this premise is derived the idea that you should create a system of information that is practical, consistent, use daily and suitable to the environments in which they are developing.

In libraries, the student does not feel motivated to enter them to search for books or journals; this said because the Research Center Pew Research Center's Internet and American Life Project detailed at the 2014 American Library Association Midwinter Meeting and Exhibits in Philadelphia in January. He reported that the total number of visitors to a physical library or a mobile library fell five percent from 2012 to 2013, from 53% to 48%. This study also reveals is the Ninety-six per cent of respondents agree that the importance of public libraries is because they promote literacy and the love of reading and who like the technological resources that provide access to bibliographic material for libraries (Macey and Morales, 2014). This is a powerful reason to turn the library into a venue that encourages the reader to enter a world of knowledge and this is should generate resources that are innovative and avant-garde so users from using them. These must be encoded in software is used daily and necessarily, and in addition, to use it with devices that use frequently, same that are called mobile devices.

SOLUTIONS AND RECOMMENDATIONS

Information Systems

Information systems are programs that help to decision-making, these ranging from the choice of a seat in the film, time and destination of a flight or the appointment with a doctor, just to mention a few, these serve to make decisions in common and everyday activities. Our ability to choice improved by using information resources, which are in part invention and improvement of the information and communication technologies, as well as express Cornford and Shaikh, (2013), who also write that information systems involve four objectives:

- Technologies are for the management of information with their features and capabilities.
- People are those who use the information.
- Tasks depend on what system does, carry out specific needs.
- Social or organizational structures are for which developed the system.

These objectives are involved with the system of search of information with AR that has implemented and you can contextualize as viewed in Figure 2:

There are several types of information systems that are categorized according to the way in which provide services to the Organization, is so are known as information systems at the operational level, at the level knowledge, at the administrative level or at the strategic level (Laudon and Laudon, 2004). However, these systems have

Figure 2. Information System. Own Source

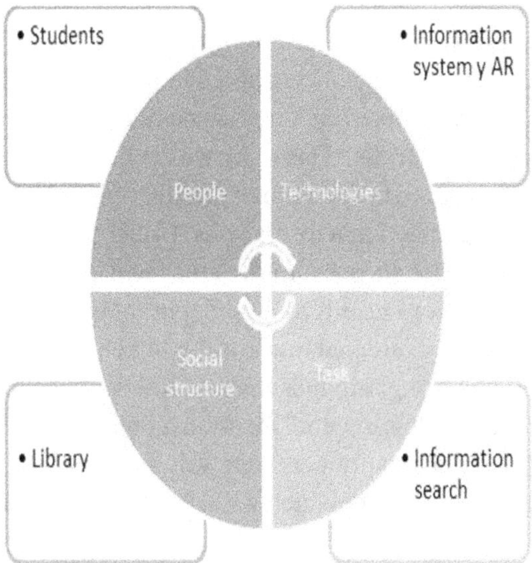

evolved to include three important factors, which are the emergence of the mobile platform, the growing use of large data for business and the growth in cloud computing (Loundon and Loudon, 2014). What this means is that the technology based on the Internet and on mobile devices represent those emerging technologies that have been included in the models of information systems.

They have arisen many technological tools that have empowered information system and augmented reality could not stay out of these systemic contexts. Rabbi and Ullah (2013) define the augmented reality as a technology through which the display of the actual environment is enhanced by elements or objects generated by a computer. There are applications that target the mass market for advertising, entertainment, and education (Azuma, 2015), and under this approach is that the AR helps to invent various application contexts, generating the convenience that will help in the design and creation of information systems. The goal for the application was to create an illusion of physical reality, augmented on a marker, being aware of the user. To do it we taken as precedent the students were born in times in which is frequent the use of electronic, tools that are easily accessible and with essential digital skills that encourage them to constantly use the technologies of information and communication. From this premise is derived the idea that should be create an information system that is practical, coherent, used daily and suitable environments that are being developed.

Design of Information System for Search With AR

An information search system is a program that assists students in locating his bibliographical material, this type of cutting-edge systems should take into account 3 fundamentals of inquiry in those academic spaces that are: collection, organization and use of bibliographic material. These 3 terms is concatenated to accomplish a main objective, which is provide the use of a bibliographic material, that lies within a collection of books organized in a formal way. Under this approach was a system where the AR superimposed to placeholders that will place from the entrance of the building for the student to take it as a guide, in order to enter the facilities and know the way that should be directed towards the search for bibliographic material.

Software engineering has guidelines that are followed for the construction of a system of information search, same that mentions, Pressman (2006), and which are included in communication, requirements analysis, modeling, design, program, test, and support, building features with which we can propose the draft of work follows:

1. Analysis of system requirements with AR
2. Formulate abstract and physical design, coding and creation of software.
3. Preparation of the files, identification and creation of test data, and finally, testing and integrating the software.

Analysis of the Requirements of the System of Search With AR in Libraries

As a first activity gets the context of the elements in the library location, taking into account and documenting the location of shelves, books, books by area classification, placement of textbooks that students used in containers prepared exclusively for this purpose. In addition, writes notes of shelves that exist, the geometry of space, stocks of books by coordinates, in short, any entity that can serve as a point of interest for the system.

The second activity is to establish the needs of having an information system where the AR is an addition to the search for information, namely to have a perspective of what you want to implement and how is required to work. It estimated that the benefits must be higher than the costs, which measured in monetary terms and in addition, measured according to the characteristics that must meet all kinds of system, Pablos et al (2012) mentions them in the following manner:

- **Flexible:** Provide your own modification to fit the changing needs of the organization.
- **Selective:** To provide the information necessary for the objective assigned.

- **Relevant**: Provide information of interest to the user.
- **Timely:** To deliver information at the required time.

To achieve these peculiarities you start the analysis by examining the functional, same requirements that describe the interactions between the system and its environment independently to its implementation (Kendall and Kendall, 2011), on this basis, the interaction required between the user and the system is summarized in Figure 3.

Requirements analysis is jointly in a diagram of case of use, which describes the functionalities of the system under the approach of universal modeling (UML) language and giving shape to the interaction that takes place between the systems and the users or between multiple systems. In the case of use described (Figure 3), makes the synthesis of the needs of the system and their interactions with users. The case shows actor representing the users of the system who may be students, teachers, or any person who occupies. Actions of the system are represented by ovals, these in turn are also known as use cases and show how the system is connected with other use cases, and these in turn with the actor, sending mutual action messages and that they represent with lines.

Figure 3. Case study of the search with AR system

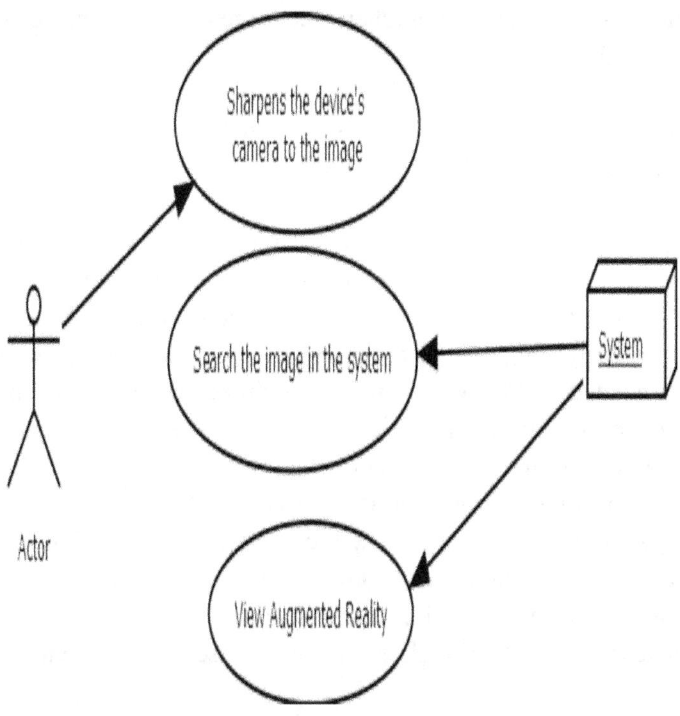

Cost-Benefit

Continuing with the definition of the requirements it is important to analyze the cost benefit of the search system in the library with AR, which should add to the benefit of creating it, so that may be feasible to its construction and implementation.

Continuing with the definition of the requirements it is important to analyze the cost benefit of the search system in the library with AR, which should add to the benefit of creating it, so that may be feasible to its construction and implementation. The gain not only refers to the economic term, rather and in this case in particular, refers to that libraries may have more followers in its facilities, which will lead to a gain that will become culture, knowledge and learning. Intangible elements but with high power of transformation, same that in turn could become tangible items such as the sale of elements derived from the application of the knowledge. Information systems based their benefits in its utility, which is to say, focus on the way in which improves the perception of individuals to the events of his daily life.

This impact seen in the frequency of use of a system, it can inferred that could be due to its intuitive and easy-to-use interface, reliable and easy-to-understand, by how flexible it is to use. This results that this information search system provides users are perceived by its usefulness in the institution that is measured by the degree in information system improves the academic performance of the person or the quality of the information system, appreciated for its ease of use, reliability and flexibility, also, relevant, comprehensible, time and complete (Bravo, Santana and Rondon, 2015).

Formulate Abstract and Physical Design, Coding and Creation of Software

The design is a significant representation of engineering of something that is going to build (Presman, 2002). The design begins with the modeling of requirements, which lead to the software to created, achieving views through the architecture of the system. The design begins with the modeling of requirements, which lead to the software that created and views through the architecture of the system. In design, it is necessary to identify the activities that the system will perform, generally it become necessary requirements for its development and detail key features on its creation. These peculiarities are; the type of architecture that will serve to shape it, the language of programming that will encode the design of the interface, the framework to use for your layout and additional hardware accessories require. Each item mentioned, requires a detailed analysis in order to choose the most optimal design tools according to their efficiency, ease of use and cost. Each one requires a detailed analysis to choose the best according to their efficiency, ease of use and cost. These tools will have a significant impact on the project and that is that they must be selected properly.

The Software Architecture

The architecture of a system is the creation of the structures of the software and its documentation, same needed to think and define the best options of construction, as well as the relationship that exists between them (Clements, et al, 2010), summarizing, the architecture refers to the modeling of the system requirements and their connections. There is a variety of styles of architecture, but on this occasion and for the type of system that they plan to build, the model view controller (MVC) is what should use. This paradigm of software architecture is useful for the development of systems where it is required to provide to the end-user of an illusion so you feel that there is a connection between his brain and memory and with the processor of the computer. The model view controller (MVC) is a software architecture that separates data from an application, the user interface, and the logic of control in three different components (model, view and controller), graphic display is shown in Figure 4.

Figure 4. Model view of controller (MVC). Source: Reenskaug and Coplien (2009).

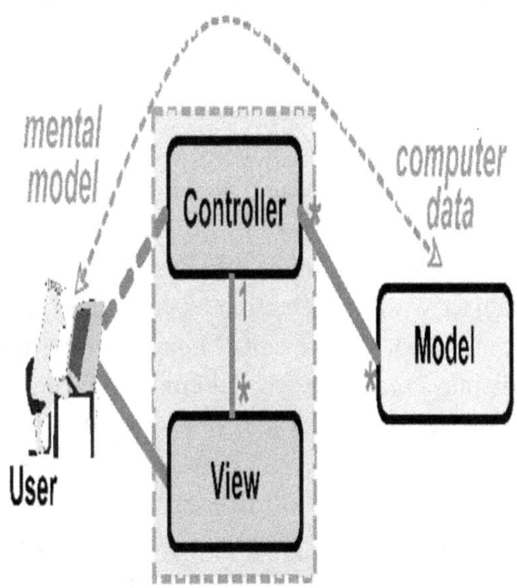

The view is the way in which you user observed the operation of the software; this translates into the interface of the system and the driver. This scheme often seen in Web application design, where the view is the page that displayed and the controller is the event that performed. Both are writing with html5 or JavaScript, which are programming languages that serve to design dynamic pages and excellent appearance; also, a model can have more than one view and each programmed to produce by a specific controller. In the proposed system, the view makes the program to launch the elements that found in the imagination of the user to the system, in this case the AR is associated with the information the user is looking for.

The MVC architecture of the search system in an AR-based library defined as follows:

View

1. The AR is displayed on the computer screen, which shows the shape of the user's face in a digitized way
2. The second tab the system display the AR in the form of virtual tour, interacting with the user to orient the location of the shelves, interactively does this whenever the user presses the keys position to access different sites.
3. The last view shows the AR through the mobile device's camera when it positions it near the marker provided as a point of interest for the AR, this is perceived as a virtual image and sound, which indicate to the user the way in which should be addressed within the library to find what you're looking.

Driver

1. The user interacts with the interface using the webcam that is into a machine arranged for that purpose and located at a strategic site, with the purpose of to serve as a reference to the visitors.
2. In the moment in which the driver receives the notification of the action requested by the user with the detection of your face (for the user), manages the event that comes through an events Manager in the system.
3. The controller displays the digital model emitting face of the user, event that gives realism to the scene and is the result of the digital superimposition on the real environment.
4. The user face detection is an event that assumed as the start and launches another request to the controller system so you visualize the structure of the library in the form of virtual tour. This action denotes in the mind of the user the composition of the library, which lets you see an overview and invites you to enter the library.

5. The user enters the library where you can listen, view and follow initial instructions of the system. In this second interaction with the driver, user focuses the camera on your mobile device to a marker that is located on a shelf and which designated by the program as a point of interest.
6. This action system launches a petition to the driver so that you associate the marker with some contents of AR that will locate it in the database and will return the answer to the view, showing a three-dimensional image with the books in that container, same that labeled according to the area that the user wishes to locate. It expresses a sound that tells you which is the route to follow to reach your goal.
7. The user follows the instructions of the system to locate markers on each shelf and return to launch the request to the handler, repeating the process of request and response between the view and the controller.

Coding and Creation of Software

The recent evolution of the mobile hardware has allowed that the AR will play on small units such as Smartphones or tablets; same that contains all the components needed for it, such as camera of high resolution and screens, accelerometers, GPS and wireless connectivity for WLAN and radio links (Honkamaa et al, 2007). It is essential to take into account the precedent that the use of mobile technology is at its peak, so this type of system reproduced on these devices so that your inquiry is frequent.

The system of search of information generated from programs that help the creation of AR, design images in third dimension, to the design of virtual tours, and the reproduction of audio and animation. Tools for the creation of the search system categorized into the following elements:

Hardware

- Camera. The smart mobile bring it with you and with this camera detects the marker of AR. Also requires a webcam on the computer where begins the operation of the AR and that should usually be placed at the entrance of the building of the library, as a process of personalized guide.
- Screen of the device with which it interacts the system. Displaying the 3D image to the user and virtual travel issued because of the inquiry, it will also contain other options that will help the user in their search for information. For this purpose, you can use a computer screen, a wide screen or the screen of your mobile device.

- Audio, also provided on mobile devices and be implemented on computers, since in many cases the AR made with sound (usually a podcast).

The functions of the search with AR System soar with the use of a camera, which at the time that detects the physical face of the user, displays it on the screen and view a virtual tour of the library, superimposed on the physical reality.

- The virtual tour responds to an inquiry carried out by the user by using search words in database on content of books organized by different themes.
- In a second interaction, AR shown when the user runs the camera of your mobile phone to each point of interest predisposed at strategic locations of the library and which will help the user to move within the path of the pursuit of knowledge.
- From start and whenever the user deploys the AR, the system directs it towards its initial goal. The way to guide you is with auditory and visual signals so the user can move quickly and confidently within the physical space of the library.

Markers

They are 2D images that are called markers of trust or references and which due to its characteristics of predefined color and shape, your information can be easily extracted (Uchiyama and Marchand, 2012). The AR marker used as a trigger that activated in the moment in which the camera detects it to provide to the user virtual objects 3D or multimedia. Some programs create markers from which the AR generated, although they can also construct with any drawing program. If this last option is used, you should take care of that marker meets certain characteristics so that they can be a point of reference for an optical instrument. Once designed the marker exported as an image of any format to print it and arrange it in strategic locations in the library. Markers provided with a framework black that contains a black and white pattern, which encoded as the marker identification, see Figure 5. There are markers whose forms of identification can vary depending on the level of recognition.

Once markers have been generated, perform their corresponding virtual models seen as 3d images, which will be superimposed as augmented reality. A 3d image is different from a 2d by the number of axes on which its design is based, the 2d has axis x and shaft, and while the image 3D is based on the axes x, and and z. There are multiple programs for the design of these elements, however, not described in this chapter of book since every design software has different characteristics and the breadth of the subject is extensive.

Figure 5. Fiducial marker

Virtual Tour

The virtual tour is an application that generated using multiple panoramic images of any installation. These images harnessed in specialized software so that with the arrow keys, the user can address virtually to a place specific. Currently programs that generate this type of applications are easy to use and there are some on the Internet. Although if required make tours more abstract, there are design programs that help to build these.

Software

The type of software for the creation of the AR should be specialized in the solution of such problems. AR applications work through the Association, in this case the AR will partner with marker to show images and output the audio and the AR also relates the user face to view the virtual tour. There are variety applications for the creation of the AR, some are free to use, but the license must purchase to use other. Others give option to download the trial software and although it does not contain all the elements arranged in a license that has been paid, it can be used for a short time for the construction of AR. Some tools are easy to use; however, others have greater difficulty, and then show an overview of each one of them:

- **Aurasma:** He is an editor of AR that be displayed in 2D images, videos and animations created in flash adobe Flash Player video.
- **Vuforia:** Software that works with Unity, effective for the development of AR, but it is not open source. It is a program of great abilities, with a degree of difficulty of use is higher in comparison with others.

- ArToolKit is software of open access with features of monitoring, guidance and recognition of patterns of markers to create AR, but that requires knowledge of programming for the construction of the AR.
- Layar is a content management system that has digital elements that of type multimedia and 3D images and their content classified by categories.

Construction of the Prototype

The prototype shows the preliminary version of the system with the characterization and behavior modeling which will serve, as the basis to project itself into the final version, is also essential since it forms the basis of the real system. For the construction of the prototype, the following actions taken into account:

1. In the moment in which the user placed in front of the webcam, the system displays the AR on the screen, which perceived as the face of the user. This action, that indicates that the AR information search system has begun.
2. The system prompts the user to enter a search term so that through your database find the AR resource. If you find the written sentence, then associates it with a media item, in this case displays a virtual tour, where is observed the way in which the library is organized. See Figure 6.
3. The next action of the AR shown through virtual, same travel that allows the user to navigate the library facilities, pressing simply buttons with labels that identify the corridors according to the topic that you want to locate. This action gives the user a global perception of the way in which the library is organized. See Figure 7.
4. As a third action, system guides the user through your mobile device, with it, focuses his camera to the markers that are placed strategically and is the way that used to guide it into the location of the shelf where are the books that you want to check. See Figure 8.
5. In this action, the AR overlaps through three-dimensional images and audio. This resource makes that user complements its guidelines, with words that allows you to listen to, for example: "follow the right" or "follow the left".

FUTURE RESEARCH DIRECTIONS

The AR applied to many disciplines, and is in information systems where it has a wide perspective for detailed consultations, in which to display results classified according to various input parameters.

Figure 6. Examples of a project with AR and virtual tour

This search system using AR could be implemented from various perspectives, the idea is that it may be a new alternative to search for location in sectors which may be convenience stores, museums, stadiums, archaeological sites and places of tourist attraction, to name a few. The central idea of this project is that the system has the ability to generate expectations of use, that it incites users so they delve to the facilities, and that derived from it, the system can wake your interest to offer their services.

The way in which the operation of the system perceived could exemplify in the following manner:

For department stores, system could guide the customer in their search for items starting with show you the contents of the store from the entrance, as well as images that demonstrate and encourage users to pursue items with designs and colors available for sale.

Figure 7. Examples of a project with AR and 3D images

It could also be available in a Museum, which will allow you to display the sections with three-dimensional images, attract the attention of visitors in order to create impact and interest in your travel.

In the places of tourist, attraction could show them the different sites that people can visit, where AR systems could make use with three-dimensional images and animations showing the tourist attractions and his operation.

Some of the areas have location and signaling systems so that the user can move within their facilities and locate the designated places, however, such systems are one-way, i.e. its communication is linear and its content is static, which leads to a monotonous reality. as opposed to systems based on AR making use of a parallel communication involving the user and the system, with active and highly dynamic

Figure 8. Markers, placed strategically

and interactive multimedia content and where their messages cause a query with delight and little vagueness in the aim of his explanation.

All of these options would be designed to be used with mobile devices and/or panoramic screens, adding audio, animation and video; You can even add hyperlinks that point to sites on the internet that have more explanation, offers or sales.

CONCLUSION

The need to have better prepared human resources and innovative ideas, because they are generated during their studies or not, encourages the research community to give you answer, albeit in a timely manner, to each of the problems generated, in turn, by those needs. In this context, it takes to create and provide a new learning environment for a specific group of students or people, especially those interested in visiting a library. The knowledge transfer has evolved gradually with the passage of time, and logical that education (which is nothing more than the process of educating) also do so. Thus, new generations of students must be prepared for the challenges which the new technologies you.

In an environment where some countries are still coming out of the global economic recession at different speeds, and some others remain in a gloomy economic environment, education plays a vital role to decrease, at the same time, the negative impact of global economic problems. In this sense, new technologies encourage education to generate human resources with a better quality of education. It topic relating to the transfer of the technology and, simultaneously, the knowledge has been object of study of multiple works of research. However, at the same time many investigations around the world have shown that aid to developing countries as only consisting of the transfer of capital, from the economic point of view, would not be sufficient if the country does not possess adequate human capital level to derive all the possible benefit of such aid. Therefore, through new technologies, is essential to create a new horizon in science and technology as to promote or strengthen the current system of learning in some, if not all, areas of knowledge.

We believe that this work is innovative from the very moment of its approach, since today there are no works that addressed the problems that we have described. In addition, we are completely certain that our contribution will help to generate new projects and research. For example, this work can be the starting point to make in the not-too-distant future and through the AR, are implemented holograms in the area of medicine and perform surgeries in real time. The challenges are many and very important, but we are aware that a contribution like ours would be of great importance to expand the current horizon of learning and not, to create new learning environments or to strengthen those that are not yet very widespread in the international arena.

The creation of new platforms for learning in any area of knowledge, through the AR, allow students to obtain a knowledge of quality as well as also a correct approach to the new technologies for timely implementation and/or development of its activities. This, no doubt, based on the assumption that to acquire the competences of the know-how, students must learn to perform new procedures or be immersed in new learning environments that motivate them in their academic activities. Some of these procedures and/or learning environments can simulate with AR. But still, different environments for learning, with these qualities, could be a proper and effective training means to have a student to assess their own learning.

We also believe that this work may well be oriented both to teachers and students up to the level called Bachelor's degree. Teachers would have new and innovative material available to their classes. That is to say, with the AR teachers can be more innovative work dynamics and, surely, new technologies would be an aspect of catalyst for students to learn in a more emotional way and therefore develop more skills and skills in their classes. However, our proposal is not limited to being only a material training or material support for teaching activities. Rather our work is a door of knowledge to scholars of the area, with or without specific knowledge on the AR, so that they feel motivated to develop new applications, processes or software that assist or facilitate the transfer of knowledge, through these new educational environments, in a classroom. That is to say, the potential readers will find in this work an innovative proposal to incorporate the dynamics of class. The embodied ideas are totally new, since nowadays there are no works that integrate proposals of this nature. While it is true that there are contributions that used Determined applications (such as GPS) make the pursuit of any reference to a public library, also is true that today there are no contributions that contain, using the tool of the AR, all a process or procedure for all a new activity with the students where the main theme is the search for references in a library. As we have already mentioned, this proposal also aims to encourage researchers to use the AR in some process, or several independent or Simultaneous, which is interesting for its dynamics of research and to serve, of course, to generate new learning environments.

Finally, we are convinced that the quality of teaching and learning will improved to create and/or promote new educational environments. In addition, not only the students but also the teachers who choose to introduce the augmented AR to their teaching activities will be able to do so. We are confident that the creation of a new learning platform, through the AR, it will allow students, in any field of knowledge, to obtain knowledge of quality as well as a correct approach to the new technologies for the timely implementation of its activities.

REFERENCES

Agrebi, S., & Jallais, J. (2015). Explain the intention to use smartphones for mobile shopping. *Journal of Retailing and Consumer Services*, *22*, 16–23. doi:10.1016/j.jretconser.2014.09.003

Alkhamisi, A. O., & Monowar, M. M. (2013). Rise of Augmented Reality: Current and Future Application Areas. *International Journal of Internet and Distributed Systems*, *1*(04), 25–34. doi:10.4236/ijids.2013.14005

Azuma, R. (2015). Location-Based Mixed and Augmented Reality Storytelling. In Fundamentals of Wearable Computers and Augmented Reality (pp. 259-276). Academic Press. doi:10.1201/b18703-15

Azuma, R., Baillot, Y., Behringer, R., Feiner, S., Julier, S., & MacIntyre, B. (2001). Recent advances in augmented reality. *IEEE Comput Graph*, *21*(6), 34–47. doi:10.1109/38.963459

Azuma, R. T. (1997). A Survey of Augmented Reality. *Presence (Cambridge, Mass.)*, *6*(4), 355–385. doi:10.1162/pres.1997.6.4.355

Bacca, J., Baldiris, S., Fabregat, R., & Graf, S., & Kinshuk. (2014). Augmented Reality Trends in Education: A Systematic Review of Research and Applications. *Journal of Educational Technology & Society*, *17*(4), 133–149.

Billinghurst, M., Kato, H., & Poupyrev, I. (2001). The MagicBook-moving seamlessly between reality and virtuality. *IEEE Computer Graphics and Applications*, *21*(3), 6–8.

Bishop, B. (2012). Analysis of reference transactions to inform library applications (apps). *Library & Information Science Research*, *34*(4), 265–270. doi:10.1016/j.lisr.2012.06.001

Bowman, D., Kruijff, E., LaVoila, J., & Poupyrev, I. (2005). *3D User Interfaces: Theory and Practice*. Addison-Wesley.

Bravo, E., Santana, M., & Rodon, J. (2015). Information systems and performance: The role of technology, the task and the individual. *Journal Behaviour and Information Technology.*, *1*(3), 247–260. doi:10.1080/0144929X.2014.934287

Brinkman, B., & Brinkman, S. (2013). AR in the library: A pilot study of multi-target acquisition usability. *2013 IEEE international symposium on mixed and augmented reality*, 241-242.

Bulearca, M. y Tamarjan, D. (2010). Augmented Reality: A sustainable marketing tool? *Global Business and Management Research: An International Journal, 2* (2-3), 237-252.

Carreón, G. (2002). *Manual de Bibliotecas*. Madrid: Fundación Germán Sánchez Ruipérez.

Caudell, T. P., & Mizell, D. W. (1992). Augmented reality: an application of heads-up display technology to manual manufacturing processes. *Proceedings of the Twenty-Fifth Hawaii International Conference on System Sciences*, 659-669. 10.1109/HICSS.1992.183317

Chang, K.-E., Chang, C.-T., Hou, H.-T., Sung, Y.-T., Chao, H.-L., & Lee, C.-M. (2014). Development and behavioral pattern analysis of a mobile guide system with augmented reality for painting appreciation instruction in an art museum. *Computers & Education*, *71*, 185–197. doi:10.1016/j.compedu.2013.09.022

Chen, C.-M., & Tsai, Y.-N. (2012). Interactive augmented reality system for enhancing library instruction in elementary schools. *Computers & Education, 59*(2), 638–652. doi:10.1016/j.compedu.2012.03.001

Choudari, A., Joshi, S., Bembalkar, A., Marathe, N. y Sankpal, L.J. (2013). Book tracking application in android for library using GPS. *International Journal of Innovative Research in Computer and Communication Engineering, 1*(1), 30-34.

Clements, P., Bachmann, F., Bass, L., Garlan, D., Ivers, J., Little, R., ... Stafford, J. (2010). *Documentación de las arquitecturas de software: Views and Beyond, segunda edición*. Boston: Addison-Wesley.

Cornford, T., & Shaikh, M. (2013). *Introduction to information Systems. Undergraduate study in Economics, Management, Finance and the Social Sciences*. University of London.

Cuendet, S., Bonnard, Q., Do-Lenh, S., & Dillenbourg, P. (2013). Designing augmented reality for the classroom. *Computers & Education, 68*, 557–569. doi:10.1016/j.compedu.2013.02.015

De Pablos, H., Agius, J., Romero, S., & Salgado, S. (2012). *Organización y transformación de los sistemas de información en la empresa*. ESIC Editorial.

Di Serio, Á., Ibáñez, M. B., & Kloos, C. D. (2013). Impact of an augmented reality system on students' motivation for a visual art course. *Computers & Education, 68*, 586–596. doi:10.1016/j.compedu.2012.03.002

Estapa, A. y Nadolny, L. (2015). The Effect of an Augmented Reality Enhanced Mathematics Lesson on Student Achievement and Motivation. *Journal of STEM Education: Innovations and Research, 16*(3), 40-48.

Ghasemi, A., & Javidan, R. (2014). A New Model as English Tutorial Assistant based on Augmented Reality. *Journal of Educational and Management Studies, 4*(3), 695–701.

Greenfield, P. M. (2009). Technology and informal education: What is taught, what is learned. *Science, 323*(5910), 69–71. doi:10.1126cience.1167190 PMID:19119220

Honkamaa, P., Jäppinen, J., & Woodward, C. (2007). *A lightweight approach for augmented reality on camera phones using 2D images to simulate in 3D*. VTT Technical Research Centre of Finland. doi:10.1145/1329469.1329490

Hugues, O., Fuchs, P., & Nannipieri, O. (2011). New augmented reality taxonomy: technologies and features of augmented environment. In B. Furth (Ed.), *Handbook of augmented reality* (pp. 47–63). New York: Springer. doi:10.1007/978-1-4614-0064-6_2

Ibáñez, M. B., Di Serio, Á., Villarán, D., & Delgado Kloos, C. (2014). Experimenting with electromagnetism using augmented reality: Impact on flow student experience and educational effectiveness. *Computers & Education*, *71*, 1–13. doi:10.1016/j.compedu.2013.09.004

Izkara, J. L., Perez, J., Basogain, X., & Borro, D. (2009). Mobile augmented reality, an advanced tool for the construction sector. *Proc. 24th CIB W78 Conference*, 453-460.

Kaufmann, H. (2002). Construct 3D: An augmented reality application for mathematics and geometry education. *Proc. 10th ACM international Conference on Multimedia*, 656-657.

Kirner, T. G., Reis, F. M. V., & Kirner, C. (2012). Development of an interactive book with Augmented Reality for teaching and learning geometric shapes. *Information Systems and Technologies*, 1-6.

Kucuk, S., Yilmaz, R., & Goktas, Y. (2014). Augmented reality for learning English: Achievement, attitude, and cognitive load levels of students. *Education in Science*, *39*(176), 393–404.

Laudon, J., & Kenneth, C. (2006). *Sistemas de información gerencial- Administración de la empresa digital*. Pearson Educación-Prentice Hall.

Laudon, K., & Laudon, P. (2014). *Management Information Systems Managing the Digital Firm*. Pearson Education Limited.

Leblanc, F., Champagne, B. J., Augestad, K. M., Neary, P. C., Senagore, A. J., Ellis, C. N., & Delaney, C. P. (2010). A Comparison of Human Cadaver and Augmented Reality Simulator Models for Straight Laparoscopic Colorectal Skills Acquisition Training. *Journal of the American College of Surgeons*, *211*(2), 250–255. doi:10.1016/j.jamcollsurg.2010.04.002 PMID:20670864

Liu, T.-Y., Tan, T.-H., & Chu, Y.-L. (2007). *2D Barcode and Augmented Reality Supported English Learning System.* 6th IEEE/ACIS International Conference on Computer and Information Science (ICIS 2007), Melbourne, Australia.

Macey, M. (2014). *ALA releases 2014 State of America's Libraries Report*. Journal American Library Asotiation.

Martín Gutiérrez, J., & Meneses Fernández, M. D. (2014). Augmented Reality Environments for Learning, Communication and Professional Contexts in Higher Education. *Digital Education Review*, *26*, 22–34.

Mekni, M., & Lemieux, A. (2014). Augmented reality: Applications, challen- ges and future trends. *Applied Computational Science Proceedings of the 13th International Conference on Applied Computer and Applied Computational Science (ACACOS 14)*, 23– 25.

Milgram, P., Takemura, H., & Utsumi, F. K. (1994). Augmented reality: a class of displays on the reality–virtuality continuum. Proceedings of telemanipulator and telepresence technologies, 2351, 282-292.

Mutiara, G. A., Hapsari, G. I., & Handayani, R. (2014). Design and Implementation Learning Media of a Computer Hardware Introduction as a Teaching Tool Based-on Augmented Reality Technology. *Contemporary Engineering Sciences*, *7*(13), 611–616. doi:10.12988/ces.2014.4667

Nicolson, D., Chalk, C., Robert, W., Funnell, J., & Daniel, S. (2006). Can virtual reality improve anatomy education? A randomised controlled study of a computer-generated three-dimensional anatomical ear model. *Medical Education*, *40*(11), 1081–1087. doi:10.1111/j.1365-2929.2006.02611.x PMID:17054617

Orlosky, J., Kiyokawa, K., & Takemura, H. (2017). Virtual and Augmented Reality on the 5G Highway. *Journal of Information Processing*, *25*(0), 133–141. doi:10.2197/ipsjjip.25.133

Perez-Lopez, D., & Contero, M. (2013). Delivering educational multimedia contents through an augmented reality application: A case study on its impact on knowledge acquisition and retention. *TOJET: The Turkish Online Journal of Educational Technology*, *12*(4), 19–28.

Pressman, R. (2002). Ingeniería de software, un enfoque práctico. McGraw Hill.

Rabbi, I., & Ullah, S. (2013). A survey on augmented reality challenges and tracking. *Acta Graphica znanstveni časopis za tiskarstvo i grafičke komunikacije, 24*(1-2), 29-46.

Reenskaug, T., & Coplien, J. (2009). The DCI Architecture: A New Vision of Object-Oriented Programming. *Artima Developer Best Practices in Enterprise Software Development*.

Reyes, R. G., Olmos, P. S., & Hernández, H. M. (2016). Private Label Sales through Catalogs with Augmented Reality. In Handbook of Research on Strategic Retailing of Private Label Products in a Recovering Economy. IGI Global.

Riddle, R. S., Wasser, D. E., & McCarthy, M. (2017). Touching The Human Neuron: User-Centric Augmented Reality Viewing and Interaction of in-vivo Cellular Confocal Laser Scanning Microscopy (CLSM) Utilizing High Resolution zStack Data Sets for Applications in Medical Education and Clinical Medicine Using GLASS and Motion Tracking Technology. *The Journal of Biocommunication*, *41*(1), 22–31. doi:10.5210/jbc.v41i1.7563

Riobó Iglesias, J., Aznar Relancio, S., Gracia Bandrés, M. A., & Romero San Martín, D. (2015). *TecsMedia: Análisis de tendencias: Realidad Aumentada y Realidad Virtual. División de Tecnologías Multimedia del Instituto Tecnológico de Aragón.* ITAINNOVA.

Savioja, P., Järvinen, P., Karhela, T., Siltanen, P., & Woodward, C. (2007). *Developing an Augmented Reality Tool for Modern Maintenance Work.* Paper presented in 12th International Conference on Human- Computer Interaction, Beijing, China.

Schall, G., Mendez, E., & Schmalstieg, D. (2008). Virtual redlining for civil engineering in real environments. *Proc. The 7th IEEE International Symposium on Mixed and Augmented Reality (ISMAR 2008)*, 95-98. 10.1109/ISMAR.2008.4637332

Schall, G., Wagner, D., Reitmayr, G., Taichmann, E., Wieser, M., Schmalstieg, D., & Hoffmann-Wellenhof B. (2008). Global pose estimation using multi-sensor fusion for outdoors augmented reality. P*roc. 8th IEEE International Symposium on Mixed and Augmented Reality (ISMAR 2008)*, 153-162.

Schmitz, B., Specht, M., & Klemke, R. (2012). An analysis of the educational potential of augmented reality games for learning. *Proceedings of the 11th world conference on mobile and contextual learning*, 140-147.

Shelton, B. E., & Hedley, N. R. (2002). Using augmented reality for teaching Earth-Sun relationships to undergraduate geography students. *Proc. The First IEEE International Augmented Reality Toolkit Workshop*. 10.1109/ART.2002.1106948

Shin, D. H., & Dunston, P. S. (2008). Identification of application areas for augmented reality in industrial construction based on technological suitability. *Automation in Construction*, *17*(7), 882–894. doi:10.1016/j.autcon.2008.02.012

Takacs, G., Chandrasekhar, V., Tsai, S. S., Chen, D. M., Grzeszczuk, R., & Girod, B. (2010). Unified real-time tracking and recognition with rotation-invariant fast features. *Proc. The Twenty-Third IEEE Conference on Computer Vision and Pattern Recognition*, 934-941. 10.1109/CVPR.2010.5540116

Tanner, P., Karas, C., & Schofield, D. (2014). Augmenting a Child's Reality: Using Educational Tablet Technology. *Journal of Information Technology Education: Innovations in Practice*, *13*, 45-55.

Techakosit, S., & Wannapiroon, P. (2015). Connectivism learning environment in augmented reality science laboratory to enhance scientific literacy. *Procedia: Social and Behavioral Sciences*, *174*, 2108–2115. doi:10.1016/j.sbspro.2015.02.009

Temkin, B., Acosta, E., Malvankar, A., & Vaidyanath, S. (2006). An Interactive Three-Dimensional Virtual Body Structures System for Anatomical Training Over the Internet. *Clinical Anatomy (New York, N.Y.)*, *19*(3), 267–274. doi:10.1002/ca.20230 PMID:16506202

Thomas, B., Close, B., Donoghue, J., Squires, J., De Bondi, P., & Piekarski, W. (2002). First Person Indoor/Outdoor Augmented Reality Application: ARQuake. *Personal and Ubiquitous Computing*, *6*(1), 75–86. doi:10.1007007790200007

Uchiyama, H., & Marchand, E. (2012). Object detection and pose tracking for augmented reality: recent approaches. *18th Korea-Japan Joint Workshop on Frontiers of Computer Vision (FCV).*

Vacchetti, L., Lepetit, V., & Fua, P. (2004). Combining Edge and Texture Information for Real-Time Accurate 3D Camera Tracking. *Proceedings of the Third IEEE and ACM International Symposium on Mixed and Augmented Reality*, 48-57. 10.1109/ISMAR.2004.24

Walsh, A. (2011). Blurring the boundaries between our physical and electronic libraries: Location aware technologies; QR codes and RFID tags. *The Electronic Library*, *29*(4), 429–437. doi:10.1108/02640471111156713

Wang, L. S., Kim, M. J., Love, P. E. D., & Kang, S. C. (2013). Augmented Reality in built environment: Classification and implications for future research. *Automation in Construction*, *32*, 1–13. doi:10.1016/j.autcon.2012.11.021

Weidenhausen, J., Knoepfle, Ch., & Stricker, D. (2003). Lessons learned on the way to industrial augmented reality applications, a retrospective on ARVIKA. *Computers & Graphics*, *27*(6), 887–891. doi:10.1016/j.cag.2003.09.001

Woodward, C., Lahti, J., Rönkkö, J., Honkamaa, P., Hakkarainen, M., Jäppinen, J., ... Hyväkkä, J. (2007). Virtual and augmented reality in the Digitalo building project. *International Journal of Design Sciences and Technology*, *14*(1), 23–40.

Wu, H., Lee, S., Chang, H., & Liang, J. (2013). Current status, opportunities and challenges of augmented reality in education. *Computers & Education*, *62*, 41–49. doi:10.1016/j.compedu.2012.10.024

Yang, M., & Liao, W. (2014). Computer-assisted culture learning in an online augmented reality environment based on free-hand gesture interaction. *Transactions on Learning Technologies*, *7*(2), 107–117. doi:10.1109/TLT.2014.2307297

Yang, Y. F. (2011). Engaging students in an online situation learning language environment. *Computer Assisted Language Learning*, *24*(2), 181–198. doi:10.1080/09588221.2010.538700

Yu, D., Jin, J. S., Luo, S., & Lai, W. (2010). A useful visualization technique: a literature review for augmented reality and its application, limitation and future direction. In M. L. Huang, Q. V. Nguyen, & K. Zhang (Eds.), *Visual information communication* (pp. 311–337). New York: Springer.

Zak, E. (2014). Do You Believe in Magic? Exploring the Conceptualization of Augmented Reality and its Implications for the User in the Field of Library and Information Science. *Information Technology and Libraries*, *33*(4), 23–50. doi:10.6017/ital.v33i4.5638

Zendjebil, I., Ababsa, F.-E., Didier, J.-Y., Vairon, J., & Frauciel, L. (2008). Outdoor Augmented Reality: State of the Art and Issues. *10th ACM/IEEE Virtual Reality International Conference (VRIC 2008)*, 177-187.

Zhou, F., Duh, H. B. L., & Billinghurst, M. (2008). Trends in augmented reality tracking, interaction and display: a review of ten years of ISMAR. *7th IEEE and ACM international symposium on mixed and augmented reality (ISMAR 2008)*.

KEY TERMS AND DEFINITIONS

Augmented Reality: A technology that superimposes a computer-generated image on a user's view of the real world, thus providing a composite view.

Educational Environment: It is a space that is organized and structured to facilitate learning.

Framework: It is a working environment with assistance defined by specific software modules, which may include programs, libraries and an interpreted language.

Information System: It is a set of elements that organized for the treatment and management of information, in order to meet a need or a goal.

New Technologies: Are the latest technological developments and their applications in computing, video, and telecommunications.

Public Library: It is an information center that provides users with all kinds of data and knowledge, regardless of age, race, sex, religion, nationality, language, or social status.

Software Engineering: It is the application of scientific knowledge into the design and construction of computer programs.

Chapter 3
Enhancing Learning and Professional Development Outcomes Through Augmented Reality

Kelly Torres
The Chicago School of Professional Psychology, USA

Aubrey Statti
The Chicago School of Professional Psychology, USA

ABSTRACT

Instructional and training approaches have evolved to become more inclusive of active learning activities that include diverse types of technologies such as augmented reality (AR). Although AR is not a novel concept, it has only recently gained more recognition as being an effective tool to use in formal learning contexts. Researchers who have focused on the use of AR in educational and organizational settings have found that it helps to enhance learners' levels of motivation and their attainment of content knowledge and critical thinking and problem-solving skills. AR tools are also considered to be beneficial since they provide users the opportunity to experience real-world events that they may not be able to experience due to cost constraints (e.g., travel) and lack of prior training (e.g., mechanical equipment).

DOI: 10.4018/978-1-5225-5243-7.ch003

INTRODUCTION

The way in which we teach, train, and acquire information has changed dramatically over the last several decades. Classroom settings now commonly contain technologically enhanced activities in which learners and employees are actively engaged via their laptops, computers, and/or mobile devices. Through the advancement of technology, educators and employers are now able to integrate a wider range of resources to supplement and enhance students' and employees' learning gains and levels of motivation and engagement. In fact, Martín-Gutiérrez and Contero (2011) suggested that augmented reality (AR) has been found to improve not only the learning process but may also result in easing the teacher's workload. Additionally, the inclusion of AR could help to enhance learners' levels of enthusiasm toward learning (Abdoli-Sejzi, 2015). Moreover, Abdoli-Seizi (2105) proclaimed that "AR is currently revolutionizing how we educate and learn" and that the creation of these types of learning experiences may be perceived by learners to be more interesting and satisfying (p. 3). These pedagogical changes may help to meet the unique learning preferences of digital learners who want and may even expect more technologically enhanced learning and training experiences. Indeed, Abdoli-Sejzi (2015) proclaimed that AR is a tool that can have a dramatic impact on contexts that include educational and training experiences.

BACKGROUND

What Is AR?

Researchers have discovered positive learning impacts for individuals who receive contextual and experiential learning experiences constructed in real-world environments with the inclusion of mobile and sensing technologies (Chu, Hwang, Tsai, & Tseng, 2010; Hung, Hwang, Lin, Wu, & Su, 2013). One way to create these types of enhanced learning experiences is through the inclusion of AR into classroom and corporate settings. AR is sometimes referred to as mixed-reality or blended reality (Zhu, Hadadgar, Masiello, & Zary, 2014) and is not a relatively new form of technology. In fact, Roesner, Kohno, and Molnar (2013) indicated that the field AR has been of interest to researchers since the 1960s. Nonetheless, AR has only recently become more popular in academic, organization, and in every day settings. Interestingly, many individuals may have even viewed AR without realizing it. Common examples of AR found on televisions include weather reports and televised sports. However, with the popularity of games such as Pokémon Go, AR has gained more popularity resulting in professionals pondering how they can more effectively incorporate it into their educational and organizational settings. For example, in 2016, Kevin Anderton, a Forbes contributor, stated that Pokémon Go will historically be perceived as the game that brought AR into mainstream. In his article, he further indicated that AR applications are becoming more popular and AR technology is projected to become a 5.7-billion-dollar industry by 2021.

In regard to defining AR, Carmigniani and Furht (2011) described this tool as having a direct and indirect impact of how we view the natural environment via enhanced virtual information that has been created by a computer. Klopfer and Squire (2008) defined AR as "a situation in which a real-world context is dynamically overlaid with coherent location or context sensitive virtual information" (p. 205). Bacca, Baldiris, Gabregat, Graf, and Kinshuk (2014) further explained that AR systems allow "for combining or supplementing real world objects or superimposed information" (p. 133). AR provides the ability to view virtual elements that are projected over real objects. Essentially, through AR tools, one's perception of his/her surrounding environment is augmented through computer and mobile applications.

Giglioli, Pallavicini, Pedroli, Serino, and Riva (2015) also shared that AR projections integrate "an automated calibration procedure [that] takes into account the structure of the surface overlapping the virtual image" (p. 12). Basically, AR helps to transform a user's environment into a digital interface through the inclusion of virtual objectives in the real world and at real time. AR applications are written via 3D programs in which the developer is able to connect animation or contextual digital information to a marker located in the real world. These types of applications are often utilized in education to enhance students' content knowledge as well as in organizations and military settings for training purposes. Additionally, these applications can be used in different platforms (e.g., personal computers, kiosks, smartphones, and glasses) and are provided in multiple formats.

Forms of AR

Location-aware and vision-based are two forms of AR that are commonly utilized for learning purposes. The first form, location-aware, is described by Dunleavy and Dede (2014) as providing learners various forms of digital media that they are able to view with a GPS-enabled smartphone or other similar types of mobile devices. The media that is utilized in location aware AR (e.g., video, 3D images, graphics) augments the physical environment via a narration, overview, and/or navigation. Paterson, Naliuka, Jensen, Carrigy, Haahr, and Conway (2010) suggested that audio play in location aware AR games has an important role in how the player is immersed in the game and the emotional connection that he/she makes to the virtual world depicted in the application.

For vision-based forms of AR, individuals must use their smartphone camera to trigger the digital image (Dunleavy & Dede, 2014). Both forms of AR incorporate several smartphone capabilities (e.g., GPS, camera) to provide "immersion" experiences (the impression that one is engaging in a realistic experience) through transformative technological enhanced learning experiences (Dede, 2009; Johnson, Smith, Willis, Levine, & Hayword, 2011).

AR has also been described as being marker-based or marked-based applications. Johnson, Levine, Smith and Stone (2010) explained that marker-based applications contain three basic components, which include: 1) booklet for marker information, 2) gripper for converting information from the booklet into another form of data, and 3) a cube which is used to augment the material into 3D-rendered information that is displayed on the screen. In regards to markless applications, these types of AR require a tracking system that includes global positioning system (GPS), compass, and an image recognition device.

Availability and Accessibility

Developments in AR have also created the need for technology to address accessibility in virtual worlds. Computer-assisted instruction (CAI) has been successful in teaching students with intellectual disabilities (ID) and autism spectrum disorders (ASD) skills such as reading, vocabulary, and retention (McMahon, Cihak, Wright, & Bell, 2015). To produce barrier-free access, platforms have been designed to transcend physiological or cognitive challenges. For instance, Smith (2011) provided examples that include "haptic input devices for the blind, virtual regions developed according to Universal Design principles, communities dedicated to people with cognitive disorders, the use of the avatar as a counselor, and customizable personae that either transcend or represent a disables person's identity" (p. 387).

Although educators may use augmented reality to teach about accessibility, these types of applications may not be accessible or user friendly for all learners. In Benda, Ulman, and Smejkalová's 2015 study, they discovered that AR activities were often too demanding and confusing for people with intellectual disabilities. Nevertheless, they believed that future research in this area could include the use of devices that allow for easier orientation and handling.

Considerations for AR Implementation

AR applications provide users the opportunity to "travel through their environment while looking at their augmented world through a mobile device" (Radu, 2014, p. 1534); however, individuals are not able to interact directly with the environment in the physical space. In fact, Steele, Hedberg, Fitzgerald, Munnerley, Bacon, and

Wilson (2012) cautioned that AR should not be perceived as a substitution of real reality but as an additional layer that adds to possible experiences and perceptions that help to "augment and enrich reality" (p. 40).

Although AR tools can provide individuals engaging "real world" experiences, they may need to be cautious when using these types of tools. For instance, Tang, Owen, Biocca, and Mou (2003) described AR users as experiencing "attention tunneling" in which their attention is cued by the system. Dunleavy, Dede, and Mitchell (2009) furthermore discovered that AR users may engage in risky behaviors such as walking into traffic due to being so engrossed in their virtual experience. Wu, Lee, Chang, and Liang (2013) advised that cognitive overload, the inclusion of multiple technology devices, and engagement in complex tasks may all be perceived as technological, pedagogical, and learning related barriers for AR activities. Another consideration for the implementation of AR is that the users' ability to access these types of applications across diverse platforms may be limited. Indeed, Kounavis, Kasimati, and Zamani (2012) cautioned that these types of tools might not be able to be accessed across all operating systems.

In regards to implementation, educators may experience difficulties utilizing AR applications due to the limited availability of industry established best practices (Hughes, 2014). Additionally, users of AR may need to be cautious of potential risks associated with computer security and privacy (Roesner, Kohno, & Molnar, 2013). However, KPMG International (2016) implied that the safety of AR users' information is largely dependent on factors such as their user behaviors including how they share their information (e.g., social media, with other AR users). They further expressed that privacy concerns may occur if AR providers experience security breaches in which users' data is compromised. In regards to healthcare considerations, KPMG International (2016) reported that AR providers in the upcoming years may need to consider how to prevent health related risks associated with conditions such as dizziness, eye strain, blackouts, and epileptic seizures.

Although there are a variety of factors that may need to be considered prior to the implementation of AR activities, the inclusion of these learning tasks has been used to enhance physical interaction and memory related learning (Chien, Chen, & Jeng, 2010) and to improve learner satisfaction (Dunleavry, Dede, & Mitchell, 2009). Furthermore, Ibáñez, Di Serio, Villarán, and Delgado Kloos (2014) found that AR applications provided students immediate feedback and increased academic performance. Similar findings were obtained by Ferrer-Torregrosa, Jiménez-Rodríguez, Torralba-Estelles, Garzón-Farinós, Pérez-Bermejo, and Fernández-Ehrling (2016) in which they discovered that students' test scores were less dispersed and they experienced general improvements in their learning when completing class activities that integrate AR tools.

There are many educational benefits to the inclusion of AR since students are afforded the opportunity to simultaneously view real and virtual objects. AR is integrated into a variety of areas including healthcare, education, counseling, and training. Nevertheless, organizations that use AR may need to consider how consumers will utilize this tool. Javornik (2016) cautioned that AR applications should be designed and implemented based on the following criteria: 1) an understanding of how consumers will use the tool, 2) higher levels of collaboration among marketers, designers, and computer scientists, and 3) strategies for how the technology will be integrated into the current consumer's journey. Although there are many factors that may need to be considered prior to implementing AR into an educational or organizational context, the use of this technology can impact learning via physical, cognitive, and contextual perspectives (Bujak, Radu, Catrambone, MacIntyre, Zheng, & Golubski, 2013)

Learning Activities

AR applications can be effective in enhancing learners' academic experiences by "provide[ing] opportunities for private contemplation or reflection, but also interaction, contestation and contribution: a multi-modal way to confront the full richness of reality" (Steel et al., 2013, p. 47). Particularly, learners' engagement in these types of activities can help them to acquire disciplinary knowledge and aid in the enhancement of skills related to critical thinking and problem-solving (West, 2012). The inclusion of AR can promote individuals' affective and content understanding of concepts that they may not be able to easily observe and/or engage with due to time and financial constraints. Additionally, AR activities afford learners the opportunity to manipulate a virtual object or a representation of a real object that would otherwise be inaccessible. By including AR activities in academic and organizational settings, educational experiences can transcend beyond the walls of a classroom or company building and as expressed by Steele et al. (2012) provides learning opportunities at the individual's current location.

Educational Settings

The inclusion of AR has been found to impact learners at all levels of education by increasing learner engagement and content knowledge. AR activities in educational settings helps to enhance learners' levels of interaction and cognition, which may result in more effective student academic outcomes (Lu & Liu, 2015) as well as increase their levels of self-efficacy (Giglioli et al., 2015; West, 2012). By using AR tools, educators are able to "think and react" to a diverse range of situations (West, 2012, p. 49). Lu and Liu (2015) expressed that "current research focused on AR applications in education suggests that learning simulations have a positive impact on learning and learner's attitudes (p. 527). This statement is illustrated in Kamarainen, Metcalf, Grotzer, Browne, Mazzuca, Tutwiler, and Dede's 2013 research in which they found that students gained a deeper understanding of classroom concepts resulting in higher levels of student interaction with course content and their peers. Essentially, AR applications provide student-centered learning approaches in which they are able to transfer knowledge to new situations with limited requirements for additional constructed learning activities (Steele, et al., 2012).

AR tools have additionally been used to augment learning across diverse educational contexts. For example, Yuen, Yaoyuneyong, and Johnson (2011) outlined five directions for AR in educational contexts that include:

- **Discovery Based Learning:** Users are provided real-world information while concurrently required to consider the object of interest. This type of AR activity is often included in content focused on museums, astronomy, and historical locations.
- **Objects Modeling:** Students are able to receive feedback on how items look in diverse settings. This application of AR can be useful for architectural courses.
- **AR Books:** The inclusion of AR in textbooks provides students access to 3D images and interactive, engaging learning experiences. AR textbooks can be found across diverse areas of study and may be particularly appealing to learners who are considered to be digital learners.
- **Skills Training:** AR can be used as a resource to train individuals to acquire specific skills. In areas such as mechanic training, AR can be utilized to provide learners textual instructions on how to resolve a situation that may arise in a given professional setting.
- **AR Gaming:** The use of AR games provides learners the opportunity to interact with virtual information in a real world setting. Through the inclusion of AR games, learners may be able to create new knowledge by gaining a deeper understanding of the relationships and connections of new taught being taught.

Students can also be involved in the design of AR activities as well. Godwin-Jones (2016) proposed that "students can be involved in creating markers, capturing images on their mobile devices, and helping to create the augmentation, which can range from text annotations to video animations" (p. 9). Prior research focused on this area has resulted in outcomes that demonstrate that student generated AR can create positive academic gains (Bower, Howe, McCredie, Robinson, & Grover, 2014; Slussareff & Boháčková, 2016).

The integration of AR activities can be effective in diverse fields of academic study. Hughes (2014) described AR as being particularly useful in scientific fields since students can be provided "bi-dimensional images from the microscopic to that of a volcano" (p. 3). Another example of AR inclusion in K-12 settings could include providing AR images of the solar system. Furthermore, AR tools have been applied in other K-12 and higher education content areas of study such as mathematics and in resources such as AR textbooks and student guides (Lee, 2012) and can be integrated directly into flashcards and other types of instructional reading materials (Abdoli-Sejzi, 2015). AR can likewise be helpful in allowing language learners to visit "virtually" another country they are studying. This can be observed in language classrooms in which educators created lessons around Pokémon Go to engage learners in their second/foreign language learning process (Godwin-Jones, 2016). Valle (2014) has found that the use of AR in language learning contexts has been successful in helping to enhance students' levels of motivation. This increase in motivation can be particularly important for areas of study, such as foreign language coursework, that are often perceived to be anxiety provoking by learners. For students who are able to study abroad, they are able to use AR applications for language translation and to learn more about cultural points of interest (e.g., museums, architecture). Language learners could also use AR applications within their homes or neighborhoods to learn new vocabulary (Kipper & Rampolla, 2012). Additionally, Kipper and Rampolla (2012) stated that updating textbooks with AR could be an effective strategy to help learners more effectively engage and interact with their course content.

In higher education, AR tools may be effective in training students in academic fields of study including areas such as counseling and nutrition. One example of this type of research is Giglioli et al.'s 2015 study focused on the effectiveness of using AR applications to treat specific phobias. The inclusion of AR into counseling related fields of study could provide students the opportunity to learn new techniques for helping their future clients. In regards to nutrition programs of study, AR tools can be utilized to help students learn how to help their future clients or patients learn healthy behaviors (e.g., portion control) (Rollo, Bucher, Smith, & Collins, 2017).

Recently, educators have gained more interest in integrating AR tools into their medical programs and curriculum. The inclusion of AR in this field of study was suggested to be particularly helpful in students acquiring essential competencies including decision-making, adaption of global resources, and teamwork (Zhu et al., 2014). Specifically, Zhu et al.'s (2014) study resulted in providing evidence that

AR can help enhance medical students' acquisition of skills and content knowledge that resulted in learning retention and higher levels of performance on cognitive-psychomotor tasks. Abdoli-Sejzi (2015) moreover suggested using AR in university settings in fields of study that include mechanical engineering, mathematics, and various sciences. Interestingly, Martín-Gutiérrez, Navarro and Acosta (2011) found that the use of AR could have an impact on dropout rates in programs such as engineering. University/college instructors can also use AR tools to provide students virtual field trips based on locations that they are currently studying. For example, instructors of Shakespeare have used AR to provide students the opportunity in order to travel "virtually" to Verona to explore historical and cultural settings of interest that were included in *Romeo and Juliet* (Godwin-Jones, 2016). Abdoli-Sejzi (2015) also contented that AR can be useful for learners and trainers to be able to discuss common virtual environments.

Organizational Settings

AR can be implemented in employee training opportunities that encompass a wide range of activities such as assembly tasks that are complex and integrate underlying skills (e.g., sensorimotor, cognitive) (Webel, Bockholt, Engelke, Gavish, Olbrich, & Preusche, 2013), medical procedures (Sutherland, Hashtrudi-Zaad, Sellens, Abolmaesumi, & Mousavi, 2013), an nuclear accident escape training (Tsai, Liu, & Yau, 2013). The use of AR for training purposes has also been perceived to be satisfying to trainees (Kipper and Rampolla, 2012) and can be replicated under normal conditions (Peniche, Diaz, Trefftrz, & Paramo, 2012).

The use of AR tools have similarly been useful in military trainings. For instance, military instructors can use AR to train students to identify fire hazards and to aid in missions such as combat, raids, and patrol (West (2012). West (2012) further shared that the military can use computers to track soldiers' reactions in these types of situations. This type of data can be essential in helping instructors more effectively and efficiently structure their trainings and to provide immediate, constructive feedback focused on learner performance and improvement. AR can likewise be included in other areas of employment including journalism (Pavlik & Bridges, 2013), aircraft maintenance (De Crescenzio, Fantini, Persiani, Stefano, Azzari, and Salti, 2011), tour guides (Kounavis, Kasimati, & Zamani, 2012; Lee, 2012), medical (Barsom, Graafladn, Schijven, 2016), and engineering (Dini & Mura, 2015). The inclusion of AR in these types of settings can help organizations to provide advanced, cost-effective training sessions in which employees are able to apply immediately the skills and knowledge that they are expected to acquire or demonstrate for their current employment.

CONCLUSION

The way in which our current generation of learners and employees acquire content knowledge, skills, and expertise is constantly changing and evolving due to advances in technology. Additionally, digital learners frequently want and expect learning and training experiences that are dynamic and technologically enhanced. Although there are challenges that need to be considered prior to the implementation of AR activities, this form of technology has the potential to have a positive impact on both cognitive and affective learning outcomes (Ibáñez, et al., 2014). Indeed, Diegmann, Schmidt-Kraepelin, van den Eynden, and Basten (2015) proclaimed, "AR should not be considered a magic bullet in educational environments" (p. 1554) and instead should be implemented based on the unique benefits that it provides to a specific learning context. Essentially, academic institutions and organizational settings need to consider first the scope of learning and training needed and the technological components that may be most effective in ensuring that learners acquire the intended learning outcomes.

Similar to integrating other types of learning activities and technological tools into educational settings, Hughes (2014) recommended that educators define their course goals. This approach is essential in both educational and organizational settings in ensuring that learners are engaged with materials that are aligned with the institutional outcomes of their course or workshop. Hughes illustrated this position (2016) in his comment that "technology should improve communication and education management" (p. 8).

As AR technologies continue to evolve, Lee (2012) predicted that the future of AR will be bright due to the high levels of interest by industry leaders, researchers, trainers, and educators. As a result, AR tools may become more commonplace in both educational and organization settings. Particularly, given that most individuals own a smart phone, tablet, or personal computer as Lee (2012) proclaimed these types of devices and other "electronic innovations are increasingly ushering AR into the mobile space where applications offer a great deal of promise, especially in education and training" (p. 14).

Given the increasing popularity of AR tools, KPMG International (2016) predicted that in 2018 more businesses will begin to use AR. They further proclaimed that by 2019 AR will begin to become a mass market product, and in 2020 businesses will begin to feel comfortable with AR technologies, and lastly that by 2021 AR technology companies will produce products that appeal to mass markets due to them being user friendly. As AR becomes more commonplace and popular, it may become increasing more imperative that we train our learners on how to engage with these types of tools. Particularly by using AR applications, we are able to support the unique learning needs of our digital learners while simultaneously preparing them to be able to utilize various forms of technology they may most likely encounter in their future academic and professional settings.

REFERENCES

Abdoli-Sejzi, A. (2015). Augmented reality and virtual learning environment. *Journal of Applied Sciences Research*, *11*(8), 1–5.

Anderton, K. (2016, November 14). *Augmented reality, the future, and Pokémon Go*. Retrieved from https://www.forbes.com/sites/kevinanderton/2016/11/14/augmented-reality-the-future-and-pokemon-go-infographic/#72acaa6b7e98

Bacca, J., Baldiris, S., Fabregat, R., & Graf, S., & Kinshuk. (2014). Augmented reality trends in education: A systematic review of research applications. *Journal of Educational Technology & Society*, *17*(4), 133–149.

Barsom, E., Graafland, M., & Schijven, M. (2016). Systematic review on the effectiveness of augmented reality applications in medical training. *Surgical Endoscopy*, *30*(10), 4174–4183. doi:10.100700464-016-4800-6 PMID:26905573

Benda, P., Ulman, M., & Smejkalová, M. (2015). Augmented reality as a working aid for intellectually disabled persons for work in horticulture. *Ecological Informatics*, *7*(4), 31–37.

Bower, M., Howe, C., McCredie, N., Robinson, A., & Grover, D. (2014). Augmented reality in education-cases, places, and potentials. *Educational Media International*, *51*(1), 1–15. doi:10.1080/09523987.2014.889400

Bujak, K., Radu, I., Catrambone, R., MacIntyre, B., Zheng, R., & Golubski, G. (2013). A psychological perspective on augmented reality in the mathematics classroom. *Computers & Education*, *68*, 536–544. doi:10.1016/j.compedu.2013.02.017

Carmigniani, J., & Furht, B. (2011). Augmented reality: An overview. In B. Furht (Ed.), *Handbook of augmented reality* (pp. 3–46). New York, NY: Springer. doi:10.1007/978-1-4614-0064-6_1

Chien, C. H., Chen, C. H., & Jeng, T. S. (2010). An interactive augmented reality system for learning anatomy structure. In T. Athanasios (Ed.), *Proceedings of the International MultiConference of Engineers and Computer Scientists* (pp. 370-375). Hong Kong, China: International Association of Engineers.

Chu, H. C., Hwang, G. J., Tsai, C. C., & Tseng, J. C. R. (2010). A two-tier test approach to developing location-aware mobile learning system for natural science course. *Computers & Education*, *55*(4), 1618–1627. doi:10.1016/j.compedu.2010.07.004

De Crescenzio, F., Fantini, M., Persiani, F., Stefano, L., Azzari, P., & Salti, S. (2011). Augmented reality for aircraft maintenance training and operations support. *IEEE Computer Graphics and Applications*, *31*(1), 96–101. doi:10.1109/MCG.2011.4 PMID:24807975

Dede, C. (2009). Immersive interfaces for engagement and learning. *Science*, *323*(5910), 66–69. doi:10.1126cience.1167311 PMID:19119219

Diegmann, P., Schmidt-Kraepelin, M., van den Eynden, S., & Basten, D. (2015). *Proceedings from the 12th International Conference on Wirtschaftsinformatik*. Osnabrück, Germany: Academic Press.

Dini, G., & Mura, D. (2015). Application of augmented reality techniques in through-life engineering services. *Procedia CIRP*, *38*, 14–23. doi:10.1016/j.procir.2015.07.044

Dunleavy, M., & Dede, C. (2014). Augmented reality teaching and learning. In M. Spector, M. Merrill, & J. Bishop (Eds.), *Handbook of Research on Educational Communications and Technology* (pp. 735–745). Heidelberg, Germany: Spring Publishing. doi:10.1007/978-1-4614-3185-5_59

Dunleavy, M., Dede, C., & Mitchell, R. (2009). Affordances and limitations of immersive participatory augmented reality simulations for teaching and learning. *Journal of Science Education and Technology*, *18*(1), 7–22. doi:10.100710956-008-9119-1

Ferrer-Torregrosa, J., Jiménez-Rodríguez, M., Torralba-Estelles, J., Garzón-Farinós, F., Pérez-Bermejo, M., & Fernández-Ehrling, N. (2016). Distance learning ects and flipped classroom in the anatomy learning: Comparative study of the use of augmented reality, video and notes. *BMC Medical Education*, *16*(223), 1–9. PMID:27581521

Giglioli, I., Pallavicini, F., & Pedroli, E. (2015). Augmented reality: A brand new challenge for the assessment and treatment of psychological disorders. *Computational and Mathematical Methods in Medicine*, *2015*, 1–12. doi:10.1155/2015/862942 PMID:26339283

Godwin-Jones, R. (2016). Augmented reality and language learning: From annotated vocabulary to place-based mobile games. *Language Learning & Technology*, *20*(3), 9–19.

Hughes, R. (2014). *Augmented reality: Developments, technologies, and applications.* Hauppauge, NY: Nova Publishers.

Hung, P. H., Hwang, G. J., Lin, Y. F., Wu, T. H., & Su, I. H. (2013). Seamless connection between learning and assessment - applying progressive learning tasks in mobile ecology inquiry. *Journal of Educational Technology & Society*, *16*(1), 194–205.

Ibáñez, M., Di Serio, Á., Villarán, D., & Kloos, C. (2014). Experimenting with electromagnetism using augmented reality: Impact on flow student experience and educational effectiveness. *Computers & Education*, *71*, 1–13. doi:10.1016/j.compedu.2013.09.004

Javornik, A. (2016, April 16). What marketers need to understand about augmented reality. *Harvard Business Review.* Retrieved from https://hbr.org/2016/04/what-marketers-need-to-understand-about-augmented-reality

Johnson, L., Levine, A., Smith, R., & Stone, S. (2010). Simple augmented reality. The 2010 Horizon Report, 21-24. Austin, TX: The New Media Consortium.

Johnson, L., Smith, R., Willis, H., Levine, A., & Haywood, K. (2011). *The 2011 Horizon Report.* Austin, TX: The New Media Consortium.

Kamarainen, A., Metcalf, S., Grotzer, T., Browne, A., Mazzuca, D., Tutwiler, S., & Dede, C. (2013). EcoMOBILE: Integrating augmented reality and probeware with environmental education field trips. *Computers & Education*, *68*, 545–556. doi:10.1016/j.compedu.2013.02.018

Kipper, G., & Rampolla, J. (2012). *Augmented reality: An emerging technologies guide to AR.* Academic Press.

Klopfer, E., & Squire, K. (2008). Environmental detectives - The development of an augmented reality platform for environmental simulations. *Educational Technology Research and Development*, *56*(2), 203–228. doi:10.100711423-007-9037-6

Kounavis, C., Kasimati, A., & Zamani, E. (2012). Enhancing the tourism experience through mobile augmented reality: Challenges and prospects. *International Journal of Engineering Business Management*, *4*, 1–6. doi:10.5772/51644

KPMG International. (2016). How augmented and virtual reality are changing the insurance landscape: Seizing the opportunity. Amstelveen, The Netherlands: Author.

Lee, K. (2012). Augmented reality in education and training. *TechTrends*, *56*(1), 13–21. doi:10.100711528-012-0559-3

Lu, S., & Liu, Y. (2015). Integrating augmented reality technology to enhance children's learning in marine education. *Environmental Education Research, 21*(4), 525–541. doi:10.1080/13504622.2014.911247

Martín-Gutiérrez, J., Navarro, R. E., & Acosta, M. M. (2011). Mixed reality for development of spatial skills of first-year engineering students. In *IEEE 2011 Frontiers in Education Conference*. IEEE.

McMahon, D., Cihak, D., Wright, R., & Bell, S. (2015). Augmented reality for teaching science vocabulary to postsecondary eduation students with intellectual disabilities and autism. *Journal of Research in Education, 48*(1), 38–56.

Paterson, N., Naliuka, K., Jensen, S., Carrigy, T., Haahr, M., & Conway, F. (2010). Design, implementation and evaluation of audio for a location aware augmented reality game. In *Proceedings from the 3rd International Conference on Fun and Games*. New York, NY: ACM. 10.1145/1823818.1823835

Pavlik, J., & Bridges, F. (2013). The emergence of augmented reality (AR) as a storytelling medium in journalism. *Journalism & Communication Monographs, 15*(1), 4–59. doi:10.1177/1522637912470819

Peniche, A., Diaz, C., Helmuth, T., & Paramo, G. (2012). *Proceedings from the WSEAS International Conference on Computer Engineering and Applications*. WSEAS.

Roesner, F., Kohno, T., & Molnar, D. (2013). Security and privacy for augmented reality. *Communications of the AMC,* 1-10.

Rollo, M., Bucher, T., Smith, S., & Collins, C. (2017). ServAR: An augmented reality guide to the serving of food. *International Journal of Behavioral Nutrition, 14*(65), 1–10. PMID:28499433

Slussareff, M., & Boháčková, P. (2016). Students as game designers vs. 'just' players: Comparison of two different approaches to location-based games implementation into school curricula. *Digital Education Review, 29*, 284–297.

Smith, K. (2011). Universal life: The use of virtual worlds among people with disabilities. *Universal Access in the Information Society, 11*(4), 387–398. doi:10.100710209-011-0254-8

Steele, J., Hedberg, J., Fitzgerald, R., Munnerley, D., Bacon, M., & Wilson, A. (2012). Confronting an augmented reality. *Research in Learning Technology, 20*(1), 39–48.

Sutherland, C., Hashtrudi-Zaad, K., Sellens, R., Abolmaesumi, P., & Mousavi, P. (2013). An augmented reality haptic training simulator for spinal needle procedures. *IEEE Transactions on Biomedical Engineering*, *60*(11), 3009–3018. doi:10.1109/TBME.2012.2236091 PMID:23269747

Tang, A., Owen, C., Biocca, F., & Mou, W. (2003). Proceedings from CHI '03*: The Conference on Human Factors in Computing Systems*. Fort Lauderdale, FL: ACM.

Tsai, M., Liu, P., & Yau, N. (2013). Using electronic maps and augmented reality-based training materials as escape guidelines for nuclear accidents: An explorative case study in Taiwan. *British Journal of Educational Technology*, *44*(1), 18–21. doi:10.1111/j.1467-8535.2012.01325.x

Valle, R. (2014). *Teaching with augmented reality is here*. Retrieved from http://edtechreview.in/trends-insights/insights/1503-teaching-with-augmented-reality-it-s-here

Webel, S., Bockholt, U., Engelke, T., Gavish, N., Olbrich, M., & Preusche, C. (2013). An augmented reality training platform for assembly and maintenance skills. *Robotics and Autonomous Systems*, *61*(4), 398–403. doi:10.1016/j.robot.2012.09.013

West, D. (2012). *Digital schools*. Washington, DC: Brookings Institution Press.

Wu, H., Lee, S., Chang, H., & Liang, J. (2013). Current status, opportunities and challenges of augmented reality in education. *Computers & Education*, *62*, 41–49. doi:10.1016/j.compedu.2012.10.024

Yuen, S., Yaoyuneyong, G., & Johnson, E. (2011). Augmented reality: An overview and five directions for AR in education. *Journal of Educational Technology Development and Exchange*, *4*(2), 119–140.

Zhu, E., Hadadgar, A., Masiello, I., & Zary, N. (2014). Augmented reality in healthcare education: An integrative review. *PeerJ*, *2*(469), 2–17. PMID:25071992

Chapter 4
Augmented Reality for Accident Analysis

Samuel Olmos Peña
Universidad Autónoma del Estado de México, Mexico

Gerardo Reyes Ruiz
Universidad Autónoma del Estado de México, Mexico

Marisol Hernández Hernández
Universidad Autónoma del Estado de México, Mexico

Maria Teresa Cuamatzi Peña
Universidad Autónoma del Estado de México, Mexico

ABSTRACT

Around the world a large number of undesirable events, commonly called accidents, occur every year. These events have implications such as injuries of all kinds, fatalities (in many cases tens, hundreds, and thousands), infrastructure losses, economic losses, and negative impacts on the environment. After a detailed analysis of most of these events and the reflection about them, two aspects are obvious: the first is that they all have multiple causal factors and the second is that most are avoidable. There are many reasons why they are not avoided, but the main reason is the inability of individuals and organizations to learn from mistakes.

INTRODUCTION

Around the world a large number of undesirable events, commonly called accidents, occur every year (Heidi, 2017; Schoijet, 1993; US-Chemical Safety & Hazard Investigation Board, 2007; Wadle, 2016; Rogers, 1986; Kunii, Akagi and Kita, 1995). These events have implications such as: injuries of all kinds, fatalities (in

DOI: 10.4018/978-1-5225-5243-7.ch004

many cases tens, hundreds and thousands), infrastructure losses, economic losses, and negative impacts on the environment. After a detailed analysis of most of these events and the reflection about them, two aspects are obvious: the first is that they all have multiple causal factors and the second is that most are avoidable. There are many reasons why they are not avoided; But the main reason is the inability of individuals and organizations to learn from mistakes.

Likewise, most of the investigations that have been made in the area accidents prevention in different areas has been, under different to the systemic approaches; see for example, Fuboa, Kepinga and Xiaominga (2016); Cohen and Felson (1979); Thomas, Int Panis, and Vandenbulcke (2017); Felson and Clarke (1998); Kauker, Kaminski, Karcher, Dowdall, Brown, Hosseini and Strand. (2016); Cornish and Clarke (1986, 1998); Garbarino, Guglielmi, Sanna, Mancardi and Magnavita (2016); Clarke (1997); Clarke and Eck (2003); Townsley and Pease (2001); US (1997); Leight et to the. (1996, 1998); Read and Nick (1998), among others. Despite numerous studies and investigations that have been carried out on failures of systems (accidents); However, there is much evidence of an investigation on the development of methodologies and models for the analysis of accidents with augmented reality.

In this context, the knowledge can be obtained in several ways, but in the vast majority of cases, it is not possible to acquire all relevant information to the event (accident) which arises, so that it is almost never possible to eliminate all elements of uncertainty. In addition to the above, in all cases there is the limitation of the time in the decision-making process: the result is undoubtedly a distinction between correct and incorrect decisions. We can be classified as good or bad decision when you have the evaluation in hindsight.

In short, for decision-making, it is necessary to perform an analysis of the system involved. I.e., a process aimed at the orderly and timely acquisition, as well as the exploration of specific information from the system in a decision taken, i.e. having a learning through events that have occurred in the past.

Various investigations have been developed in use of augmented reality for the development of learning environments or improves these. Foster (2016) is developing a project to create a customizable application usable on a smart phone that implements a selective processing to make it easier for students with visual disabilities to participate and learn from the conferences. Giap, Yin, Hong and Ee (2016) proposed a learning environment with augmented reality for study and compression of the 4 course of biology matter in secondary schools in Malaysia using markers such as pointing devices, is a long-term study that aims to improve the perception and comprehension of students about the processes and phenomena in biology. The use of augmented reality in learning environments not only in classical topics in the development of students, for example, Orman, Price, and Russell (2017), raised the viability of using a learning environment to improve musical abilities.

On the other hand, including reviews of the literature on learning with augmented reality environments have been made. Medical complex, sequential tasks must be mastered and the objective of the review made by Barsom, Graafland and Schijven (2016) was to investigate to what extent the augmented reality applications that are currently used to support the training of medical professionals are of help in this training. The authors conclusions are that: a) to be of value, the application must be able to transfer information to the user, and b) Although the advancement of technology is promising, the literature to date is insufficient to support this evidence. The above items are a small part of the research in augmented reality learning environments. (for more examples see;) Ibanez, Di Serio, Villarán, And Delgado Kloos, 2016; Kurubacak and Altinpulluk, 2017; Vassigh, Elias, Ortega, Davis, Gallardo, Alhaffar, Borges, Bernal and you, 2016; Wu, Lee, Chang and Liang, 2013, among others).

This chapter addresses, first, elements of the General systems theory to help understand more deeply accidents, then displays fault for accidents analysis trees from systemic, or multifactorial approach is exposed as it should be dealt with the technique of the tree's fault for qualitative factors, these trees are a systematic method to acquire information about an accident viewed as a system, information that is obtained can be used in the taking of decisions, a brief explanation is given of how accidents are analyzed from the technical point of view, a model is finally proposed to develop content for trees of faults with augmented reality, then, have a compression more deep and graphic of the factors that contributed to make it happened given accident. In this context, the research project arises from the need to look at the past to learn from mistakes and thus contribute to the prevention and mitigation of the consequences of system failures. A learning environment supported in the augmented reality for the accident analysis is the subject of the investigation of this project of chapter of book.

BACKGROUND

Given the above, we start to a brief approach to the analysis of systems. The word "system" is frequently used and talk about social systems, environmental systems, control systems, computer systems, solar system, philosophical systems, biological systems, among others. The fact that the word is used in very different contexts indicates the complexity of the concept itself. But without engaging in linguistic or semantic we can say that a system is a set of elements (parts) interrelated each other with a purpose in common, that have inputs and outputs, you interrelations, in addition that develops in an environment. For details of the origins, concepts and development of the science of systems, see for example, Emery (1981), Bertalanffy

(1981), Forrester (1961), Kim (1993), Flood (2001), Checkland (2013), Checkland and Scholes (1999).

Checkland has proposed four systems kinds necessary to describe the "everything" in the real world, these are: {a} natural systems, {b} designed physical systems; {c} designed abstract systems; and {d} systems of human activity (Figure 1).

They described below very briefly each of them, for more details see Checkland (1995).

1. **Natural Systems:** They are those whose origins lie in the "origin of the universe", and the author argues that they are the result of the forces and processes that characterize this universe; for example, living systems which are observed on Earth.
2. **Designed Physical Systems:** Are those which are designed as a result of some human purpose and that exist to serve a purpose; for example, any technological system.
3. **Designed Abstract Systems:** These systems represent ordered "product aware" of the human mind; for example, mathematics, poems, philosophy, among others.
4. **Human Activity Systems:** These are less tangible than the natural and designed systems systems. Checkland (1995) argues that in the world you can see clearly innumerable groups of more or less orderly human activities, as a result of any purpose or mission; for example, "the habits of study of the students of UNAM" is an example of a human activity system.

Figure 1. Systems kinds according with Checkland (1995)

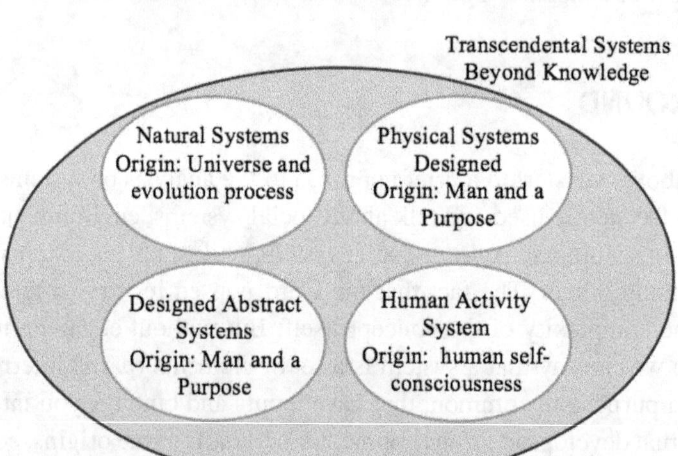

Checkland also argued a combination of the above, and defines (1995, p. 141) social systems as a mixture of rational Assembly of activities together (a set of human activity) and a group of relations that are established in a Community (for example, a natural system). An approach purely behavior, based on the idea of a man as a gregarious animal, will deny the power and influence of rational design; but an approach that assumes that human beings are conscious automata and ignore its cultural dimension, nor pay attention to the problems. In this context, within systems theory the methodologies are divided into "soft" and "hard", in general are divided into two camps:

1. Mathematical theory of "hard" systems (Jensen, 1998; Bayraktar, et at., 1979).
2. Systems of human activity ("soft") (Checkland, 1995; Checkland & Scholes, 1999; Flood, 2001).

"Hard" systems thinking is directed to a target that you want to achieve (Checkland, 1999). The use of these methods in "soft" problems are more difficult to execute, because "the goals" are less clear or depend on the perspectives of those involved in the system. Methodologies can be seen as a spectrum of "soft" and "hard" systems (see Figure 2).

The methodologies of "hard" systems, as for example the research operations (OR), may be appropriate for cases where:

1. Structured problems can be formulated explicitly in a language that implies that it is available a theory relating to their solutions. For example, how can transport product "x" from A to B, with a minimal cost?;
2. The "system" is well defined;
3. There is consensus among stakeholders about the objectives.
4. There is no conflict of interest;
5. Among others.

A typical example of a "hard" methodology could be the design of an air conditioning system.

Figure 2. Spectrum of methodologies, where the methodologies of systems "soft" and "hard" are shown as opposite ends. (Adapted from Beard, et al. 2005)

At the other end of the spectrum are 'soft' methodologies; for example the methodology the system soft (SSM for its acronym in English). For a detailed description of the SSM, see Checkland (1995). In general, the features of soft systems methodologies are the following:

1. Unstructured problems that are manifest in a feeling of concern but that not to be asked explicitly without the apparent attempt to simplify the situation.
2. Not there is consensus among stakeholders about the objectives.
3. There are conflicts of interests; This is there are different perspectives.

The foregoing the following question takes direction: where fault tree is can be located with reality augmented within systems theory? In general, fault trees can be considered as an intermediary metodology, since there are different proposals for analysis and design where it makes use of mathematical theories or look for investigating qualitative factors, in particular those related to the human factor and management (Figure 3).

Risk Tree

Accident analysis approaches traditionally focus on the immediate causes of an unwanted event. This type of events or faults are known as active faults and can be considered as human errors or violations that have immediate impact on the integrity of the system (Grabowski and Roberts, 1996; Andreas, 1999; Anjana, 1997; Perrow, 1984; Black, 1989). Researchers have found that the human factor is one of the key factors that contribute to the occurrence of disasters and major accidents.

However, in recent years the understanding of the nature and importance of organizational errors caused that latter also will be in the attempt of reducing the frequency of accidents and major disasters. The errors inherent in organisations are appointed as latent failures. Frequently, these faults are performed on the stages of design, management and communication, although they can also be deficiencies in the structure of the Organization (Grabowski and Roberts, 1996; Embrey, 1991; Martin

Figure 3. Trees of failures in the context of "soft" and "hard" systems methodologies. (Adapted from Beard, et al. 2005).

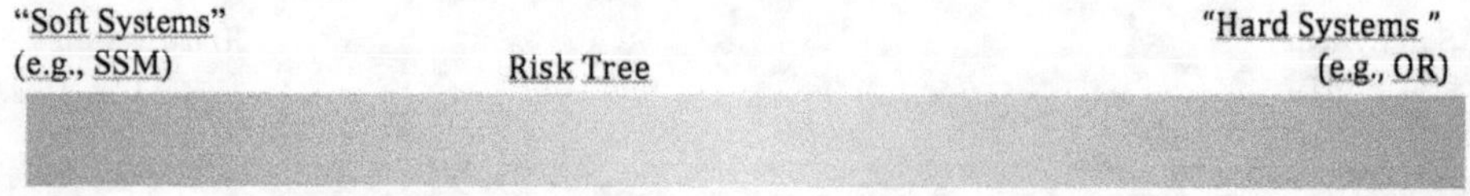

and Siehl, 1990). It is clear that studying and treating organizational failures is as important as focusing on the human or technical causes of accidents. In this regard, the recognition that all events have multiple causes is fundamental in the study of failures of technological systems. This means that each event is the result of a set of causal factors; in other words, each event has multiple causes. The undesirable event (an injury, fatality, among others) is not a single cause-effect relationship.

As shown in Figure 4, the event P has causal factors A, B, C, D and E. According to the approach of the traditional methods ("hard" systems) A, B, D and E must be constant in order to find the effect of the factor C. On the other hand, the fault tree takes into account the fact that the phenomenon is explained by the action of various causes. Thus, a fault tree is an analytical procedure to determine causes and factors that contribute to unwanted event. This tree is focused in the main event and provides a method to determine the causes of an event. The unwanted event is happening in a fault tree built for a given system diagram and usually involves a total or catastrophic failure. The careful choice of the main event is important to the success of the analysis. If it is too general, the analysis becomes unmanageable; If it is too specific, the analysis does not offer a sufficiently broad view of the system. Fault tree analysis can be a costly exercise and time-consuming and cost must be considered against the cost associated with the occurrence of the relevant unwanted event (Vesely, Goldberg, Roberts and Haasl, 1981).

Unforeseen events are those that produce damage or harm, i.e., loss. Losses occur when a harmful agent comes into contact with a person, or a material good. This contact can occur either because of a lack of prevention or as a regrettable, but acceptable, result of a hazard that has been correctly evaluated (the so-called "assumed risk"). Analysis of the accident must always assess the route of the "failure" before

Figure 4. The difference between fault trees and other methods of risk analysis. Own elaboration.

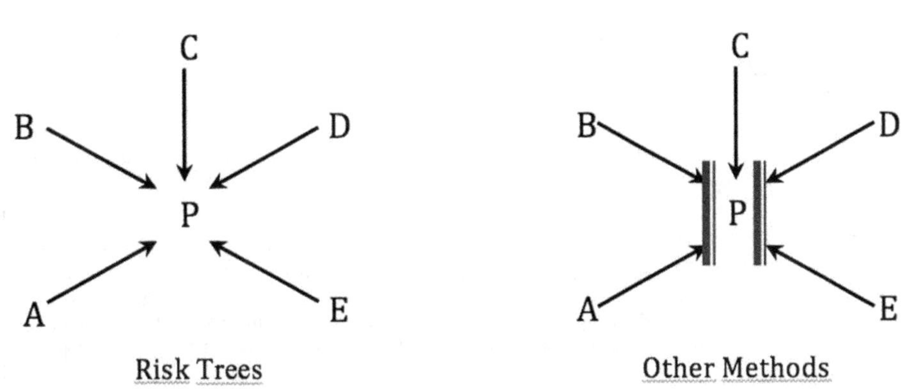

considering the hypothesis "assumed risk". This type of method you have different applications and proposed construction and analysis, see for example; Ming-Hung and Hsue-Cheng Jing-Rong, 2006; Dong and Yu, 2005; Durga, Gopika, Sanyasi-Rao, Kushwaha, Verma and Srividya, 2009.

Conventions of the Fault Tree

For the scope of the chapter, this section introduces the conventions and symbols used in the tree from the failure of a basic form and not delve into aspects of the mathematical description of probabilistic way events, jointly described the step of construction and analysis (see table 1 and 2).

To understand the application of previous symbols, Figure 5 gives an example of an unwanted event called "fire".

In the fault tree events follow a ranking system that reflects the structure of the graph, for this reason, for the construction of this required the participation of experts in the scenarios that are required to raise (DOE, 2008; Johnson, 1980). In addition, the analysis is carried out of up/down and left/right. Fault tree analysis

Table 1. Elemental symbolism of a fault tree (adapted from Vasely et al, 1981; DOE, 2008).

Symbol	Description
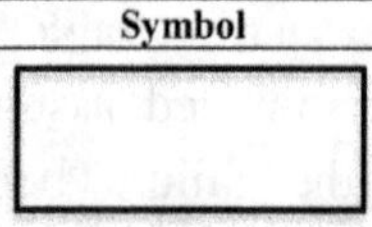	Intermediate or main event. An event that occurs because of one or more causes that act through the gates "and" and "or".
	Basic event. The circle means that event which has been researched more and elemental.
	Gate at their level (and). The generic tree events (intermediate) decompose in its elements grounds using a hierarchical logic and joins reasons with logic gates, 'And' (and) and "O" (or). In this case, it is necessary to ensure compliance with all of the events below immediately.
	Gate or (O). The generic tree events (intermediate) decompose in its elements grounds using a hierarchical logic and it unites causes with logical gates, 'And' (and) and "O" (or). In this case, necessary, met at least one of the immediate lower events.
	Risks assumed. The risks that have been evaluated and properly accepted as something inherent practice of particular activity or almost zero occurrence. To do so, however, they would have to establish the reasons for this decision to a satisfactory level of testing. In practice, this will involve the review of the evaluation of the risk and the cost-benefit analysis that supports the decision.

Table 2. Proposed steps to carry out an evaluation of failures and potential risks.

Step	Description
I.- Understanding the problem	The knowledge of the possible scenarios of failure of expert systems is carried out in this step. In this step are collected testimonies from witnesses, interviews, videos, among others. Together, relevant information has been collected to properly structure failures.
II.- Select top event (fault)	The main event is an event that occurs due to mismanagement of risk, in this case an accident. It should be with the minimum words that provide a clear and concise understanding of the problem. You should be considered the type linked to the event gates, these can be inclusive or exclusive ("or" or "and").
III.- Define assumed risks.	In the application, this involves the thorough review of the assessment of risk and the analysis cost - benefit that supports the decision. I.e., verify that these were properly evaluated
IV.- Build events intermediate to basic events	Define with the help of experts and through scenarios intermediate events within tree decomposing them in its causal elements, using a hierarchical logic and joining the causes with logical gates, this until you reach the basic events. Construction always the type of gate that requires the result should take into account. It is necessary to clarify that there will be both intermediate events depending on the complexity of the accident, which relates directly to cn the amount of factors that produced the accident.
V.- Assess risk factors	The last step in the qualitative analysis is to explain possible faults that led to undesired event. This allows conclusions and take action against possible scenarios. The form of presentation of these results varies depending on the purpose of the application of the fault tree, can be from a manual of risk management into policies of the organization. In summary, you get a learning based on own feedback giving the fault tree.

on causal components are known as input events and their effect is called an output of the (main) event. For example, in Figure 5 the three input events: "Source of ignition", "Fuel" and "Oxygen" produce 'Fire' as an output event. Where all entries are necessary to produce the results, as in the case of fires, input events are added by a gate 'and' to give an output event. Where only an input event is sufficient to produce the result, gate "or" is used. To have a control specific location at an event can be numbered or coded these for ease of analysis.

Accident Investigation

Incident investigation (accident) has made significant progress in recent years, and the methodology to be followed is already well established. The general stages of a typical accidents investigation are shown below in Figure 6.

The following describes briefly each of the stages.

Compilation of information. The data collection stage includes: {a} to obtain and archive any relevant information (manuals, procedures, among others); {b} obtain the testimony of witnesses; {c} conducting direct interviews; {d} among others. A

Figure 5. Example of hierarchical logic of fault tree (adapted from DOE, 2008).

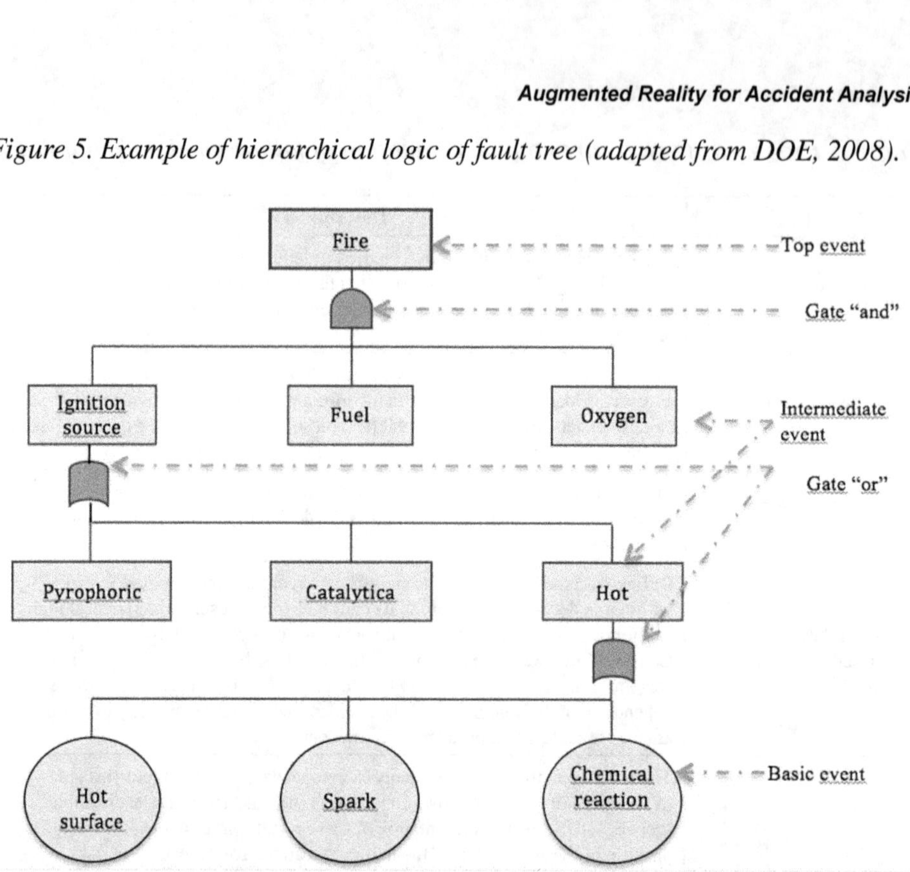

Figure 6. General stages of accident investigation

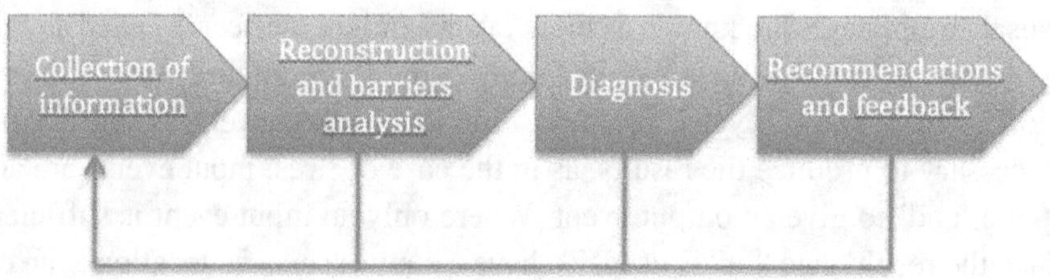

problem of this stage is that in the majority of cases it is not possible to obtain all the relevant information. Missing information may lead to the lack of clarity and the uncertainty in the analysis. For this reason, it is very important to gather the most information at this stage of the investigation that is.

Reconstruction and analysis of barriers. Reconstruction focuses on what took place (happened). At this stage, it is possible to use models of accidents to capture the generic aspects of the adverse event. Some models focus on the chain of events, while others take into account more the changing relationships between individuals and organizations involved. As part of the reconstruction often develops a timeline of what happened. Bias in the research team is a factor that can affect the results of the investigation. The analysis of "barrier and flow of energy," or simply "barrier analysis", produces a clear set of "episodes" that you want to analyze (Ramzali, Lavasani and Ghodousi, 2015;) Khan, Rathnayaka, and Ahmed, 2015). By "Power" refers to harmful agents that threaten or cause actual harm to a "target", which is exposed to it. Although the "energy" and "Energy flow" are the most commonly used terms, the harmful agents may include environmental conditions (for example, biological hazards, the limitation of oxygen, among others).

The "objectives" can be people, things or processes - nothing, in fact, that must be protected or that it would be better if it is altered by the "energy". For this research project, an accident must produce a loss, therefore, at least one of the objectives in the sequence of accidents has to be valuable. However, incidents (sometimes called near misses or almost hits) are also of interest. An incident may be as a result of exposure to a flow of energy without damage or injury, or damage to a target without intrinsic value. The latter case may still be a valuable item for analysis.

On the other hand, "barrier" refers to the means by which the "objectives" are kept safe from "Energy". Indeed, the "barrier analysis" includes not only the barriers (of nature which are purely of protection), but also the work/process controls, because that can also provide protection energies (and objectives) in a safe way.

Very often, an accident reveals a series of episodes where energies are the objectives in unwanted interactions; the analysis of barriers is locate all these and make them available for analysis. This means that in practice Table 3 can have multiple rows, each corresponding to an episode of the interaction of energy with a target.

Analysis of barrier aims to give an account of all undesired interactions between energy and the objectives that must be available for further analysis in the research

Diagnosis. This stage trying to find because the accident occurred. Usually there is feedback between stages of analysis, reconstruction and compilation of data (information) because a greater understanding causes the information in the early stages is parsed more closely. In the analysis phase it is possible to identify root causes and causal factors of event

Table 3. Format of the barrier analysis

Energy flow or harmful agent, the adverse condition of the "environment"	Target or person vulnerable	Barriers and controls for separate "Power" and "Objective"

Recommendations and feedback. As conclusions of the diagnosis of the accident, can identify and implement corrective actions. The processes have to monitor that corrective actions are effective and complete. The most difficult task is usually to make the most profound changes in the structure or in the administration. The conclusions and recommendations must be targeted to the needs of staff who will use. The main objective of this stage is the dissemination of lessons learned. This may be a planned process of the efficient exchange of information at the local level to create an overview at regional, national and international levels.

MAIN FOCUS OF THE ARTICLE

Issues, Controversies, Problems

Several methods have been developed over the years with the aim of investigating accidents. For example, during the 70s and 80s the Department of energy of the United States developed technical for the "reconstruction of incidents", as well as techniques of "argument"; for example, the method of "Analysis of changes" (DOE, 2000; Van Vuuren, 2000), among others. It is worth mentioning that these methods have limitations because concentrating on find the immediate causes of the accidents. On the other hand, the trees of failures to analyze accidents do not seek to find a unique or immediate cause of an undesirable event, on the other hand, explores all those so dissimilar causal factors due to deficiencies in organizational, communication, human aspects among others (Johnson, 1980).

The decision making which has resulted in accidents, in the majority of cases, is a very complex process; any decision is based on the existing understanding of the present situation. This knowledge comes in part from direct experience about the relevant situation or that related to similar situations. This knowledge can be increased through analysis, design, implementation and adequate evidence of the results: i.e. through experimentation. At the same time, the degree of knowledge can be based on conjecture: this will be conditioned by the State of optimism or pessimism of who makes the decision, for example, can believe in Murphy's law: "If something can go wrong, will go wrong" (Vesely, Goldberg, Roberts and Haasl, 1981).

In this context, the operation of a system can be considered from two perspectives: enumerate various forms of system success; otherwise, assume various ways in which the system can fail. This investigation work, proposes a methodology that complements the accidents analysis across fault tree model with developing augmented reality, therefore, it has proposed as guides for accidents analysis, where these will work like architects in its learning.

Then the chapter presents the proposal of a much more comprehensive accident analysis, addressing the problem from the systems approach with fault trees, based on augmented reality for a better compression and simulation of situations in accidents.

SOLUTIONS AND RECOMMENDATIONS

First, we present a model for development of applications with reality of increased very linked to the analysis of accidents.

Phase I: Analysis

Subphase I: Environment of Accident

The environment of a system are all those factors external to this affecting in a negative or positive way the performance of the system. An accident and its results can be approached as a system. The importance of how the environment influences in a set has been dealt with in various studies, see; Bertalanffy (1969); Turnipseed, (1994); Child, (1997); Aldrich, (2008); Rice (2013), among others.

Task I: Understand the Accident Environment

The first work to build trees of faults with reality augmented is to identify the context of the place where happened the accident; identify the space/time, regulatory framework if applicable, objective of the different actors in place, among other aspects that apply to the system in particular. In this task, it is important to collect documents that contribute to the analysis of the accident.

If the accident occurred in an organization, it is priority to know leading its vision and mission, organization skills, strategies and goals, among other factors (Raynor, 1998). Regulations, laws, regulations, manuals of procedures, guides and all document that interferes with the different functions of the Organization must collect in the relevant areas for this purpose

Task II: Identify Organizational Structure

In the accidents occurring in organizations, it is necessary to know the structure of this. This helps to locate the functional areas that were involved with the accident t guide about who interview and who can provide valuable information that reinforce the analysis of the accident. How is divided work and functions are delegated, it synthesizes what is the organizational structure (Mintzberg, 2001). A simple technique which helps to observe organizational structure graphics way are charts.

Task III: Identify the Area Where the Accident Occurred

Depending on the size of the Organization, it is important to know if there are plans, objectives, raison d ' être of the area, etc. Where it happened (see task I) accident. A view you specify where it happened accident is the objective of this proposed task. A good starting point to analyze accidents is to understand how functions are performed and how they interact each part of the organization.

Use case diagrams is a technique that unfolds in a way graphic how interacting users with system. Models both internal users and external users.

The symbols (see Figure 7) use case diagrams which follow are; i) actor: he is the person who performs actions with the system, players are out of the system and can even be other systems; ii) use cases: are the actions that occur within the system; iii) relationships: are connections that are between actors and use cases or the same cases, there are different types, but for this proposals only cover the General; iv) border of the system, is the main barrier between the system itself and the actors (John and Muthig, 2002; Dijkman and Joosten, 2002; Sousa, Kelvin, days, and De Carvalho, 2017; Monda, Das, and Banerjee, 2014).

Task IV: Identify the Involved Procedures

For the simplicity of symbols, for the identification of processes (DFD´s) data flow diagrams are recommended. These diagrams are a graphical technique that shows how flows the information in an organization through different processes (Jonglei and Chenho, 2003; Gorm, Plat and Toetenel, 1994; Coleman, 2013; Khot, Mudur, Thorat and Doulatramani, 2017). The symbolism is simple; a} rectangles or circles representing the process that transforms an input into an outlet, including at the top, a line where encodes the process to which it refers; b} lines that represent the data flow; c} rectangles without the right end line refer to data warehouses (see Figure 8).

In addition to the data flow, the DFD's show different levels of recursion in the transformation of information, starting from a zero level to the level of abstraction determined by the same organization. These levels are encoded as threads of diagrams. Then develops a brief example (zero, level one) on the process of manufacturing of a product.

Figure 7. Basic symbols of use case diagrams

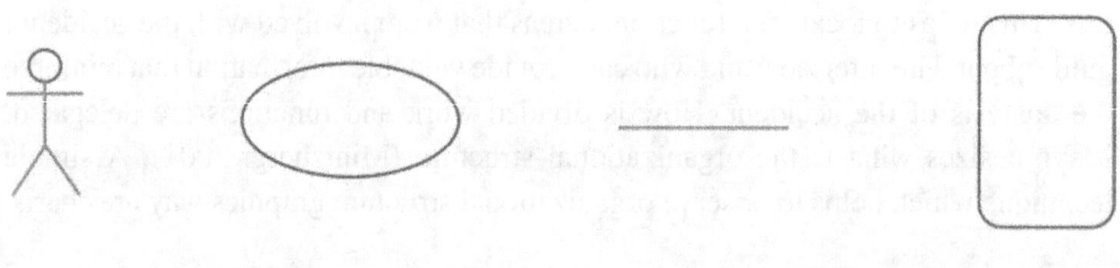

Figure 8. Symbolism of data flow diagrams

The diagrams of data flows give guidelines to identify the processes that transform inputs into outputs. Together, they help identify deficiencies in the process in general. As an example for Figure 9, the processes are described briefly:

P.1. The raw material through mechanism will enter already developed and involved machinery makes precise cuts based on measurements and patterns already established.

P.2. After making cuts is transferred to a subsequent process in which arms following a sequence already programmed. The process involves a quality assurance on the Assembly of the product which provides validation for packaged.

P.3. Starting from the previous process, is wrapped product according to standards that could be applied. All the taks involved at this stage looking for a understanding more broad on the environment of the accident, i.e., to know those external factors that contributed to the accident.

Figure 9. DFD's level one on manufacture of any product

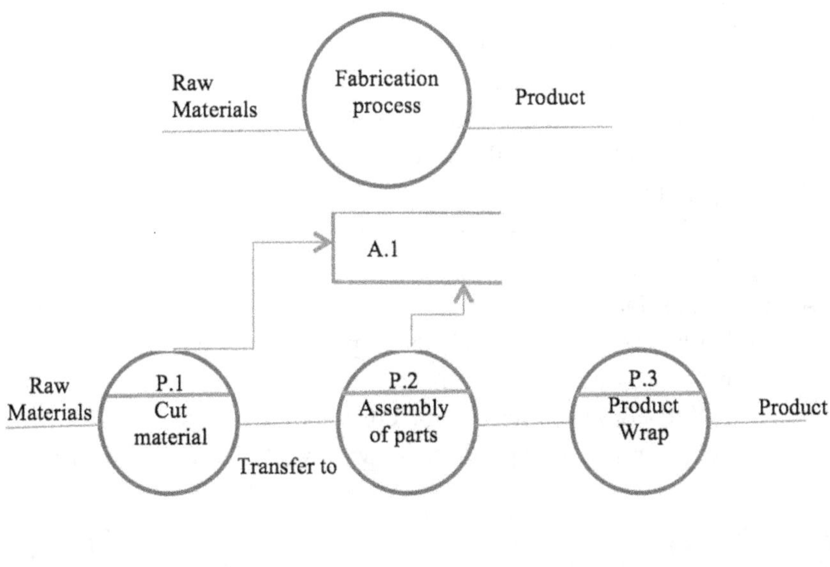

Subphase II: Analysis of Processes

The second stage proposal investigates more in detail on the processes that led to the accident.

Task V: Understanding Accident Elements

To carry out this action is necessary to ask about the accident, these questions are proposed:

- About the processes involved:
  - Who or what and where does the process start?
  - What or who are the processes (areas, data, etc.)?
  - How often do processes start?
  - What do data are needed to process the information?
  - What do data are generated and which are data stored?
  - What do data are originate from sources external to the company?
  - How do it is advisable to present the information?
  - What do processes separate, stages or functions make up the sales process?
  - How long does each activity last?
  - What do factors control the amount of total time?
  - What do delays occur or can they occur?
  - How does the interaction with external elements occur?
  - What is the cost of operating the current systems?
- About the data:
  - What do data are entered into the system and what is its origin?
  - How is the data received? Are stored them? or what is done with them?
  - What do data are stored in the system as part of its activities?
  - Who does uses the information produced by the system? What is it for?
  - What do not parts of the system are used? What do data are missing frequently?
  - How do data are encoded or abbreviated and how are these activities performed?
- About the interfaces:
  - What inputs or outputs are used or produced by the system?
  - What processes create them?
  - What files or Databases do you create or use?
  - Who generates or employs them, with what distribution, in what form?

- About the volumes:
  - How often does the activity occur?
  - Does the activity occur according to a cycle?
- About the controls:
  - What do activities need specific control?
  - What are control methods used in the various activities?
  - What are used parameters to measure and signal performance?
  - Are any national or international standards used?
  - What are methods of fault detection used in the control?
  - Are specific safety precautions taken to safeguard against unauthorized activity?
  - Are there methods to transgress the system? How and why can they occur?
- Other questions:
  - Who are the people who stick to the system?
  - Because are they important?

Subphase III: Solution

Subphase III seeks to develop the trees fault showing as did the accident, in order to determine which images will be developed as augmented reality.

Task VI: Analysis With Fault Trees

Task synthesized through of fault trees an accident viewed as a system, the above supporting phase 1, seeking to know all those external to the accident factors that might contribute to this together with stage ii that inquires about the processes of the accident itself.

Phase II: Design and Construction of the Fault Tree With AR

Fault Tree Design

Since the proposal of accident analysis, which seeks to understand and determine what hapenned in an undesirable event, the requirements are obtained for creating a fault tree with AR. At this phase, it proceeds to develop the design and construction under the actions described in subsequent paragraphs.

Task VII: System Architecture

The establishment of the system architecture, data structures, and Sketches of interfaces and algorithms, is the design of a system. That is to say, it is process that translates the requirements and specifications to technical language (Senn, 2001).

Task The aim of the this phase is to propose the behavior of the solution. Design seeks improvements into systems by adding efficiency, effectiveness, speed, economy and quality visual content. The order, interaction and hierarchical structure of the modules of the computational system are raised in the design of the architecture (Pressman, 2002). However, because its seeked to illustrate by making use of augmented reality to explain what happened in an accident, many of the techniques of data modeling are left for future work by the nature of the fault tres.

Task VIII: Outputs Design and Construction

It is very common that for users, the most important feature of information system based on computers, is the way that produces. If the output is not of quality, you can think systemwide is not good, necessary or proper, therefore, avoid their use or even cause errors (sabotage) generating system to fail.

Logical design of outputs. The concept 'out', applies to any information produced by a computer or computer system, either: printed, folded, verbal, multimedia or the network. It is very common that for users, the most important feature of information system based on computers, is the way that produces. If the output is not of quality, you can think systemwide is not good, necessary or proper, therefore, avoid their use or even cause errors (sabotage) generating system to fail.

The second part of the proposal is seen in Figure 10.

Figure 10 describes the proposal of learning with augmented reality environment to analyze accidents, this environment is given with combination of three methodologies; i) analysis of accidents, ii) fault trees and iii) RA to complement development methodology of fault trees. In the figure you can see the correspondence of each one of the stages with other similar ones of the other methodologies

To develop a learning environment with augmented reality in the analysis of accidents should be made that graphically in the figure, i.e. make a construction from the three methods resulting in robust learning environment. The following paragraphs illustrate briefly analysis of accidents with augmented reality in the case of a car accident. In the analysis it makes use of the fault trees and is exemplified as augmented reality contributes to accidents compression and encourages proposals for new factors favouring that happened an accident.

Figure 10. Proposal of integration of a learning environment for analysis of accidents with augmented reality

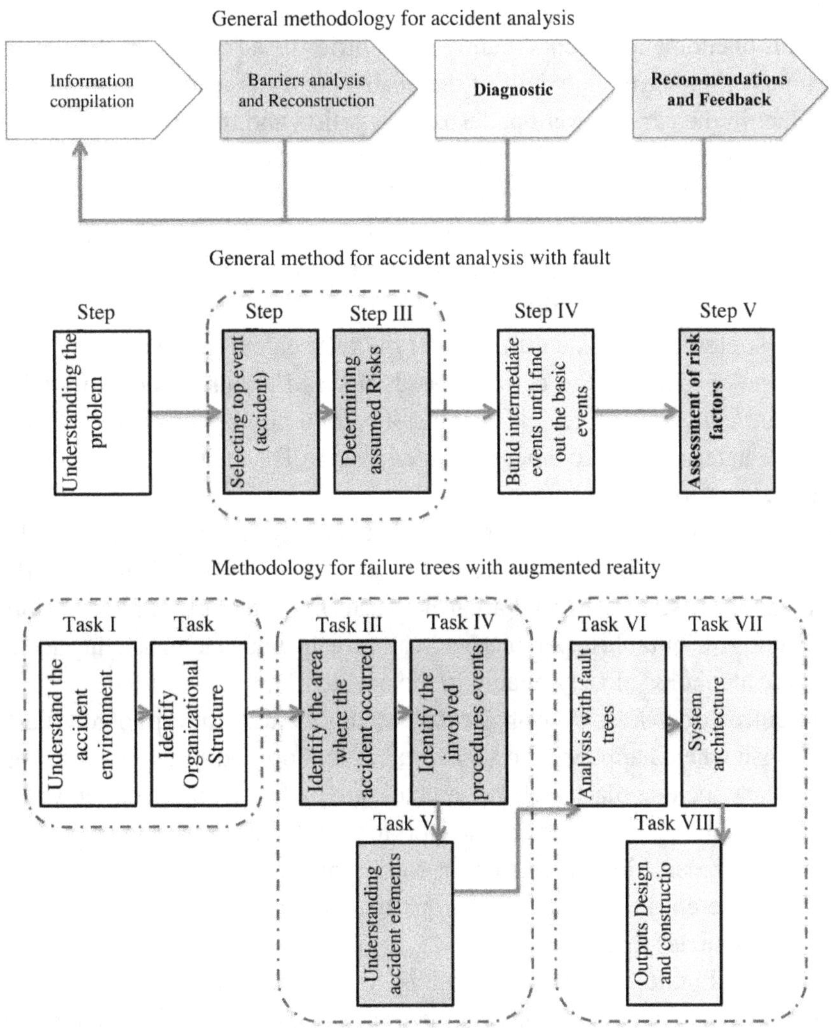

Understanding the Problem

A car accident is that unwanted event that occurs unexpectedly on the road public, are not planned nor controlled, most of the time defined by inadequate conditions; car/ road; acts reckless many of these factors are attributable to the human factor causes and; climate-related conditions. Except for studies that seek to prevent them, there is no experimentation, but data a posteriori of the facts. In this sense, in accident analysis looking for separation and distinction of an event looking for inquire into those faults that were raised which had as a result the final event.

Traffic accidents annually cause the death of millions of people around the world, this phenomenon occurs mainly in countries listed outside of the first world. Unfortunately approximately half of the deaths are users who were not at the time of accident in the car, i.e. were pedestrians, cyclists and motorcyclists. The World Health Organization predicts that such accidents have caused nearly two million deaths by 2020. The Organization of the United Nations mentioned that the main victims of these accidents are young in age range of 15 to 29. The above figures are only people killed by this type of accident, should add them injuries and lost economic impact directly to the people.

The first element is to determine the type of accident that happened, can be a clash of one or more cars to certain speed, also fall within this classification the road kill are collisions of vehicles against a certain number of people. Any of the two types can lead in turn to other unwanted events. The results of any accident can always lead to people.

Another element to determine the accident is the type of vehicle involved in the accident, they can be from goods vehicles up to motorcycles. Then try to identify specific characteristics of driver that can help determine its degree of responsibility in the accident. Attributable to persons behaviors are the main factor causing accidents, such as the alcohol is closely related to the accident.

An element to consider is the physical place, this includes the type of road designed for the transit where happened the accident; a neighborhood street, Avenue, road, or highway, may include places where vehicles, are parked along the town where the facts occurred should be included, this refers to the inhabited place no matter the size.

The last element, in general terms, to be considered is factor climate, those conditions inherent in weather conditions that adversely affect the conditions of security for vehicles management.

Following Figure 10, the proposal is to perform to; stage 1; information compilation; b} step I; {undertanding the problem, c} task I and II; understand the environment of the accident and identify the organizational structure if applicable. Therefore implies, gather information which will contribute to the understanding of the accident.

Structuring the Accident

The second phase to build the learning environment is structured the undesired event, for it to be carried out; stage 2; analysis of barriers and reconstruction; b} step II and III; {Select the main event and determine the risks involved, c} task III, IV and V; identify the area where it happened the accident; identify, if any, procedures involved and understand the elements of the system by questioning of the accident. For the proposed example of a motor vehicle accident is built Table 4 and Figure 11. This gives a structure to the problem, this means, collect loose acts, give them an order and build consistent models that represent the best way the accident with them. They must be reasonable and understandable.

Learning Environment for Analysis of Accidents With Trees of Faults and Augmented Reality

This phase involves; a} step 3; diagnosis; b} step IV; build intermediate events select the main event and determine the risks involved, c} task VI, VII and VIII; develop augmented reality.

For the example that develops, a clash of a car against a concrete column, first explains the structure of the branches, to then illustrate with images of augmented reality the branch of environmental factors that influence the accident.

As previously explained, the environment of a system (an accident is analyzed as a system) are all those external factors that are constantly changing, are temporary and can influence the driving unexpectedly, resulting in an accident, according to the issues raised these are:

- **Fog:** With fog on the road, the vision and the brain are forced to react in the proper front from outside stimuli. Some barriers that reduce this danger are lights for these conditions, as well as the decrease in speed and longer distances between cars.

To support the analysis of accidents with augmented reality you can see figures 12, 13 and 14 that illustrate place the fog effect and it can look at it from different angles to understand deeper this factor in the accident.

Table 4. Example of barrier analysis to research an vehicular accident

Energy flow or harmful agent, the adverse condition of the "environment"	Target or person vulnerable	Barriers and controls for separate "Power" and "Objective"
Fog	Occupants of the vehicle	Lights for fog, vehicular equipment
Bumps on the road	Occupants of the vehicle	Suspensión of the vehicle
Heavy rain	Occupants of the vehicle	Windscreen wiper, vehicle equipment

Figure 11. Risk tree for vehicular accident

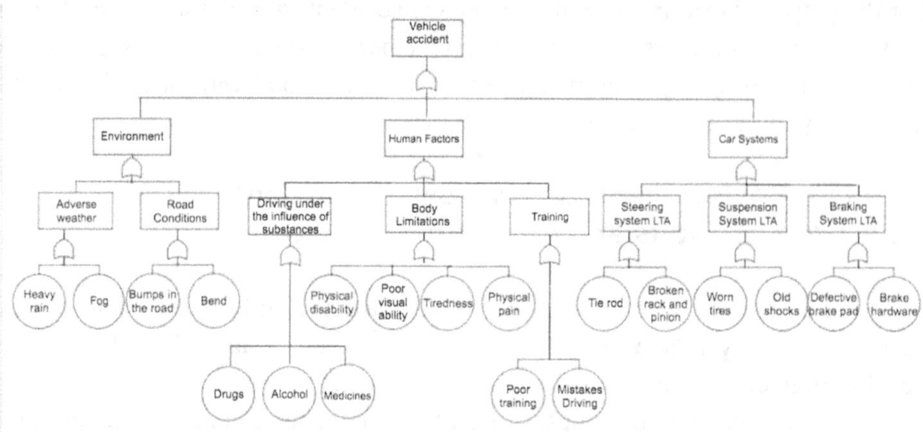

Figure 12. Image with the use of augmented reality from an "a" perspective

Figure 13. Image with the use of augmented reality from an "b" perspective

Figure 14. Image with the use of augmented reality from an "c" perspective

- **Heavy Rain:** A lubricant layer between the tyres and the asphalt, is formed when it rains, decreasing the adherence of the vehicle. Driving at speeds lower than normal and increase the distance between vehicles is one of the recommended action to reduce this type of risk. Like the previous factor, augmented reality helps to pose as the accident influences the environmental element.

Other factors related to the environment, are those related to the paths where it circulates the vehicle, i.e. the conditions of the road.

- **Bumps on the Road:** These defects in the road get worse driving when it rains, also if the visibility is poor often forcing drivers to change its path suddenly aggravate it. Potholes on the road to invite accidents that hinder driving. A problem of this type of deformations of the road are the own fault of the car resulting in accidents. Also augmented reality based on this factor, here first magnify the bump without fog (Figure 15) and then with it (Figure 16).
- **Bends:** Always closed curves which are taken with too much speed are transformed into a latent risk. A dangerous path, accompanied by a defective signaling, contribute to these events. If the curve in addition, it has some degree of inclination increases the risk. See Figure 17.

It is important to mention that the learning environment for the analysis of accidents with augmented reality aims to show how influence elements so that accidents happen modeling reality with causal factors.

From a first analysis, we found new factors that can have an impact such as environmental components, these are:

Figure 15. Image with the use of augmented reality with a bump

Figure 16. Image with the use of augmented reality with a bump and fog

Figure 17. Image with the use of augmented reality with a bend

- **Heavy Wind:** At high intensities the wind increases the risk of tip-over and instability in driving. As in the previous speed is decreased and the distance increases, depending on the risk it is recommended to park in safe places.
- **Ice:** In terms of adherence is much more dangerous than the rain. Although the visibility is not affected. The application of brakes should be soft.

Human Factors

The main cause of accidents in any scenario is the human factor (for this driver analysis), the vast majority of accidents involve sometime a failure of persons.

Driving Under the Influence of Substances

- **Drugs:** Any drug has adverse affects on the human body, many of these affect the nervous system directly involved when driving, others have a numbing effect on various vital functions, result reflexes become more slow and sometimes vision becomes less clear. Within the consequences of using drugs and handle this one resulting in aggression toward other motorists. In this event, if an analysis is required more profound may pose the type of drug consumed that have specific behaviors on the consumers of these
- **Alcohol:** The main cause of fatal accidents is given by such behaviors. Manage alcohol produces the driver serious errors that cause accidents. Some of the effects of alcohol are from falling asleep at the wheel to make decisions outside the common reasoning.
- **Medicines:** The use of certain medications affect people in different ways. These effects range from drowsiness to adverse moods that cause making erroneous decisions.

Body Limitations

- **Physical Disability:** Although the majority of disabled people can drive a car tailored to your needs, it is necessary to find out if a temporary or permanent disability contributed to the accident.
- **Poor Visual Ability:** It is necessary to inquire if the driver had Visual problems that affected their reactions to make decisions when driving. The lack of a proper vision or elements that minimize this problem can cause accidents. For example, you did not read that output to their destination was next until he was too close and this pulled the driver to exit suddenly.

- **Tiredness:** The effect of long working hours, for example, causes body reactions that are counterproductive when driving, the most common is falling asleep. Another can make risky decisions and increase the speed to get the House soon. It should inquire about this item with the driver.
- **Physical Pain:** Late responses to stimuli or inability to perform certain actions to mention only some effects are the result of driving with physical pain due to temporary or chronic injuries. Press brake with a suffered sprain road the car may cause an accident.

Training

Poor training. Poor or no training for driving causes accidents when handling. This derives from the training to manage and make decisions often unforeseen, and that a good training simulates scenarios of this type.

Errors while driving. Related to the previous point, the errors while driving involved most frequently on the vehicle accident, the distraction is one of the major errors that have been committed. This error are presented in different forms and/or situations. For example, the use of cell phone, reading ads, talks with passengers, read messages/maps/texts, light cigarettes, among others.

Vehicle With Faults in Its Systems

A car also can be analyzed as a system, different subsystems can be assessed for the purposes of this example only raise three. If the vehicle has mechanical imbalances this predestined to suffer a mishap, only needs a possible combination of circumstances to make happen by accident.

- **Steering System:** The direction of a vehicle, as well as other systems, are composed of several elements that have a major stake in the priority operation. The direction aims to control trajectory that follows the car. A fault may cause fatal accidents. It is necessary to inquire if it had a failure in this system.
- **Suspension System:** Worn tires can cause sudden punctures that depending on the speed of the car accidents with fatal consequences, defective braking due to low adhesion with the only pavement are some of the defects that influence an accident. Also, within the suspension, shock absorbers play a role within the acceptable conditions and making sure a car.
- **Brake System:** Pads worn and/or defective items within this system has serious consequences on the auto control. In the analysis of the accident it is common to find faults in this type of elements.

The subsystems that compose the vehicle can decompose to a degree far greater detail but due to the expansion of the present chapter, only by way of example to understand how the analysis of the accident can be developed through trees of faults with the support of augmented reality.

FUTURE RESEARCH DIRECTIONS

According to the literature review presented, the topic of learning environment for accident analysis has, among others, three areas of future job opportunity:

1. Although the investigations that have been conducted in the area of analysis of accidents and failures of systems are oriented towards socio-technical systems, there has been no significant development in models or approaches that make use of augmented reality learning environments.
2. On the other hand, the present chapter just introduced to the analysis in an educational environment, therefore it is important to explore new fields of application in the field practice, where surely the proposal for analysis of accidents with RA will be strengthened with new proposals for action.
3. Finally, it is important to mention that specifically the section on technological reality development increased this just at an early stage by which would be interesting to develop specific applications in the area of accident analysis.

CONCLUSION

Those who have the power of decision making within the structure of a nation, company or organization are committed to create conditions of security more robust, these must be created from learning in situations longer periods or with the approach of scenarios that help to this end.

Decision makers must have active systems of monitoring that they can be defined as those that have as main objective the provide feedback on the performance of a system before the occurrence of an undesirable incident. This includes the monitoring of the achievement of specific goals and plans, the given organization operation and compliance with the performance standards. Reactive systems together should be of the monitoring, which can be defined as those that take place after an undesirable event.

In other words, this means that it must conduct an investigation of each accident to learn from failures and prevent such events in the future. This can be achieved through the development of new models or methodologies for the analysis of accidents such as that proposed in this project that relies on the use of augmented reality. This would allow to find systemic causes a failure of certain using the RA for similar scenarios that could occur in real time. To reduce failures of this type, not just the institutions Government and companies have to get involved but also individuals in general; for example, the population must do hear their views on items deemed hazardous under certain circumstances, highlight existing problems and require respective security solutions since there is a risk of observing these with resignation or oblivion. In this context, the research to analyze accidents should contribute to this objective, together there must be proposals for the use of technology to make analysis more robust and new approaches of how an unwanted event really happened. Augmented reality proposes other approaches in the understanding of reality, encourages the approach of new scenarios in the accident analysis simulating effects of conditions which occurred in certain event.

REFERENCES

Aldrich, H. E. (2007). *Organizations and Environments*. Stanford University Press.

Andreas, W. (1999, May 22). Wake up call. *The Scotsman*, 1-2.

Anjana, A. (1997, January 27). Accidents and the human factor. *The Times*, 17.

Barsom, E. Z., Graafland, M., & Schijven, M. P. (2016). Systematic review on the effectiveness of augmented reality applications in medical training. *Surgical Endoscopy*, *30*(10), 4174–4183. doi:10.100700464-016-4800-6 PMID:26905573

Beard, A. N., Thompson, P., Santos-Reyes, J., & Goodwin, J. (2005). *Risk assessment and safety management module*. Edinburgh, UK: H-W University.

Bertalanffy, I. Von. (1981). A systems view of man: collected essays. Boulder, Co: Westview Press.

Black, D. (1989, March 20). The human element at the core of disaster. *The Independent*.

Checkland, P. B. (1995). *Systems Thinking, System Practice*. John Wiley and Sons.

Checkland, P. B. (2013). *Systems Thinking, Systems Practice*. Wiley.

Checkland, P. B., & Scholes, J. (1999). *Soft Systems Methodology in Action*. Chichester, UK: Wiley.

Child, J. (1997). Strategic Choice in the Analysis of Action, Structure, Organizations and Environment: Retrospect and Prospect. *Organization Studies*, *18*(1), 43–76. doi:10.1177/017084069701800104

Clarke, R. V. (Ed.). (1997). *Situational Crime Prevention: successful case studies* (2nd ed.). Harrow and Heston.

Clarke, R. V., & Eck, J. (2003). *Becoming a Problem-Solving Crime Analyst: In 55 Small Steps*. London: Jill Dando Institute of Crime Science.

Cohen, L. E., & Felson, M. (1979). Social change and crime rate trends: A routine activity approach. *American Sociological Review*, *44*(4), 588–608. doi:10.2307/2094589

Coleman, J. (2013). Data Flow Sequences: A Revision of Data Flow Diagrams for Modelling Applications using XML. *International Journal of Advanced Computer Science and Applications*, *4*(5), 28–31.

Cornish, D., & Clarke, R. V. (1998). Understanding Crime Displacement: An application of Rational Choice Theory. In *Criminology Theory Reader*. New York: New York University Press.

De Sousa, T., Kelvin, L., Dias, C., & De Carvalho, C. G. (2017). A Formal Semantics for Use Case Diagram Via Event-B. *Journal of Software*, *12*(3), 189–200. doi:10.17706/jsw.12.3.189-200

Dijkman, R., & Joosten, S. (2002). *Deriving use case diagrams from business process models*. Technical Report 02-08. CTIT.

DOE. (2008). *Department of Energy (DOE)*. Washington, DC: Guideline Root Cause Analysis Guidance Document, Nuclear Energy and Office of Nuclear Safety Policy and Standards.

Dong, Y., & Yu, D. (2005). Estimation of failure probability of oil and gas transmission pipelines by fuzzy fault tree analysis. *Journal of Loss Prevention in the Process Industries*, *18*(2), 83–88. doi:10.1016/j.jlp.2004.12.003

Durga, K., Gopika, V., Sanyasi-Rao, V. V. S., Kushwaha, H. S., Verma, A. K., & Srividya, A. (2009). Dynamic fault tree analysis using Monte Carlo simulation in probabilistic safety assessment. *Reliability Engineering & System Safety*, *94*(4), 872–883. doi:10.1016/j.ress.2008.09.007

Embrey, D. (1991, October). Bringing organizational factors to the fore of human error management. *Nuclear Engineering International*, 50–52.

Emery, F. E. (Ed.). (1981). *Systems Thinking* (Vols. 1–2). Harmondsworth, UK: Penguin.

Felson, M., & Clarke, R. V. (1998). Opportunity Makes the Thief: practical theory for crime prevention. Police Research Series, Paper 98.

Flood, R. L. (2001). *The relationship of "Systems Thinking" to Action Research. In Handbook of Action Research-Participative Inquiry & Practice*. Sage.

Forrester, J. W. (1961). *Industrial Dynamics.* MIT Press.

Foster, P., & Cunniff, S. (2016). *Augmented Reality in the Classroom* (Honors Thesis). Loyola Marymount University.

Fuboa, S., Kepinga, L., & Xiaominga, X. (2016). Railway accidents analysis based on the improved algorithm of the maximal information coefficient. *Intelligent Data Analysis, 20*(3), 597–613. doi:10.3233/IDA-160822

Garbarino, S., Guglielmi, O., Sanna, A., Mancardi, G. L., & Magnavita, N. (2016). Risk of Occupational Accidents in Workers with Obstructive Sleep Apnea: Systematic Review and Meta-analysis. *Sleep, 39*(6), 1211–1218. doi:10.5665leep.5834 PMID:26951401

Giap, N., Yin, O., Hong, L., & And Ee, T. (2016). An Augmented Reality System for Biology Science Education in Malaysia. *International Journal of Innovative Computing, 6*(2), 8–13.

Gorm, P., Plat, N., & Toetenel, H. (1994). A Formal Semantics of Data Flow Diagrams. *Formal Aspects of Computing, 6*(6), 586–606. doi:10.1007/BF03259387

Grabowski, M., & Roberts, K. H. (1996). Human and organizational error in large scale systems. *IEEE Trans Systems man Cybernet Part A. Systems Humans, 26*(1), 2–16. doi:10.1109/3468.477856

Heidi, E. (2017). *Kinds of accident in Great Britain, 2016.* Health and Safety Executive.

Ibáñez, M. B., Di Serio, A., Villarán, D., & Delgado-Kloos, C. (2016). *The Acceptance of Learning Augmented Reality Environments: A Case Study.* 16th International Conference on Advanced Learning Technologies (ICALT), Austin, TX. 10.1109/ICALT.2016.124

Jensen, H. J. (1998). *Self organizad criticality. Cambridge Lecture Notes in Physics.* Cambridge University Press. doi:10.1017/CBO9780511622717

John, I., & Muthig, D. (2002). Tailoring Use Cases for Product Line Modeling. *Proceedings REPL 02. International Workshop on Requirements Engineering for Product Lines.*

Johnson, W. G. (1980). *MORT Safety Assurance Systems.* New York: Marcel Dekker.

Kauker, F., Kaminski, T., Karcher, M., Dowdall, M., Brown, J., Hosseini, A., & Strand, P. (2016). Model analysis of worst place scenarios for nuclear accidents in the northern marine environment. *Environmental Modelling & Software, 77*, 13–18. doi:10.1016/j.envsoft.2015.11.021

Khan, F., Rathnayaka, S., & Ahmed, S. (2015). Methods and models in process safety and risk management: Past, present and future. *Process Safety and Environmental Protection, 98*, 116–147. doi:10.1016/j.psep.2015.07.005

Khot, N., Mudur, K., Thorat, O., & Doulatramani, Y. (2017). A Management Information System on Cloud. *International Research Journal of Engineering and Technology, 4*(4), 372–380.

Kim, D. H. (1993). *Systems Archetypes: Diagnosing systemic issues and designing high leverage interventions.* Pegasus Communications. USA.

Kunii, O., Akagi, M., & Kita, E. (1995). Health consequences and medical and public health response to the Great Hanshin Awaji Earth-quake in Japan: A case study in disaster planning. *Medicine and Global Survival, 2*, 32–45.

Kurubacak, G., & Altinpulluk, H. (2017). *Mobile Technologies and Augmented Reality in Open Education.* IGI Global. doi:10.4018/978-1-5225-2110-5

Leigh, A., & Read, T. (1998). *Brit Pop II: problem-oriented Policing in Practice.* Home Office.

Martin, J., & Siehl, C. (1990). Organizational culture and counterculture: an uneasy symbiosis. In B. D. Sypher (Ed.), *Case studies in organizational communication. Gilford Press.*

Ming-Hung, S., Hsue-Cheng, Ch., & Jing-Rong, Ch. (2006). Using intuitionistic fuzzy sets for fault-tree analysis on printed circuit board assembly. *Microelectronics and Reliability, 46*(12), 2139–2148. doi:10.1016/j.microrel.2006.01.007

Mintzberg, H. (2001). *Diseño de organizaciones eficientes.* New York: Penguin University Books.

Monda, B., Das, B., & Banerjee, P. (2014). Formal Specification of UML Use Case Diagram - A CASL based approach. *International Journal of Computer Science and Information Technologies*, *5*(3), 2713–2717.

Orman, E. K., Price, H. E., & Russell, C. R. (2017). Feasibility of Using an Augmented Immersive Virtual Reality Learning Environment to Enhance Music Conducting Skills. *Journal of Music Teacher Education*, *27*(1), 24–35. doi:10.1177/1057083717697962

Perrow, C. (1984). *Normal accidents: living with high risk technologies*. New York: Basic Books.

Pressman, R. (2002). Ingeniería de software, un enfoque práctico. McGraw Hill.

Ramzali, N., Lavasani, M. R. M., & And Ghodousi, J. (2015). Safety barriers analysis of offshore drilling system by employing Fuzzy Event Tree Analysis. *Safety Science*, *78*, 49–59. doi:10.1016/j.ssci.2015.04.004

Raynor, M. E. (1998). That vision thing: Do we need it? *Long Range Planning*, *31*(3), 368–376. doi:10.1016/S0024-6301(98)80004-6

Read, T., & Nick, T. (1998). *Not Rocket Science? Problem-solving and Crime Reduction.* Home Office.

Rice, A. L. (2013). *The Enterprise and Its Environment: A System Theory of Management Organization*. London: Psychology Press.

Rogers, W. P. (1986). *Report of the presidential commission on the space shuttle challenger accident*. Washington, DC: US Government Printing Office.

Schoijet, M. (1993). Accidentes tecnológicos. *Ciencias*, *30*, 55–60.

Senn, J. A. (2001). Analysis and design of information systems. McGraw Hill.

Thomas, I., Int Panis, L., & Vandenbulcke, G. (2017). On the location of reported and unreported cycling accidents: A spatial network analysis for Brussels. *Cybergeo, European Journal of Geography*, *818*, 1-22.

Townsley, M., & Pease, K. (2001). *What makes a good SARA?* Merseyside Police.

Turnipseed, D. (1994). The Relationship Between the Social Environment of Organizations and the Climate for Innovation and Creativity. *Creativity and Innovation Management*, *3*(3), 184–195. doi:10.1111/j.1467-8691.1994.tb00172.x

US. (1997). *Facilitator's Guide – The Mechanics of Problem Solving: Train-the-trainers. The Community Policing Consortium, supported by the US Department of Justice*. Office of Community Oriented Policing Services.

US-Chemical Safety & Hazard Investigation Board. (2007). *Investigation report-refinery explosion and fire*. Author.

Van Vuuren, W. (2000). *Organizational Failure: An Exploratory Study in the Steel Industry and the Medical Domain* (PhD Thesis). Institute for Business Engineering and Technology Application, The Netherlands.

Vassigh, S., Elias, A., Ortega, F. R., Davis, D., Gallardo, G., Alhaffar, H., . . . Rishe, N. D. (2016). *Integrating Building Information Modeling with Augmented Reality for Interdisciplinary Learning*. International Symposium on Mixed and Augmented Reality (ISMAR-Adjunct), Mérida, Mexico. 10.1109/ISMAR-Adjunct.2016.0089

Vesely, W. E., Goldberg, F., Roberts, N. H., & Haasl, D. F. (1981). *Fault Tree Handbook*. Washington, DC: D.C. Nuclear Regulatory Commission.

Von Bertalanffy, K. L. (1969). General system theory: Foundations, development, applications (rev. ed.). New York: George Braziller.

Wadle, M. (2016). *Update: Fire at the North Harbor in Ludwigshafen. News Release*. BASF.

Wu, H., Lee, S., Chang, H., & Liang, J. (2013). Current status, opportunities and challenges of augmented reality in education. *Computers & Education*, *62*, 41–49. doi:10.1016/j.compedu.2012.10.024

Yonglei, T., & Chenho, K. (2003). Formal definition and verification of data flow diagrams. *Journal of Systems and Software*, *16*, 29–36.

Chapter 5
On the Development of VR and AR Learning Contents for Children on the Autism Spectrum:
From Real Requirements to Virtual Scenarios

Gerardo Herrera
University of Valencia, Spain

Javier Sevilla
University of Valencia, Spain

Lucia Vera
University of Valencia, Spain

Cristina Portalés
University of Valencia, Spain

Sergio Casas
University of Valencia, Spain

ABSTRACT

Autism spectrum disorder (ASD) is an umbrella term used to group a range of brain development disorders. The learning profile of most people with ASD is mainly visual, and VR and AR technologies offer important advantages to provide a visually based mean for gaining access to educational contents. The prices of VR and AR glasses and helmets have fallen. Also, a number of tools that facilitate the development and publication of AR and VR contents have recently appeared. Therefore, a scenario of opportunity for new developments has appeared in this field. This chapter offers guidelines for developing AR and VR learning contents for people on the autism spectrum and analyses those guidelines from the perspective of two important case studies developed in previous years.

DOI: 10.4018/978-1-5225-5243-7.ch005

INTRODUCTION

This chapter approaches the development of VR and AR learning contents for autism considering the important evidence-based knowledge available from the research in social sciences, in order to maximize impact and effectiveness of technological tools to be developed in this area. The chapter starts introducing the formal definition of Autism Spectrum Disorder and the relevant concepts and terms in the area of serious games.

ASD Definition

The term Autism Spectrum Disorder groups a range of brain development disorders. Before 2013, it was widely accepted that people with autism had a 'triad of impairments': in social communication, social interaction and the presence of restricted and repetitive behaviors and interests (according to the DSM-IV by the American Psychiatric Association or APA). Things changed in 2013 when the APA proposed that all autism-related diagnoses (including Autism and Asperger's Syndrome) be given the label 'Autism Spectrum Disorder' (ASD).

The DSM-5 (APA, 2013) provided a definition that described a dyad of impairments in: (1) persistent social communication and interaction deficits in multiple contexts, and (2) restricted, repetitive patterns of behavior, interests, or activities. Both aspects of the dyad must be present for a diagnosis. Most studies indicate that at least 1% of the population have ASD (Atlanta Centre for Disease Control) and it is estimated that 25-50% of individuals with autism also have intellectual disability/learning difficulties.

Visual Learning Style and Technology Use in ASD

No medical treatment is available for the core symptoms of Autism. Students with autism progress much better when specific educational supports are provided. Visual supports for both receptive communication (daily agendas, individual work-systems, tasks structures, etc.) and expressive communication (alternative communication systems based on picture-exchange to communicate what they need, and to share ideas with others) are examples of autism-specific supports that have evidence for their effectiveness. Very often, these visual supports are provided by means of technologies, taking advantage of the visual capabilities of innovative technologies. Lots of technological solutions are available for people with autism, with hundreds of apps for smart devices available on Google Play ® and Apple AppStore ® Markets and with an increasing number of VR and AR solutions running on game consoles or PCs. Given the rapid decrease of the prices for VR and AR solutions produced in the recent years, with the appearance of a number of low-cost VR and AR helmets or glasses, and with the increasing availability of software development tools to facilitate the process of creation of educational contents (such as Unity, Unreal Engine, CryEngine), the interest towards this subgroup of technologies is rapidly increasing.

Terminology and Concepts in the Area of Serious Games

Terms such as Virtual Reality (VR), Augmented Reality (AR), Video games, Educational games, Edutainment or Serious games are currently present in our life. But, what are the differences between them? How can we identify the kind of technology used in a specific application? Before analyzing the state of the art in the area of methodologies used to develop educational applications, we will review this kind of technological concepts that underlie the developments described in this paper.

There are several definitions of VR, because it is a term that evolves and specializes its meaning depending on the evolutions of technologies used and the hardware available for that. The basis of the term is described in Sherman (2003) as a computer-generated 3D environment that allows the user to enter and interact with alternative realities. The users are allowed to “immerse” themselves into an artificial world and interact within it in a great variety of forms. As we can read in Giraldi et al. (2003) the term “Virtual Reality” was coined by Jaron Lanier, founder of VPL Research, and after the appearance of this term, some other terms related to VR can be found in the literature, such as “Artificial Reality”, “Cyberspace”, “Virtual worlds” or “Virtual Environments”. A more complicated definition, more actual and technology-independent is the one found in Steven (2017) where the author defines VR as “inducing targeted behavior in an organism by using artificial sensory stimulation, while the organism has little or no awareness of the interface”.

Another important term needed to clarify the scenario of our study, is the Augmented Reality (AR) definition. Carmigniani and Furht (2011) define AR as “a real-time direct or indirect view of a physical real-world environment that has been enhanced/augmented by adding virtual computer-generated information to it”. In AR applications, there are real and virtual objects. Steven (2017) introduce a different definition of Augmented Reality and Mixed Reality (MR) and the difference between them. They identify AR as “systems where visual stimuli are propagated directly through glasses or cameras to the eyes and some additional structures appear to be superimposed onto the user’s world”. In the case of MR, the term refers more to a combination of VR, AR and normal reality.

The next terms such as video game, educational games or serious games, are more related to the previous terms in that they use some kind of technology for their development. Some of them are based only in virtual worlds, others in VR with some kind of immersion and some others use VR or MR to enhance the engagement of the user. In Esposito (2005) a Video Game is defined as "a game which we play thanks to an audiovisual apparatus and which can be based on a story". This definition involves terms as game, play, interactivity and narrative. In the literature, there are several studies that analyze the benefits and advantages of the educative use of games and video games. Griffiths (2002) reviews the big possibilities and benefits of using Video games for teaching concepts, addressing specific problems or teaching/training certain skills. It was in this environment where terms such as Educational games, Edutainment or Serious Games started to appear, trying to identify a specific use of games for training, learning or teaching while the user is playing and enjoying.

In this specific area related with games, education and learning is where our work has been developed. The following sections are aimed at helping readers to consider the research supporting the background of this area, identifying current problems to be considered and proposing solutions in the form of guidelines to be applied when developing AR and VR learning contents for students with ASD. Finally, two serious game projects are exposed, explaining how they follow the guidelines.

BACKGROUND

In the development of applications for education and learning, some kind of methodology is needed to guarantee the correct achievement of the objectives of each project. In the literature, we can find several methodologies for the development of games and educative games, but none of them is considered to be a standard, so there is no common criterion in the phases and steps needed for a correct development of educative contents for children.

Regarding the game development methodologies, we can find that Sánchez et al. (2009) consider that the methodologies used in video game development are similar to those used in software development, adding some elements specific for games (such as virtual worlds, scenarios, characters design, etc.). For that purpose, they analyze the necessary inclusion of the Playability concept in all the phases of a game development in order to guarantee its quality. Normally, the game testing in traditional methodologies is done in the final testing and validation phase, at the end of the development, but to get better playability results, they add tests with the workgroup and some players in all the phases of the development process, not only in the testing and validation one. The diagram of their methodology is shown in Figure 1.

Slimani et al. (2016) compare different methodologies of game design trying to offer a classification which can help other authors in the decisions making of

Figure 1. Methodology based in playability

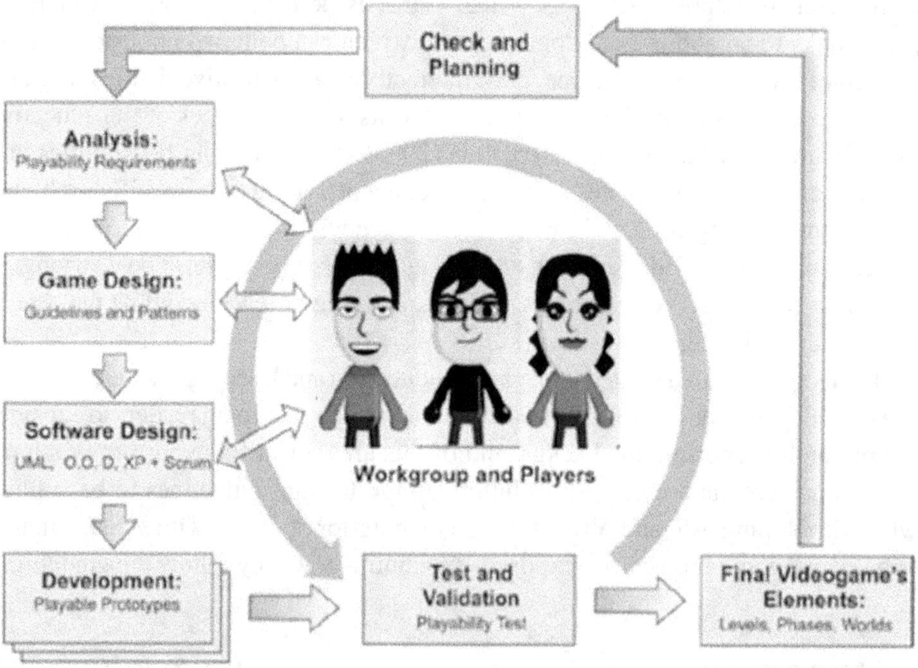

the adequate methodology to be used in their game development. They offer a comparative study of 14 existing methodologies of serious games (from 2004 to 2015), creating a classification between 18 and 99 subcategories. With the analysis of these methodologies, they offer a classification of serious games design based on eleven related design subjects: category, level, layers, purpose, orientation, tools, process, applications, player, users and evaluation. Using those subjects, they create a table with the classification and comparison of the different methodologies.

Al-Azawi et al. (2014) consider that there are many methodologies used in traditional systems and software development, some of them include Waterfull, Incremental and Spiral methods (Boehm, 1988). In game development, one of these is used or a hybrid/combination version of them. Attending to that, they consider two archetypical development models, the predictive and the adaptive models. *Predictive models* create a planning of the work, as a separate task prior to the development and would be preferable when the goals and the customer requirements are clear and completely defined. In the case of *Adaptive models*, the requirements and goals are not completely clear and the customer is allowed to add new goals and requirements in every stage of the project. So, the process is based on prototypes, tests and refinements (Figure 2).

Figure 2. Schematic view of the a) Predictive development methodology, b) Adaptive development methodology

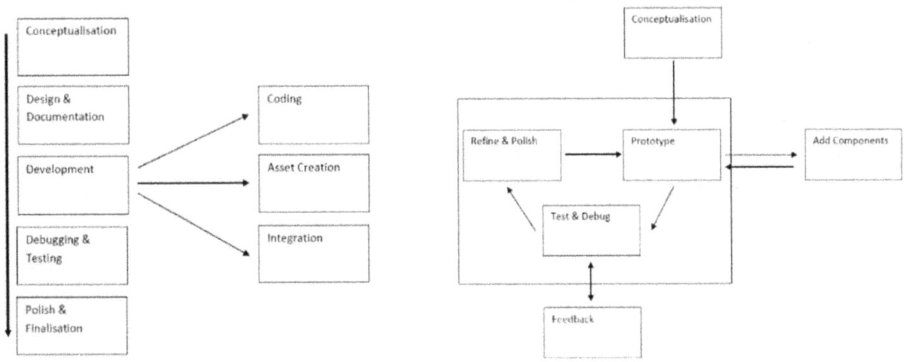

Then they review two specific methodologies, AOSE as a predictive one and Agile as an adaptive one. Finally, they propose an Agent-Agile game development methodology (AAGDM) with an adaptive and predictive development lifecycle. Each iteration includes analysis, design, implementation, testing and evaluation (Figure 3).

Predictive models might be very useful for non-flexible application areas but very inadequate for creating IT solutions for ASD. In this particular area, the application domain is not so clear (or at least it is not clear from the very beginning)

Figure 3. Agent-Agile game development methodology

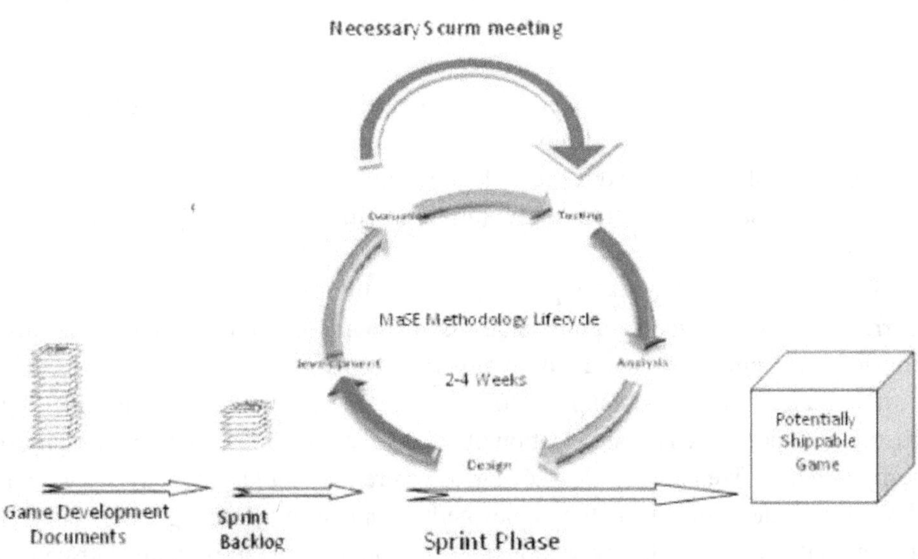

because application conditions can be very different for each final user with ASD, also requiring adaptable solutions that evolve as the user acquires more skills. For this particular case, it is usually more appropriate to apply adaptive models, as the detailed functionality, the design and the implementation may evolve when all the stakeholders have the opportunity to gain access and to test the prototypes of the solutions they envisaged.

Adaptive models are also more useful when the background of the participants involved vary very much from one to another, as it happens in a multi-disciplinary design. This is because not all the people involved can predict the consequences of the decisions made during design and development. Participatory design –where the final users are active participants in the design process- also benefits from this perspective, as these co-designers usually do not have any expertise in these processes and therefore they are not so aware of the consequences of their decisions.

Finally, adaptive models also facilitate fine-tuning of the tools being produced to increase their usability. Usability is a composed measure of the *effectiveness* (the tool works well for the function it was defined, the *efficiency* (in terms of economical and time resources) and the user satisfaction (considering how friendly the tool is). The testing stage, a necessary step in the last part of the development, can also include usability measures that can help to improve the prototype in the following iterations.

In the area of Serious games (Zyda, 2005), there are some studies oriented mainly to methodologies for educational games. Aslan and Balci (2015) describe a complete methodology consisting in 4 phases (Game Design Phase, Game Software Design Phase, Game implementation and Publishing Phase and Game-based Learning and Feedback Phase), and several stages in each phase (see Figure 4). They try to establish a complete methodology for the correct development of a digital educational game of every complexity and size. Also, the authors establish a very complete procedure to accomplish Quality Assurance in the game development and result.

Ibrahim and Jaafar (2009) made a review of three models for the development of Educational Games, and proposed a specific model combining three factors of the models analyzed: game design, pedagogy and learning content modelling, with emphasis on usability, multimodality, fun, problem solving and syllabus matching (see Figure 5).

The concept of a Methodology for Adaptive Educational Game is reviewed in Carro et at. (2002), where authors analyze the meaning of educational games also considering them to be a good tool to motivate the users to test the knowledge they own, to improve it by practicing and to learn what they do not know while enjoying. Also, this paper makes a classification of the educational games in two types: those composed by a fixed sequence of scenarios where the user has to interact with, and those where the user selects the game she/he wants to play among a collection of games. With this in mind, they propose a methodology for adaptive games structured

Figure 4. GAMED development methodology

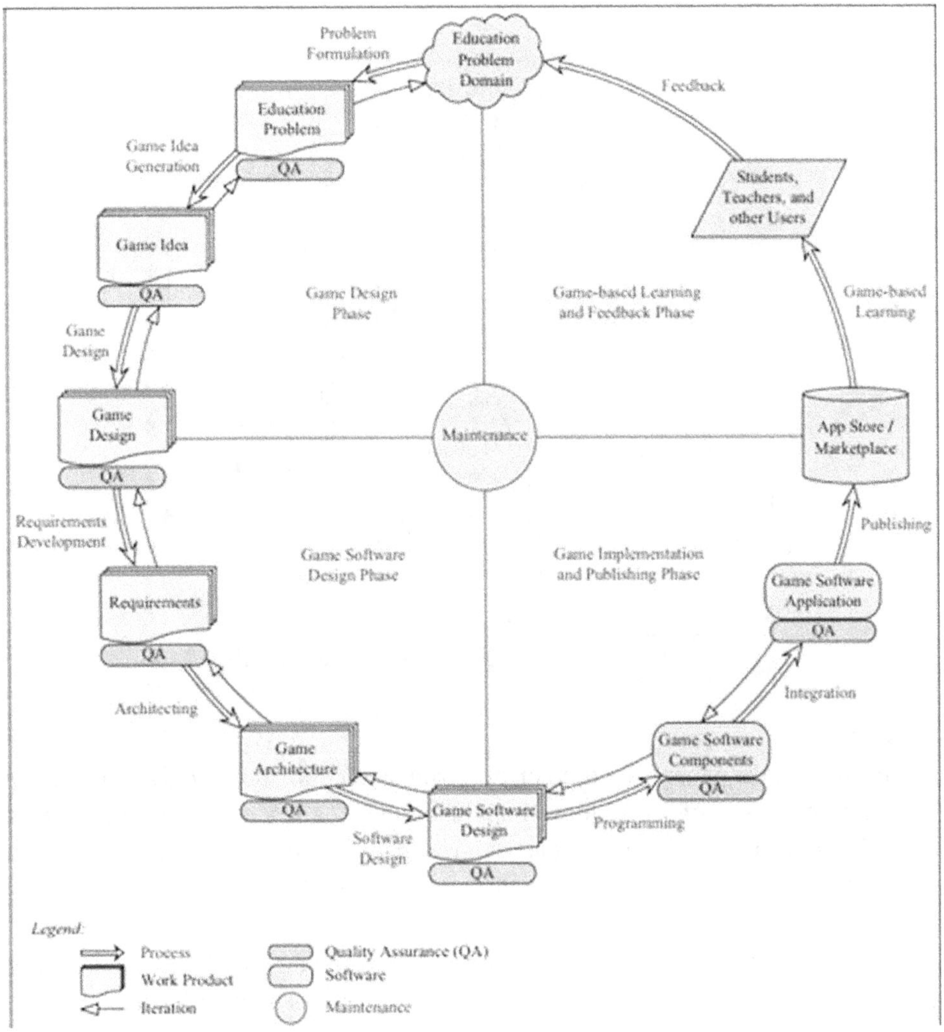

in 5 main steps: target user identification, game goals specification, computer game development, educational methods classification and final description of stories.

Finally, Hanna et at. (2004) evaluate a different methodology where the users, in this case, a small group of children around eight and nine years old, are involved from the very initial stages of the game design. They try to create a method to obtain games of big interest to this kind of public, and also a very big level of engagement. For that reason, the methodology is based on the evaluation of each stage, from initial concepts to prototypes, with a small sample of future users.

Figure 5. Educational Game Design based on Pedagogy and learning content modelling

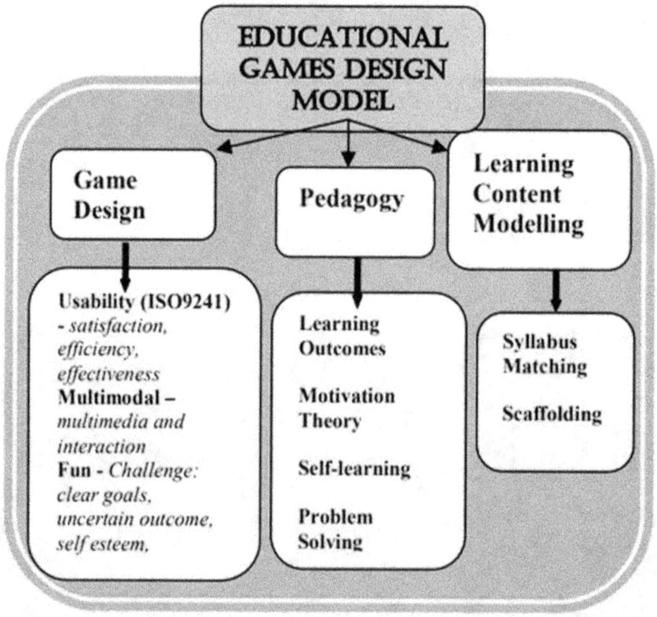

In our case, the paper is focused on proposing a set of methodological guidelines for the development of technological applications or games with learning contents for children with special needs, in particular Autism Spectrum Disorders (ASD) and other related learning difficulties. For that reason, we will focus on the required steps needed to complete the system development to guarantee the quality, the design of the correct contents for the specific skills to be trained and the final evaluation of the resulting game developed, obtaining a level of success in line with the proposed objectives.

Participatory Design: Developing Technologies for and With People With ASD

People with ASD can play a key role in the process of designing tools created for them. A priori, communication and socialization difficulties, together with restricted interests can be considered as 'barriers' to their participation. However, if they receive the support and structure they require, their participation then becomes an opportunity to practice communication and socialize, while at the same time it can improve the usefulness of the tool being created.

Participatory design can help improve the individual self-esteem (as he/she will have the opportunity to see and test the impact of their contributions), improve her/his communication skills and provide the satisfaction of being one of the authors of a tool (Benton et al, 2012). It also contributes to the creation of solutions that are suited to her/his particular needs.

The other members of the team have a collaborative function, complementing the contributions of the individual with ASD with their knowledge and expertise.

During the last years, the knowledge around the process of participatory design have quickly evolved. Some of the more important works include:

Druin (1999) defined a model of 'cooperative inquiry' with different levels of involvement for a child within the technology design process, describing four distinct roles: User, Tester, Informant and Design Partner. According to Benton et al (2012), these roles range from the child having minimal involvement and influence (User) to being seen as an equal stakeholder with the same opportunities to be involved and to contribute as adults (Design Partner). Benton et al (2012) reflect about the role children with special needs such as ASD could potentially undertake, and how dependent their level of involvement is on specific support to overcome their inherent difficulties.

Other authors, such as Keintz et al. (2007) have counted on parents and interventionists of children with ASD as informants and, sometimes, as designers. This is of special relevance when tools are aimed to people who have not developed their communication skills enough as to be able to understand what is going on and provide their own ideas.

Benton et al (2012) created a methodology for participatory design in ASD named IDEAS (standing for Interface Design Experience for the Autistic Spectrum) that is explained in detail within a further section in this chapter.

A good participatory design involves deep knowledge of the participants with ASD and also having updated knowledge about ASD. Considering the unique perspective each individual has about how to approach her/his own difficulties is very enriching for all the participants involved in the design process.

Technologies Being Used for Both Mainstream Curriculum Delivering and to Help Individuals With ASD Overcome Their Autism-Specific Difficulties

The goal of serious games aimed at students with Autism can be related to any curriculum area of interest. Some mainstream videogames are very popular among high-functioning youngsters with ASD (such as Minecraft, a game about placing blocks and going on adventures) and this can be used as a reinforcer to those learners.

Within the autism spectrum, those with higher function may not really need the types of visual supports we mention below, although they can find them helpful in most situations. For those with more difficulties (autism with intellectual disability), these visual supports are essential.

The educational contents of serious games created for autism, can also be aimed at overcoming their difficulties (not only to gaining access to the mainstream curriculum). In fact, over the last decades, the skills trained with VR are very varied. Some studies have trained students to cross street as a safer alternative than the real environment (Strickland et al, 1996), other have trained on social conventions (Mitchell et al, 2007) or imagination (Herrera et al, 2008).

MAIN FOCUS OF THE CHAPTER[1]

Issues, Controversies, Problems

Is It Possible to Benefit From Research Results From Social Science and Apply Them to Technology Design?

In ASD, early intervention programs (usually aimed at children from 0 to 6 years old) have been demonstrated effective for supporting the development of a relevant percentage of children with autism. The most effective programs have a behavioral base (such as the Applied Behavior Analysis or ABA, Cohen et al. (2006)) or cognitive-behavioral base (such as Early Start Denver Model or ESDM, Rogers and Dawson (2010)).

Intervention programs in autism can be classified as focused-intervention (FI) programs (Wong et al, 2015), usually designed for improving a particular ability (or a reduced set of abilities) or comprehensive treatment models (CTM) that are much wider and are based on a holistic approach of the child development (Odom et al, 2010). Some of these programs use technologies as a basis of documenting the child progress, and some other use technology for very particular tasks. However, none of these programs are genuinely based on any particular technology. When available, innovative technologies are used for Focused Interventions rather than as Comprehensive Treatment Models.

Most research evidence available on technologies for ASD relay mainly on the use of particular communicator apps on tablet devices while the evidence on other areas seems to be anecdotal or at least not enough explored (Lorah, 2014). Thus, a fundamental question in this area is if it is possible to benefit from the knowledge coming from the research in social sciences and to apply it for technology design.

Is It Justified to Use VR and AR in ASD?

Brok & Sterkenburg (2014) reviewed the use of virtual environments in ASD. They explain that, in the papers reviewed by them, other technologies were available to work on each study goals, but VR was the technology that better matched with those goals. In six out of the nine studies they reviewed, the argument for selecting VR was the possibility of adapting the environment to participant needs (by simplifying it). Other arguments include interactivity, ecologic validity (assuming an –at least potentially- better generalization from virtual to real environment) and simulation.

There are other reasons why VR is a priori interesting for ASD. Within a virtual environment, it is possible to control the learning process and pace; to control the stimulation load; to provide a safe environment with minimum risks; to provide a predictable environment (where things can happen always in the same way, if desired); and to provide an environment where personalization is easy to implement. However, these are potential beneficial reasons, rather than proven facts, as the level of evidence available in the area is still low.

Is It Important to Personalize Technology for Students With ASD? If So, How Can This Personalization Be Delivered?

Although all individuals with autism share social communication and restrictive patterns of interests and behaviors, the way in which autism affects each individual is very different from one person to another. As a consequence, the needs of each individual are also very different and it is widely accepted that there is no 'best technology for autism' and different efforts are being made to facilitate the way of finding the best technology for each individual with autism (see SMART-ASD project at http://smart-asd.eu).

When it comes to the development of VR/AR solutions, personalization is very important and lots of actions can be developed in order to maximize the motivation and opportunities for learning.

But, how can this personalization be delivered? Later on, this chapter provides guidelines about how to personalize software for individuals with ASD.

Is the Knowledge Acquired in a Virtual Environment Automatically Transferred to the Real Environment?

The effectiveness of the VR/AR environments and tools for training students with ASD to acquire relevant knowledge can be measured in many ways. Standard psychological tests are used to measure progress in the acquisition of social communication skills, flexibility of thinking and behavior or problem solving. Different measures are applied depending on the goals of the games developed.

A very important and common effect that should be measured is generalization. In other words, was the knowledge acquired within the VR/AR transferred to the real world? Most empirical research on VR/AR applied to autism has found important acquisition of knowledge within the virtual environment, however more research is needed when it comes to the transfer of that learning to the real world (Brok and Sterkenburg, 2014).

Wass and Prayska-Pomsta (2013) developed a systematic review focusing on the transfer of knowledge from virtual to real environments, considering mainly VR but also other related technologies. They found several studies reporting negative results in generalization and, in contrast, some other more optimistic, but with a weaker research design. These authors suggest that those negative results might be related to the well-known generalization difficulties people with autism have (Brown and Bebko, 2012). They also suggest that another factor contributing to this lack of knowledge transference are the big differences we can find between both types of environments (virtual and real). As an example, the sensory load such as the environment noise (that makes any task more difficult to perform) is very well controlled within a VR setting and is much more difficult to control in a real setting.

A priori, Augmented Reality and Mixed Realities may facilitate transfer more than Virtual Reality, as the real world is already a component of those AR/MR. But, again, this is more a promise than a proven fact and more research is needed.

SOLUTIONS AND RECOMMENDATIONS

In this section, we describe guidelines for applying existing knowledge coming from the research in social science to design technologies for autism and to deliver personalization for them.

A Proposal to Deliver Personalization in Computer Games

Technological supports for learners with ASD can gather a higher amount of personal data than regular tools or games for mainstream population. This is because this information will be used to adapt the game to the profile of the learner. This data may include:

- **Personal Data:** Real picture or realistic avatar to identify the user within the game; favorite colors in order to adapt the appearance to that preference;

sensory sensitivities (e.g., non-invasive devices for individuals with hyper-sensitivities); etc.

- **Learner Profile:** Including communication skills, level of understanding of abstract information, autonomy, device management skills (e.g., autonomous navigation with controller), token systems, fine motor skills, cognitive function; and other information that can be relevant to adapt the technology to the individual profile.
- Reinforcers, including pictures, videos and audios that can be used to increase motivation to learn within the game (providing positive feedback…)

Another important way to provide personalization is to give students with ASD the opportunity of bringing their unique perspectives and needs by participating in the process of technology design. This will always produce solutions meeting their individual needs, although these needs may enormously vary from one individual to another.

The IDEAS Methodology (from Benton et al, 2012) is a good way of involving participants with ASD in the process of design.

This methodology is structured along six sessions of participatory design:

- **Session 1 – Team Building:** This involves structured activities such as agreeing to a team name, drawing each other's 'team portrait,' thinking of team rules and participation turns.
- **Session 2 – Context Setting:** This means discussing the children's prior experiences of receiving feedback and being rewarded in school. This will inform designers about how to reward them within the technological tools and also helps the children generalize past experiences within this new context and then the concrete examples of the design topic support potential difficulties grasping the topic context, i.e. a math game.
- **Session 3 – Idea Generation:** This implies demonstrating an existing previous solution for the same purpose that was poor at giving feedback and rewarding the player. An initial task in this session is that each team member can produce their own ideas, onto three separate paper template interfaces for what happens if the user provides a correct answer (correct feedback), what happens if they get it wrong (incorrect feedback) and how the game should reward them for winning. After this, these ideas are presented to the rest of the team. Benton et al. suggest that templates are better than a totally blank piece of paper, as this may be too difficult for some children. The individual ideas are then combined into three team ideas (correct, incorrect, reward), with each child responsible for making decisions as to which ideas to include

for one team idea (supported by an adult). By doing it this way, the idea generation process begins with paper prototyping and then moves to more sophisticated materials with the help of a designer with appropriate technical skills (who is also part of the multi-disciplinary design team).

- **Session 4 – Design Development:** This involves showing team members the combined group ideas for the prototyped tool, now on the computer to help make the ideas more concrete. The team members then collectively discuss and agree on how to animate the prototype game, annotating ideas on a paper version of the interface. Between sessions 4 and 5 an animated computer-based prototype can be developed, by a researcher from the design team who has the necessary skills to do so.
- **Session 5 – Design Refinement:** This means refining the team's ideas into a product of higher quality. Between sessions 5 and 6 a researcher refines the computer-based prototype to include these further ideas.
- **Session 6 – Evaluation and Reflection:** This involves evaluating the final prototype and reflecting on the participatory design experience both from an emotional and technical points of view.

This model considers a 1:1 ratio of children/people with ASD and adults to be implemented. Their authors suggest several additional principles to be applied in order to adapt the process as much as possible to the profile of each individual with ASD:

- At the beginning of each session, deliver a timetable or visual panel anticipating the sequence of steps to be followed, where the participant can mark as complete every step already done. Also provide visual explanations of each task and explanations of the rules previously agreed upon, together with pictures and other reminders from previous sessions.
- Remember the difficulties people with autism have to get the whole picture and their tendency to focus on non-relevant aspects. Using an interactive digital board where all the ideas are projected, highlighting the most relevant issues at each moment, may help the participant with ASD keep the focus during the sessions.
- Select a quiet environment with as few distractors as possible. This will help participants get a positive experience.
- Manage anxiety with the participation of some professional who knows in-depth the interests and preferences of the person. He/she will be able to mitigate impulses related to their special interests and will also be able to control their anxiety (that may raise if the participation in the sessions imply important changes in their daily routines).

Scaffolding in Games Development and Autism Interventions

Another important guideline to be considered when personalizing VR and AR solutions is to provide a visual structure and support within the game design. This guideline takes advantage from existing knowledge and research results from social sciences.

The most extended autism-specific program of intervention on educational settings is, without a doubt, TEACCH (standing for Treatment and Education of Autistic and Communication related handicapped CHildren). TEACCH is a comprehensive treatment model that is well known mainly because its visual strategies.

Within TEACCH, different visual supports are provided in order to deliver educational content to the student with autism. At first, TEACCH is very much about 'learn to learn', rather than about learning specific contents. Once the student is familiar with the learning structure, any kind of educational content can be delivered with the support of visual aids.

One of the main strategies of TEACCH is what it is known as 'individual working system' (Figure 6), a visual structure where the students count with well-defined areas for the entry tray (tasks to be done, usually at the left), working area (where tasks are done, usually in front of the student, over the table) and finished work tray (where to put all the tasks once completed, usually at the right). A visual panel located in the wall is typically used to show the sequence of tasks the child is expected to do, with pictures, pictograms or object miniatures used for representing each of the tasks. This sequence is usually composed with Velcro type or magnets and are different from one session to another.

The tasks the child has to develop (usually stored within an 'entry tray') also count on a visual structure (Figure 7), as visual clarity is one of the fundamental principles to teach students with autism.

Figure 6. Example of an individual working system

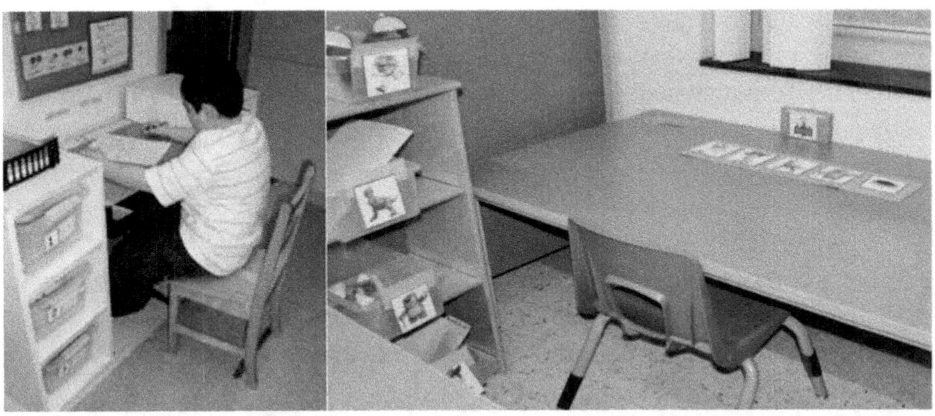

Figure 7. Examples of TEACCH activities

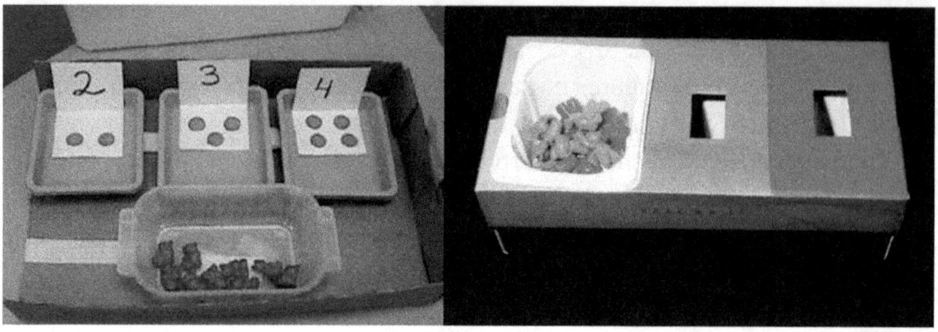

The overall objective of this structure is to provide anticipation (the child knows at every moment what he/she is expected to do), guidance (visual explanations are self-contained within each task so that the child finds it easy) and completion feedback (the child can see the amount of activities already done, together with those that are still pending).

Managing Motivation to Learn in Serious Games for ASD

Handling motivation is a key element in every autism intervention. Within serious game design, principles of playability and engagement should be carefully managed to produce effective games. Typical reinforcers of regular (mainstream) videogames can be meaningless for many individuals with autism, who may need personal reinforcers.

Personal reinforcers can include standard media content, such as pictures of favorite things (a toy, a cartoon character, …), sounds (favorite songs or melodies) or videos (favorite cartoons films or extracts). Those reinforcers can come alone or better accompanied by a well-structured method to inform the user about their meaning within the game and with complementary feedback. Examples of this are the use of tokens that can be obtained as a reward of a given short game and accumulated throughout different screens and finally exchanged by the visualization of one of those reinforcers (seeing an episode of a favorite TV series or listening to a favorite song).

This is the most reasonable and always viable way to implement reinforcers, although more complex ways are also possible. As an example, the themes of the games can be adapted to suit the player's interests. Common interest of some (usually high functioning) individual with autism include trains, space and astronomy, and games where the script is related to these themes can be considered of a highest potential benefit for learners with ASD.

Fostering Generalization From Virtual to Real Environments

Wass and Prayska-Pomsta (2013) suggest new uses of VR where more properties from the real environments are gradually included in the VR world, thus reducing differences between both environments as part of the training (i.e. increasing the noise in the VR setting to facilitate transition to the real setting).

Other gradual transitions can be implemented as well. In robot-based interventions for autism, the less human appearance and behavior of the robot seems to be a facilitator for interaction for children who find it difficult to interact with real people. In a similar way, virtual agents or characters participating in the virtual environments can behave more like robots at the initial stages of an intervention and, later on, prior to moving to real environments, they can be programmed to behave and look more human for facilitating this transition.

Moving from a completely virtual setting to an augmented and/or mixed reality setting (were elements from the real world are already present) may also facilitate the final transition to the real world with no supports available. In any case, it is possible that the individual with autism still needs supports in the real environment (with augmented elements or with any other type of support), as it happens with any other intervention in autism, whether it is technologically-based or not.

CASE STUDIES

SAVIA Project

The main objective of the SAVIA project was to provide support to the educational and training interventions that professionals and families perform with people with Autism Spectrum Disorders (ASD).

SAVIA intended to establish a prototype of virtual and augmented reality environments where it was possible to frame all the educational contents necessary to provide educational support to people with ASD, with or without Intellectual Disability. It was designed to work on interactive platforms and natural interaction methods (Figure 8).

Goals

Among the main goals of the project were to provide added value to the agents involved:

Figure 8. Savia environment

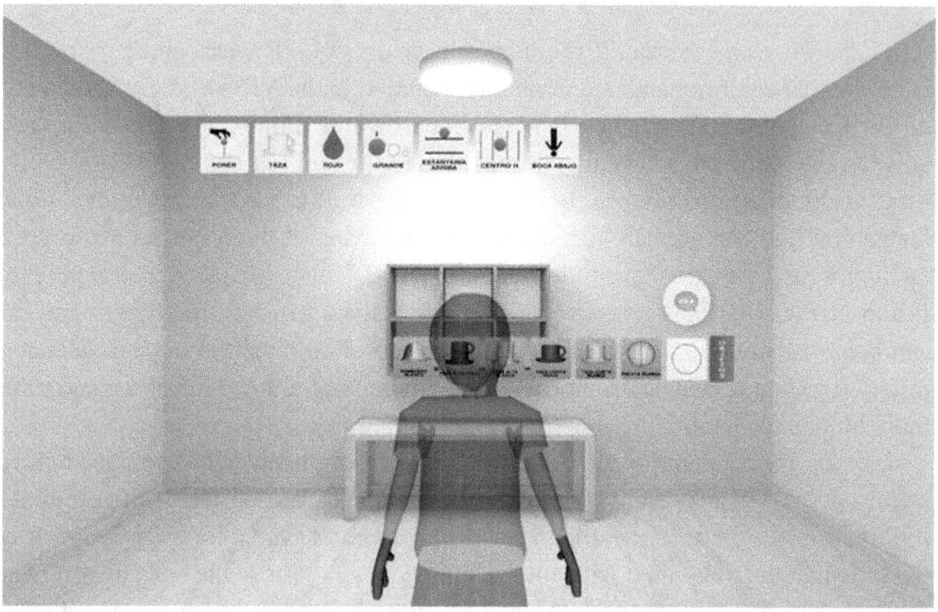

- For the group of people with ASD and Intellectual Disability, trying to offer a working environment that they will find pleasant, controlled and understandable, to enhance their abilities and develop those on which they present more problems, improving as much as possible their life quality.
- For families, trying to offer an element with which to learn and facilitate learning in a simple, and understandable way, being able to actively collaborate in the development of their children.
- For professionals in the area, who work daily with people with intellectual disabilities, offering them the possibility of having a workspace where they can obtain educational tools with highly configurable interfaces and contents that can be adapted to each profile of person they are going to work with, and where to share experiences and new contents with other professionals of the area.
- Finally, for the general public, offering an interesting tool for school-age children as an educational game that is easy to understand, reliable and with contents that are thoroughly analyzed and tested.

In the scope of the project were to provide an educational game with new interaction systems more usable and natural for the final user, advanced interfaces with tools to personalize the game for each specific profile of the user, and new technologies to create and structure the contents of each game. Also, virtual environments with high level of interaction and complete functionality were provided, based on educative contents, and visualization systems for the user to feel comfortable and immersed in the educative setting that the tool offered.

As a complete tool, the project was not only focused on one type of educational content, but it included also a very broad set of educational concepts and games that deal with a wide variety of aspects and educational needs. Some of them are:

- Concepts of the school curriculum related to basic learning (large, small, far…).
- Concepts related to the skills for everyday life (personal hygiene, dressing, eating ...).
- Concepts related to other curricular skills such as group work and understanding of relationships (emotions, hopes, social situations ...).
- Aspects related to the abilities that are reached in the child's development when there is no alteration (imagination, play ...).

How General Principles of ASD Intervention Were Applied

In the development of the SAVIA project, all the general principles of ASD intervention mentioned above are considered. In some ways, they were included from the definition and specification of the project to the final game developed. Each principle is reviewed and its application in this project is analyzed.

Usage of VR/AR

SAVIA is based on a virtual environment where activities in first person are developed. All the components, games and contents are designed as virtual models and spaces, based on the basis of Virtual Reality interaction. Also, the Augmented Reality technology is somehow included in this game because the user is represented by an avatar fully controlled by the player. It is not a pure AR, is more Mixed Reality where some part of the real world comes into the virtual world. In this case, it is the motion of the real person the component integrated in the virtual world to control his/her own avatar (Figure 9). For that, Kinect is used as the technology for developing motion capture to control the motion of the user and adapt it to the virtual character configured to represent each user.

Figure 9. Savia VR/AR environment

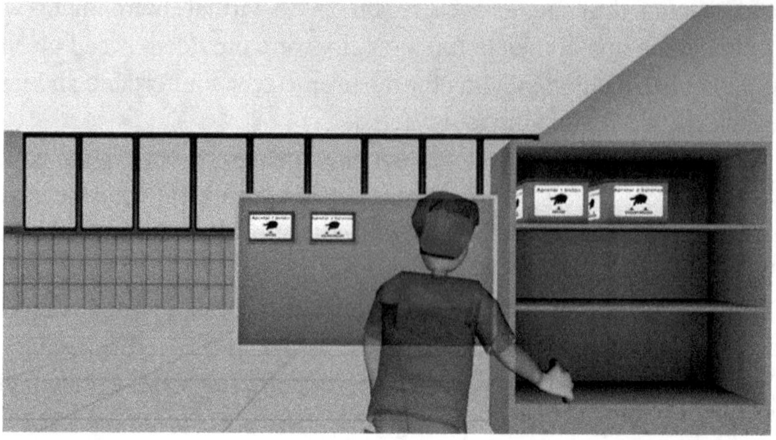

Personalization

One of the most important objectives included in the scope of the SAVIA project, were to develop an advanced interface for the personalization and adaptation of the games to the specific profile of each user (Figure 10).

Included in this personalization, the application allows the configuration and adaptation of the following aspects:

Figure 10. Configuration interface to adapt the game

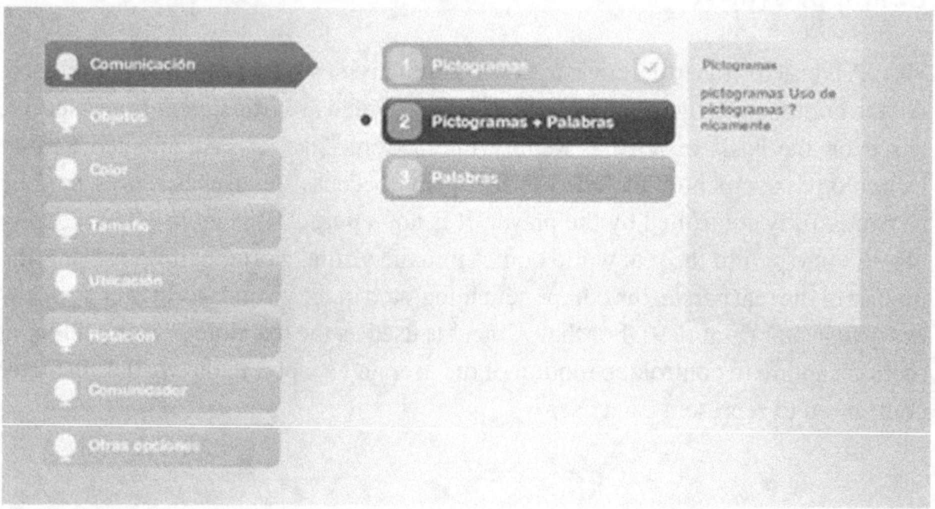

- **Communication:** It is possible to configure the communication method used in the game. The options offered by the tool are: communication by means of pictograms, using words or a combination of both.
- **Objects, Color, Size, Location and Rotation:** In the interface, it is possible to configure these elements that will be included in the games, selecting only the ones that are completely recognizable by the user (for example, specific objects, some colors, etc.)
- **Communicator:** Allows the configuration of some aspects of the communicator used between the teacher or tutor and the user in one of the games included.
- **Other Options:** Such us the kind of feedback given to the user in each activity.

SAVIA has a global configuration created and associated to each user, but also, it is possible to configure each game in particular, to adapt it to the player, obtaining with that more engagement and better performance results in this case.

Profile of Learner

To play in SAVIA, the teacher or tutor has to create a profile inside the game for each specific user, selecting a virtual avatar and some other characteristics. The specific profile of the user is stored in a database including the game configuration required for that user and some data related to each learning profile. Also, all games have a detailed evaluation of the performance done by each player, storing his/her evolution, allowing the improvement of each user learning through the evolution of the games, offering more complicated configurations as the user learn the specific skills proposed.

The Basis of TEACCH

As was mentioned above, TEACCH is a referent in the area of educational settings for the intervention in children with learning difficulties. For that reason, SAVIA has a specific game called Learn to Learn, based in the concept and structure of TEACCH. In this game, the user learns about a specific learning structure, developing very simple tasks always using the same structure. A virtual environment was used to simulate the areas where the user has to go to select and develop each activity. This game establishes the bases on which the rest of the games included in the tool are developed (Figure 11).

Figure 11. TEACCH learning structure in a VR environment

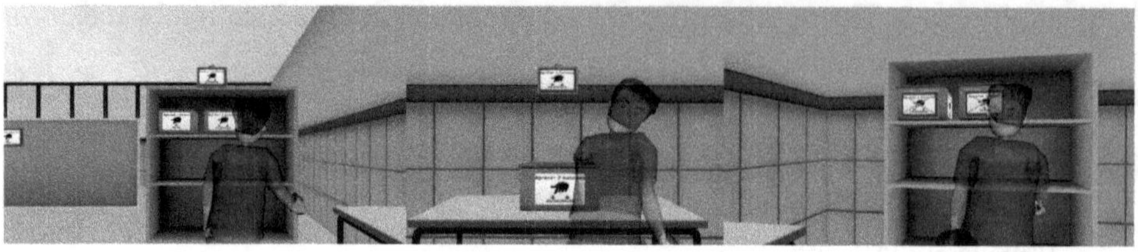

Motivation

In the case of SAVIA, the motivation or personal reinforcers are based in the feedback given to the user after the work done in each activity. There is no personalized reinforcers or feedback. The teacher or tutor can configure when the user will receive a standard feedback, immediately or at the end of the activity, depending on the specific learning profile of the user. After the use of the tool, any positive reinforcers of the user's liking can be offered by the teacher or tutor if it is appropriated.

Curriculum

Some games included in SAVIA are based on the specific school curriculum for children. Spatial, size, color, quantitative or visual concepts are included and available in the games. Also, the tool makes a very important contribution for the development of the communication skills in children with ASD and other learning difficulties (Figure 12).

Figure 12. Concepts and communication learning in SAVIA

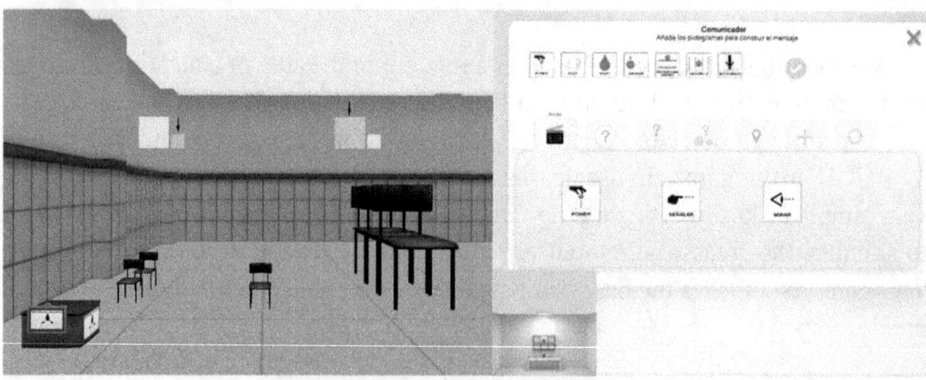

Generalization to Real Word

All the concepts included in SAVIA are eligible to be generalized to the real world. The games included in Learn to learn, are important to acquire a specific learning structure that can be used later in a classroom or at home. The concepts included in the Knowing the environment game, are very useful for their daily life, as they include concepts from the school curriculum. And finally, the Referential Communication game tries to improve the communication skills of the users, with an important part of generalization, because with the learning acquired in the tool, it is possible to improve the communicative capacities in the daily life of these children.

PICTOGRAM ROOM

The Pictogram Room (Casas et al, 2012; Herrera et al, 2012) is a set of educational video games for children and adults with autistic spectrum disorder (ASD). These video games support learning of educational goals related to key areas of development, where people with ASD normally have difficulties, like body language, joint attention and imitation.

In Pictogram Room, a camera-projector system is required, where the child's own image is reflected and supplemented with a series of graphic and musical elements to guide his/her learning. In the next figure (see Figure 13) is exposed a scheme that represents how the user experiments the augmented mirror (Portalés et. al, 2016).

Figure 13. A scheme that represents how the Pictogram Rooms displays the augmented scene

The games are designed to be played by the person with ASD, but they also consider the possibility of an additional player: the educator.

Goals

The main goals of the Pictogram Room are related to the four blocks of games offered by the application:

- **The Body:** This first set of games includes several groups of activities designed to train on body recognition. These are "mirror" games, where the learner gradually increases his/her attention to different parts of the body and the puppet used to represent them. The puppet is graphically designed like a set of lines that define the human silhouette.
- **Postures:** These games are intended to take the development of the human body one step further, working on imitation and communication. During the "posture" games, the students are intended to gain more and more awareness of their bodies, and learn to differentiate between different postures as they start to adopt them.
- **To Point at:** These blocks of games rely on the knowledge acquired during the previous games to teach how to point at, with the hand and with the eyes.
- **To Imitate:** This last set of games promotes the observer/imitator roles interchange. The majority of the games are targeted to work with the visual-motor aspects of imitation (Heyes, 2001), but some of them also work with its cognitive aspects (Van Vuchelen et al, 2007) related to rhythm, or the characters representation, like a bear, a clown, etc.

How General Principles of ASD Intervention Were Applied

In the design and development of the Pictogram Room project the general principles of ASD intervention are considered, previously exposed in this chapter. Next, each principle and its application in the Pictogram Room is reviewed and analyzed.

Usage of VR/AR

Pictogram Room is based on an Augmented Reality environment that acts like a mirror. The learner and/or the educator (if plays) see their own images reflected on the mirror (screen) and around them, all the virtual elements are displayed. Depending on the difficulty level set for the game, the presence of virtual elements changes. For instance, in easy games, the person can see him/herself like he/she is, and the same with the background, through a real video image. As the difficulty grows the virtual elements will cover the real elements, and in the most difficult activities the user cannot see real elements: the person, the background and all the elements are virtual.

Personalization

This application offers two customization methods (see Figure 14). The first one, web based, is the most generic. It allows the definition of the learner preferences. The elements that can be set are:

- The colors of the puppet. The user can decide the color of the lines to be drawn over the learner and the educator body image that are displayed in the screen.
- User photo.
- Background color. In many activities, the real background image is replaced by a user defined color background.
- The possibility of use music or videos associated with different virtual elements reproduced when the user performs a determined interaction activity.
- The selection of background music.
- Activate the possibility of play with an advanced and initially blocked game.

The second way is by changing the local options of each activity, before the start of the game. There is a button that allows the definition of local aspects of many elements of the activity. For example, some of these elements are:

Figure 14. Every activity can be fully customized from the website (left) and partially from the application (right)

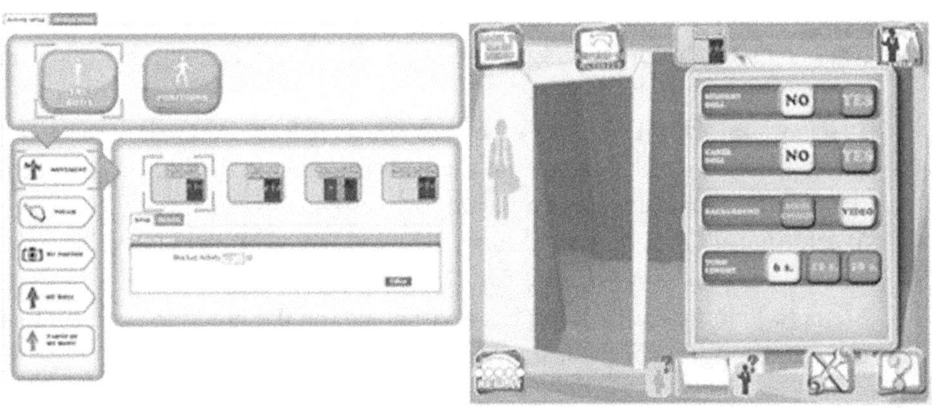

- Shift duration.
- Speed of the elements.
- Activate/Deactivate the learner puppet visualization.
- Activate/Deactivate the educator puppet visualization.
- Visualize the real background or a virtual plain color background.
- Etc.

Profile of Learner

All the games can be adapted to the preferences of each student. You can customize them in line with each student's rhythm of learning, and his/her visual and musical preferences. To configure this tool, you need to register on the project website. Once registered, you can download the application and, on the website, access the details of each student and customize each and every game available. The changes made on the website will automatically be synchronized with the application installed on your computer, provided you have an internet connection.

In order to assess the autistic student's progress, at the end of each game the tutor is asked to respond to a question by which the student can score a maximum of three points if the task is completed without any verbal or physical help, and a minimum of zero points if the task was not completed. These results are visible in the application interface, with little graphical changes in the interface and with more detail at the website, in the "results" tab of every game.

The Basis of TEACCH

The entire Pictogram Room interface is based on the philosophy of the structure proposed by the TEACCH methodology (see Figure 15). There are many common features and different well marked areas for responding to the visual structure requirements:

- **Task Panel:** The different activities (games) of the Pictogram Room are displayed horizontally.
- **In-Tray and Out-Try:** The activities are displayed from the easiest (on the left) to the most difficult (on the right). Every activity has a graphical representation that exposes graphical changes when is done.
- **Work Space:** Once the game starts, the whole screen is the place where the activity action is performed.
- **Steps to Follow:** Every game has a visual aid, on the top of the screen, that shows the progress of the learner inside the activity.

Figure 15. Screenshots of the application that shows the structure of an activity (game)

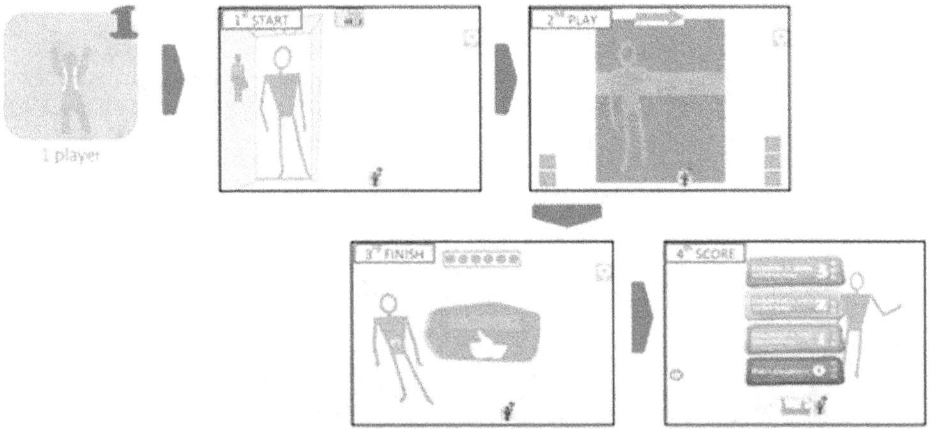

- Making the activity self-explanatory. Every activity has visual aids to indicate the student what to do. For instance, if the user must wait in a place, a decreasing time bar is shown over his/her head; if the user must move to a place, an arrow indicates where to move; if the user must touch an element, that element has a border with the same color that his/her puppet, etc.

Motivation

The motivation of the student is mainly performed by the reproduction of personalized songs and videos that can be defined in the user preferences section of the website. In a number of studies (Wimpory et al., 1995; Christie et al., 1992) the success of music-assisted communication has been used to develop an interactive relationship between parents and their autistic or intellectually disabled child, as this relationship is a key precursor to other social interaction. By using live music, the pro-social behavior in pairs (formed by a child and his/her main tutor, or a child and one of his/her parent) is emphasized and reinforced. The music is played like a background song, and/or when he/she finalizes a part of the activity (touching the required element, for example) (see Figure 16). In many games a little video appears, which is reproduced and stopped depending on the success or errors of the user.

Curriculum

The targeted educational goals pursued by Pictogram Room are related to areas where people with ASD normally have difficulties. Then, the games of this project

Figure 16. Screenshot of the application. A child is playing with his educator. If he touches the square with a musical note, his favorite song is reproduced

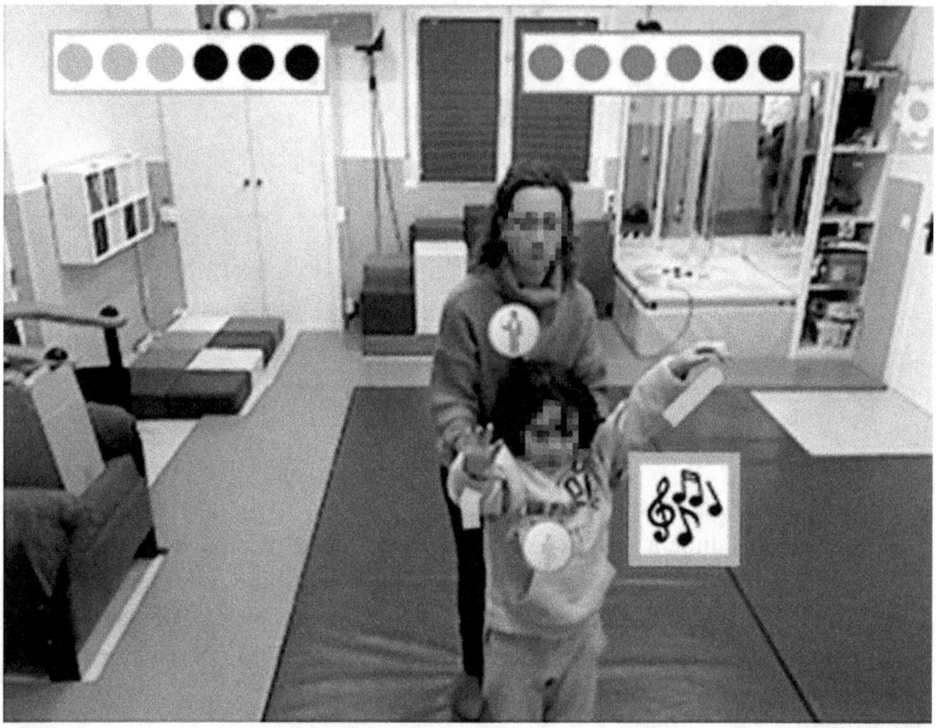

are really involved in the development of the skills of those areas (language, joint attention and imitation). These are the main goals, but there are many educational goals that the student can learn by playing with the Pictogram Room, like training in social interventions (hello, and good-bye activity), fine motor skills (moving positions activities), etc.

Generalization from Virtual to Real Worlds

The Pictogram Room project is designed for understanding the augmented world starting from games with the 95% of real world images, to games with the 100% of virtual images. Then, it is designed to enter, step by step, in an augmented world. Other question is, if the student can apply what he/she learns in the augmented world, to the real world.

In order to measure the effectiveness of the Pictogram Room for training students with ASD in the acquisition of relevant knowledge, two studies have been published as part of doctoral dissertations.

In the first study, (Mademtzi, 2016) evaluated the improvement in sensory-motor skills with 5 children with ASD. The study concludes that those skills improved in many environments (classroom, playground and home).

In the second study, (Perez-Fuster, 2017) evaluated the response with joint-attention with 7 children with ASD in a school environment. The study results are that response with joint-attention skills improves by using the application.

Then, there are scientific evidences that confirm the effectiveness of the Pictogram Room for training students with ASD. In the project, there are many educational goals that are not evaluated, but at least for the researched areas, it is demonstrated that Pictogram Room is a good tool to work with people with ASD, because it improves their skills and they enjoy during the learning process.

FUTURE RESEARCH DIRECTIONS

There is no a quality standard for the development of VR/AR learning contents for ASD. This lack of standards and methodologies can –at least partially- explain the little scientific evidence available about its effectiveness in ASD. Therefore, a first challenge to advance will be to convert the guidelines provided in this chapter, together with other existing knowledge, into solid methodologies for technology development in ASD. A first step for doing so may involve the generalization of participatory design, as it will help technologies to be adaptable to the diversity of autism. Also, any methodology in this area should include issues such as personalization, visual clarity and optimal functioning as necessary requirements.

Another important challenge to overcome is the lack of syllabus contextualization of technologies. We can often find tools to approach specific difficulties (related to focused interventions) but they are not integrated within wider programs. As an example, most evidence-based practices in ASD do not include any technological supports.

A very attractive challenge is the integration of technological developments from affective computing discipline into the VR/AR learning contents. Technologies are now able to read much more about internal status of the user and about how things happening in the virtual environments affect them. Devices such as Embrace or Empatica E4, among others, have these capabilities and this is a very important step when we talk about users who have big communications difficulties, who usually cannot communicate when they feel bad or even when they are in pain. By means of analyzing subtle variations in hearth rate or electro-dermal activity it is possible to infer the internal status of the individual and to use that information to adapt the educational intervention in real time. The combination of VR/AR technologies with affective computing technology will clearly open new horizons of intervention and help individual with autism to learn not only regular educational contents but also others related with self-regulation and emotional well-being.

Another area of opportunity is the application of language technologies for the personalization and user profiling with AR/VR games. In the last decade, many projects have been developed that were focused on Human Computer Interaction related to persons with disabilities. For instance, the ACCESIBLE (ACCESIBLE, 2017) project assessed the accessibility level of a web interaction, the VUMS cluster project (VUMS, 2017) aims to develop a standard user model considering people with different range of abilities and common data storage format for user profiles. All these projects used ontologies and technologies based on semantic web research field. The GPII project (GPII, 2017) purpose is "to ensure that everyone who faces accessibility barriers due to disability, literacy, digital literacy, or aging, regardless of economic resources, can access and use the internet and its information, communities and services for education, employment, daily living, civic participation, health and safety". This ambitious and needed goal, has received large funding from the governments of US, Canada and the European Comision. Nowadays the main result is the Cloud4All (Cloud4All, 2017) project that finished in 2015, and Prosperity4All (Prosperity4All, 2017), the last part of GPII, which is still ongoing. This project uses an ontology to represent the user model and automatically adapt any device to the user preferences and needs. Due to this, and the impulse of the governments, the user data could be represented though an ontology in the very near future. Then, the customization of the projects for persons with autism, and disability in general, must consider the need to extend the ontology of GPII project, in order to process the needs and preferences of the learner.

CONCLUSION

The prices of VR and AR glasses and helmets have fallen. Also, a number of tools that facilitate the development and publication of AR and VR contents have recently appeared. Therefore, a scenario of opportunity for new developments has appeared in this field. This chapter provides a set of guidelines that may facilitate the development of new solutions and also methodologies for the development of AR and VR for ASD. The level of scientific evidence in this area is still very low and important research efforts should be made to demonstrate the effectiveness of AR/VR technologies for the purpose they are designed. Some quality standards are available for both single case research (Horner et al, 2005) and for group designs (Gersten, et al 2005). Both types of experimental designs can be combined for determining evidence-based practices in any type of intervention in ASD and Reichow (2011) provided a method for doing so. Systematically developing and studying AR/VR contents may drive research in this area to a point where evidence-based knowledge is available and can be applied as a good practice in regular intervention in ASD.

ACKNOWLEDGMENT

SAVIA project was developed with the financial support of the Spanish Ministry of Science and Technology and PICTOGRAM ROOM project was developed also with the support of that Ministry and Orange Foundation.

REFERENCES

ACCESIBLE. (n.d.). *Home page of the ACCESSIBLE project*. Retrieved July 20, 2007, from http://www.accessible-eu.org/

Al-Azawi, R., Ayesh, A., & Al-Obaidy, M. (2014). Towards agent-based agile approach for game development methodology. *Proceeding of the 2014 World Congress on Computer Applications and Information Systems* (WCCAIS). 10.1109/WCCAIS.2014.6916626

American Psychiatric Association. (2013). *Diagnostic and statistical manual of mental disorders* (5th ed.). Washington, DC: Author.

Aslan, S., & Balci, O. (2015). GAMED: Digital Educational Game Development Methodology. *Simulation, 91*(4), 307–319. doi:10.1177/0037549715572673

Benton, L., Johnson, H., Ashwin, E., Brosnan, M., & Grawemeyer, B. (2012). Developing IDEAS: supporting children with autism within a participatory design team. In *CHI '12 Proceedings of the SIGCHI Conference on Human Factors in Computing Systems*. Association for Computing Machinery (ACM). 10.1145/2207676.2208650

Boehm, B. W. (1988). A Spiral Model of Software Development and Enhancement. *Computer, 21*(5), 61–72. doi:10.1109/2.59

Brown, S. M., & Bebko, J. M. (2012). Generalization, overselectivity, and discrimination in the autism phenotype: A review. *Research in Autism Spectrum Disorders, 6*(2), 733–740. doi:10.1016/j.rasd.2011.10.012

Carmigniani, J., & Furht, B. (2011). Augmented reality: An overview. In B. Furht (Ed.), *Handbook of augmented reality* (pp. 3–46). New York, NY: Springer. doi:10.1007/978-1-4614-0064-6_1

Carro, R. M., Breda, A. M., Castillo, G., & Bajuelos, A. L. (2002). A Methodology for Developing Adaptive Educational-Game Environments. In *Proceedings of AH 2002: Adaptive Hypermedia and Adaptive Web-Based Systems*, Malaga, Spain: Springer. 10.1007/3-540-47952-X_11

Casas, X., Herrera, G., Coma, I., & Fernández, M. (2012). *A kinect-based augmented reality system for individuals with autism spectrum disorders. Grapp/ivapp, 440-446. Center for Disease Control.* Atlanta, GA: CDC. Retrieved from https://www.cdc.gov/ncbddd/autism/data.html

Christie, P., Newson, E., Newson, J., & Prevezner, W. (1992). An interactive approach to language and communication for non-speaking children. In Child and Adolescent Therapy: A Handbook. Milton Keynes, UKs: Open University Press.

Cloud4All. (n.d.). *Home page of the Cloud4All project.* Retrieved July 20, 2007, from http://www.cloud4all.info

Cohen, H., Amerine-Dickens, M., & Smith, T. (2006). Early intensive behavioral treatment: Replication of the UCLA Model in a community setting. *Developmental and Behavioral Pediatrics*, *27*(Supplement 2), 145–155. doi:10.1097/00004703-200604002-00013 PMID:16685181

Den Brok, W. L. J. E., & Sterkenburg, P. S. (2014). Self-controlled technologies to support skill attainment in persons with an autism spectrum disorder and/or an intellectual disability: a systematic literature review. *Disability and Rehabilitation Assitive Technology*, 1-10.

Druin, A. (1999). Cooperative inquiry: developing new technologies for children with children. In *Proc. CHI*. ACM Press. 10.1145/302979.303166

Esposito, N. (2005). A Short and Simple Definition of What a Video Game Is. *Proceedings of DiGRA 2005 Conference: Changing Views - Worlds in Play.*

Gersten, R., Fuchs, L. S., Compton, D., Coyne, M., Greenwood, C., & Innocenti, M. S. (2005). Quality indicators for group experimental and quasi-experimental research in special education. *Exceptional Children*, *71*(2), 149–164. doi:10.1177/001440290507100202

Giraldi, G. A., Silva, R., & Oliveira, J. C. (2003). *Introduction to Virtual Reality*. LNCC Research Report #06/2003, National Laboratory for Scientific Computation. Retrieved July 20, 2007, from http://gpii.net/

Griffiths, M. D. (2002b). The educational benefits of videogames. *Education for Health*, *20*(3), 47–51.

Hanna, L., Neapolitan, D., & Risden, K. (2004). Evaluating computer game concepts with children. *Proceedings of the 2004 conference on Interaction design and children: building a community*, 49-56. 10.1145/1017833.1017840

Herrera, G., Casas, X., Sevilla, J., Rosa, L., Pardo, C., Plaza, J., & Le Groux, S. (2012). Pictogram room: Natural interaction technologies to aid in the development of children with autism. *Annuary of Clinical and Health Psychology*, *8*, 39–44.

Herrera, G., Alcantud, F., Jordan, R., Blanquer, A., Labajo, G., & de Pablo, C. (2008). Development of symbolic play through the use of virtual reality tools in children with autistic spectrum disorders: Two case studies. *Autism*, *12*(2), 7–21. doi:10.1177/1362361307086657 PMID:18308764

Heyes, C. (2001). Causes and Consequences of Imitation. *Trends in Cognitive Sciences*, *5*(6), 253–261. doi:10.1016/S1364-6613(00)01661-2 PMID:11390296

Horner, R. H., Carr, E. G., Halle, J., McGee, G., Odom, S., & Wolery, M. (2005). The use of single-subject research to identify evidence-based practice in special education. *Exceptional Children*, *71*(2), 165–179. doi:10.1177/001440290507100203

Ibrahim, R., & Jaafar, A. (2009). Educational games (EG) design framework: combination of game design, pedagogy and content modeling. *Proceedings of the International Conference on Electrical Engineering and Informatics*, 1, 293-298. 10.1109/ICEEI.2009.5254771

Kientz, J. A., Hayes, G. R., Westeyn, T. L., Starner, T., & Abowd, G. D. (2007). Pervasive computing and autism: Assisting caregivers of children with special needs. *IEEE Pervasive Comp. Magazine*, *6*(1), 28–35. doi:10.1109/MPRV.2007.18

Lorah, E. R., Parnell, A., Whitby, P. S., & Hantula, D. (2014). A systematic review of tablet computers and portable media players as speech generating devices for individuals with autism spectrum disorder. *Journal of Autism and Developmental Disorders*, 1–13. PMID:25413144

Mademtzi, M. (2016). *The use of a kinect-based technology within the school environment to enhance sensory-motor skills of children with autism* (Doctoral dissertation). University of Birmingham.

Mesibov, G. B., & Howley, M. (2003). *Accessing the Curriculum for Pupils with Autistic Spectrum Disorders*. London: David Fulton Publishers.

Mitchell, P., Parsons, S., & Leonard, A. (2007). Using virtual environments for teaching social understanding to adolescents with autistic spectrum disorders. *Journal of Autism and Developmental Disorders, 37*(3), 589–600. doi:10.100710803-006-0189-8 PMID:16900403

Odom, S. L., Boyd, B. A., Hall, L. J., & Hume, K. (2010). Evaluation of comprehensive treatment models for individuals with autism spectrum disorders. *Journal of Autism and Developmental Disorders, 40*(4), 425–436. doi:10.100710803-009-0825-1 PMID:19633939

Perez-Fuster, P. (2017). *Enhancing skills in individuals with Autism Spectrum Disorders through technology-mediated interventions* (Doctoral dissertation). University of Valencia.

Pictogram Room. (n.d.). Retrieved July 20, 2007, from http://www.pictogramas.org

Portalés, C., Gimeno, J., Casas, S., Olanda, R., & Giner, F. (2016). *Interacting with augmented reality mirrors. In Handbook of Research on Human-Computer Interfaces* (pp. 216–244). Developments, and Applications. doi:10.4018/978-1-5225-0435-1.ch009

Prosperity4All. (n.d.). *Home page of the Prosperity4All project*. Retrieved July 20, 2007, from http://www.prosperity4all.eu/

Reichow, B. (2011). Development, procedures, and application of the evaluative method for determining evidence-based practices in autism. In B. Reichow, P. Doehring, D. V. Cicchetti, & F. R. Volkmar (Eds.), *Evidence-based practices and treatments for children with autism* (pp. 25–39). New York, NY: Springer. doi:10.1007/978-1-4419-6975-0_2

Rogers, S. J., & Dawson, G. (2010). *Early start Denver model for young children with autism: Promoting language, learning, and engagement*. New York, NY: Guilford Press.

Sánchez, J. L. G., Zea, N. P., & Gutiérrez, F. L. (2009). From Usability to Playability: Introduction to Player-Centred Video Game Development Process. *Proc. of 1st Int. Conf. HCD 2009*.

Sherman, W., & Craig, A. (2003). *Understanding Virtual Reality: Interface, Applications and Design*. Morgan Kaufmann Publishers.

Slimani, A., Sbert, M., Boada, I., Elouaai, F., & Bouhorma, M. (2016). Improving Serious Game Design Through a Descriptive Classification: A comparation of Methodologies. *Journal of Theoretical and Applied Information Technology*, *92*(1), 130-143.

Steven, M. (2017). Virtual Reality. Cambridge University Press.

Strickland, D., Marcus, L. M., Mesibov, G. B., & Hogan, K. (1996). Brief report: Two case studies using virtual reality as a learning tool for autistic children. *Journal of Autism and Developmental Disorders*, *26*(6), 651–659. doi:10.1007/BF02172354 PMID:8986851

Vanvuchelen, M., Roeyers, H., & Weerdt, W. (2007). Nature of motor imitation problems in school-aged boys with autism: A motor or a cognitive problem? En Autism: An International. *Journal of Research Practice*, *11*(3), 225–240. PMID:17478576

VUMS. (n.d.). *Home page of the VUMS project*. Retrieved July 20, 2007, from http://vums.it.gr/

Wass, S. V., & Porayska-Pomsta, K. (2013). The uses of cognitive training technologies in the treatment of autism spectrum disorders. *Autism*, *18*(3), 1–21. PMID:24129912

Wimpory, D., Chadwick, P., & Nash, S. (1995). Musical interaction therapy for children with autism: An evaluation case study with a two year follow up. *Journal of Autism and Developmental Disorders*, *25*(5), 541–552. doi:10.1007/BF02178299 PMID:8567598

Wong, C., Odom, S. L., Hume, K. A., Cox, A. W., & Schultz, T. R. (2015, July). Evidence-Based Practices for Children, Youth, and Young Adults with Autism Spectrum Disorder: A Comprehensive Review. *Journal of Autism and Developmental Disorders*, *45*(7), 1951–1966. doi:10.100710803-014-2351-z PMID:25578338

Zyda, M. (2005). *From visual simulation to virtual reality to games*. IEEE Computer Society.

Chapter 6
Aura:
Augmented Reality in Mobile Devices for the Learning of Children With ASD - Augmented Reality in the Learning of Children With Autism

Marva Angélica Mora Lumbreras
Universidad Autónoma de Tlaxcala, Mexico

Méndez-Trejo María de Lourdes
Universidad Autónoma de Tlaxcala, Mexico

Sanluis-Ramírez Ariel
Universidad Autónoma de Tlaxcala, Mexico

ABSTRACT

A person with autism or autism spectrum disorder (ASD) presents conditions characterized by challenges with social skills, repetitive behaviors, speech, and nonverbal communication. Augmented reality (AR) combines reality with virtual aspects such as sound, video, graphics, or GPS data. Specifically, Aura is a mobile augmented reality application applied in the learning of children with ASD with the purpose of helping them in their relationships with the outside world and especially in their learning. Aura consists of five modules and 42 activities. The modules are Learn Basic Shapes, Repeat Basic Habits, Draw, Learn to Write, and Learn Values and Empathy. This project was tested by children of the Angelitos Mios Foundation, located in Apizaco Tlaxcala. The test showed favorable results. Tests were conducted with students in the age range of 4-8 years with ASD. The foundation is currently working on the acquisition of mobile devices for the implementation of Aura.

DOI: 10.4018/978-1-5225-5243-7.ch006

INTRODUCTION

Autism is a complex neurological disorder that usually all the life stays. It is part of a group of disorders known as autism spectrum disorders Autism Spectrum Disorder (ASD) (Benito, 2016) and (García, 2004). The most recent statistics indicate that one in every 10,000 Mexicans live with ASD at different levels.

The scientific research that have been made in "unique case" groups have demonstrated the effectiveness of global interventions where children with autism learn skills through set of techniques based on applied behavior analysis. These techniques help people with autism adapt to their environment and have shown that they can increase their IQ by about 20 points (Rodríguez, 2017).

The purpose of the project is to be part of the methods used in the education of children with autism in a range of 4 to 8 years. The AURA project focuses on supporting the significant learning of these children, considering all the elements necessary for this, such as a well ordered space, application of significant graphic elements, and other aspects.

The importance of Aura and its relationship with Augmented Reality remains in the possibility of adding virtual information to the real world, allowing to enrich the user's enviroment.

Throughout the project we have reviewed different works that other authors have done along with their respective contribution to autism, as well as the state of art that surrounds our research, which is reflected in the article. The Aura project and its evaluation are also presented.

BACKGROUND

Background of Augmented Reality

The Augmented Reality (AR) is a variation of Virtual Reality. Virtual Reality technologies wrap users in a completely synthetic environment, shifting the real world around them. Augmented Reality AR, however, allows the user to see the real world, in which virtual objects are superimposed, such as animations, 3D objects (Lara, 2004). Therefore, the Augmented Reality does not replace reality, but complements it (González, 2011). The Augmented Reality in mobile devices has a great impact, because it is very easy to work with this type of devices, giving way to great possibilities to generate Augmented Reality by relating images in real time, geographic position of the user, markers with information stored in the Fombona (Fombona, 2012). Platforms like Vuforia (Vuforia, 2017) currently allow us to implement AR with texture-based tracking (Markeless, 2013), which gives us more freedom when superimposing our models within the real world and do not need to put another element on some side to recognize it; the application will intelligently know where and how it should run.

Within the Augmented Reality animation can be included, in this project 2D animation will be used, 2D animation is a process that allows to give the sensation of movement to images, drawings or other inanimate objects (plasticine, paper, etc.). It is normally considered an optical illusion. There are numerous techniques for performing animation that go beyond familiar cartoons (Cogua, 2017).

The beginnings of the Augmented Reality date from 1962, when Morton Heilig, who was a cinematographer, made a system called Sensorama which included stimulation for the sense of smell, taste and touch. Later in 1973 Ivan Sutherland invented the Head Mounted Display, which is a helmet for visualization of images created by computer.

The term Augmented Reality was coined in 1992 by Tom Caudell, who used it to describe a screen that would be used by Boeing's electrician technicians, who mixed virtual graphics with physical reality.

Background of Computational Vision

Computational vision is the ability of a computer to analyze and recognize patterns of images in real-time.

Facial recognition is subdivided into several challenges:

- **Position of the Face:** The images that can be taken from a face will show changes in the degrees of inclination of the face.
- **Existence of Structural Components:** The different types of additions that a face can have (such as mustache, beard, lenses, earrings) adds complexity to the facial recognition task.
- **Facial Expressions:** Another factor to consider are facial expressions.
- **Obstruction:** In the environment where facial recognition is performed.
- **Environmental Conditions of the Face:** Lighting, camera characteristics, focus, among others, are determining factors in facial recognition.

For the development of AURA we made use of an Open Source library developed by Qualcomm called FastCV (FastCV, 2017) and the implementation of its algorithm, called FAST.

The mix between FAST and FREAK (Stringhini, 2011) is ideal for mobile devices and augmented reality because both use little processing time.

The computational vision is fundamental in the development of systems of Augmented Reality like Aura, since it is the one that gives the ability to recognize the place of the virtual elements. The dawn of this branch of technology came about in 1961, when Larry Roberts created a program with the ability to "see" a block structure, to later analyze what they contained and make a reproduction of it from another perspective. This demonstrated that the image that had been sent to the computer through a webcam had been processed well.

In later years, important advances were made in this field, which allowed for ever more powerful systems. The most advanced fields within the Computational Vision are the following:

- Detection, localization, segmentation and recognition of objects within the images in real time.
- Evaluation of the results obtained in the segmentation and registration.
- Real-time tracking of objects.
- Mapping scenes to be able to generate a 3D model of the scene.
- Estimation of human postures.
- Search for images according to their content

Background of Support Systems for People with ASD

Autism was recognized as a syndrome in 1943 by Leo Kanner who identified the same characteristics to a group of children, he detected two essential characteristics: extreme isolation and concern for the invariability in the environment (Kanner, 1943).

Scientific research has shown the effectiveness of global interventions where children with autism learn skills through techniques based on applied behavior analysis. These are used for children with autism to adapt to their environment and have shown that they can increase their IQ by 20 points.

The importance of Aura is that it is applied in specific interventions, which, contrary to global interventions, show the effectiveness of psychological techniques when taught appropriately and intensively. It is effective, for example, the use of reinforcers, which depend on each child and the acceptance of them in the usual environment. Different techniques have been effective in teaching basic behaviors such as looking at the eyes or imitating appropriate behaviors, teaching language (repeating words, asking properly, naming objects, asking or answering questions, using prepositions correctly, etc.) or teaching skills how to initiate and hold talks.

Visual communication is key for parents and teachers who support the education of children with this disorder, all visual materials, whether drawings, pictures, photographs or symbols, are a great help to children with autism, both for learning, the development of communication, and to increase their understanding and regulate their behavior.

Converging different technologies, such as facial recognition, speech recognition and augmented reality, we can developt applications to provide many benefits to society.

The current release of Open Source libraries for system development is a big push for developers. The problem before was that knowledge was not shared as easily as today, but thanks to advances in computer science, we live in an era where knowledge is transmitted in a simpler way. We believe that the next step that computing must take is to improve current systems and technologies and generate advances using them, because the tools are now at our disposal.

The Augmented Reality in mobile devices is experiencing a very large increase, partly because it is easier to find and work with such devices. We can see systems that mix Augmented Reality with the gyroscope that comes in the cell, or the compass, or the GPS system, and of course the microphone and the integrated horns inside these devices.

Platforms such as Vuforia (Vuforia, 2017) now allow us to implement Augmented Reality with texture-based tracking which gives us more freedom to superimpose our models in the real world and they do not need to put another element on some side to recognize it; the application will intelligently know where and how it should run.

People suffering from Autism Spectrum Disorder require new physical implementations in technological devices that allow them to have a better accessibility to them. On the other hand, it is necessary when developing such applications to select resources according to their characteristics, for example, that the software has a clear, dynamic, agile, graphic language and with clear instructions, in addition to that it must have different levels of difficulty which will allow the customization of activities.

One of the most important applications is ZAC Browser, which is the first web browser that was developed especially for children with ASD, and allows them to interact and play autonomously. It offers games and various activities that fit the needs of people with autism, such as difficulties in social interaction and communication, repetitive patterns of activity and difficulties in social interaction.

State of the Art

This section presents the state of the art related in behavioral therapies for the learning of children with autism through mobile devices.

Midori: Video Game for the Learning of Children with Autism in the Language and Communication Areas (García, 2015)

Midori was developed in 2015, Midori aims to make the user learn while he plays, his approach being the support for children diagnosed with autism and specifically with problems in the area of Language and Communication. The video game is based on the description of people, objects, places and phenomena of its environment, belonging to the expected learning of the Language and Communication training field of the Preschool Education Program 2011, currently program. Midori is composed of three different stories that are narrated and described graphically through three different scenes. Scenes and animations are created in the Unity game engine and 3D objects, which make up these scenes, are modeled in SketchUp software. As an essential part of the Midori project, a feasibility study focused on the degree of interest of 20 specialists in autism, teachers of the Multiple Care Center. The video game Midori uses three stories with which the child can interact, based on suggestions and comments from the specialists, and it is always about transmitting the realism of stories through different 3D scenarios with sounds, in which it is possible to carry out tours. the idea is that the child interacts and then is induced to answer some questions in the story, Midori is guided by a teacher and it is possible to make virtual tours for direct interaction with each scene.

The first story is entitled "The Dream of Carmen", this story talks about a girl and her school, which is described through a story. In the history primary characteristics like the color of the school, the elements that conform to the gardens and their forms, etc. are defined. It also describes the actions Carmen performs.

The second story called "Robert and his ball" tells Roberto's desire to get a ball and how he gets it. The story describes the characteristics of Roberto as well as the ball, taking into account its shape and color. Two basic elements in the description of objects.

In the third story "The hat of Augustine" addresses the situation that happens to Agustín losing his hat in the forest and how he recovers. This story describes the environment surrounding the main character, as well as the basic characteristics of the hat used by Augustine.

The student's task is to participate in each story, through the scenes modeled in 3D. As part of the route that the student performs within the scenes are the main objects and from which the questions are subsequently made. The student has the possibility of being one more element of the history to be present of virtual way. The expected learning in each story lies in the identification and description of objects, characters and places. Fulfilling what is marked in the Preschool Education Program 2011. Autistic children may exhibit a large number of symptoms such as: hyperactivity, brief attention episodes, impulsivity, aggressiveness, self-injurious behaviors, uncertain responses to sensory stimuli, eg hypersensitivity when listening to sounds, exaggerated reactions when they see lights, as well as lack of response to real dangers or intense fear of stimuli that are not dangerous. So the Midori project has been inclined to a natural 3D interface, allowing the user to navigate freely and directly, with the idea of facilitating its use. It has chosen to use short stories that use the senses of sight and hearing. The tests so far have been of two types: development and usability. At the development level, modular and project integration tests were carried out. At the level of usability has been revised the content of the project, the degree of interaction, the response of the scenes, navigability and design. It is important to emphasize that during the development of this project we have had an approach with the teachers of the Multiple Attention Center No. 1 of the State of Tlaxcala, who have observed the acceptance of the technology in autistic children in Tlaxcala, they explain that children in general have a positive adaptive behavior, and that this type of projects can reinforce knowledge seen in class.

The mobile application based on the Android platform focus on the Arachnophobia (Cuamatzi, 2017). provides a series of activities for the visualization of phobic environments (based essentially on Arachnophobia) through Augmented Reality, allowing the user to interact with a three-dimensional world generated through the mobile. Virtual reality has been incorporated as an alternative to the field of phobias treatment, for that reason the development of this system aims to provide a virtual environment, in where the user can perceive emotions, reactions and thoughts very similar to those that would be given in the real situation, by means of a mobile device.

The project Museum of Memory of Tlaxcala with Augmented Reality includes a photo gallery and 3D-models of Ocotlan (Mora, 2017)., different galleries of ranges such as Santa Agueda, Soltepec, San Pedro and San Diego Tenexac. Also, photo Galleries of the Codex of Huamantla and canvas of Tepeticpac agricultural tools modeladed in 3D. The implementation was carried out in one year. The project includes several sections, for example, the San Pedro Tenexac ranch, this ranch is located in Terrenate, Tlaxcala, the National Institute of Anthropology and History (INAH) declared Historic Monument of the Nation for their conservation in 1982. The gallery included photos of the San Pedro Tenexac ranch and details of the ranch.

The CompHi project, which is a virtual museum focused on the evolution and operation of computers is created using Augmented Reality technology for mobile devices (Bello, 2016), specifically for the Android operating system, this project is supported by the connectivism and we intended to act as a teaching tool for students, increasing at the same time the technological culture.

Autism Series (Web Team Corporation, 2015)

It is a set of applications developed by WebTeam Corporation where more than 100 mini-applications meet so that children with ASD can learn about the alphabet, time, colors, numbers, signs, objects, etc. An example is the module called Number Sequence in which the child is allowed to learn the sequence of numbers. This learning is considered vital for preschoolers.

Grace - Picture Exchange for Non-Verbal People (Dominican, 2016)

This application helps people with autism and other special needs communicate efficiently by constructing semantic sequences taken from relevant images in order to be able to form sentences using the Image Based Communication System

(Ilene, 1998). It offers diverse advantages, among them favors the independence of the person, improves the consistency in the communication, and increases the social interaction with the environment. This application was developed by Steven Troughton-Smith and Mary Moroney with support from O2 Telefonica. His analysis is important for our project since it opens the panorama referring to the different ways of communication that people with autism may need.

Let Me Talk (Jens-Uwe Rumstich, 2015) It is an Android application that helps people with special abilities like Autism, Asperger Syndrome, Amyotrophic Lateral Sclerosis, as well as children with Down Syndrome, to communicate anytime, anywhere.

This app allows you to transmit a message by aligning images in a row, making the images make sense. This way of communication is called Incremental and Alternative Communication (Abadin, 2010). It contains a database with more than 9,000 images, in addition the user can add his own with the included camera. Its approach to the treatment of people with communication limitations is interesting, and allows projects like Aura to be developed. The important thing for our project is the interaction between the user and his mobile device, and the benefits it offers to the people who use it.

MOBIS. Augmented reality application for mobile allowing multimodal interaction in order to guide students with autism during training in object recognition and recognition therapy. In this system an algorithm of vision of recognition of objects is implemented to be able to associate visual and verbal cognitive suggestions towards the object that is being recognized.

Look At Me. Monica Tentori is the person behind this project, and in one of her most important works (Tentori, 2012) describes how the use of augmented reality can help children stay focused on their work; this was applied in this project. Being an application that involves Augmented Reality has a greater similarity with our project, and by investigating a little more we can find similarities in Aura modules that involve learning, such as Learn.

Application developed by Samsung (Samsung, 2015) is aimed at improving the ability of individuals with autism to make eye contact, as it is well known that people with this disorder have problems with that. The application is currently under clinical testing to verify its effectiveness. Helps the concentration and motivation of children using the camera of mobile devices. Each module in the app requires interaction between parents and children to foster positive relationships and connections. Aura will also feature facial recognition in order to improve the interaction between the application and the user.

EDUCATIONAL AND CULTURAL CONTENTS

The development of Educational and Cultural Contents using innovative technologies is not recent:

The Fraunhofer IGD institute in Darmstadt (Germany) developed an application called "20 Years since the Fall of the Berlin Wall" (Zoellner, 2009), which sought to revive the long and rich history of Berlin on the anniversary of the fall of the wall, was exhibited at the CeBiT 2009 in Hannover (Germany). To show this inside the premises of a hypothetical museum, a large surface was designed with a satellite image of the city of Berlin, on which the visitor, with a UMPC, saw on the map the three-dimensional reconstruction of the Berlin Wall and the urban development of the city from 1940 to 2008, thanks to the use of aerial images of the city taken over the last few years. In this case augmented reality technology is used without the need to create three-dimensional (3D) virtual graphics, but rather uses the digitized (2D) images available in the city cartographic file.

A Future for the Past, a project carried out at the Allard Pierson Museum in Amsterdam to commemorate the 75th anniversary of its creation (Zoellner, 2009), used an enlargement of an old photograph of the Allard Pierson collection showing the remains of the Foro Romano, dated 1855, that was placed inside the exhibition in front of a movable screen with a built-in camera, in which the user, when making a panoramic route through the photograph, saw the remains of the forum, and marked as points of interest, the virtual reconstructions of several buildings (Temple of Saturn, Via Sacra, Coliseum, etc.), along with additional information about them.

The Virtual Showcase (Bimber, 2001), although designed as a traditional showcase in its dimensions and configuration, relied on virtual reality and augmented reality as mediators to present the pieces in an attractive way, in which the use of new technologies and the traditional museographic discourse are united to show the cultural object.

Tuscany + is the official augmented reality application of Tuscany. It allows through the iPhone to have Augmented Reality live for details on a specific location, restaurant or museum. All points of interest are the color coding category in restaurants, sightseeing, accommodation and entertainment, both live and view map (Tuscany, 2017).

Patents Related With Augmented Reality

1. Apple continues to work on Augmented Reality technology and has two patents registered by Metaio, an Augmented Reality and Virtual Reality firm that Apple bought in 2015. The first patent describes a device with "minimum one camera", one screen, one ideal user interface for augmented reality glasses

or mobile device. The system would have a double camera to use algorithms (like those used by the iPhone 7 Plus camera for Portrait mode that highlights the main purpose of the whole environment). The second patent describes the interface and the methods to show augmented reality in real objects, this, through a translucent screen or that of a smartphone. This patent also describes the need for a dual camera for mapping (Gutiérrez, 2017).

2. As part of the Ericsson Research team, there is a project called AR Collaboration, which involves using an augmented reality (AR) device to encourage teamwork among remote collaborators across the network. It is a great way to adapt the existing environment and settings, showing additional information about the world today. This relates to the work of Ericsson Research Media Technologies to improve the quality of the media experience, such as refining how audio and video are delivered and consumed. In Silicon Valley, work has been done on content discovery, referral systems and even 360° videos (Ericsson, 2017).
3. Facebook registered a patent of some glasses "that increase the view of the physical world, real, with elements generated by computer. The system will be integrated in a frame that is placed on the view and with a screen assembled, so that it presents the result in the form of content in front of the user's eyes. On the screen, according to the indications given, a two-dimensional scanner is integrated to integrate the current Oculus system. In this way, they will be able to cover the three options that until now are proposed: augmented reality, mixed and virtual, in the same device (Facebook, 2017), (Synthesis, 2017).

MAIN FOCUS OF THE CHAPTER

Problem Definition

Autism is a complex neurological disorder that usually lasts a lifetime. It is part of a group of disorders known as Autism Spectrum Disorders (ASD). In 2007, the Autism Society of America reported that in Mexico there were 150 000 people with this disease and it is estimated that there are about 40 000 children living with this disease, however, there are no official data on the disease, number of Mexicans living with autism. The most recent statistics indicate that one in every 10,000 Mexicans live with ASD at different levels.

-The relationship these people have with the outside world is generally difficult and therefore their learning is diminished from an early age. The symptoms are lack of social interaction: they show difficulty in relating to other children of the same age, have little or no visual contact, avoid physical contact, do not respond to being called by name, usually do not have language and if they have alterations, repeat many movements, have little tolerance to frustration, laughter or tears for no apparent reason, are hyperactivity or are very passive, there is no symbolic play and lack creative play.

The lack of quality material for the education of these children often hinders their learning and, therefore, their personal development; therefore it is considered of vital importance to implement this application, which intends to use the most innovative methods of psychology and pedagogy (in the teaching part), in addition to the Augmented Reality, so that together they will help children with this problem to be able to improve.

Justification

Scientific research that single case groups have conducted has demonstrated the effectiveness of global interventions where children with autism learn skills through bundles of techniques based on applied behavior analysis. These help people with autism adapt to their environment and have shown that they can increase their IQ by about 20 points.

Aura and its relationship with Augmented Reality are important because of the possibility of adding virtual information to the physical world allowing to enrich the user environment. In the educational sector, for example, it begins to take force because of its efficiency in relation to the process of reading comprehension, the basis of learning and without doubt, essential for the individual. The information is more interactive and visual, bringing the students closer to the real world, increasing in them the interest to learn. It also provides the possibility to complement a didactic book with the added information that contributes the virtuality of its contents, making learning faster and better understood.

In the application with children with autism, the implementation of virtual worlds and controlled environments, which are in turn comprehensible and adaptable, is vital to their success, since as we have mentioned in previous paragraphs, due to their suffering their interaction with the systems is different and Aura will have that approach.

SOLUTIONS AND RECOMMENDATIONS

Objectives

To be part of the methods used in the education of children with autism from 4 to 8 years. The AURA project will focus on the meaningful learning of these children, taking into account all the elements necessary for this, such as space is well ordered, application of significant graphic elements, instructions will be as clear as possible, and will be given to user an immersive sense of empowerment, as well as a constant repetition of the elements to learn, since the new usually generates anxiety.

The specific objectives are as follows:

1. Develop a functional application in Augmented Reality that converges technologies such as image recognition.
2. Have Aura have the five proposed modules that are: Learning figures, Repeating habits, Learning to write, Drawing and plotting, Practicing values and empathy.
3. Develop a system that is useful in teaching children with autism.

Autism and Video Game

Etymologically, the term autism comes from the Greek word eaftismos, which means "Enclosed in oneself." The word was introduced by Eugen Bleuler in the work Dementia Preacox or the Group of Shizophrenias (Cuxart, 2000). He used the word to define one of the symptoms of schizophrenia. Autism is a neurological disorder that mainly affects three areas in the individual detected with it: Difficulty for social interaction, limitations for Communication and Language and finally differences in behavior. Some specialists recommend the use of musical therapies, occupational therapy, language, etc. as a treatment. as there is no cure for this disorder. On the other hand, videogames are defined as playful instruments that require an electronic support, that is to say a silver-form electronic game and the participation of one or several players in a physical or network environment (Frasca, 2001). Video games have undergone a constant evolution until we reach what today we know and continue towards more dynamic elements that come in a more realistic experience using these video games.

Drawing on both concepts, AURA is focused on children with autism, specifically in language, based on the fact that language is a system of codes that are designated to the objects of the outside world, considering their actions, qualities and relationships between them (Luria, 1977), giving a meaningful and intraindividual transmission of information (Pavio, 1981).

AURA: AUGMENTED REALITY IN MOBILE DEVICES FOR THE LEARNING OF CHILDREN WITH ASD

Aura is a project aimed at helping children with autism spectrum disorder preschoolers, so that they can learn everything necessary for that age. The development platform will be Android, since according to statistics, is the Operating System for mobile devices most used (44.62% of users use it).

Requirements Analysis

Aura is a project aimed at helping children between 4-8 years of age who have autism spectrum disorder, so that they can learn everything necessary for that age. It will be programmed based on the following strategies:

1. **Structured Environment:** The physical structure of a place is the way spaces are distributed. What the child sees in a place informs or suggests the activity to be performed, as well as the materials or virtual objects that can be used and those who do not. In addition, each activity will last only a short time (5-10 minutes).
2. **Visual Strategies:** It is well known that children with this problem have a very large visual memory, so in order to improve their understanding of the world around them, make their learning faster, and regulate their behavior, they will get clear images about actions that will be done.
3. **Plan of Activities:** Aura is planned to be used during the preschool stage of these children during a regulated time, depending on what parents or instructors decide, so plans will be made daily. It is planned to make modules so that the child can: learn figures, repeat habits, practice speech, basic writing, basic reading and draw.
4. **Clear Instructions:** Children with autism often do not follow the instructions they receive and continue in their activity as if they do not hear, because they do not understand the words they are told. It is fundamental for their development that they learn the meaning of the instructions given to them and that they fulfill them.
5. **Acknowledgments and Praise:** Children with ASDs, as mentioned above, tend to keep little interest and their views are very rigid. For this reason, they need many strategies that help them broaden their interests, take into account what others think, and focus on other people's reactions to how to behave appropriately. When they achieve some progress in these aspects they should be praised for their effort. On the other hand, they can be frustrated if they fail or things do not work out well. This is why it is very useful to use positive phrases and actions that tell children that what they have done is what we expect. Aura will praise them every time they complete a unit or module, and invite them to do things right if they do not do it right.

All the requirements that are made through the application will be according to the age of the user, so that he does not lose the concentration nor the interest in the same.

General System Methodology

The methodology chosen for the system is Scrum, which is a process of software development in which different good practices converge to create systems.

In Scrum, partial deliveries of the developing system are made, which are given a priority order based on the benefit that each module produces. This methodology specializes in complex projects that need results soon, in addition to behaves well in the face of changes in requirements, and is good for implementing innovation, flexibility and productivity.

The advantages of Scrum are as follows:

1. The final product is delivered in different stages
2. Productivity and high performance in software development
3. Mitigation of risks

In the process of research our thesis will follow a methodology on theoretical and laboratory issues, because the tests are applied in a controlled environment

SCOPE AND LIMITATIONS

Scope

1. The present work will explore the possible convergence between the Augmented Reality and the computational vision, in order to be applied in teaching children with autism.
2. Research will focus on the behavior of people with ASD, in order to provide a system capable of meeting their learning needs.
3. Five proposed modules will be built and assembled: Learning figures, Repeating basic habits, Learning to write, Drawing and plotting, Practicing values and empathy. All modules are required for the system to work.
4. A proposed solution to the learning problem in children with autism will be provided, so that it can be applied in the future.

Limitations

1. The system will be limited to a certain age range (4-8 years) so the results in their application to different age users may vary.
2. The hardware will play a fundamental point in this system, so users who use it must meet the requirements specified below.

Implementation of AURA: Augmented Reality for the Learning of Children With Autism

Below is a description of the equipment and software that was used for the development of Aura:

Hardware:

Laptop TOSHIBA Satellite L505D

- AMD Turion (tm) II Dual-Core Mobile M500 (2 CPUs), 2.2GHz
- 4.09 GB of RAM
- BIOS InsydeH2O Version 1.00
- Windows 7 Ultimate 32-bit
- ATI Mobility Radeon HD 4200 Series video card
- 320GB Hard Drive

Laptop HP Pavilion g4 Notebook PC

- Intel (R) Core (TM) i3-2350M CPU (4 CPUs), 2.3GHz
- 8,192 GB of RAM
- BIOS InsydeH2O Version 03.72.32F.25
- Windows 7 Home Basic 64-bit (6.1, Build 7601) Service Pack 1
- Intel (R) HD Graphics Family Video Card
- 500GB Hard Drive

Mobile hardware: The mobile hardware that we occupied was two cell phones: Moto G 3rd Generation

- 5.0 inch display with 2180x720 resolution
- Internal Memory 16GB
- Android 5.1 Lollipop
- Qualcomm Snapdragon 410 Processor
- 13 Megapixel Main Camera
- RAM Memory Capacity: 1 GB

Software:

Let us make clear that the team we occupy is the one that was within our reach to develop in time and form the application. It is important to emphasize that the Qualcomm Snapdragon processor is necessary for the development since this allows the calculations necessary so that the Augmented Reality can be shown to the user.

For the implementation of the system the following software was used:

1. Android Studio 1.3.2, Free Software
2. Mono Develop V4.01, Free Software
3. Unity 4.6, Free / Paid Software
4. Blender 2.74, Free Software
5. Vuforia 5.0.5, Free / Paid Software
6. Photoshop CC, Software Paid
7. Ilustrator CC, Software Paid
8. Android SDK 5.2, Free Software
9. Smart Voice Recorder 1.7.1, Free Software
10. Cubase 4.7, Software Payment
11. Unity Remote 4 1.1, Free Software

The importance of Aura is that it is applied in specific interventions, which, unlike the global interventions, they show the effectiveness of psychological techniques when they are taught appropriately and intensively. It is effective for teaching children, for example, the use of reinforcers, which depend on each child and the acceptance of them in the common environment.

Different techniques have been effective in teaching basic behaviors such as looking in the eyes or imitating appropriate behaviors, teaching language (repeating words, asking properly, naming objects, asking or answering questions, using prepositions correctly, etc.) or teaching skills of how to initiate and hold talks.

Visual communication is key for parents and teachers who support the education of children with this disorder, all visual materials, whether drawings, pictures, photographs or symbols, are a great help to children with autism, both for learning, for the development of communication, to increase their understanding and regulate their behavior.

General Diagram of the Aura Project

The Aura project is structured as shown in Figure 1.

Aura is a support tool focused on learning of children with autism consisting of an emerging technology called Augmented Reality.

Figure 1. General diagram

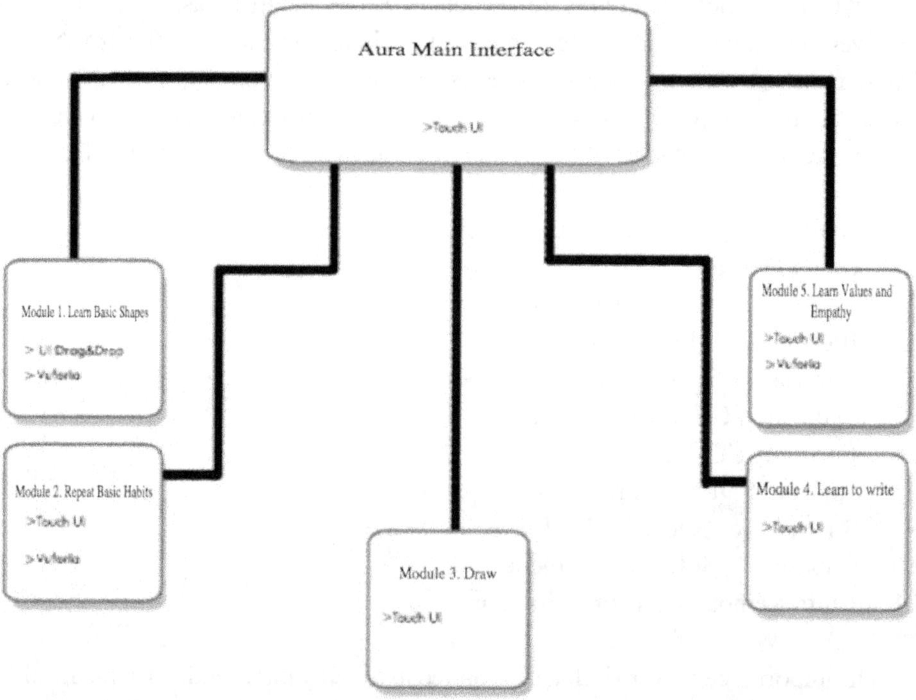

Considering the characteristics that the children have and the comments of the experts in the teaching area of the Angelitos Mios Foundation, 5 important modules were proposed for their learning, the modules are:

1. Learn Basic Shapes
2. Repeat Basic Habits
3. Draw
4. Learn to write
5. Learn values and empathy

Aura Interface

Aura has a touch interface. With the type of interaction that this interface offers the user will feel comfortable using the application. The elements are ordered based on their importance and have colors that capture the child's attention, the modules are described below:

Learn Basic Shapes

This Aura module is especially for children to learn basic figures, with a Drag and Drop interface. On the left side are the basic shapes: Square, rectangle, triangle, rhombus, trapeze, circle. The figures that the child will practice are: Train, flower, bicycle, house, bed, car.

In order to motivate the child's learning is shown at the end of each level successfully completed a third-dimensional modeling in augmented reality according to the level. Figure 3 shows the reward at the end of the activity in Figure 2, in which the child has to assemble a train with the basic figures available. This figure has animation and sounds that attract the attention of the user.

The modeling is superimposed over the predefined marker which helps us to show augmented reality through the camera of the mobile device.

The purpose of this module is that the user learns to recognize the figures and relate them. Aura will remind the child what's the figure name that he managed to put in the center.

At the end of forming the figure shown Aura will show the user the same figure but in 3D using the camera of the mobile device in such a way that the child understands that it is a reward for him and with this is motivated to continue doing the activity.

Figure 2. Learn basic shapes

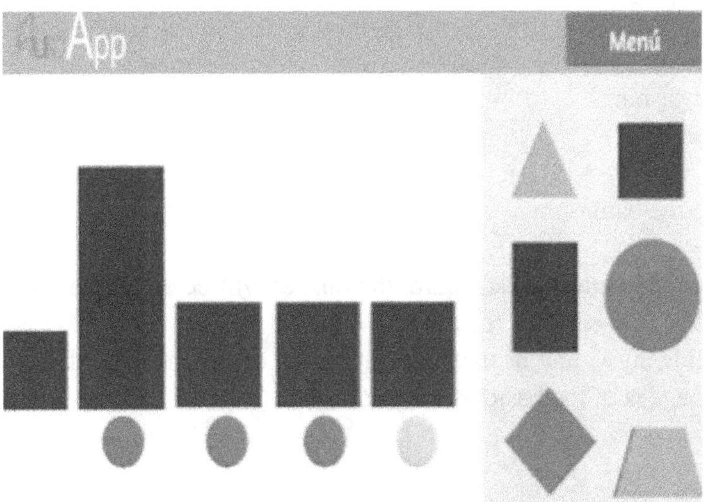

Figure 3. Augmented Reality reward at the end of the level

Repeat Basic Habits

For children with autism is difficult to do certain activities at home or elsewhere so this module is important so they can learn to do things and remember them. This module works with a list of pictograms in order that the child can order the images of the activities according to the process of the real life.

- Brush your teeth
- Handwashing
- Take a bath
- Eat
- Go to the bathroom

Following the interface standard, the images will be on the left side and in the center will be the sequence that the child should follow.

The following is one of the Aura interfaces of the mentioned module. In this case the image is of the basic bathing habit.

Draw

When we learn to write normally the first thing teachers taught us was to quicken the fingers of the hand as well as make strokes, such as lines, arcs, consecutive circles, which are grafomotricity exercises. These types of exercises are included

Figure 4. Repeat basic habits

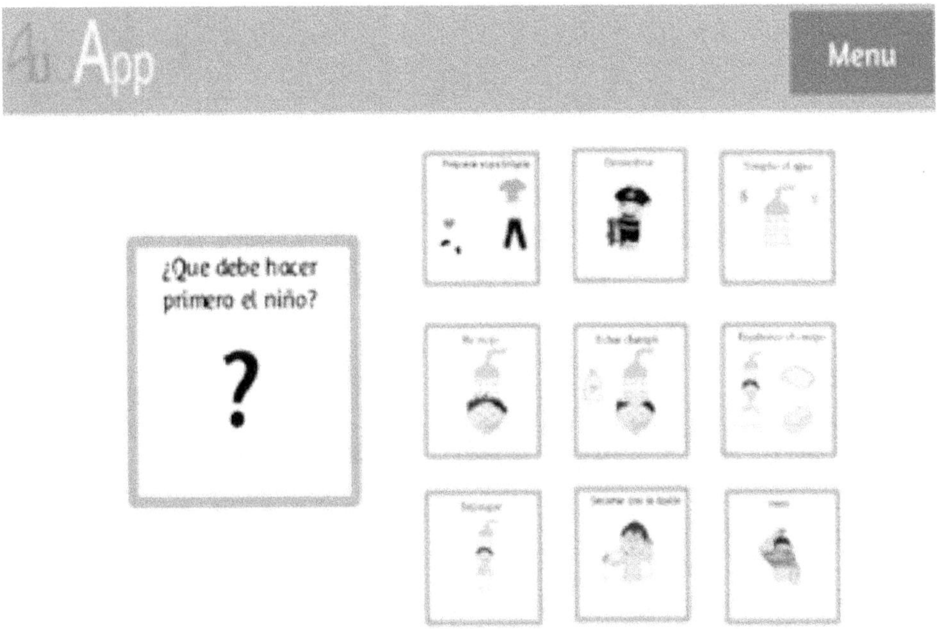

in the Draw module, considered as the first step before beginning with the Learn to Write module. The child will stroke with his finger on the touch interface that Aura shows, there is an introductory video of pictogram images about how the child has to do the activity in this section, see Figure 5.

Learn to Write

Once the child has mastered the realization of basic graphs, the application will allow you to access the Module of Learn to write that as sample includes the letters, vowels and the alphabet. The mode of interaction with the user is similar to the previous module because in order to complete the activities the child has to trace the corresponding letters with his finger on the screen.

Practice Values and Emphaty

In order to the user to have a more complete understanding of human values and their application in everyday life, this module is used, in which the child is presented with a situation and asked about the correct reaction. Among the applied values are:

Figure 5. Draw

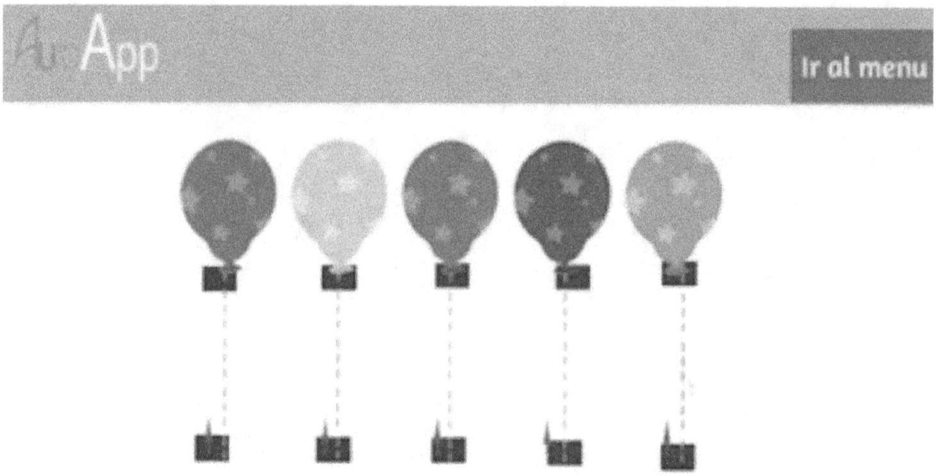

Figure 6. Learn to write

- Kindness
- Respect
- Love
- Friendship
- Emphaty

Through the use of pictograms and a touch interface where we have to drag and drop the images, the user can to learn to relate with other people.

Figure 7. Repeat values and emphaty

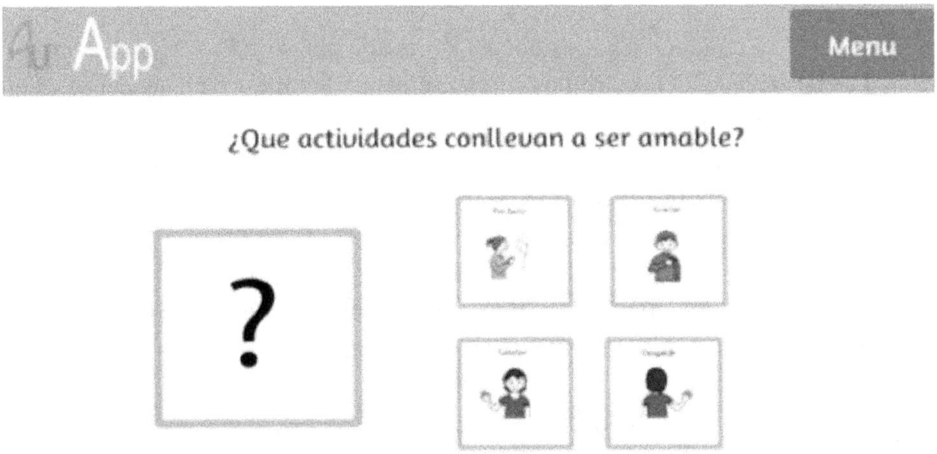

Tests and Results

The following describes how was the execution of the tests, the compilation and analysis of the results obtained.

On february 17th, 2016 we visited to Foundation Angelitos Míos located at Avenue Zaragoza number 412, Apizaco, Salón Ferrocarrilero, in order to request permission to do the tests of the Aura project.

We talked with Elizabeth Sánchez Flores, Director of the foundation, was approached to whom the project was proposed for the benefit of children with autism. She found out that it was a system with a high profit margin and had a positive attitude about the project being applied in the children's learning, she commented how it is in fact the situation of the interaction that children with autism have with their External world and what could be implemented to improve the user experience.

The director of foundation asked us if we was familiared with the subject of autism, in that moment we had already investigated and with the support of the foundation improved some parts of the project.

The tests were performed with three children, furthermore, we had the support of a professional therapist, in order to guide them in the use of the device.

Prior to this we had the approval of the parents on March 2nd, 2016 and showed them the basic aspects of the application, the modules that it has and how the Augmented Reality would motivate children's learning.

Aspects to emphasize in the use of Aura

- Tests were conducted with students in the age range of 4 to 8 years.
- People with ASD have different requirements that must be considered when they occupy some software.
- The child should know how to pick up a mobile phone and hold it with his hands without throwing it away and understand the “Drag and Drop” interaction.
- The figure support instructor should always be present when the child interacts with the application. Based on the instructions of the institution we established as maximum time of use 15 minutes per module.

The tests were performed as follows:

1. The children were gathered in the room designated for the activity
2. The instructor in turn gave a mobile device to the first child in order to start the activity
3. The weather level was successfully passed and the child learned about of the pictograms shown
4. Later the children acceded to the modules.

Results

1. In the module Learning Basic Figures with the help of the instructor the child learned how to proceed with the activity levels and when he saw the different rewards he was excited to continue using the app.
2. In the module Repeat Basic Habits the child was able to differentiate the pictograms shown and managed to put them in order. However he had some errors, which were notified by the application and corrected later by the child.
3. In the Draw module the intuitive interface allowed the child to do the different paths that Aura was requesting, a task that the child achieved in an acceptable way, but it was noticed that it requires improvement.
4. In the Learn to Write module, it was seen how the audio of the letters allowed the children to relate the draw together with the name of each letter which moved the child.
5. In the Practicing Values and Empathy module the pictograms were successfully recognized and there was no problem in the sequence of the application.

FUTURE RESEARCH DIRECTION

Currently the technological development has allowed intelligent mobile devices to be available to the general public, which has allowed the Augmented Reality is being used a lot in areas such as entertainment, education, tourism, etc.

In the other hand, Higher Education Institutions have created different virtual laboratories that allow all aspects of Augmented Reality to be worked. So you can see projects that were previously unimaginable, such as applications in diseases such as autism, phobias, human skeleton, etc. Giving the possibility of interacting very dynamically. It is important to mention that the Augmented Reality is being required by professionals from other fields, such as medicine, biology, space exploration, chemistry, etc; many times for teaching. For example, medical students can learn from complementary activities with Augmented Reality. Biologists can see simulations of organisms through Augmented Reality, from different perspectives. Chemicals can see dangerous chemical combinations, but from a mobile device without causing any dangerous reaction.

In the Institutes of Higher Level also is doing investigation using Augmented Reality, Universities such as the Autonomous University of Tlaxcala (UAT) have developed different works such as Augmented Reality Applied in the Museum of Memory of Tlaxcala completed in 2017(Mora, 2017). The CompHi project: History of Computers with Augmented Reality was concluded in 2016 (Bello, 2016). The Veterinary Medicine through Augmented Reality developed in 2016 (Herández, 2016). Arachnophobia with Augmented Reality completed in 2017 (Cuamatzi, 2017).

It can be said that we can see that the area of Augmented Reality will continue to be booming, especially now that many devices have been reduced in cost and therefore more flexible to acquire. It can be mentioned that the applications in mobile devices with Augmented Reality combined with lenses also of Augmented Reality have become fashionable, since even in toy shops can be acquired at moderate prices.

CONCLUSION

During the development of this project we obtained experience in different topics from the Augmented Reality until knowledge of autism. The fact of gaining knowledge about a topic as interesting as the Augmented Reality give us the bases to continue developing projects and innovating in the area.

At the end of this project the general and specific objectives were met, so we consider that the implementation of the system has been successful and the design of the UI is attractive, which benefits the children, who will use the application.

We reviewed the state of the art, which expanded the panorama about applications focused on people with disabilities. The different features were analyzed, and based of these, we were able to design an application based on the unique needs of that sector of the population.

In the same way we were able to know and have a good basis in relation to the theory that involves the different topics of this thesis: Autism, Augmented Reality and Recognition of images and patterns. The field of development of a computer engineer is much broader than just programming, since we had to analyze even psychology topics and read pioneering authors who began in the discovery of this disorder in children.

Throughout the project it was seen that software engineering is elementary to structure a system, and the use cases were used to define the process of structuring Aura, helping us to shape the operation of the application modules.

FUTURE WORK

In the future we will implement more levels that will increase the level of complexity of the application, which will allow children with autism to have access to a more complete and constant development. The continuous advances in hardware make possible new and better forms of interaction between the mobile devices and the user. Aura is a system that is constantly updated and therefore in the future will converge with the available hardware upgrades to improve the App.

REFERENCES

Abadin, D. D. S. C., & Ángela, V. C. (2010). Increasing and Alternative Communication. CEAPAT.

Bello, R. M. A., Mora, L. M. A., Alberto, P. F., Sánchez, P. C. R., & Carmona, F. M. E. (2016), CompHi: History of Computers with Augmented Reality. *Revista Revista CiBIyT, 11*(31), 17-20.

Cuxart, F. (2000). Autism, Descriptive and therapeutic aspects. Málaga. *Ediciones Aljibe S.*

Elena. (2016). *A propósito D. Autism. The importance of the family in the intervention.* Colegio Oficial de la psicología de Castilla- La Mancha.

Ericsson. (2017). *4K and Augmented Reality*. Retrieved from https://www.ericsson.com/mx/en/networked-society/live-sports-experience/4k-and-augmented-reality

FastCV-sdk Documentation. (2017). Retrieved from https://developer.qualcomm.com/software/fastcv-sdk

Fombona Cadavieco. (2012). *Pascual Sevillano María Ángeles, Madeira Ferreira, Galindo Dolores*. Augmented Reality in Museums, Social Museum.

Frasca, G. (2001). *Videogames of the Oppressed: Videogames as a Means for Critical Thinking and Debate*. Institute of Technology.

García Eligio de la Puente. (2004). Psychology in care for people with disabilities. Psychology in Care, (23), 355-362.

González, C., Vallejo, D., Albusac, J. A., & Castro, J. J. (2011). *Augmented Reality: A Practical Approach with ARToolKit and Blender*. Bubok Publishing S. L.

Izak. (2017). *The special need ware, the proud creator of Autismate365 and TeachMate365*. Retrieved from autismate.com

Lara, B. L. (2004). *Augmented reality: A technology waiting for users. Revista Digital Universitaria*. UNAM.

Leo, K. (1943). Autistic disturbances of affective contact. *Pathology*.

Luria, A. (1977). *Evolutionary Introduction to Psychology*. Barcelona: Fontanella.

Maribel, C. M., & Mora, L. M. A. (2017). Augmented Reality Focused on Arachnophobia. *Revista Iztatl Computación, 6*(11), 32-39.

Marisol, H. H., & Mora, L. M. A. (2016). Veterinary Medicine through Augmented Reality. *Revista Iztatl Computación, 5*(10), 49-56.

Markeless, A. (2013). Augmented Reality Tracking for Enhancing the User Interaction during Virtual Rehabilitation. *XV Symposium on Virtual and Augmented Reality*.

Marva-Angélica, M.-L., Sergio, M.-G., & Carolina-Rocío, S.-P. (2017). *Augmented Reality Applied in the Museum of Memory of Tlaxcala. In Software Engineering: Methods, Modeling, and Teaching* (Vol. 4). Editorial Universidad de Medellín, Pontificia Universidad Católica del Perú, and Universidad Nacional de Colombia.

Metaio. (2017). Retrieved from http://www.metaio.com

Mónica, T. (2013). Innovative technologies for Autism. *First International Conference: The Autism Spectrum. A Different Perspective*.

García Flores &Mora Lumbreras Marva. (2015). Midori: Video Game for the Learning of children with Autism in the Area of Language and Communication. In *Emerging Technologies in Education, Memory of the National Encounter of Computer Science*. Sociedad Mexicana de Ciencias de la Computación.

Oscar, G. (2017). *New Apple patents show interest in augmented reality, C / net in Spanish*. Retrieved from https://www.cnet.com/es/noticias/apple-realidad-aumentada-patentes/

Pavio, A., & Begg, I. (1981). *Psychology of language*. Prentice-Hall.

Rodríguez, C. (2017). Animation studies in Colombia: Acrobatics in the Timeline. Pontificia Universidad Javeriana.

Rodríguez Escalona Mirelle. (2017). *Autism*. Retrieved from http://www.academia.edu/14904027/A_UTISMO

Samsung. (2017). *The Look at Me Project*. Retrieved from http://pages.samsung.com/ca/whoeyeam/English/

Stringhini, M. (2011). *High Level Computer Vision using OpenCV*. Sao Paulo, Brazil: Faculdade de Computacao e Informatica, Universidade Presbiteriana Mackenzie.

Troughton-Smith. (2016). *Grace - Image exchange for people with verbal disabilities*. Academic Press.

Tuscany. (2017). *Tuscany+, Application Aggregation AppAgg*. Retrieved from https://appagg.com/ios/travel/tuscany-849156.html

Vuforia Documentation Qualcomm. (2017). Retrieved from https://www.qualcomm.com/products/vuforia

WTC. (2017). *Technology For Smart Education*. Retrieved from www.webteamcorp.com

Zoellner, M. (2009). An Augmented Reality Presentation System for Remote Cultural Heritage Sites. In *Proceedings of the 10th International Symposium on Virtual Reality, Archaeology and Cultural Heritage*. University of Malta.

KEY TERMS AND DEFINITIONS

Android: Is a mobile operating system developed by Google, based on the Linux kernel.

Augmented Reality: AR, however, allows the user to see the real world, in which virtual objects are superimposed, such as animations, 3D objects.

Autism: Person with two essential characteristics: extreme isolation and concern for the invariability in the environment.

Autism Spectrum: Also known as autism spectrum disorder (ASD). Features of these disorders include social deficits, communication difficulties, stereotyped or repetitive behaviors and interests, sensory issues, and in some cases, cognitive delays.

Blender: Is a professional, free, and open-source 3D computer graphics software toolset used for creating animated films, visual effects, 3D printed models, interactive 3D applications, and video games.

Computational Vision: Is the ability of a computer to analyze and recognize patterns of images in real time.

Smart Voice Recorder: Is designed to provide high quality long recording with function to skip relative silences.

Unity: Is the ultimate game development platform. Unity allow building high-quality 3D and 2D games for mobile, desktop, VR/AR, consoles and smart tv.

Unity Remote: Is a software application that makes the Android device act as a remote control for your project in Unity Editor.

Vuforia: Is an augmented reality software development kit (SDK) for mobile devices that enables the creation of augmented reality applications.

Chapter 7
Characterization of English Through Augmented Reality

Marisol Hernández Hernández
Universidad Autónoma de Tlaxcala, Mexico & Universidad Autónoma del Estado de México, Mexico

Marva Angélica Mora Lumbreras
Universidad Autónoma de Tlaxcala, Mexico

ABSTRACT

Children who begin to learn English usually associate words with images and sounds; this facilitates the assimilation of knowledge and increases their educational interest. This premise grounded this research using augmented reality-based applications designed for people who want to learn English vocabulary. The set of useful terms for students to learn are put together in various categories such as animals, colors, and things. The vocabulary is stored in a database in different formats that are text, 3D image, and audio, which are associated with items containing a vocabulary that represents abstract entities and that are necessary to complement the learning of the English language. The words are associated with the images and with the corresponding audio in order that the students learn to read, write, listen, and consequently, to pronounce the words. This research is projected for more promising applications based on the multi-lingual teaching process.

INTRODUCTION

Globalization has resulted in the daily life require people who have as a basic knowledge of several languages to enter a world so competitive in terms of work, economic and cultural, to mention some aspects, this is the reason why learning different languages is one of the activities that are becoming more frequent in elementary schools.

DOI: 10.4018/978-1-5225-5243-7.ch007

From that perspective, educational technology has been constantly working to offer different language learning tools, which should be used from basic education in order to take advantage of the powerful cognitive system that children have at that age. Technological tools for learning the English language should consist of a series of skills that enable people to communicate effectively and diverse educational contexts have been developed whose characteristics promote learning; that is why they are required to generate educational contexts whose implementation characteristics are not enormous costs, rather than tools that are easy to manage and implement, but above all that their cost is measured in low monetary terms, in counterpart with the educational benefits it may provide that must be high.

Technological development has shown many advances in support of teaching-learning strategies. This progress is overcome by more efficient technologies whose mission is to help students and teachers in their educational process. Educational technologies are embedded with various devices and media, they have been making use of the Internet, mobile devices, the cybernetic cloud and various technological objects to support in a more efficient way the task of teaching and learning; however, augmented reality has emerged as a technology that also supports educational environments, but within its most salient features it is how it helps to make abstract educational content easier for students to understand.

Derived from the above premises, it is necessary to generate educational contexts whose characteristics help to learn and to build their knowledge and it has been observed that the Augmented Reality has been an ideal complement for diverse educational applications and for the teaching of English is also useful. Its basic characteristics define it as a technology through which the visualization of the real environment is increased by elements or objects generated by a computer (Rabbi and S. Ullah, 2013).

The English language is used as a means of communication in different parts of the world, so it is necessary for children to learn that language with the prospect that when they need it, it is easier to enter into a globalized context. To complement this task, technological tools are needed to help students easily acquire English language learning and augmented reality technology is being proposed for use by students studying preschool or primary levels, including for any a person who wishes to learn an English vocabulary in order to develop more tools that complement the teaching process of the English language, which is inexpensive and that encapsulates suitable characteristics for students to learn using different learning styles during the process of teaching children, with the background that they require like games or activities that really motivate them to want to learn.

This research was done on the basis of the above precepts and will describe how it can work as training in students who want to learn or are learning English and that as already mentioned, if it is not the most spoken, it is the most used in the developed countries that are generators of knowledge and consequently the results of the investigations that they realize are published in this type of language.

This document describes a software engineering methodology based on the four-plus-one model, which describes step-by-step and with diagrams, the way in which this application has been developed, UML diagrams with which it is described the system is to clarify the concepts of it, in addition, it lists the types of software and hardware that should be used in its development, emphasizes the cost benefit of this educational technology and promotes this technology in future research.

Finally, it is concluded that the use of RA as an educational technological task that uses various scenarios of virtual reality with the objective of simulating the operation of abstract elements, so that through various visual and multimedia effects, students can to abstract meaningful learning and to relate it to their previous knowledge in order to learn and identify words in English. It is thus that use of augmented reality in the educational processes of children, and more specifically in the teaching of a second language, manages to demonstrate that if the characteristics of the different learning styles that are auditory, kinesthetic and visual are encapsulated which prove to be suitable for them to be used together would develop their cognitive potential to the fullest.

BACKGROUND

Globalization requires the training of people with knowledge in different subjects and mainly with appropriate skills of communication towards people with other lifestyles and more than anything with different languages of communication, this with the aim of being able to enter a competitive world of work as functional worldwide. Information and communication technologies are a guideline for this to be achieved and people understand each other, regardless of the variety of their ideological and cultural areas. The learning of another language different from the one that each individual has in his native environment is a constant need every day and on which the schools are based so that the students begin to teach English at an early age. The learning of different languages is one of the activities that are most frequently done in elementary schools, as a result of studies which state that the lower the age of individuals for learning other languages, it is greater the cognitive plasticity of the individual to assimilate a foreign language (Alcedo, Yesser, Chacón, Carmen, 2011).

The English language is predominant in the developed world in reading, writing and speaking, this is mainly perceived because in addition to people whose main language is English, this language is studied at different levels of education systems in multiple countries. The reason for this second language choice is that it is a language used in more than 60 countries, which is used to write books, newspapers, airports and air traffic control, international business and academic conferences, science, technology, medicine, diplomacy, international competitions, pop music, and advocacy, in addition the scientific investigations are written in English mostly, which means that millions of children study English in their different educational levels (Cristal, 1987, quoted by Pennycook, 2017).

Consequently, the knowledge that is found in libraries around the world and that is available for scholars to use it is embodied in several languages, but mainly in the multiplied English language. This generates the need to innovate strategies that help the learning process of this language and to generate educational tools that are supported by the various current technologies, such as translators, which have evolved over the years and have been perfected more and more becoming a daily query software as it is the tools of google translator, program of free access and designed for all kinds of people who already knows how to read and write in a fluid way.

Thematic contents of the English language schools contain tools to aid in their teaching and training. In addition, various tools have been designed to support learning in this subject, which is offered to students from the preschool level, basic and professional level and even anyone who wishes to obtain that knowledge. The language can be learned at any age or situation of people and different materials have been developed to help both teachers and learners in this task; in the same way, there are several tools to help people in this task to learn new vocabularies that facilitate them to move through different countries fluently. From this perspective, educational technology has been constantly working to offer different language learning tools, which should be used in preschool education in order to take advantage of the powerful cognitive system that children have at that age. Technological tools for learning the English language should consist of a series of skills that enable people to communicate effectively and have developed diverse educational contexts whose characteristics promote it.

Times changes along with the way to communicate, to obtain information and to learn, and therefore, the educational contexts have to be modified as well, these must combine elements that promote the learning in students of this century, who are restless and who have born in a digital age where technological resources fill their space and life. For this reason, the traditional way of teaching and learning must migrate to new educational approaches, based on the fact that true learning requires experience and that the more senses are involved (sound, sight, touch, emotions, etc.), is more powerful is for learning. (Pérez-López and Contero 2013). It is in this way that augmented reality can be an essential part of teaching, helping to create new educational environments that should be designed to motivate students to use their visual, auditory and kinesthetic senses to learn. Peaceful students listening to lectures or exhibitions are falling behind, new ways of teaching and learning are needed, and ways that by inserting knowledge into students it will make them feel it, live it and enjoy it. This may sound a bit poetic, but now there are technologies with which these goals that can be achieved.

The augmented reality is a tool that has entered the educational option, with various tools that strengthen the task of helping the student to learn, this helps to develop skills such as space, practical skills and conceptual understanding of students who are provided by the image-based AR (Cheng and Tsai, 2013). This technology is based on showing pupils abstract elements in a virtual way and overlapping physical reality, in addition RA provides an interactive and attractive interface for students to reinforce their learning using 3D images or other multimedia resource, several studies show that classroom implementation helps improve the learning process, increases motivation and facilitates teacher work (Martín-Gutiérrez & Contero, 2011, mentioned by Gutiérrez, 2014).

AR has been used to translate texts; such is the case of the Google Word Lens app that bases its operation on positioning the camera over the text and will automatically display its translation. Word Lens translates between English, Spanish, French, German, Italian, Portuguese and Russian languages and has additional features such as erasing and inverting words and searching for words in a dictionary. Another tool that uses AR to help people learn English is the Wordbook, which bases its operation on markers that allow the selection of words correctly written in English for the student to practice reading English (Vate-U- Lan, 2012).

Augmented reality has not only been used to teach English, systems have also been designed to help learn other languages such as the May Lottery application, which helps in learning Maya language based on a Mayan lottery that bases its operation on the interaction between images and audio that were used to implement the AR, this application is a game that works with 89 images that are used as markers so that the student learns how to play with other teammates where they can make equipment out of it. The way to understand and interact with abstract elements shown by images, makes the words that are shown and their meaning are recorded in the repertoire of student knowledge (Miranda et all, 2016).

MAIN FOCUS OF THE CHAPTER

Issues, Controversies, Problems

Phase I: System Analysis

In a world where everyday life encompasses the management of new technologies focused on facilitating people's lives and knowing that individuals must be endowed with the skills to face problems and provide solutions in contexts where knowledge revolves around different issues that are written by different researchers in different languages, learning environments are required to prepare students with appropriate skills that involve the dialectic between the real and the virtual with tools based on cutting-edge educational technology.

The English language is used as a means of communication in different parts of the world, so it is necessary for children to learn that language so that when they need it, it is easier to enter into a globalized context. Under this approach it is important that students whose first language is different from English that they learn it, although it is important to mention that this language can be object of learning at any age and / or educational level; however it is of better benefit than learning as early as possible, to take advantage of the cognitive flexibility of the students as already mentioned, for it requires a teaching process different from traditional, where with the support of didactic elements learning is highly effective.

This is based on the experience that during the process of teaching learning children are easily distracted, requiring games or activities that motivate them to want to learn and concatenated to that are needed of technological tools that contribute to the academic training result be easy, pleasant and therefore motivating; to achieve this, tools are needed that help in the teaching-learning process, strategies in the classroom that promote the acquisition of knowledge and that cause joy to learn in the students and also, that induce that learning is for them a laudable opportunity, rather than a need. To achieve this, it is necessary to use state-of-the-art technology that builds educational contexts whose implementation characteristics are not high-cost, but are easy to manage and implement, and above all, their cost is measured in low and counter-part monetary terms and their increasing cognitive benefits.

SOLUTIONS AND RECOMMENDATIONS

The Augmented Reality has been an ideal complement for various educational applications and for the teaching of English is also useful for its basic characteristics that define it as a technology through which the visualization of the real environment is enhanced by elements or objects generated by a computer (Rabbi and S. Ullah, 2013). To demonstrate this idea requires applications that encapsulate the elements that interact in a system of augmented reality and that are united in the design of systems that interact with the students, that allows them to visualize the real world and that associate it with the physical world.

A system is developed using a methodology of software engineering that allows you to take step by step each part of the system so that in the end it encapsulates them and emits a result. An information system (IS) is a set of interrelated components that collect, process, store, and disseminate data and information, and provides monitors with feedback mechanisms and operations control that result in the objectives for which they were designed, ie good systems produce excellent results (Stair and Reynolds, 2008). The main parts of an IS are people, who during the use of the software increase the productivity of their work, groups of those same people and in turn companies that interrelate these groups of people. In this context, an IS of AR would be an analogy as seen in Figure 1.

It is necessary to generate educational systems that generate contexts whose characteristics of implementation are not high cost, but rather, contain tools that are easy to manage and implement, but above all that their cost is measured in low monetary terms and in counterpart that its benefits are high. Several studies indicate that augmented reality can improve students' academic performance (Chiu, De Jaegher & Chao, 2015), so it is important to continue to make systems that use this

Figure 1. Information system for teaching English with AR

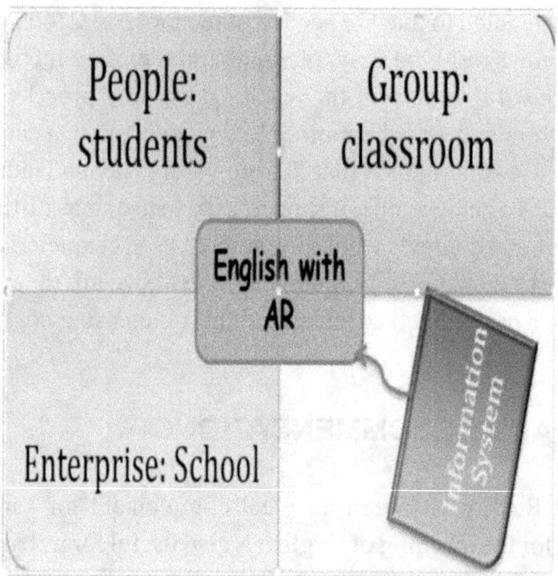

technique, and although many tools have already been made that enrich the contexts educational, there is always a way to improve what has already been invented, because it is important to mention that RA has been implemented in different fields such as military, medicine, engineering design, robotics, manufacturing applications, in maintenance and repair, in teaching and learning, in entertainment, in psychological treatments, etc. (Azuma, 1997; Azuma, 2001).

The analysis phase seeks in the learning environments how and where the English language training system can be accommodated, which makes it a necessity that must be approached from different types of technologies, but in this case it will be designed this context of learning using RA as the main element. This requirement or need may consist of a form of training that is based on capturing and processing data and then producing desirable information. Under this sequence of activities, identifying the requirements includes investigating the case study, analyzing the information to find out what these requirements are, which is why it is necessary to elaborate an outline of what is required to do the procedures that will be involved in the project, determining and allocating the time required for each of these activities, which needs to be reflected in a work program.

Reyes, Olmos and Hernández (2016), observed that identifying the time requirements for each of the activities of a project, allows knowing the number of days, weeks or months that are necessary to integrate the time program, is also essential as in all types of projects, allocate a margin of time to counter any event that implies the delay of the project term and it is necessary, as in all types of projects, to allocate a margin of time for setbacks, as well as punctuate all policies, regulations, norms and restrictions to which the development and operation of the system with RA should be subjected and to define the functional bases of the system, for which it is necessary to establish the information flows, documents to be used, reports to be produced, controls, times and responsibilities within the organizational areas of those involved in some way with the system being built .

Therefore, before beginning with the design of the system, it is necessary to investigate how the teaching and learning of the English language is currently carried out, what methods are used for that activity, and how the educational technology is involved in them, how the augmented reality is used in these methods in case it is used and in what way; and what benefits brings both (technological and non-technological) and compare those results, so as to clearly show the needs and functions that will add our AR system in this field of knowledge.

Once the above results have been investigated, discussed and shaped, the system design is continued, defining the functions that the system will perform and how these functions will stimulate the cognitive process of the students, and not only that, sequence of operation, the information required and the characteristics on which these requirements are based. Once the analysis has been carried out, the idea of the software that satisfies these requirements, the feasibility of the realization of the system, as well as the resources is determined and from this it is defined which is the most adequate, also and according to the resources the company chooses the programming language to be used for the construction of the system, so that the selected tools will have a significant impact on the process and cost for the development of the AR system.

Finally, and as an important part of the development and implementation of the English language learning system with AR, it is a cost-benefit analysis that will determine if there is a financial feasibility to make such a system, taking into account that the development of a system does not is based only on the coding of the system, also requires software licenses, hardware tools and qualified personnel to carry out these tasks; In addition, cost-benefit analysis not only connotes monetary terms, rather, and in this case abstract benefits, which in the long term could help students in their academic development and, of course, more efficient achievements, and understanding the case more, not only at the level of student and person, the benefits could also be measured at the level of prestige of educational Institution and achievements of students at state, national or even international levels. The cost benefit is complex to analyse, there will always be variants to take into account and the results that each information system gives are perceived by their utility in institutions, which are measured by the degree to which it improves the performance of the person or quality of the information system (ease of use, reliability, flexibility) and the type of information it provides (relevant, comprehensible, complete and timely) as measured by the use of the information system and user satisfaction (Bravo, Santana and Rondon, 2015).

Once the analysis of the system as a whole is made, it lists the activities to be carried out, organizing them in a general way depending on the methodology to be used for the abstract and physical design, the codification and creation of the software, the preparation of the files to create test data and test itself, test and integrate the software and make the order, purchase and installation of the equipment, if applicable, implementation and release.

Applications must be organized in a way that allows for scalability, security and robust execution under stressful conditions, and its structure or architecture as it is commonly called must be clearly defined so that a later error can be quickly found and corrected. A properly designed architecture benefits any program regardless of the complexity of the system or enterprise, it must work excellently well during scalability, it must also be reusable to facilitate system restructuring and reuse of code, which is stored in libraries to be available in later projects (UML, 2005).

Based on what has been explained, the first mission is to look for the way the current system works, this is done through the representation of the system through diagrams, which use their symbology to explain in a very understandable way the operation of the system. One practice recommended for the simplicity of its symbology is the Unified Modeling Language (UML) diagrams, which is a universal language that models software systems, and is backed by Object Management Group (OMG).

This language is used to visualize, specify, construct and document a system, offering standard diagrams describing a system model that describes concepts, processes, functions and specific aspects of the system, as well as expressions of programming languages, database schemas and recycled compounds (see official site uml.org).

The software engineering methodologies make use of some diagrams, which adapt to the paradigm, that is, not necessarily have to use all the diagrams, in fact only some are used and are very necessary to show the architecture of the system. The symbology of these models is simple and easy to understand; there are diagrams with specific objectives, depending on the angle of the system to be modeled, the diagrams will complement various methodologies, such as the following diagrams described in OMG UML (2015) and described below:

Class diagram, these diagrams show the classes in which a system is divided and is denoted in a box with the name at the top, the attributes at the center and the operations or methods at the bottom; classes are related for large systems.

- **Diagram of Components:** This shows the structural relationship of the components of a software system and serves for complex systems, the components have the characteristic of communicating with one another, through interfaces using connectors.
- **Deployment Diagram:** It shows the hardware of your system and the software of that hardware, which are deployed on several computers with a unique configuration.
- **Diagram of Objects:** They are similar to the class diagrams and show the relationship between the objects that are used to show how a system will look.
- **Packet Diagram:** Shows dependencies between different packages on a system.
- **Diagram Of activities:** These represent the workflows graphically. They can be used to describe the enterprise workflow or the operational workflow of any component of a system.
- Usage diagrams it is the UML diagrams that are best known, offers an overview of the actors involved in a system, as well as the different functions that these actors need and how these different functions interact.
- **State Diagram:** They are used to describe the behavior of objects that act differently depending on the state in which they are in the moment.
- **Global Diagram of Interactions:** They are similar to those of activity, but they show an interaction of a sequence diagram in these diagrams are

visualized to the objects interacting with each other in an ordered way, that is to say, they are realizing the events depending on the sequence in which they are produced, showing the processes vertically and interactions as arrow.

- **Time Diagram:** These represent the behavior of objects in a specified time frame, although they can also occur in a type with interactions involved.
  - Continuing with the development of the research proposal, the system begins with the design, which is defined as the determination of the architecture of the system, this means that it is the hierarchical structure of the program modules shown visually, as well as the way of interacting between its components and the structure of the data used by these modules. (Rodríguez et al, 2013). By the nature of the system, the design of the system is based on Kruchten's proposal, Philippe (1995), who shows the architecture as the perspective of the Software from 4 + 1 types of views that are defined below:
  - **Logical View:** The organization and functionality of the system is what can be observed in this view, this means that it is the structure and functionality of the system. To represent it, UML diagrams are used, specifically represented with Class Diagrams or Sequence Diagram.
  - **Development View:** A component diagram is used to show from the view of the programmer, that is, shows the programmer that makes each part of the code.
  - **Process View:** With dynamic views shows and explains the processes of the system, and details the way in which they communicate, considering aspects such as concurrency, distribution, performance and scalability that are represented by activity diagrams.
  - **Physical View:** Represents the topology of software components and uses the deployment diagram to represent it.
  - In addition to the aforementioned views, scenarios are contemplated, which are represented by use cases, they describe the sequences and interactions between objects and between processes; also serve as a starting point for testing the prototype of the system.

Phase II: System Design

As it has been observed, the details of the elaboration of the system have been gathered, which are compiled in the analysis of the system, where it is sought to understand for what and how the system works to learn the English idiom with RA and, proceeds to elaborate the design and construction under the actions described in later paragraphs. Pressman (2002) describes the design of a system such as the establishment of data structures, the general architecture of the software and the representations of the interfaces and algorithms; that is, the process that translates the requirements into software specifications.

The objective of the design phase is to make known the behavior of the proposed solution; this is conceived taking into account that the design is a pre-phase that initiates the construction of programs and / or processes of activities that are normally carried out by the users, who seek to improve themselves adding speed, efficiency, efficiency, saving and design visual.

System Architecture

The first action that begins with the design is the determination of the system architecture, which is the hierarchical structure of the program modules, the way of interacting of its components and the structure of the data used by these modules (Presman, 2002). Of the multiple architectural software systems that exist, as already mentioned, the methodology "four views plus one" was chosen for its development. Each view has already been described and it is now appropriate to note the development of each stage.

Logical View

In this view it is possible to see the actions sequentially performed by the system, in which all entities that interact for the proper operation of the system are immersed. For the case of the system object of this investigation, the entities are the students, the camera, the system and the database. This view is represented by a sequential diagram and shows the actions performed by the system during the interaction with the entities, since the camera focuses on the student so that by means of pattern recognition he detects that it is his face and then asks him to write the word in English he wants to learn to write, to recognize and to speak in English, that way the system shows him the three-dimensional image of the abstraction of the word in case it is correct, as well as the pronunciation audio in English of the written word, these digital files are superimposed on the physical reality that in this case is what is called AR. But if the word has been spelled incorrectly, the system will show you options by asking which word you want to know how to write, the student writes it in Spanish and the system is shown in English; with that suggestion, the student retests the training of writing the word in English. This process is shown in figure 2.

This phase notes the requirements of the proposed system and how to approach them, that is, looking for several hardware and software elements, the most suitable and feasible for their execution.

Figure 2. Sequence diagram of the AR system

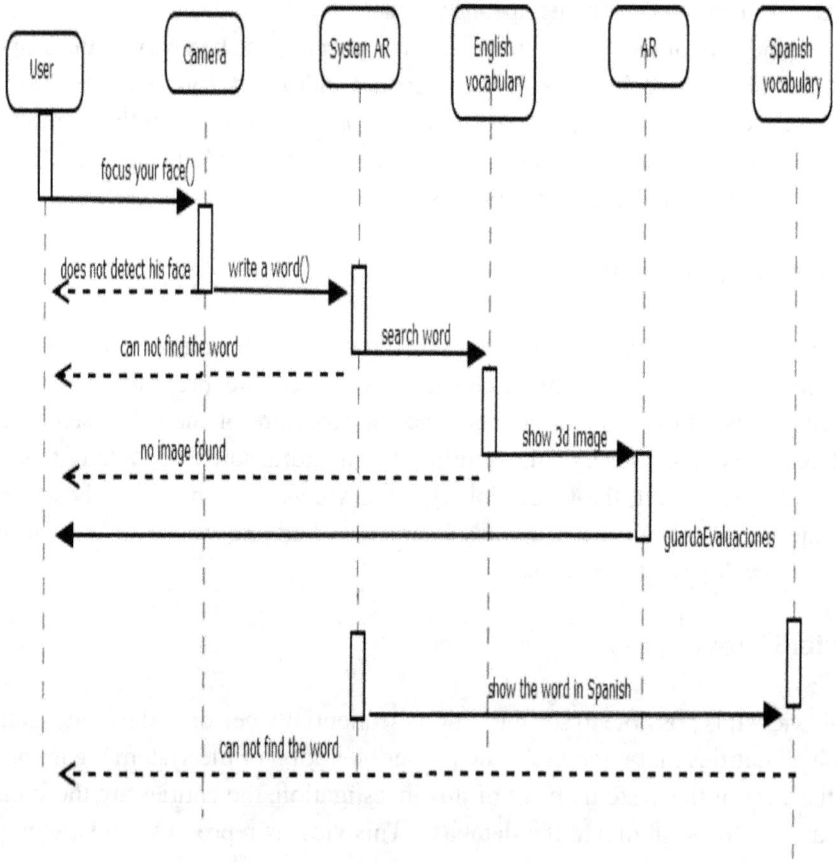

Hardware

The hardware that is required to display the AR system in the comment is listed as follows:

- **Camera of Photographs:** With this camera the AR is triggered, it is indispensable to superimpose the virtual elements on the real face of the user. Every avant-garde device has one, both on a computer and on a mobile device.
- **Display of the Device:** This is contained in any computer device (tidy or mobile) and in this AR system, it is used to display the virtual elements, messages, the user's face and in general the entire environment of this educational technological system.

- **Keyboard:** It is provided in any device of the aforementioned, although they can also be added as accessories and used in the system to be able to interact with it, when words are written that are wanted to be searched in the database, both in English and in Spanish.
- Audio, also provided on mobile devices, included in computers or as an accessory, this audio is very useful, since the AR of the system also incorporates sounds with the words of the en spoken in English, so that the student, not only associate the image with the writing, also with the diction.

The above elements as already commented are included or acquired, but are basic and common in everyday life. The recent evolution of mobile hardware has allowed the RA to be reproduced in small units such as smartphones or tablets, which contain all the components necessary for it, such as: high resolution cameras and screens, accelerometers, GPS and wireless connectivity by WLAN and radio links (Honkamaa et al, 2007).

Software

The software required for the implementation of the AR system should be selected taking into account cost, feasibility, access and even ease of handling. For 3D images to be clear you need a design software, although there are images of free download on the internet that can be used to save time, although it takes time and patience to find the one you are looking for. In order for the audio where the words are heard, it is required that they be recorded with a good diction, or to display the AR have been implemented a variety of browsers, some of free use and others will have to be bought.

AR Browser

There are several types of software (some licensed for free use and others licensed for exclusive use) dedicated to the construction of RA. Some types of these are: Vuforia Aurasma, Layar, ArToolKit, Total Immersion, Mixare, ARPA and Unity3D, ARCore. Some others were designed to show AR on specific topics, for example: LearnAR, WordLens, Wikitude World Browser, TAT Augmented ID, Monocle Point & Find, TwittARound, Lookator, Google Goggles, Google Sky Map.

Development View

The components of the system will serve to guide the programming that is conceived from the view of the programmer and serves to implement the software through the diagram of components. The diagram that represents this system of AR shows as components the processes that the system will perform, such as: recognition of the image before the camera, association of the written word in English in the database, as well as the search for written word in Spanish and the messages generated by emitting the correct answer, as well as the display of the AR shown with multimedia elements in this case three-dimensional images and audio, in addition and if that were not enough, an accountant of the achievements that students are having, which in the end, gives the score obtained and a message. The components are shown in Figure 3 and are listed as shown below:

Process View

The RA system model to learn how to write a vocabulary in English proposes that in its process view show the design of the images, the design of the programming, the searches in the database, the shooting of the AR, this is shown in the activity diagram, as can be seen in Figure 4. In the activity diagram the programming paradigms require a structure that integrates modules and that are interconnected,

Figure 3. Diagram of components of the AR system

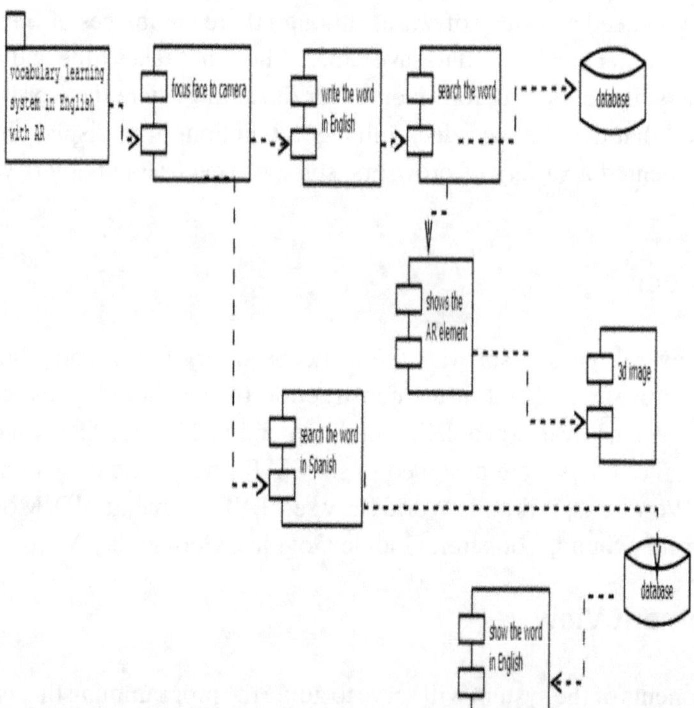

Figure 4. Activity diagram of the AR system

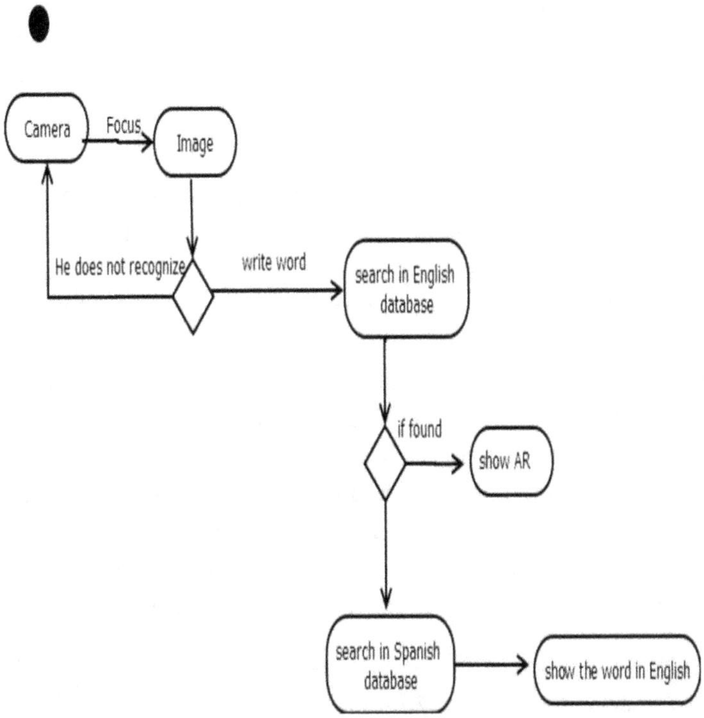

but at the same time, that can operate individually, this is can graphically display in the system architecture a diagram that integrates the operation of the system, starting from the moment the user is in front of the computer to start the system and ends until the moment the user wants to finish the training.

SketchUp Make is used for the design of three-dimensional images, as it is a free version, although images of other free sites can also be downloaded, such as 3D Warehouse. These images are saved in a database and are associated with the correct words that the user enters in the system, in case the words that were captured are not located in the list of stored words, the system will ask the user to enter the word in Spanish, you want to learn to write in English, that way the system locates the word in Spanish and associates it with the English word, which shows the user in a message with the indication that the word you want knowing how to write is written as follows showing the word in English, spelled correctly.

The procedures of the system can work separately, because if the user initially wants to know how to spell a word in Spanish, choose the corresponding menu, which will ask you to type the word and do the process described above. Otherwise, if the student starts his training without wanting to know how to spell the word he captured in English, so that he forced himself to remember the way he is written, he can do it without choosing the second option.

In this view, we can observe the programming, the association of words with images and the search of words in Spanish to show their translation in English.

- **Physical View:** As already mentioned, the topology of the software components is represented and the deployment diagram is used to represent it. In the case of the writing system of the vocabulary with RA the components are: camera, databases, interaction. In the interaction will be applied through the keyboard of the computer and overlapping augmented reality in digital format using images in 3D, audio and text formats, which will be shown according to the point of interaction of the student to the system. The language that performs the interaction is JavaScript with Html5, which is well known as it handles the programming with events, which are the ones that trigger the buttons and menus and whose diagram can be visualized in the figure 5.
- **The Additional View:** The referenced methodology is represented by the use-case diagram, which represents the general functioning of the system from the point of view of the user, that diagram can be observed in figure

Figure 5. Use case diagram of the AR system

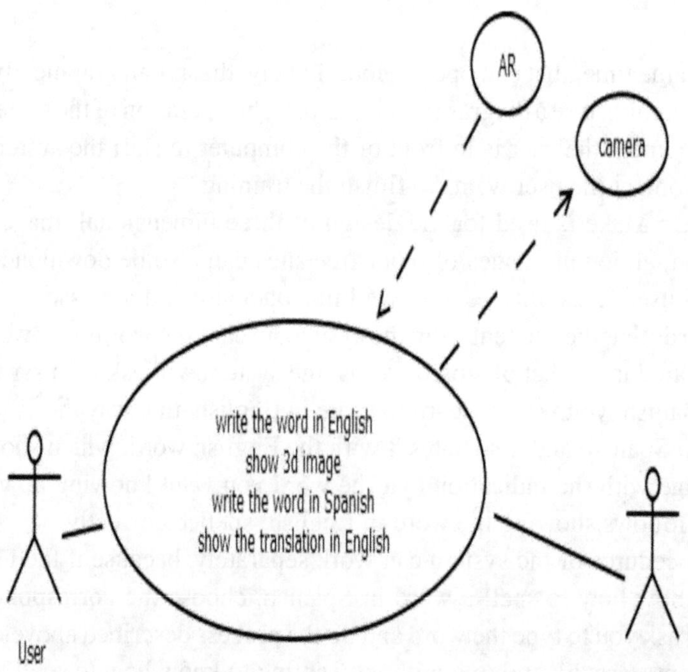

5, which shows the way in which the user interacts with the system in cases of translation and search of words, as well as the overlapping of augmented reality.

Construction of the Prototype

To finalize the design and construction, a prototype of the system is made. That is, it shows how the system would be in a way more approximate to the final system. In this case, the sequence of actions necessary to reproduce the RA is shown, starting from the image of the user before the web camera as perceived in figure 6.

When the student selects the option to write in English (click on the button), the system asks to type the English word and if the search in the database is a success sends the three-dimensional image and the audio that corresponds to that word (Figure 7 and Figure 8).

The user has the option to choose to write the word in Spanish and the system searches it in the database, if the locates the returned translated into English (Figure 9 and 10).

Figure 6. Image that triggers the RA system

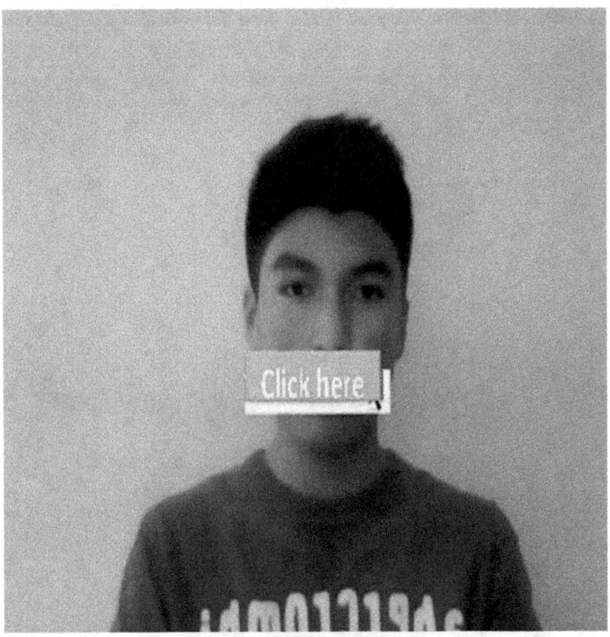

Figure 7. The system asks to write the word in English

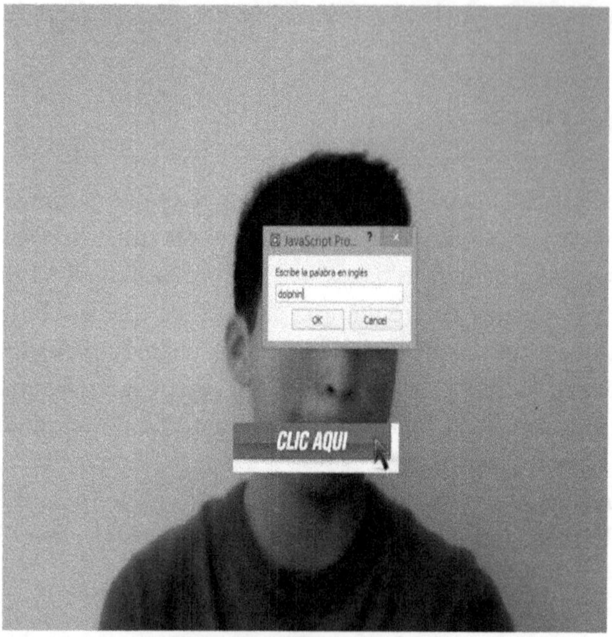

Figure 8. The system displays the RA if the word is in the database

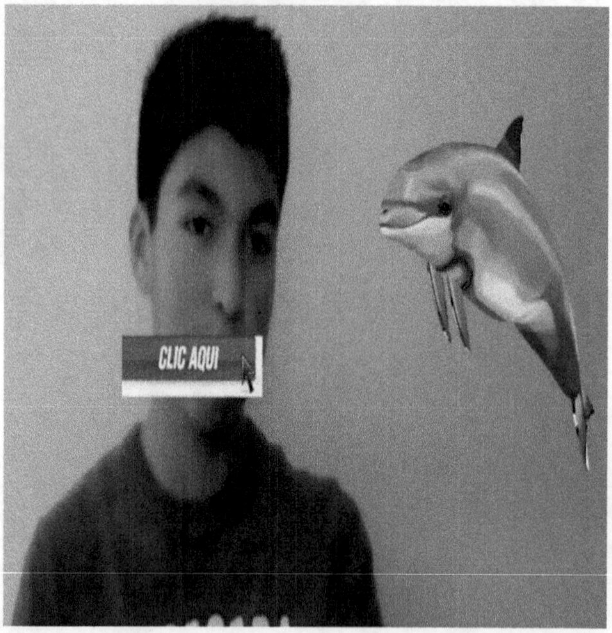

Figure 9. The system asks to write the word in Spanish and the sample in English

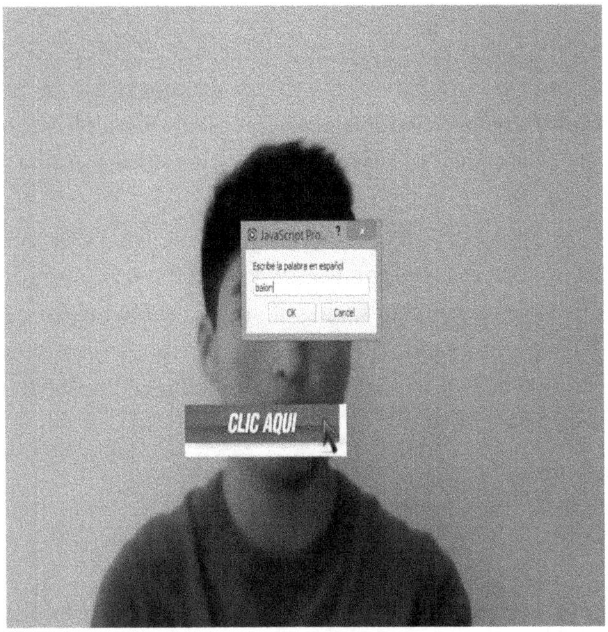

Figure 10. The system displays the word shown in English as AR

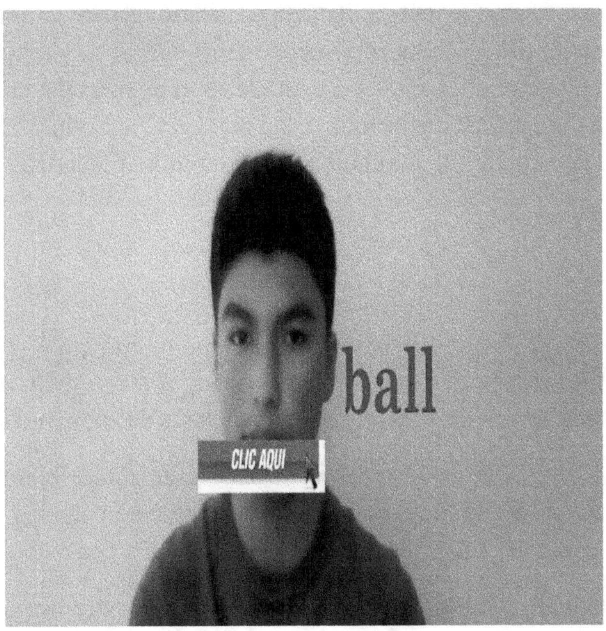

FUTURE RESEARCH DIRECTIONS

For future research, RA is an element that as a complement in educational technology results in many benefits. Improvements to this system could be investigated, and even adapted to new languages, where its pedagogical characteristics would promote the training of those languages, which would generate the construction of useful and efficient knowledge.

This type of systems works as classes and objects, where the reuse of them is a highly usable resource for the construction of new systems, in addition the interaction that promotes this type of systems makes it applicable to any discipline. In future research could be supplemented with tactile interaction, which although it is in the initial phase, could be added so that the student managed to have the sensation of a more physical virtual reality.

CONCLUSION

The use of RA implies an educational technological task that uses different scenarios of virtual reality with the objective of simulating the operation of abstract elements, so that through various visual and multimedia effects, students can abstract meaningful learning and relate to their previous knowledge, in order to learn and identify words in English. The use of augmented reality in the educational processes of children, and more specifically in the teaching of a second language, shows that if it is possible to encapsulate characteristics suitable for students to learn as the different learning styles such as auditory, kinesthetic and visual that each individual has and that used together would develop to the maximum their cognitive potential.

REFERENCES

Alcedo & Chacón. (2011). *El Enfoque Lúdico como Estrategia Metodológica para Promover el Aprendizaje del Inglés en Niños de Educación Primaria*. SABER. Revista Multidisciplinaria del Consejo de Investigación de la Universidad de Oriente.

Azuma, R. (2015). Location-Based Mixed and Augmented Reality Storytelling. In Fundamentals of Wearable Computers and Augmented Reality (pp. 259-276). Academic Press. doi:10.1201/b18703-15

Bravo, E., Santana, M., & Rodon, J. (2015). Information systems and performance: The role of technology, the task and the individual. *Journal Behaviour & Information Technology.*, *1*(3), 247–260. doi:10.1080/0144929X.2014.934287

Cheng, K. H., & Tsai, C. C. (2013). Affordances of augmented reality in science learning: Suggestions for future research. *Journal of Science Education and Technology*, *22*(4), 449–462. doi:10.100710956-012-9405-9

Chiu, J. L., DeJaegher, C. J., & Chao, J. (2015). The effects of augmented virtual science laboratories on middle school-students' understanding of gas properties. *Computers & Education*, *85*, 59–73. doi:10.1016/j.compedu.2015.02.007

Gutiérrez, M. (2014). Augmented Reality Environments in Learning, Communicational and Professional Contexts in Higher Education. *Digital Education Review*, *26*, 22–35.

Honkamaa, P., Jäppinen, J., & Woodward, C. (2007). *A Lightweight Approach for Augmented Reality on Camera Phones using 2D Images to Simulate in 3D*. VTT Technical Research Centre of Finland.

Kruchten, P. B. (1995). The 4+1 View Model of architecture. *IEEE Software*, *12*(6), 42–50.

Miranda Bojórquez, E., Vergara Villegas, O. O., Cruz Sánchez, V. G., García-Alcaraz, J. L., & Favela Vara, J. (2016). Study on Mobile Augmented Reality Adoption for Mayo Language Learning. *Mobile Information Systems, 2016.*

Pennycook, A. (2017). *La política cultural del inglés como lengua internacional.* Taylor and Francis.

Pérez-López, D., & Contero, M. (2013). Delivering educational multimedia contents through an augmented reality application: A case study on its impact on knowledge acquisition and retention. *TOJET: The Turkish Online Journal of Educational Technology, 12*(4).

Presman, R. (2010). *Ingenieria del Software*. McGraw-Hill.

Rabbi, I. & Ullah, S. (2013). A survey on augmented reality challenges and tracking. *Acta Graphica znanstveni časopis za tiskarstvo i grafičke komunikacije, 24*(1-2), 29-46.

Reyes, R. G., Olmos, P. S., & Hernández, H. M. (2016). Private Label Sales through Catalogs with Augmented Reality. In Handbook of Research on Strategic Retailing of Private Label Products in a Recovering Economy. IGI Global.

Stair, R., & Reynolds, G. (2008). *Fundamentals of information systems*. Course Technology Press.

UML. (2005). *To OMG's Unified Modeling Language*. Retrieved from http://www.uml.org/what-is-uml.htm

Vate-U-Lan, P. (2012). Una realidad aumentada 3D Pop-Up Book: El desarrollo de un proyecto multimedia para la enseñanza del idioma inglés. *2012 IEEE Conferencia Internacional sobre Multimedia y Expo*.

Vázquez, R. S., & Salinas Alguacil, L. N. (2013). Arquitectura organizacional para soluciones empresariales de software. *Revista Cubana de Ciencias Informáticas, 7*(3), 1-13. Retrieved from http://scielo.sld.cu/scielo.php?script=sci_arttext&pid=S2227-18992013000300001&lng=es&tlng=es

KEY TERMS AND DEFINITIONS

Augmented Reality: A technology that superimposes a computer-generated image on a user's view of the real world, thus providing a composite view.

Educational Environment: It is a space that is organized and structured to facilitate learning.

Globalization: It is a process that allows dynamic that society generates and allows communication and between countries in economic, technological, political, social, and cultural terms.

Information System: It is a set of elements that organized for the treatment and management of information, in order to meet a need or a goal.

Languages: Also called language, is a system of verbal communication that can be oral or graphic; there is a great variety of language.

Learning Environment: It is a medium in which significant learning is generated among students.

Significant Learning: It is a type of learning in which the user relates the information he acquires with what he already has, in a way that builds new information.

Software Engineering: It is the application of scientific knowledge into the design and construction of computer programs.

Chapter 8
Second or Foreign Language Learning With Augmented Reality

Aubrey Statti
The Chicago School of Professional Psychology, USA

Kelly Torres
The Chicago School of Professional Psychology, USA

ABSTRACT

The following chapter will discuss the impact of technology use and mobile learning, specifically augmented reality (AR), in the process of learning a second or foreign language, namely English and Spanish. The chapter will begin with an overview of AR and then include a discussion of the theoretical framework, language learning contexts, as well as AR tools and applications in the process of second or foreign language learning. An overview of the benefits of AR in language learning will also be included, as well as an introduction to AR applications and specific AR systems, platforms, and case studies in language learning. The research will also provide a discussion of the challenges of using AR in language learning contexts, including specific attention to challenges with AR and learning, AR and language learning, and mobile learning as a whole. The chapter will conclude with final thoughts from the authors in terms of potential areas of AR development that are in need of further attention.

DOI: 10.4018/978-1-5225-5243-7.ch008

INTRODUCTION

The advancement of wireless applications in addition to the wide-spread use and popularity of mobile devices have contributed to the development of technological opportunities and advantages in learning (Ho, Hseigh, Sun, & Chen, 2017). Research indicates that while in the past the role of technology was still under evaluation, presently the case for the inclusion of technology in the classroom has been clearly made and therefore technology in learning is here to stay (Hoopingarner, 2009). As Holden and Sykes (2011) best stated: "in moving forward, it has been come increasingly necessary to redefine what it means for our students to learn and do, as well as simultaneously find new ways of trying to understand when and how this transformation takes place" (pp. 2-3). Additionally, as Godwin-Jones (2011) explained, "learning becomes more real and permanent when tied to learners' lives outside the academic environment. Mobile devices are a great way to achieve that goal" (p. 8).

The following chapter will discuss the impact of technology use and mobile learning, specifically augmented reality (AR), in the process of learning a second or foreign language, namely English and Spanish. The chapter will begin with an overview of AR and then include a discussion of the theoretical framework, language learning contexts, as well as AR tools and applications in the process of second or foreign language learning. An overview of the benefits of AR in language learning will also be included, as well as an introduction to AR applications and specific AR systems, platforms, and case studies in language learning. The research will also provide a discussion of the challenges of using AR in language learning contexts, including specific attention to challenges with AR and learning, AR and language learning, and mobile learning as a whole. The chapter will conclude with final thoughts from the authors in terms of potential areas of AR development that are in need of further attention.

Overview of AR Technology

With the current advancement of various technology tools and applications used in the field of education, an emphasis has been placed in the engagement of the learner through these platforms. Mobile learning (m-learning) utilizes mobile computing technologies, such as phones and tablets, in order to enhance the learning experience anytime and anywhere (P.L. Liu, 2014; T.Y. Liu, 2009). Augmented reality (AR is a specific tool of engagement through mobile learning that is currently trending in education and therefore in need of more research and review.

Historical Use of AR in Industry

Although in some professional contexts, such as the military, AR tools have been utilized for more than 50 years, AR has only more recently been made available for the broad public (Sommerauer & Muller, 2014). Movies and science fiction have utilized AR-like technology as far back as the 1980s in films such as *The Terminator* (1984) and *RoboCop* (1987). However, Tom Caudell, a researcher for The Boeing Company (Mullen, 2011), did not officially coin the term until 1990. As Mullen (2011) explained in his description of the history of AR, "Caudell and his colleagues at Boeing worked on developing head-mounted display systems to enable engineers to assemble complex wire bundles using digital, AR diagrams superimposed on a board over which the wiring would be arranged" (p. 3). AR has developed tremendously since its onset and has become a tool used by individuals at a variety of ages, experience and education levels, and professional status. Currently, the advances in m-learning have allowed AR tools to be available to anyone with access to a mobile camera, GPS, and Internet access (Sommerauer & Muller, 2014). AR has also recently become popular in the fields of: advertising, travel and tourism guides, navigation and city guides, architecture, medicine, translation, marketing and sales, entertainment and games, and social networks (Cabero & Barroso, 2016).

Definitions and Uses of AR

Azuma (1997) defined AR as the technological blend of real world and virtual images through real-time interaction. AR technology allows for the use of 3D objects, 2D images, videos, and animations and can be implemented through various means including desktop computers, laptops, portable devices, and smart phones (Kirner, Reis, & Kirner, 2012; Kucuk, Yilmaz, & Goktas, 2014; Wang, Kim, Love, & Kang, 2013).

Furthermore, AR technology allows flexibility for learners, enhances creative thinking skills, and develops interpretation and problem-solving abilities (Solak & Cakir, 2016). Learning activities on mobile devices, including AR, allow learners to engage with the material and to actively construct their knowledge, rather than passively receiving information from a teacher, text, or guide (P. Liu & Tsai, 2013). Instead of simply being recipients of content, students are exposed to experiential, explorative, and authentic models of learning, thus affording students the opportunity to create knowledge by taking an active role in the gathering and processing of information (EDUCAUSE, 2005). Furthermore, because of its focus on different phases, stages, or parts and the viewing of an object through various points of understanding, AR facilitates the knowledgeable command of complex phenomena and concepts (Cabero & Barroso, 2016).

In contrast to virtual reality, AR does not create a simulation of reality (EDUCAUSE, 2005). Instead, the intent of AR is to add contextual data, information, and meaning to a real object or place, thus expanding the learner's understanding of the subject matter in real life (Cabero & Barroso, 2016; EDUCAUSE, 2005; Ho, Hseigh, Sun, & Chen, 2017). Moreover, due to the authentic design of AR, learners are able to experience real feelings and emotions while exploring new content, similar to real world interactions (T. Liu, 2009). Users of AR are provided with a more meaningful learning experience of a place or thing through the addition of audio commentary, location data, and historical context. Godwin-Jones (2011) noted of the responsive touchscreen interface and its ability to "create a more personal, even intimate relationship between user and machine" (p. 6), positing that the devices themselves "encourage a new kind of relationship between user and machine" (p. 6).

AR Technologies and Popularity

AR programs work using a range of technologies, thus exposing learners to a variety of innovative technology programs and tools. Headgear, build-in cameras, PDAs, GPS sensors, Internet access, and mobile devices can be utilized to provide students with a dynamic, interactive, and context-aware real world learning environment through audio, visual, or text-based data (EDUCAUSE, 2005; Ho, Hseigh, Sun, & Chen, 2017). Cabero and Barroso (2016) predicted that AR will reach a high level of dissemination into education centers, including primary, secondary, and university settings within a 3-to-5-year horizon. Additionally, Anderton (2016) forecasted that the AR market will grow from a 515 million dollar industry in 2016 to 5.7 billion dollar industry in 2021, with the majority of the revenue coming from subscription and license fees.

THEORETICAL FRAMEWORK

This discussion of language learning through the lens of AR is contextualized through the theoretical framework of cognitive theory of multimedia learning and situated learning theory. Both theories are discussed at length, leading to an explanation of the process of ubiquitous learning. In addition, this chapter defines and reviews the theoretical principles of task-based language learning and teaching and their relation and applicability to AR systems.

Cognitive Theory of Multimedia Learning

The cognitive theory of multimedia learning (CTML) offers a theoretical explanation of why AR tools may be used to improve learning (Sommerauer & Muller, 2014). In explanation of CTML, Mayer (2009) proclaimed that individuals are able to learn more deeply through the combination of words and pictures than through the simple inclusion of words alone. However, simply incorporating words with pictures may not enhance students learning outcomes. As such, Mayer (2009) suggested that there are three main assumptions associated with multimedia learning: 1) auditory and visual channels are separate and both used to process information, 2) auditory and visual channels both having a limited capacity, and 3) active processes that filter, select, organize, and integrate information based on an individual's prior knowledge, which allows new information to be combined with prior knowledge.

Grounded in these theoretical postulations, CTML suggests design principles for the effective use of multimedia instruction and best practices. Through the use of CTML principles, Sommerauer & Muller (2014) proposed that if AR systems are designed and applied correctly, they "inherently incorporate a subset of these design principles, namely, the (1) multimedia principles, (2) the spatial contiguity principle, (3) the temporal contiguity principles, (4), the modality principle, and (5) the signaling principle" (p. 60). Rather than words alone, the multimedia principles explain that individuals learn better from words and pictures. AR implements this principle through the technique of overlaying printed texts with virtual picture content and vice versa. Examples of this AR method includes integrating videos into a textbook or displaying labels and measures over a technical object. The spatial and temporal contiguity principles posit that when the space and/or time between unequal but related elements of information is minimized, learning is most improved and enriched. AR systems have the ability to implement the contiguity principles "by superimposing virtual content onto physical objects in real-time and therefore spatially and temporally aligning related physical and virtual information" (Sommerauer & Muller, 2014, p. 60). Additionally, in alignment with the modality principle, which states that learning is improved and deepened when an auditory format accompanies related visual content rather than a visual format, AR tools have the ability to play spoken text, instead of displaying printed text only. Lastly, the signaling principle concludes that learning is improved when the organization of essential information in a learning environment is highlighted by cues. AR systems "can implement signaling by directing and guiding people through learning environments using geographic location information and visual triggers" (Sommerauer & Muller, 2014, p. 60).

Additionally, in their research, She, Wu, Wang, and Chen (2009) explained that according to CTML's individual-differences principle, the design of the multimedia instruction has a more significant impact on learners with less knowledge of the subject, than learners with more advanced awareness of the content. Also, this principle explains that the design has a greater impact on visually oriented learners than on non-visually oriented individuals. Therefore, according to CTML, the appearance of AR systems can both significantly enhance the learning process or distract the learner.

Situated Learning Theory

Ubiquitous learning (u-learning), a term defined later in this chapter and also a component of AR, is well described through the lens of situated learning theory. Situated learning theory explains that "learning cannot be achieved or looked at separately from the context in which it occurs, therefore a deconstructualized approach to technology is unlikely to be successful" (Bell, Maeng, & Binns, 2013, p. 350-351). Orgill (2007, as cited in Bell, Maeng, & Binns, 2013) explained that according to situated learning theory, the understanding of a concept is constantly in process of change. Additionally, this theory posits that knowledge often is a result of the interactions between individuals and thus a focus on context is key in situated learning theory. AR has the potential to enhance education in a variety of curriculums due to its focus on background and context (Educause, 2005), therefore the learning of foreign language through AR will be further explored through the framework of situated learning theory.

Based on the principles of situated learning theory, McLellan (1996, as cited in Bell, Maeng, & Binns, 2013) developed a model of instruction that aimed to create a practical framework for constructing a learning program aligned with the concepts of situated learning theory. McLellan's framework emphasized social interactions during learning by including the following components: *cognitive apprenticeship and coaching*, *opportunities for multiple practice*, *collaboration*, and *reflection*. Fundamental to the situated learning model is *cognitive apprenticeship*. Throughout cognitive apprenticeship, the instructor provides the students with authentic problems to solve. The teacher also gives students the opportunity to apply the skills learned in other situations through a gradual increase of task complexity. Central to this process is *coaching*. Rather than instructing the students with exactly what they need to know, teachers guide students through a scaffolding of learning and coach students to understanding and competence. Through this process, students are given ample time to *practice* and refine their new learning skills. Focused on the importance of the social construction of knowledge, *collaboration* offers students the opportunity to learn through discussion and teamwork in the construction of knowledge and the understanding of new learning ideas. Lastly, this model of instruction encourages the importance of *reflection* throughout the learning process. Reflection can be encouraged through the facilitation of time, thus allowing students the opportunity to make predictions, make observations, and to summarize their learning.

Ubiquitous learning defined. The integration of situated learning theory and McLellan's learning model provides an effective approach to incorporating technology in the learning process (Bell, Maeng, & Binns, 2013). Ubiquitous learning creates an environment of learning that is "context-aware, interoperable, pervasive, and interactive learning architecture that integrates, connects, and shares learning resources among the appropriate parties" (Ho, Hsieh, Sun, & Chen, 2017, p. 175). Ho et al., (2017) investigated AR in the context of learning English as a foreign language and determined the effectiveness of AR language learning as a means of ubiquitous learning. Their research concluded with a development of Ubiquitous Learning Instruction System with Augmented Reality features (UL-IAR), an AR system geared specifically towards English language learning, which will be explored further in this chapter. Prior to investigating their work, it is important to gain a solid understanding of the term ubiquitous learning.

Ubiquitous learning focuses on the actual learning context of the learning process. U-learning is the process that allows learners to obtain the needed resources for learning anytime and anywhere (Chen, Yu, & Chiang, 2017). Chen, Yu, and Chiang (2017) described a dynamic ubiquitous learning resource model as including the following parts: contents, resource context, association information, and context interface. As Kolb (1984) emphasized, "learning is constructed and contextualized which relies on engagement with social interactions and experience form the real world" (Ho, Hsieh, Sun, & Chen, 2017, p. 176). Moreover, Weiser et al. (1999) explained that "ubiquitous computing refers to the use of computer systems in everyday environments that enable user interaction at any time" (T. Liu, 2009, p. 516).

Additionally, ubiquitous computing opens the learning environment to the physical world integrated with computational elements, sensors, displays, and actuators, interwoven to everyday objects of life, relationships, and communication (Weiser, et al., 1999). Ubiquitous computing happens all around the learner, whether the student is aware or not (T. Liu, 2009). Beaudin, Intille, Tapia, Rockinson, & Morris (2007) posited that ubiquitous learning is useful for microlearning, when a difficult task is broken down into a series of very quick learning interactions, since it can reach users in various locations and times throughout their day. Their research indicates that learners are better able to retrieve the learned data when they associate the material with cues needed at the time of retrieval. Additionally, highlighting the context in learning is useful in that "learners are most receptive to information, ideas, and skills that are relevant to their current needs and actions" (Beaudin, et al., 2007, p. 2). Furthermore, Kipper and Rampolla (2013) explained that the method of "pegging" is a memory technique that acknowledges the importance of associating new information to knowledge that a learner already possesses in order to support the learning process. Their research indicates that AR programs allow users to identify and describe an object or action in the targeting language, therefore building a stronger memory bond to the term or vocabulary through the location, or context, of the item and their previous experiences with this location.

Ho, Hsieh, Sun, and Chen (2017) contended that "the application of augmented reality with context-aware ubiquitous learning systems offers considerable advantages for English as a foreign language learning" (p. 176). The premise of AR systems usefulness to language learning in ubiquitous environments will be discussed further throughout the chapter.

Theoretical Framework of Language Learning

In addition to the theoretical approaches of Cognitive Theory of Multimedia Learning and Situated Learning Theory as well as the value of ubiquitous learning, this chapter also evaluates the role of task-based language teaching and learning in the instruction of foreign and secondary languages.

Task-Based Language Teaching and Learning

Task-based Language Teaching (TBLT) is a well-established approach to language instruction that stimulates learning by prompting students to achieve a goal or complete a task (Seedhouse et al., 2014; T.Y. Liu, 2009). In Task-based Language Learning (TBLL), students are provided a task and then required to use language in order to complete or solve the task. According to TBLT principles, 1) meaning is primary, denoting that language use is more important that form; 2) classroom tasks should relate directly to real world activities and work to solve communication barriers; and 3) assessment is measured in relation to outcomes (Ellis, 2003). Essentially, the inclusion of task-based learning activities has transformed language learning settings from being teacher-centered to student-centered. In order to expand interaction and autonomy, learning tasks in the TBLT method should be carried out in pairs or small groups. A TBLT approach is said to increase student conversations, create a relaxed classroom atmosphere, and reinforce student comprehensive input (Nunan, 1992, as cited in T.Y. Liu, 2009). According to Ellis, "there is a clear psycholinguistic rationale (and substantial empirical support) for choosing 'task' as the bases for language pedagogy" (2003, p. 320; as cited in Seedhouse et al., 2014).

Skehan's (1998; as cited in Seedhouse et al., 2014) TBLT framework described three phases of learning: *pre-task*, *during-task*, and *post-task*. The *pre-task* phase serves as a time of preparation for the oncoming activity to be completed in the *during-task* phase. An example of *pre-task* might be the presentation of new language or a clarification of existing language knowledge. The *during-task* phase is the actual performance of the task. During this phase of the task, "Skehan claimed learners' attention can be specifically manipulated through a range of features such as time pressure, support, and surprises" (Seedhouse et al., 2014, p. 7). Lastly, the *post-task* phase is a time of evaluation and consolidation as learners analyze and reflect on the task and process after its completion. Task-based learning can also be used in order for instructors to provide their students more personalized learning experiences. Indeed, Griffiths (2001) stated that the use of tasks in foreign and second learning environments may result in students have the opportunity to work at their own pace.

The Impact of AR Systems on Language Learning

As with all fields of education, language learning courses have also begun to focus on the use of technology in the classroom (Hoopingarner, 2009). Contemporary research critiques the traditional approach to language learning due to its focus on acquiring vocabularies, grammar and pragmatic features without the inclusion of real situations (Y. Wang, 2017). Often language learning is a practice of students rehearsing the language rather than learning to use the language to in order to carry out tasks (Seedhouse et al., 2014). Instead, Y. Wang (2017) stressed the importance of immersion in order to improve the learners' language proficiency and communicative competency. Wang, Liu, and Hwang (2017) explained that "autonomous learning in various socio-cultural contexts with the support of location aware systems has been recognized as an important learning approach for language learning" (p. 654). Current approaches to second language acquisition emphasize localized, contextual learning and authentic relations to the real world. With the ability to utilize add-on digital assets to visit and explore scenes and locales from the real world, AR demonstrates an apparent connection to second language learning (Godwin-Jones, 2016). Namely, rather than creating new worlds, AR is an effective teaching method to supplement existing worlds by bringing experiential and location-based learning to students (EDUCAUSE, 2005).

Currently, AR has been well explored for most effective learning and teaching strategies in history, arts, languages, natural science, medicine, and engineering as well as in educational levels including K-12, universities, museums, parks, and zoos (Cabero & Barroso, 2016; Sommerauer & Muller, 2014). Still, the effectiveness of AR with specifically English language learning is in need of further investigation, understanding and application.

English Language Learners and Foreign Language Contexts

Research and practice indicate that the most efficient way to learn a foreign language is to spend time in the community where the target language is spoken (Seedhouse et al., 2014; Yang, 2011). However, full immersion is not always feasible for language learners due to financial and time constraints. Thus, an authentic learning and cultural environment can be stimulated through the use of AR technology in the language classroom (Solak & Cakir, 2016). As explained through situational learning theory, students are more likely to comprehend what they are learning and remember it better later when they are provided a broad context for exploring and understanding the real world (EDUCAUSE, 2005).

Furthermore, Lee (2005) and Davis and Berland (2013) supported the notion that English learners are most successful in the learning process in a highly-contextualized environment that includes hands-on activities, concrete objects, and visual cues. Additionally, the linguistics burden for content comprehension is lessened because these learning activities are less based on mastery of academic terms in the development of content area understanding (Lee, 2005). Learning activities, such as inquiry learning, benefits the English language learner through the use of oral, gestural, and graphic modalities (Davis & Berland, 2013; and Lee, 2005).

The Use of Technology in Language Learning

Hoopingarner (2009) explained that language teaching can be enhanced through the effective use of educational technology. In his research, Hoopingarner explores the uses of technology as a whole in the field of language teaching. He defined the best practices in supporting language learning through the use of technology as viewing "technology as a tool that can enhance teaching and learning by augmented input, providing additional opportunities for language practice, and serving as a platform for interaction and tasks-based learning activities" (Hoopingarner, 2009, p. 222). In addition to task-based learning, Hoopingarner (2009) argued that technology can be used to teach discrete language skills such listening, speaking, reading, and writing. He further explained that technology cannot serve as a methodology nor as a teacher in and of itself. Additionally, technology should not be viewed as holistically beneficial to learning; implementation is a primary consideration for the benefit of technology to the learning process (Godwin-Jones, 2014).

Computer Use in Language Learning. Still, computer-based exercises are beneficial to student learning by increasing interaction and engagement in the classroom. Additionally, technology and the use of computer programs, such as speech recognition software and signal analysis software, have demonstrated the ability to help learners improve their pronunciation.

Despite the need for context and applicability in language learning, vocabulary remains an essential component in foreign language learning (P.L. Liu, 2016) and therefore cannot be forgotten. With the ability to include vocabulary, grammar, pronunciation, and linguistics, current research demonstrates the promise of using technology in the instruction of English and foreign language learners (Andrei, 2017; Godwin-Jones, 2008, 2011, 2016; Hoopingarner, 2009; and Kipper & Rampolla, 2013).

Mobile learning in language instruction. Mobile phones are an integral part of students' everyday lives. As a result, educators may able to easily integrate classroom activities into their lessons that incorporate this type of technology. Lindaman and Nolan (2015) stated that "the long standing desire to make use of digital technology and multimedia in language learning classrooms, in part, has been satisfied by the recent developments of applications for mobile devices" (p. 1). However, educators may not be certain of how to integrate effective forms of educational technology into their classes. In fact, in a survey conducted by Lindaman and Nolan (2015) they found that language instructors typically use applications that provide them the opportunity to lookup definitions, watch videos, and view statistic, but they were uncertain of how to use effectively other forms of technology.

Nevertheless, there are a diverse range of applications that instructors can use to help their students acquire higher levels of foreign or second language proficiency. For instance, research indicates that specifically English vocabulary is effectively acquired through mobile learning (P.L. Liu, 2016). While vocabulary knowledge is deemed one of the most significant elements in foreign language competency, many language learners feel overwhelmed by the task of memorizing large amounts of vocabulary words and phrases and applying them correctly. However, text recognition and gamification options in m-learning provide an effective and entertaining method of learning and practicing language vocabulary and grammar skills (Dita, 2016). Therefore, the mobile mode of learning provides benefits that non-technological environments could not offer.

Digital gaming in language learning. Considering the popularity of gaming in the everyday lives of adolescents and young adults in developed countries, a rise in the explosive growth of educational games is not surprising. Godwin-Jones (2014) posited that digital gaming can have appropriate benefits to pedagogical approaches in language learning provided that the games are appropriately selected, students are trained in order to correctly participate, and the game has a well-designed format. Dita (2016) argued that motivation in learning through digital gaming is increased because of the impact that the gaming process has on a student's emotion, cognitive, and social areas.

Additionally, Peterson (2010) explained the benefits that an immersive gaming environment can offer a language learner. For example, in order to move forward in a game, players must interact verbally with other players or game objects and therefore must use the target language in a real and meaningful way. Additionally, digital gaming in language learning teaches users about the studied culture and customs, thereby teaching students how to use the targeted language in socially appropriate ways. Throughout the gaming environment, students are more likely to be exposed to new cultural and linguistic knowledge that they might not encounter in the traditional classroom setting or in the pages of a textbook (Godwin-Jones, 2014).

Pragmatics. Furthermore, Holden and Sykes (2013) posited that game-based approaches to instruction offer a uniquely effective method for learning language pragmatics. As Godwin-Jones (2014) stated, "in the game context grammatic appropriateness is more important than grammatical accuracy" (p. 10). Pragmatics has been defined as "the study of language from the point of view of users, especially of the choices they make, the constraints they encounter in using language in social interaction and the effects their use of language has on other participants in the act of communication" (Crystal, 1997, p. 301; as cited in Bardovi-Harlig, 2013, p. 69). Bardovi-Harlig (2013) also defines pragmatics as "the study of how-to-say-what-to-whom-when and that L2 [second language learner] pragmatics is the study of how learners comes to know how-to-say-what-to-whom-when" (2013, pp. 68-69). Godwin-Jones (2016) explained that "pragmatic behaviors are difficult to teach, due to the absence of clearly defined rules, the considerable various in appropriateness depending on context and individual, and the always present possibility of a speaker choosing not to use a particular learning pragmatic feature for personal reasons" (p. 13).

In the game format, choices can have significantly dramatic consequences, some as extreme as life and death or great success and substantial failure. However, this format provides a safe environment for pragmatic choices, as the game can be turned off or restarted. Holden and Sykes (2013) warn that miscommunication when a learner receives initial pragmatic feedback in a language can often have detrimental consequences if the feedback occurs in a high stakes environment, such as during a study abroad experience, host family interactions, or a scholarship or job interview. However, mobile virtual AR games allow learners to experience pragmatic errors in a safer environment where these missteps can lead to a relevant and meaningful interaction with a more positive outcome and lesson learned (Godwin-Jones, 2016).

Motivation and Military Use. Virtual learning games and simulations can have a significant impact on the learner, especially if the student is motived by external factors to practice specific linguistics or cultural topics (Godwin-Jones, 2016). Effective game-based learning systems present users with experiences "that are challenging enough not to be boring, but not so challenging as to be frustrating and discouraging. They build learner confidence, as learners master each game level and progress to more advanced levels" (Johnson, 2010). Successful games seek to develop and maintain learner interest and motivation.

In addition to the motivation to learn or to accomplish a task in the virtual game setting, highly motivating factors might include a passing grade, college acceptance, visiting a new country, or applying for a job in the spoken language. Even more extreme examples of learning motivation include life or death situations faced by military members deployed in other cultures. US military personnel utilize the Tactical Language and Culture Training System (TLCTS) from Alelo in order to develop natural language understanding and processing, practice speech recognition, and to prepare for interactions with native speakers through simulated encounters in the targeted culture and environment (Johnson, 2010). The first prototype of TLCTS, titled Tactical Levantine, concentrated on the spoken Levantine Arabic language. The second learning system, titled Tactical Iraqi, focuses on teaching military members the Arabic language and culture. The game includes instruction and practice in culture and language, as well as a focus on specific mission-oriented and task-oriented communication skills. Additionally, at the conclusion of the game and training program, military users completed a final mission rehearsal exercise in a mock Iraqi town in order to practice their communication skills in the Arabic language while completing their military mission.

Johnson's (2010) research evaluated the effectiveness of the TLCTS program on a specific group of Marines prior to, during, and post deployment. He specifically noted the role of the game atmosphere for learning as well as the depth of the language and cultured learned by the Marines throughout the program. Remarkably, this specific Marine battalion did not suffer a single combat-related injury or fatality during their deployment. Post-deployment data indicated through participant interviews and questionnaires that the deployed Marines who had participated in the TLCTS program regarding their language and culture training to be effective in operations during employment. Due to the lack of availability of translators, the studied battalion was able to use their language skills learned during the virtual game in real life interactions. In response to the virtual tool, one company commander stated: "I can tell you that it did greatly enhance our operational capability…It just increased our tempo, it increased our understanding, it increased most importantly our relationship with them. They understood that we came in with a basic set of knowledge and that we were also willing to learn and be able to communicate and those communication skills came through" (Johnson, 2010, p. 191).

In addition to the TLCTS program which are assumed to reach over tens of thousands of users, Alelo has developed other virtual gaming systems for the military that include: Tactical Pashto, which teaches the culture and language of the Pashtuns in Afghanistan, and Tactical French, a game developed to teach the dialect of French spoken in sub-Saharan Africa along with a focus on the culture of the

Sahel region. These Alelo language systems uses the virtual game environment to develop a higher level of language proficiency as well as learner confidence in their abilities to construct their own sentences, instead of relying solely on memorized phrases, an important ability in language aptitude (Johnson, 2010).

Computer-Assisted Language Learning and Mobile-Assisted Language Learning Fields

Computer-assisted Language Learning (CALL) is a growing field of research that looks to explore linguistics, second language acquisition, language pedagogy, and computer science. CALL research offers successful case studies and offers best practices for technology inclusion with language learning (Hoopingarner, 2009, T.Y. Liu, 2009; and Peterson, 2010). CALL training approaches have faced two primary difficulties though: 1) students often lack sufficient opportunities to practice English conversation with teachers, classmates, and native English speakers and 2) schools lack significant English learning environments as well as language learning software and hardware. Likewise, CALL does not provide a clear guide for successful instructed language learning (Hoopingarner, 2009).

Therefore, mobile-assisted language learning (MALL) has potentially replaced the dominance of CALL fields due to its flexibility, low cost, small size, accessibility, and user ability. For these reasons, MALL activities and environments demonstrate success in implementing English and other language learning (T.Y. Liu, 2009).

AR Applications for Language Learning

The inclusion of AR can help to engage learners throughout various types of learning activities (Ho, Hseigh, Sun, & Chen, 2017; P. Liu & Tsai, 2013). Particularly, AR has been utilized to enhance language learners' levels of motivation toward learning a target language. For example, Mahadzir and Phung (2013) conducted a study on the use of AR pop-up books to increase English foreign language learners' levels of motivation and confidence toward the language learning process. They concluded that AR can be beneficial in enhancing students' levels of intrinsic and extrinsic motivation, goal orientation, and academic performance. Additional language learning applications and tools include programs such as campus tours (P. Liu & Tsai, 2013) and games that allow students to solve historical legal cases (Holden & Skyes, 2011) which have been found to enhance students' vocabulary skills and motivational levels.

Kucuk, Yilmaz, and Goktas's (2014) study demonstrated that students who utilize AR applications in the English learning process have a high level of achievement, show a positive attitude towards AR technology, and are required to exert a lower amount of effort during the implementation process. Additionally, students indicate an intention to use AR applications in the future, are satisfied with the implementation of the technology, and have low levels of anxiety while using this technology. Solak and Cakir's (2016) research indicated that AR application in the elementary-level language classroom increases student academic performance and helps learners to store new vocabulary words in their memory longer than through traditional methods of teaching vocabulary (e.g., finding definitions in the dictionary, repetitiously writing words). Through their research of examining the role of AR technology in Spanish teaching, Ibanez et al. (2011) and Perez-Lopez and Contero (2013) suggested that the use of AR in Spanish learning increased student motivation as well as learning outcomes. Moreover, as Godwin-Jones (2011) explained, the small screen size and touch interface of a mobile device used for AR require that students focus on the task being presently learned, rather than multi-tasking between several browsers which is more common during the use of regular desktop computers. This heightened level of attention, in addition to increased motivation, boosts comprehension, knowledge, and learning.

Benefits of AR in Language Learning

Holden and Sykes (2011) contended that foreign language educators often are successful at preparing students for tests, papers, and academic exercises, but often overlook the importance of developing productive, multilingual members of society. Students may need the opportunity to have immersive language experiences in order to proficiently acquire a target language and culture. However, most individuals are unable to travel abroad in order to be immersed in an environment that provides them these types of immersive experiences.

As a result, educators may seek alternative forms of classroom activities, such as AR, that provide students a virtual language learning experience. Indeed, Yang and Liao (2014) expressed that AR can provide immersion experiences to language learners through the merge of virtual and real-world objects and images. In their 2014 study, Yand and Lio found that the use of AR enhanced cultural and language learning experiences and improved teachers' and students' interpersonal communication skills. Additionally, Chen (2014) proclaimed that AR allows students to be "teleported" to different places which can "stimulate various real-life scenarios and make learning more fun and meaningful (p. 50)" which can result in learners experiencing higher levels of motivation, engagement, and autonomy. As Cabero and Barroso (2016) explained, with AR, "information resides in the real content; and the digital content only augments and completes it" (p. 45). Therefore, AR systems indicate an appropriate use of language learning in that the focus of learning remains on the language itself, rather than the additional technology or digital content. Still, these tools can be used to deepen and enhance both the quality and enjoyment of language learning.

Specific AR Systems, Platforms, and Case Studies in Language Learning

The following section will address current AR platforms used in language learning as well as the case studies that were conducted to research the tools. The following AR games and projects will be discussed: Pokémon GO, The European Digital Kitchen project, TANGO, HELLO, Imparapp, Mentira, and UL-IAR. Additionally, both marker-based AR and location-based AR systems will be defined. Lastly, the ARIS platform and Participatory Augmented Reality Simulations (PARS) will be reviewed.

The Pokémon GO Phenomenon

In the summer of 2016, the popularity of the Pokémon GO mobile game created public attention as well as the curiosity of educators for the use of AR tools in the classroom (Godwin-Jones, 2016). In fact, Anderton (2016) predicted that Pokémon GO will serve in history as the game that brought AR technology to the masses. As of August 2016, more than 40 million people were actively playing Pokémon GO and the game itself had been downloaded over 500 million times. Pokémon GO was created by Niantic and made available to players through iOS and Android devices. The game itself involves players interacting with reality, in areas such as parks, malls, restaurants, and other pedestrian areas, in order to earn game assets such as eggs and Poké Balls and thus find Pokémon (pocket monsters). Additionally, PokéStops are specific locations, such as monuments, town squares, or museums, where players can find Pokémon or other game rewards. Despite some criticism for potential safety concerns due to distracted users while walking, Pokémon Go does encourage physical activity, walking, and outdoor play because a player must be active in order to be successful at the game. The eggs, for example, turn into a Pokémon player depending upon the distance walked by the player (Godwin-Jones, 2016).

Due to the popularity of Pokémon GO and its focus on location, second language instructors have concluded the potential benefits of AR during the foreign language learning process (Godwin-Jones, 2016). Godwin explained that the social interactions required of the game offer an abundant opportunity for language use and learning. Additionally, as Pokémon GO continues to spread geographically, learners will have expanded global and multilingual learning experiences through social connections with a multicultural online community. However, the game itself was not intended specifically for language learning and though its wide-spread popularity might have a more engaging impact on young learners, other AR systems potentially provide equal language learning opportunities.

Marker Based AR Learning Language Systems

Despite the popularity and entertainment value of Pokémon GO, not all AR games offer the same high quality of design. Because most language learning AR systems are developed by research-educators, they can be rather limited in their design, functionality, and sophistication (Godwin-Jones, 2016). Instead of using physical location to create the AR experience for students, often these applications utilize an optical sensor, such as a camera mounted on a computer or a camera embedded into a handheld device. Also, this type of AR tool relies on images hard-coded into an application, known as markers, which then trigger some type of action in the system. In this format, markers are tagged to specific objects, attached to walls, or embedded in books and once an "AR app recognized that a marker has come into view through the user's camera, an action is generated, such as displaying a text, showing an image, or playing a sound clip" (Godwin-Jones, 2016, p. 10).

The European Digital Kitchen Project. An example of an AR marker-based tool is the European Digital Kitchen project (Seedhouse et al., 2014). The project was an EU-funded language learning tool designed to engage learners in the following languages as well as culture and cuisine: English, German, Spanish, French, Catalan, Italian, and Finnish. This game uses sensors embedded in various kitchen items such as ingredient containers, appliances, and utensils. Following the principles of Task-Based Language Teaching, the marker-based game is designed for pairs to learn to cook as well as practice their command of the language by assisting one another based on the feedback given from the game in the targeted language. Initial data analysis of the game demonstrated that students were able to learn both tasks simultaneously (Seedhouse et al., 2014), potentially creating a garnered interest in the language, cuisine, and culture of the studied nation.

TANGO. Similar to European Kitchen (Seedhouse et al., 2014), Beaudin, et al (2007), utilized TANGO (tag added learning objects) in their project to tag various items in a house in the language learning context. Additionally, sensors in the design recognize actions in the house such as opening a door, closing a cabinet, or flushing a toilet (Beaudin, Intille, Tapia, Rockinson, & Morris, 2007; Godwin-Jones, 2016). The TANGO application can assist students in learning language vocabulary by making the context relatable and the learning process appealing.

Hand-held English Language Learning Organization (HELLO). The Hand-held English Language Learning Organization (HELLO) is a sensor and handheld augmented related-supported ubiquitous learning environment designed to enhance students' language learning (T. Y. Liu, 2009). HELLO is composed of two subsystems: An English learning management system and a u-learning tool. HELLO was created specifically to target the methods of English learning in Taiwan, Japan, and Korea in order to combat the unique difficulties of English education in these countries. Liu (2009) explained that traditional English education in these countries does not focus on life skills but rather knowledge acquisition. Therefore, the rote recitation of words, reading of papers, and focus on syntax does not enhance student motivation in the learning process. Additionally, there are few opportunities for students to practice English outside of the classroom.

HELLO, like many AR tools designed for the educational setting, includes the following characteristics which can also be applied to other AR platforms:

1. **Permanence:** Learning processes can be recorded in the learning system and stored permanently.
2. **Accessibility:** Learners can easily access audio and video learning materials anywhere.
3. **Immediacy:** Learners can immediately access audio and video learning materials at any time and can get an immediate response from the test tool.
4. **Interactivity:** Learners can operate learning objects and interact with peers.
5. **Situation:** Learners practice listening and speaking in real situations.
6. **Seamlessness:** The learning process is not interrupted when the location of the learners changes.
7. **Immersion:** Learners can talk with virtual teachers in the real world.
8. **Context Awareness:** Learners can hear context-aware audio language materials in specifics zones.
9. **Social Interactivity:** Learners can collaboratively complete a story.
10. **Individuality:** Learners can select proper learning materials according to personal ability, interest, requirement, objective, and schedule. (T. Liu, 2009, p. 518)

HELLO is comprised of two subsystems: the HELLO learning server and u-Tools, a soft-ware application. To test the effectiveness of HELLO, T. Liu, (2009) used a case study method to explore the use of the tool in Taiwanese high school classrooms. During the eight-week course, researchers used the following HELLO tools and English language teaching strategies: context-aware ubiquitous pedagogic strategies; 'Campus Environment', a self-study learning game; 'Campus Life', a context-aware learning game, 'Campus Story', a story relate race, and a series of formative tests. The results of the study indicated that the average grade on the assessments from the experimental group exceeded those of the control group. Additionally, the tests taken during the learning activities were also significantly better by the experimental group rather than the control group. Lastly, participant interviews demonstrated that students improved their learning of the English language and felt encouraged in their creative abilities, indicating that overall effectiveness of HELLO as an AR tool in the development of English language learning (T. Liu, 2009).

Location Based AR Learning Language Systems

While students demonstrate an increased interest in the targeted language, learning gains through the use of marker-based AR systems have been deemed modest (Godwin-Jones, 2016). Therefore, location based AR language systems have also been developed in the aim of increasing not only enjoyment of learning but also learning gains by the user. In their research, Holden and Sykes (2011) "ascribe to the fundamental ecological notion that place is not a mere particularity, an allocation for academic knowledge, but has a profound influence on what and how we learn, and is itself generative" (p. 4). Location based, also referred to as place-based, AR allows the learner to read, listen, speak and write in the targeted language. Additionally, well designed location based games can also provide for student engagement and entertainment. Sensors such as GPS, gyroscope, compass, accelerometer, as well as data retrieved through the camera on a handheld device can provide AR systems with location based information about a learner's physical surroundings. With this detail of information, students can engage in the context of their learning, specifically their location. Examples of place-based learning through AR include the student serving as a digital tour guide in a particular area or participating in a scavenger hunt while practicing the foreign language (Godwin-Jones, 2016).

Imparapp. Imparapp, a mobile game developed by Coventry University for learning basic Italian, has learners complete a treasure hunt, or, in the more updated version, solve a time travel mystery. Throughout the game students are asked to complete tasks such as counting and reporting the steps up to the Coventry Cathedral, asking for directions, or answering other queried information. Additionally, the design of Imparapp allows students the practice of using an Italian map and conversing with other players in Italian (Godwin-Jones, 2016).

Mentira. Mentira is the first place-based AR mobile game created for learning Spanish (Holden & Sykes, 2011). The mobile game is set in Los Greigos, a neighborhood in Albuquerque, New Mexico. The creators of the game designed Mentira with the intention of knowledge building as well as increased participation in the learning process. The location of Los Greigos was selected due to its "connection to the Spanish language, documented history, diverse use and architecture, and walkability…the neighborhood is currently a diverse residential district" (Holden & Sykes, 2011, p. 5). The game was specifically evaluated in a fourth semester college

Spanish class in the attempt of guiding the learning from a basic understanding of the language towards a more in-depth language learning experience for students at the lower proficiency of the language in hopes of encouraging students to move forward in their study of the language. The researchers anticipated that the implementation of this learning experience, prior to advanced language course work or study abroad experiences, would best serve students in preparation for the skills and behaviors needed for these advanced levels.

The game, played over a three to four-week time period through iPod Touches loaned out to students, focused on the essential components of learning through mobile devices: an immersed understanding of the place, ubiquity of access, and a personalization of the learning experience. In order to achieve this goal, the creators of the game developed a mystery format in which "the players must solve the prohibition-era murder of Dionisio Silve in order to clear their family's name and absolve the family of any guilt" (Holden & Sykes, 2011, p. 6). Students are initially introduced to the setting, the murder, and their role in one of four the implicated families. Throughout the game, students are sent to various locations in Los Greigos to collect and investigate clues and to eventually solve the murder. Players practice Spanish language through conversations with fictional characters in order to investigate and solve the crime. Students receive support as well as reinforced learning from the related course curriculum that takes place in the classroom (Holden & Sykes, 2011).

Although studies indicate that students may often rebuke the notion of educational games, specifically games in which educational researchers are the designers, Holden and Sykes (2011) contend that students were not simply going through the motions but were truly playing the Mendira as indicated by the length and frequency of play sessions. Additionally, through observation and participant interviews, their study indicated the students' enjoyment of place-based games and real world interface. Moreover, students also indicated an excitement to engage in the local culture of the game as well as to connect their understanding of the Spanish experience and language to their own learning.

U-Learning Instruction System with Augmented Reality Features. Ho, Hsieh, Sun, and Chen (2017) developed U-Learning Instruction System with Augmented Reality Features (UL-IAR) focused on English as a Foreign Language (EFL). The UL-IAR system was developed on the Android smartphone using Android SDK and Wikitude SDK. The primary features of the program "include GPS position, the highlighting of local features, mark-up, scaffolding instruction, and real-time tests…the UL_IAR system which integrated learning strategies and real-time quizzes helped users to learn English in real life contexts was one of the pioneering applications in the field of education" (Ho et al., 2017, pp. 179-180). The results of their study indicated the effectiveness of the enforcing learning strategy utilized in the UL-IAR program. This strategy "is defined to help learners recapitulate and integrate what was explicitly displayed in the instructional materials and techniques that contribute to the memorization and understanding of learning contents" (Ho et al., 2017, p. 182). Enforcing strategy is an effective learning strategy with significant contributions to individual learning performance. As well, their results echoed Kolb's (1984) premise that an integration of both learning and life produces a mature learning environment for students.

ARIS Platform

Well-known place-based games available on mobile devices have been created with the ARIS (Augmented Reality and Interactive Storytelling) platform (Godwin-Jones, 2008; Godwin-Jones, 2016), such as Mentira described earlier in the chapter. Developed by David Gagnon et al. at UW-Madison, ARIS is an open-source game editor and engine software and is designed for the use of nonprogrammers and educational researchers (Godwin-Jones, 2016). The creators of Mentira selected this specific platform because it is a free and open source and therefore an on-site programmer was not necessary in the creation or implementation of the design of the place-based game for mobile devices. Furthermore, ARIS is noted as having very low technical requirements, yet still having the capability of intricate design and player interaction abilities, an essential for the development of mobile games (Holden & Sykes, 2011). Other language based learning AR systems created with ARIS were created through the University of Oregon's Center for Applied Second Language Studies (CASLS) include *Explorez*, a game geared towards the study of first-year French, and *Why Butterflies are Silent*, a game designed to practice grammar skills of the indigenous language Tohono O'odham. Additionally, CASLS has also used ARIS to create Analy Nyuwiich, a game designed to teach players about the Mojave culture, a Native American community in Arizona (Godwin-Jones, 2016).

Participatory Augmented Reality Simulations (PARS)

Davis and Berland (2013) explored the use of Participatory Augmented Reality Simulations (PARS) with English language learners, specifically in the K-12 science classroom. PARS relies on various components, including audio and graphic components, in order to scaffold learners' understanding. PARS facilitates engagement through creative problem solving, a collaborative jigsaw structure, and the technology component itself. Additionally, PARS games generally include "small group discussion, multiple paths to success, hands-on activities, multi-modal components, and highly contextualized language use occurring in an authentic context" (Davis & Berland, 2013, p. 297).

Challenges of AR in Language Learning Contexts

Despite the numerous positive benefits, the use of AR in language contexts is not without challenges (Godwin-Jones, 2008, 2011, 2014, & 2016; Hoopingarner, 2009). To begin with, AR projects are often costly to develop and maintain. The implementation of combining technology and the real world requires specific or customized hardware and is often technically complex (EDUCAUSE, 2005). In addition, currently many AR programs provide for individual users to experience the learning process and are not always geared towards group learning. Also, the pedagogical value of AR tools has been questioned due to their resemblance of entertainment. Educators utilizing AR tools in the classroom should reinforce the educational value of these programs and dissuade students from being obsessed with simply the technology component. For example, focusing on finishing a race in a game-based AR tool, rather than pausing to understand and solve the problem (Davis & Berland, 2013, EDUCAUSE, 2005).

Potential Struggles With AR Specific to Learning Skills and Abilities

Additionally, AR tools necessitate that both students and teachers have spatial ability, technology self-efficacy, mathematical prediction, problem solving skills, and collaboration qualifications in order to implement and manage the process effectively (Kucuk, Yilmaz, & Goktas, 2014). Studies indicate that there are difficulties with AR implementation if students do not possess these skills and that students may feel cognitively overloaded by the significant amount of information they encounter, the various technological devices used in the process, as well as the complex tasks required (Wu, H., Lee, S., Chang, H., & Liang, J., 2012). Ongoing technical literacy training is necessary for both students and teachers to fully engage and benefit from technology and AR learning tools (Hoopingarner, 2009). Furthermore, research indicates that students with learning and intellectual disabilities may find AR activities to be too demanding or confusing (Benda, Ulman, Smejkalová's, 2015).

Challenges of AR Specific to Language Learning

In relation to the challenges of utilizing AR with language learning, it must be recognized that the way in which computers and humans process language is fundamentally different. Human listening comprehension involves a two-part process:

acoustic and linguistic. Speech recognition programs must also use the same process to understand and respond to spoken language. Technology must first parse the speech signal and then interpret the linguistic message, a technological capability that has improved exponentially. However, despite the remarkable innovations to speech recognition through technology, computers and computer based programing may never be able to communicate in a true human-like way (Hoopingarner, 2009), which would limit the way in which students solely learn language through AR tools.

Disadvantages of Mobile Learning

Furthermore, disadvantages unique to m-learning include no keyboard or mouse, a small screen size, a short battery life, and devices that often have insufficient size of memory for complex systems. Moreover, the screen display may be unclear under strong sunlight during outdoor learning. Furthermore, school districts also face the challenge of purchasing additional devices and learners also face the inconvenience of carrying secondary devices (T. Liu, 2009). Lastly, the potential safety concerns of mobile tools cannot be ignored (Kipper & Rampolla, 2013). Just as mobile phone usage impacts the safety of one's driving, so do these tools affect the attentions of pedestrians engrossed in a game or the learning material. Therefore, instructors and program developers must take extreme caution and provide relevant warnings to users of potential dangers of walking, especially in AR games that take place in specific outside locations, while playing the game.

CLOSING REFLECTIONS

In closing, research has demonstrated the positive impact of AR tools in education and specifically in the language learning process (Cabero & Barroso, 2016; Kucuk, Yilmaz, & Goktas, 2014; Godwin-Jones, 2016; Solak & Cakir, 2016). Particularly, the use of AR helps to increase students' language learning skills and levels of motivation toward the language learning process. These skills appear to be particularly important as the world becomes more multilingual and multicultural.

Moreover, research also demonstrates the need to consider design elements of AR systems (Cabero & Barroso, 2016). Additionally, the technical training of teachers and students is an additional factor to consider during the planning and implementation process of new AR tools. Thus, AR systems must specifically consider accessibility in the development and implementation phases, because when done correctly, computer-assisted instruction (CAI) has shown promise for teaching students with intellectual disabilities (ID) and autism spectrum disorders (ASD) significant skills including: vocabulary, reading, and retention (McMahon, Cihak, Wright, & Bell, 2015), all vital skills in both first and second language learning. Likewise, developers should be mindful that not all students will be enthusiastic gamers and some students will have much more gaming experience than others. Therefore, it is important to provide sufficient gameplay scaffolding for non-gamers in addition to suitable challenges in order to maintain the attention of more experienced and eager gamers (Godwin-Jones, 2016). Furthermore, Holden and Sykes (2011) highlight that developers should also strive to find an appropriate balance between game quality and language learning potential. While language learning should be maximized, AR systems also should address player interest in order to engage students in the learning process. By language instructors using appropriate technological tools in their classroom activities, students will receive engaging learning experiences that will help them to effectively interact in a society that is becoming more linguistically and culturally diverse.

REFERENCES

Anderton, K. (2016, November 14). *Augmented reality, the future, and Pokémon Go*. Retrieved from https://www.forbes.com/sites/kevinanderton/2016/11/14/augmented-reality-the-future-and-pokemon-go-infographic/#72acaa6b7e98

Andrei, E. (2017, June). Technology in teaching English language learners: The case of three middle school teachers. *TESOL Journal*, *8*(2), 409–431. doi:10.1002/tesj.280

Azuma, R. T. (1997). A survey of augmented reality. *Presence (Cambridge, Mass.)*, *6*(4), 355–385. doi:10.1162/pres.1997.6.4.355

Bardovi-Harlig, K. (2013). Developing L2 pragmatics. *Language Learning*, *63*(1), 68–86. doi:10.1111/j.1467-9922.2012.00738.x

Beaudin, J., Intille, S., Tapia, E. M., Rockinson, R., & Morris, M. (2007). *Context-sensitive microlearning of a foreign language vocabulary on a mobile device*. Retrieved from http://web.media.mit.edu/~intille/papers-files/BeaudinIntilleETAL07.pdf

Bell, R., Maeng, J., & Binns, I. (2013). Learning in context: Technology integration in a teacher preparation program informed by situated learning theory. *Journal of Research in Science Education*, *50*(3), 348–379.

Benda, P., Ulman, M., & Smejkalová, M. (2015). Augmented reality as a working aid for intellectually disabled persons for work in horticulture. *Ecological Informatics*, *7*(4), 31–37.

Cabero, J., & Barroso, J. (2016). The educational possibilities of augmented reality. *New Approaches in Educational Research*, *5*(1), 44–50.

Chen, J. (2014). *Proceedings from EUROCALL Conference: CALL design principles and practices*. Groningen, Netherlands: Academic Press.

Chen, M., Yu, S., & Chiang, F. K. (2017). A dynamic ubiquitous learning resource model with context and its effects on ubiquitous learning. *Interactive Learning Environments*, *25*(1), 127–141. doi:10.1080/10494820.2016.1143846

Crystal, D. (Ed.). (1997). *The Cambridge encyclopedia of language* (2nd ed.). New York: Cambridge University Press.

Davis, D., & Berland, M. (2013). Supporting English learners with participatory augmented reality simulations. *On the Horizon*, *21*(4), 294–303. doi:10.1108/OTH-01-2012-0001

Dita, F. A. (2016). A foreign language learning application using mobile augmented reality. *Informações Econômicas*, *20*(4), 76–87. doi:10.12948/issn14531305/20.4.2016.07

EDUCAUSE Learning Initiative. (2005). *7 things you should know about augmented reality. Advancing learning through It innovation*. Retrieved from http://www.educause.edu/ir/library/pdf/ELI7007.pdf

Ellis, R. (2003). *Task-based language learning and teaching*. Oxford, UK: Oxford University Press.

Godwin-Jones, R. (2008). Mobile computing trends: Lighter, faster, smarter. *Language Learning & Technology*, *15*(2), 3–9.

Godwin-Jones, R. (2011). Mobile apps for language learning. *Language Learning & Technology*, *12*(3), 3–9.

Godwin-Jones, R. (2014). Games in language learning: Opportunities and challenges. *Language Learning & Technology*, *18*(2), 9–19.

Godwin-Jones, R. (2016). Augmented reality and language learning: From annotated vocabulary to place-based mobile games. *Language Learning & Technology*, *20*(3), 9–19. Retrieved from http://llt.msu.edu/issues/october2016/emerging.pdf

Griffiths, A. (2001). Implementing task-based instruction to facilitate language learning: Moving away from theory. *TEFLIN Journal, 3*(1), 49–59.

Ho, S. C., Hsieh, S. W., Sun, P. C., & Chen, C. M. (2017). To activate English learning: Listen and speak in real life context with AR featured u-learning system. *Journal of Educational Technology & Society, 20*(2), 176–187.

Holden, C., & Sykes, J. (2013). Place-based mobile games for pragmatic learning. In N. Taguchi & J. Sykes (Eds.), *Technology in interlanguage pragmatics research and teaching* (pp. 1–15). Philadelphia, PA: John Benjamins. doi:10.1075/lllt.36.09hol

Holden, C. L., & Sykes, J. M. (2011). Leveraging Mobile Games for Place-Based Language Learning. *International Journal of Game-Based Learning, 1*(2), 1–18. doi:10.4018/ijgbl.2011040101

Hoopingarner, D. (2009). Best practices in technology and language learning. *Language and Linguistics Compass, 3*(1), 222–235. doi:10.1111/j.1749-818X.2008.00123.x

Ibanez, M., Kloos, C., Leony, D., Rueda, J., & Maroto, D. (2011). Learning a foreign language in a mixed-reality environment. *IEEE Internet Computing, 15*(6), 44–47. doi:10.1109/MIC.2011.78

Johnson, W. (2010). Serious use of a serious game for language learning. *International Journal of Artificial Intelligence in Education, 20*, 175–195.

Kipper, G., & Rampolla, J. (2013). *Augmented Reality: An Emerging Technologies Guide to AR* (1st ed.). Amsterdam: Elsevier. doi:10.1016/B978-1-59-749733-6.00001-2

Kirner, T.G., Reis, F.M.V., & Kirner, C. (2012). Development of an interactive book with Augmented Reality for teaching and learning geometric shapes. *Information Systems and Technologies (CISTI)*, 1-6.

Kolb, D. A. (1984). *Experiential learning: Experience as the source of learning and development.* Englewood Cliffs, NJ: Prentice Hall.

Kucuk, S., Yilmaz, R., & Goktas, Y. (2014). Augmented reality for learning English: Achievement, attitude, and cognitive load levels of students. *Education in Science, 39*(176), 393–404.

Lee, O. (2005). Science education with English language learners: Synthesis and research agenda. *Review of Educational Research, 75*(4), 491–530. doi:10.3102/00346543075004491

Lindaman, D., & Nolan, D. (2015). Mobile-assisted language learning: Application development projects within reach for language teachers. *International Association for Language Learning Technology Journal*, *45*(1), 1–22.

Liu, P. E., & Tsai, M. (2013). Using augmented-reality-based mobile learning material in EFL English composition: An exploratory case study. *British Journal of Educational Technology*, *44*(1), E1–E4. doi:10.1111/j.1467-8535.2012.01302.x

Liu, P. L. (2016). Mobile English vocabulary learning based on concept-mapping strategy. *Language Learning & Technology*, *20*(1), 128–140. Retrieved from http://llt.msu.edu/issues/october2016/liu.pdf

Liu, T. Y. (2009). A context-aware ubiquitous learning environment for language listening and speaking. *Journal of Computer Assisted Learning*, *25*(6), 515–527. doi:10.1111/j.1365-2729.2009.00329.x

Mahadzir, N., & Phung, L. (2013). The use of augmented reality pop-up book to increase motivation in English language learning for national primary school. *Journal of Research & Method in Education*, *1*(1), 26–38.

Mayer, R. (2009). *Multimedia Learning* (2nd ed.). Cambridge, UK: Cambridge University Press. doi:10.1017/CBO9780511811678

McLellan, H. (1996). Situated learning: Multiple perspectives. In H. McLellan (Ed.), *Situation learning perspectives* (pp. 5–17). Educational Technology Publications.

McMahon, D., Cihak, D., Wright, R., & Bell, S. (2015). Augmented reality for teaching science vocabulary to postsecondary education students with intellectual disabilities and autism. *Journal of Research in Education*, *48*(1), 38–56.

Mullen, T. (2011). *Prototyping Augmented Reality*. Indianapolis, IN: John Wiley & Sons.

Nunan, D. (1992). *Research Methods in Language Learning*. Cambridge, UK: Cambridge University Press.

Orgill, M. (2007). Situated cognition. In G. M. Bodner & M. Orgill (Eds.), *Theoretical frameworks for research in chemistry/science education* (pp. 187–203). Upper Saddle River, NJ: Prentice Hall.

Perez-Lopez, D., & Contero, M. (2013). Delivering educational multimedia contents through an augmented reality application: A case study on its impact on knowledge acquisition and retention. *TOJET: The Turkish Online Journal of Educational Technology*, *12*(4), 19–28.

Peterson, M. (2010). Computerized games and simulations in computer-assisted language learning: A meta-analysis of research. *Simulation & Gaming*, *41*(1), 72–93. doi:10.1177/1046878109355684

Seedhouse, P., Preston, A., Oliver, P., Jackson, D., Heslop, P., Balaam, M., ... Kipling, M. (2014). The European Digital Kitchen Project. *Bellaterra Journal of Teaching & Learning Language and Literature*, *7*(1), 1–16.

She, J. H., Wu, C., Wang, H., & Chen, S. (2009). Design of an e-learning system for technical Chinese courses using cognitive theory of multimedia learning. *Electronics and Communications in Japan*, *92*(8), 393–400. doi:10.1002/ecj.10204

Skehan, P. (1998). *A cognitive approach to language learning*. Oxford, UK: Oxford University Press.

Solak, E., & Cakir, R. (2016). Investigating the role of augmented reality technology in the language classroom. *Croatian Journal of Education*, *18*(4), 1067–1085.

Soomerauer, P., & Muller, O. (2014). Augmented reality in informal learning environments: A field experiment in a mathematics exhibition. *Computers & Education*, *79*, 59–68. doi:10.1016/j.compedu.2014.07.013

Wang, H. Y., Liu, G. Z., & Hwang, G. J. (2017). Integrating socio-cultural contexts and location-based systems for ubiquitous language learning in museums: A state of the art review of 2009-2014. *British Journal of Educational Technology*, *48*(2), 653–671. doi:10.1111/bjet.12424

Wang, L. S., Kim, M. J., Love, P. E. D., & Kang, S. C. (2013). Augmented Reality in built environment: Classification and implications for future research. *Automation in Construction*, *32*, 1–13. doi:10.1016/j.autcon.2012.11.021

Wang, Y. F., Petrina, S., & Feng, F. (2017). VILLAGE-Virtual immersive language learning and gaming environment: Immersion and presence. *British Journal of Educational Technology*, *48*(20), 431–450. doi:10.1111/bjet.12388

Weiser, M., Gold, R., & Brown, J. S. (1999). The origins of ubiquitous computing research at PARC in the late 1980's. *IBM Systems Journal*, *38*(4), 693–696. doi:10.1147j.384.0693

Wu, H., Lee, S., Chang, H., & Liang, J. (2012). Current status, opportunities, and challenges of augmented reality in education. *Computers & Education*, *62*, 41–49. doi:10.1016/j.compedu.2012.10.024

Yang, M., & Liao, W. (2014). Computer-assisted culture learning in an online augmented reality environment based on free-hand gesture interaction. *Transactions on Learning Technologies*, *7*(2), 107–117. doi:10.1109/TLT.2014.2307297

Yang, Y. F. (2011). Engaging students in an online situation learning language environment. *Computer Assisted Language Learning*, *24*(2), 181–198. doi:10.1080/09588221.2010.538700

Chapter 9
Augmented Reality for Evaluating Low Environmental Impact 3D Concepts in Industrial Design

Omar E. Sánchez Estrada
Universidad Autónoma del Estado de México, Mexico

Mario Gerson Urbina
University Autonomous of the State of Mexico, Mexico

Raymundo Ocaña
University Autonomous of the State of Mexico, Mexico

ABSTRACT

This work uses augmented reality (AR) as a supplementary tool in teacher's evaluation of low environmental impact 3D concepts in industrial design, which are part of contents in subjects taken by fifth semester undergraduate students of Industrial Design at the Autonomous University of the State of Mexico (UAEM), specifically in the Tool Design Workshop. Design criteria are presented and they will be used to evaluate 3D concepts through the use of AR. The project is developed in three stages: 1) presenting the 3D concept through AR scenarios in order to be evaluated, 2) visual evaluation with established technical criteria, and 3) evaluation feedback so as to improve the 3D concept. The aim is to reduce evaluation subjectivity in order to reduce production costs, waste generation, and energy use in producing mockups and models.

DOI: 10.4018/978-1-5225-5243-7.ch009

INTRODUCTION

Nowadays, technology development has enabled exploring and making use of different strategies in order to have a favorable impact on education. Augmented Reality (AR) in teaching abstract concepts and morphologic evaluation of objects is an important technological tool for Higher Education Institutions (HEI). Likewise, it is an opportunity to innovate in the teaching-learning process. As pointed out by Billinghurst (2002) interactions with tangible objects and efficient transition between reality and virtuality may generate new educational experiences. Therefore, this technology along with its three main characteristics: a) combining real with virtual, b) real time interactions and, c) three-dimensional records (3D), allow to make a combination among objects, people and contexts that are part of real environments and virtual objects, making them seem as if they coexist in the same space as in the real world (Azuma, 2001).

Nowadays, teacher's perception on aspects of structure, use, function and morphological analysis applied to objects is a permanent action and, evaluating 3D concepts that could subsequently be built leans towards a professor's experience and tendencies to conceptualize. Further, evaluation and approval of a 3D concept in Industrial Design is usually defined by design requirements, which are proposed by students as variables that must fulfill a quantitative and qualitative solution due to regulations the project must follow, whether it is a use, function, structural, ergonomic, esthetic formal and/or productive technical requirement, among others (Rodríguez, 1988). Precision criteria change very little from one concept to another; function, use, morphology and esthetic structure are applied in most cases. Meanwhile if requirement for the designed project is governed by a low environmental impact, it is possible to categorize and prioritize how they will be solved from complementary subjects such as: life cycle, required energy use, raw material extraction or production processes.

Due to the above and the different variables an evaluation may have, it is possible to include some didactic resources and determined processes to evaluate 3D concepts through AR; also when adding conventional instruments such as evaluation documents, signatures or evidence folders, as well as software that is easy to access and use by the teacher. Within these activities, both Industrial Designer and evaluator aim to decrease evaluation subjectivity, representation and improvements of three-dimensional models (3D). Therefore, it is viable to add or eliminate objects from the real environment and to use graphic coverings to hide or remove environmental parts if the evaluation requires it according to complexity level.

BACKGROUND

In recent years, AR research has improved and extended to different study areas, while the same thing has happened in data processing and development of devices that include digital cameras, state-of-the-art sensors and global positioning systems. However, authors such as Uva, Cristiano, Florentino and Monno (2010) affirm that tools for computer-aided technologies do not provide good support when carrying out a review of design's concepts, prefiguration and figuration, mainly for the following matters: (a) subsequent applications integration; (b) finite element methods (FEM); (c) usability; (d) complex design knowledge; (e) system configuration management and; (f) web contents support. In a different way, AR improves perception of industrial objects with digital and multimedia data annotations (Friedrich, Jahn, & Schmidt, 2002).

On that basis, AR facilitates an interrelation among virtual representation systems and creative activity of industrial designers. According to Huang (2002) design review plays an important role in the product life cycle (PLC) as it allows to identify fails or errors in productive processes in advance. For their part, Uva, Fiorentino, and Monno (2011) affirm that computer tools are developed to facilitate certain tasks; however, they are more complex every time, for example computer-aided design (CAD) must improve in the following aspects: (1) interfaces reconfiguration to favor interaction and to optimize usage time required by inexperienced users and teachers; (2) making technical support simple and; (3) facilitate understanding of 3D geometries among virtual and real models. Consequently, the possibility of adding innovative technologies to the business sector opens up.

Such is the case of Volkswagen, the German Company that has implemented AR to their product development processes. In that sense, Ostermann, a computer engineer, tells how a 1:4 scale model of a Golf automobile, after being analyzed using mixed reality lenses named "HoloLens" and a Microsoft computer that projects virtual content in a physical object through gesture control and voice commands, was modified by changing its side mirrors and tires and replacing its tail lights in just seconds. The software used was developed in the engineering virtual lab. Nowadays, uses of AR and Virtual Reality (VR) have become tools for technical development, which allows for changes in equipment or design of new components in virtual vehicles, while saving time, development costs and having a low environmental impact for that process. The company has 6 engineering virtual labs operated by the IT team at Volkswagen, in Wolfsburg, Berlin, Munich and San Francisco and, the last lab is already operating in Barcelona, Spain. (Netmedia, 2017).

On the other hand, Sampaio and Almeida (2016) proposed to determine a group of technical criteria to integrate AR systems into the classroom, to evaluate whether introduction of such technology provides significant advances, as well as to identify, explore and evaluate different strategies for integrating AR devices and functions into the teaching-learning process, specifically with students of the Information and Communication Technologies (ICT) area. The proposal was structured in four cycles, each one includes introduction of a prototype and evaluation of uses by students.

In the first one, it was proposed to set an interrelation among transparencies (acetates) with an AR system that integrates a real object with a virtual one in a real environment. This was achieved through acetates that were printed with space configuration problems, and once they were overlapped on the answer sheet, they revealed the response. For the second cycle, a prototype was designed for it to observe activities and consequences of the first cycle; this was based on searching techniques and material flow in the ecosystems. Students worked with a specific application, using code reading (QR). In order to solve the problem, they connected multimedia contents related to questions assigned in paper, in that way they obtained instant information on their cellular phones, while they completed the task. Authors highlighted to introduce more technology increased motivation; however, concentration seemed to be affected. The following two cycles were used to evaluate and obtain more precise conclusions on the AR use.

For their part, Cuendet, Bonnard, Do-Lenh, and Dillenbourg (2013) suggest implementing five principles to design a learning environment in the classroom: integration, awareness, empowerment, flexibility and minimalism, and through their use of AR and tangible user interfaces (TUI), it could be an active for learning. In that sense, a TUI is that where a person interacts with digital information through a physical environment. The GUIs that arise at the same time allow for users to manipulate objects in a virtual space using real objects (Ullmer & Ishii, 2000). In order to understand if usability among a user and a system is acceptable, it is necessary to obtain performance measures, errors rate or user satisfaction, taking user's experience or skills into account as well as his cognitive load; this was defined as the first usability circle (Dillenbourg et al., 2011). Interaction of two or more users, through technologies (usability levels) can be measured by quality of their conversations, gestural expressions and easiness to take turns. The third usability circle is defined by classroom limitations. Likewise, Hutchins (1995) defined a cabin as a distributed cognitive system and therefore, a classroom must be adapted into an adequate learning environment.

Also, the international conference named: Innovative Methods in Designing Products, presented at the International Symposium on Mixed and Augmented Reality (2011), given by researchers at the Bari Polytechnic, highlighted how to develop different scenarios during figuration phases of a product, applying specific tests from each stage, based on interrelation among AR support phases (technical drawing, design evaluation, visualization software, components evaluation, virtual assembling and dimensional inspection) and the concept, design, analysis, manufacture, assembling, quality control and maintenance (Uva et. al., 2011). In that way, users interact and make adjustments and new proposals, due to incorporation of elements that prefigure different contexts for their application to the physical environment, as well as to an industrial product or even to technical drawings. Besides taking care, of data access, visualization, simulation and alternatives review, through practical applications.

Previous, Evaluation and Design

Doing an evaluation of the designed process conceptual phase is very important, as having integrated and precise stages or a dividing line for future activities depend on it. A bad decision on the initial phase can never be compensated with a good detailed design (Wynne & Irene, 1998). Therefore, a fundamental aspect of an efficient design process means understanding a solution with alternatives, considering its potential and limitations. Regarding evaluation of 3D concepts, it is important to mention that fast evolution of demands for product functions has considerably reduce their life cycle. All of these have to be considered in a design concept evolution, as the proposal must include requirements that meet the needs of possible users, as well as those who will pay to get the product.

Nowadays, several design approaches and methods for the development of products have been applied in different areas. These methods include reverse engineering, value engineering, Taguchi method and quality function deployment (QFD); the first three focus on product functions and on the other hand, QFD is more centered in clients' demands and coordinating the production process (Liu, 2011). For Lockamy and Khurana (1995) the QFD method enables interdepartmental collaboration and offers more technical elements. According to Bottani and Rizzi (2006), such method is comprised of four successive matrices: (1) client's requirement planning matrix; (2) product's features deployment matrix; (3) process and quality control matrix and; (4) operative instruction matrix. For the 3D design concepts evaluation these matrices preset a considerable number of design requirements that are completely assessable.

It is important to highlight that evaluating and making decisions are important actions for the design process. According to De Boer (1990) there are four reasons for paying attention to the evaluation: (a) it increases the problem size of making decisions; (b) people have limited work memory and when they must make decisions they are likely to be very selective when acquiring and processing information and, unstable to evaluate consequences; (c) it increases pressure due to the competitiveness environment in companies as they are looking for successful products and therefore, decisions that create better products and; (d) it requires for objective and explicit procedures so that all departments work holistically. According to Roozenburg and Eekels (1996) there must be at least three conditions in order to make decisions: (1) there will be alternatives; (2) alternatives must conclude towards different results and, (3) there must be goals to be reached.

Another reason to focus on evaluation and decision making is that new solutions will usually provide more than the old ones, as it is more difficult to evaluate innovative technologies than the already known. Dentsoras (2008) affirms that most methods or techniques for concept evaluation consider attributes that punctually respond to quantitative and qualitative requirements in order to define its values regarding design specifications; the needs from users or clients that will be attended are quantified. Therefore, concept evaluation is a process where multiple characteristics are subject to a systematic evaluation process regarding one or more design requirement and, as a result only one concept is selected, it can be one of the initial concepts or a new synthesis that combines attributes that set a difference in value from the initial concepts. On the other hand, Ullman (1992) mentions several evaluation methods and two categories stand out: (a) methods compare each concept with a number of design requirements determined by the designer and; (b) relative comparisons are made among concepts.

Also, the shape of a design object is very important not only to evaluate what a new product would be, but also to hold a designed object before market competitiveness. A common *trade-off* in a product's design is shape versus functioning. While function is analyzed and studied through users in order to gather information, there is not the same interest for visual shape. However, the need for a better preference analysis has increased, in fact "shape" has become a market differentiating factor that is more important every time (Jarod, 2007). Disciplines such as psychology, marketing and engineering have studied preference research methods that allow to link different design variables with an attractive shape. The PREFMAP method can be used to analyze and understand preference linked to amounts of determined products, such as size or sweetness of a product. For Chang and Carrol (1972) the PREFMAP method describes a stimulus space for preference data and it generates an external preference cartography, based on data independently obtained from the preference evaluation.

Thus, designers optimize their concepts by means of different quantitative attributes in a product, such as function, size, volume or cost. However, these attributes do not consider the esthetic part as important, nor attributes that do not have a functional relationship among potential values and consumer's preference (Turner, 2010). For example, color research as part of esthetic go back to1890; however, there have not been conclusions on it after 100 years (Eysenck, 1941). Therefore, a recurrent problem among color preferences is given when people are asked to evaluate a product or application independently speaking. This creates a logical problem before preference, as it is very likely for people not to choose one same color when buying an object. So it is necessary to carry out a research with a product type or field considering a group of colors (Grossman, Randi, Wisenblit & Joseph, 1999).

Some researchers affirm that design has influence on processing characteristics, when esthetic and functions performance are in conflict (Hoegg, Alba & Dahl, 2010). Also, Silvera, Josephs and Giesler (2002) say that people trust a variety of heuristics in memory and judgement tasks, they also demonstrated through color experiments that people greatly depend on information that is computationally easy and therefore recognize patterns in objects. Likewise, physical size that works as an incitement for esthetic impressions (Silvera, Josephs & Giesler, 2002), prototypes and unity (Kumar & Garg, 2010; Veryzer & Hutchinson, 1998), exposure frequency and interaction among design complexity, act in the same way (Cox & Cox, 2002). Other researches have worked on people's responses individually before visual design (Bloch, Brunel, & Arnold, 2003; Yang, Zhang & Peracchio, 2010). In a more global way, researches have focused on different ways in which esthetic contributes to evaluating a designed object from its prefiguration to a prototype development.

Now, it can be said that esthetic aspects are a source of pleasure for both designer and consumer (Holbrook & Zirlin, 1985). Therefore, the result of esthetic influence does not only have an impact on the marketing strategy, product's quality and differentiation and competitive advantage, but also on tendencies for developing new products. Although there is a general conscience on the different areas of industrial design, there is limited experimental research that proves specific hypotheses about how esthetic answers are related to product's design. Nevertheless, designed concepts evaluation cannot do without certain criteria. Along previous visual aspects we can consider unity and fast prototype to be determining for congruence among a design's elements so they seem as a visual connection among different parts of the same design (Veryzer & Hutchinson, 1998).

Esthetic answer as a complex behavior turns out to be a series of factors that differ in their generality degree, on the one hand, there are different abstract principles of perceptual organization that have been discussed in art and esthetic experimentation by authors such as Berlyne 1971, Holbrook 1995; Lauer 1979; Lombardo 1991; Martindale et Alabama. 1990; on the other hand, there are specific responses to determined objects or categories by Gordon and Holyoak 1983; Loken and Ward 1990; Rosch 1978, in such a way that determinants of esthetic answers can be highlighted, because notion of such determinants, which are influenced by experience, can be collected including external interventions such as market behavior, fashion tendencies and norms.

Low Environmental Impact Design

Due to the nature of the present work, it is necessary to locate the factors that will have an influence on design requirements such as structure, shape, composition and whatever is related to life cycle of a future designed object, as it most place itself among those with low environmental impact. Sustainable design considers environmental economic and social impacts produced throughout the product's life cycle (Bhamra & Lofthouse, 2007). According to Papanek (1972) designers configure products and services development, which have a direct impact on society and environment.

Likewise, education for low environment impact projects is a key element in production of goods and services. Through the use of AR and redesign of objects or buildings, it is possible for students to understand different considerations of sustainable design, in such a way that they generate, visualize and evaluate performance of new design alternatives in order to determine the best approach possible (Ayer, Messner, & Anumba 2016). Such research is centered in assigning activities to students regarding redesign of objects and buildings; they had to design, visualize and evaluate exterior wall designs and other objects in order to adapt an existing installation and improve its sustainable performance. Educational gaming based on augmented reality called *ecoCampus* had influence on teaching-learning process of designers. Also, the LSI architectural study in London, Norwich is focused on sustainable projects, using the Augment software of AR, which gives 2D animation to construction drawings previously made in order to promote interaction with clients, and in a motivating way, they can visualize, interpret and get involved in designs with an approach towards sustainability (Lsiarchitects, 2017).

New Learning Environments

AR is having a strong impact on education and technological competence development within training future industrial designers. *Knowledge arises when a person considers, interprets and uses information in a combined manner with his own experience and capacity* (Mazo, 1998, p. 26). In that sense, it can be affirmed that knowledge is intrinsic for people and therefore, it increases its value when utilized, its use can be reflected on innovation, decision making, materialization of a product or service and, even creation of new knowledge (Garnica & Calderon, 2015).

It is important to highlight that AR can be applied in a learning virtual environment, which makes reference to physical space where new technologies such as internet, multimedia and satellite systems, and interactive television interact and have developed in such a way that they have left traditional school environment behind (in fact, there are researches that affirm such environments will be the educational process of the future) and they favor knowledge and contents appropriation, experiences and pedagogic-communicational processes. The main characteristic of such environments is that they are made of space, students, advisers, educational contents, evaluation and, information and communication media (Herrera, 2002). On the other hand, UNESCO (1998), through its world report on education defines virtual environment of learning as an interactive computer program of pedagogic character that has an integrated communication capacity, which means related to New Technologies.

PROBLEMATIC

Over time different evaluation perceptions have been presented and in each one of them, there underlies a way of thinking and interpreting reality according to a historic moment where there is special interest on determined evaluation objects (Abreu, 2013). Conceptual design evaluation is generally subjective and it is carried out based on the evaluator's experience and training. For the present work, detecting needs in a determined environment, through the development of tridimensional objects that are susceptible of being produced according to available technologies and conjunction of ergonomic, technological, productive, esthetic, semiotic and sustainable elements and aspects in a determined context, are the parameters that delimit evaluation of a low environmental impact 3D concept in Industrial Design. Therefore, new strategies are required not only to accelerate the process, but also to facilitate and make such activity more efficient.

For the current evaluation to flow positively, the teacher must have a new attitude towards information collection, gathering it and implementing process planning on students' achievement, while creating clear instruments where activities are a support complement (Cizek, 1997). In order to evaluate specific competences referred to 3D concepts, it is necessary to validate the grounds for tridimensional objects that are susceptible to be produced according to available technologies and national production methods.

General Considerations

The information outlined below are the project's three stages. It is important to highlight that conditions to carry out evaluations change from one institution to another. In the case of the UAEM, there are particular criteria that have been considered to generate new teaching evaluation strategies.

- In order to meet the demand to get a bachelor's degree, teachers at the Autonomous University of the State of Mexico work with groups of about 40 students, which means an important effort to carry out an efficient and fast evaluation. They have an academic load of about 20 hours per week, which means working with 120 students divided into four groups and different levels, besides an average of 20 hours a week for management activities.
- An important number of students do not have personal equipment nor adequate software to carry out their practices, so they work at the computer labs of the University Center, which means facilitating the student with the presentation of their concepts in a practical manner and using any computer within the lab.
- The University works with a model based on competences, therefore an alternative evaluation to the traditional one is required and it has to include knowledge, abilities and attitudes of students in performing a specific activity, simultaneously providing useful information for teachers and students about such performance.

First Stage

To begin the process it is necessary for the student to have worked previously on the problematic to be attended with the highly complex tool design, besides design requirements, and thus, the teacher will have knowledge of the problem being assessed for the evaluation. The designer must develop the 3D concept with software used in regular sessions (*Solid Works* or any other compatible with AR software -Augment) to present different perspectives in the real environment to the teacher making use of any mobile device. It is necessary to capture some representative images that work as evidence of such appraisal.

Figure 1, 2 and 3. Analysis of 3D design concepts through AR.

Second Stage

The teacher will consider the following design criteria as reference in order to make a 3D concept evaluation and to make notes. During the visual evaluation the teacher must fill out the evaluation card with the items that are part of it.

Technical elements of evaluating:

1. **Structural Analysis,**
   a. To analyze the 3D design concept, through studying components, parts and elements that form it, taking the following as reference:

Figure 1. Washer bottles, (analysis of proportion), design: Moreno Grecia and Silva Beatriz.

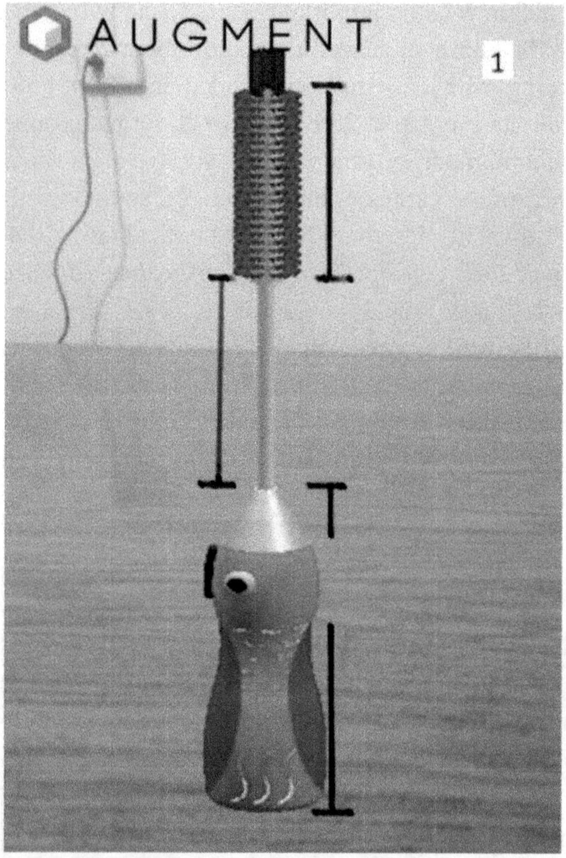

i. The number of components, parts and elements that will give shape to the concept.
ii. A carcass as a mean of protecting internal mechanisms of the 3D concept.
iii. Connection systems that will make a coherent link of the designed concept.
iv. Stability, referring to concept's gravity center.

2. **Functional Analysis.**
   a. To analyze the 3D design concept, through a general study of physical, chemical and technical principles of functioning, considering the following as reference:
      i. Mechanisms that will give functionality to the concept.
      ii. Reliability manifested by user before the concept's functioning.

Figure 2. Drill, (analysis of proportion with subsystems), design: Vazquez Daniel.

Figure 3. Toilet opener, (analysis of correlation between 3D concept and context objects), design: Espinoza Zahori and Castillo Esmeralda. Students of second degree in design Industrial of the Centro Universitario UAEM Valley of Chalco. Adviser Omar Sanchez. Full time Professor.

iii. Possibility that the concept fulfills different functions.
iv. Resistance to compression, tension or impact.
v. Final appearance of concept's exterior.

3. **Utilization Analysis.**
   a. To analyze the use of a 3D design concept, through a general study of interactions among user and concept, taking as reference:
      i. Easiness of use according to interaction between user and concept.
      ii. Security, the concept cannot compromise user's security.
      iii. Adequate manipulation, relationship between concept and user in terms of biomechanics.
      iv. Anthropometry, dimensional relationship between concept and user.

Table 1. Visual evaluation card for a 3D concept using AR

	Visual Evaluation	Excellent 10-9	Good 8-7	Sufficient 6	Not satisfactory 5-0
Visual evaluation of the structural requirements of the concept.	Feasibility of the number of components of the concept with the context.				
	Tool housing suitable for user safety				
	The stability of the concept is evident to the factors or interfaces that surround it.				
Visual evaluation of the requirement of function concept	The concept should reflect the function for which it was created				
	Functions of the 3D concept must be perceptible.				
	The relationship between concept, subsystems and context will be viable.				
	The proportions of the concept are adapted to the different interfaces of the context.				
	The basic requirements of biomechanics are evident.				
Visual evaluation of the selection of materials	The selection of materials was made considering environmental care.				
	The concept presents visual balance based on the selection of materials.				

v. Ergonomics, adequate relationship among ergonomic variables (weight, barycenter, vibration, noise limits, heat, etc.) and user.

4. **Morphological Analysis.**
   a. To analyze morphological evaluation of a 3D concept through a general study of interaction of the main function of concept and user at the beginning, development and end of the interaction.
      i. Angles (biomechanical frame) of user's physiological structure.
      ii. Functional assessment.
      iii. Concept adjustments of design and utilization technique (Rodríguez, 1988).
5. **Material Selection**
   a. Materials suggested have low environmental impact.
   b. The concept represents visual balance for a determined context.

Third Stage

For feedback with student, teacher will give the favorable characteristics and those that can be improved for developing renewed conceptual proposes, giving a copy of the evaluation card, considering different stages of AR presentation analysis, as well as suggestions to assess items required. Therefore, the 3D concept will be projected after improving it as a differentiated object that will comprehensively attend a specific need. (Feedback results).

Figure 4, 5 and 6. Improvements to the 3D concept through the evaluation and feedback with the student. Design: Garcia Laura and Ortiz Jonathan. Adviser Omar Sanchez.

- **It is also possible to prove concept's characteristics if student is required to validate the following questions:**
  - What was done?
  - Why was it done?
  - What for?
  - For whom?
  - Where was it done? (context)
  - What technology was used?
- **It is also important to do the evaluation considering the following:**
  - It is a product or system of products.
  - Reason for its production.
  - Finality.
  - Proposed amount to be made.

Figure 4.

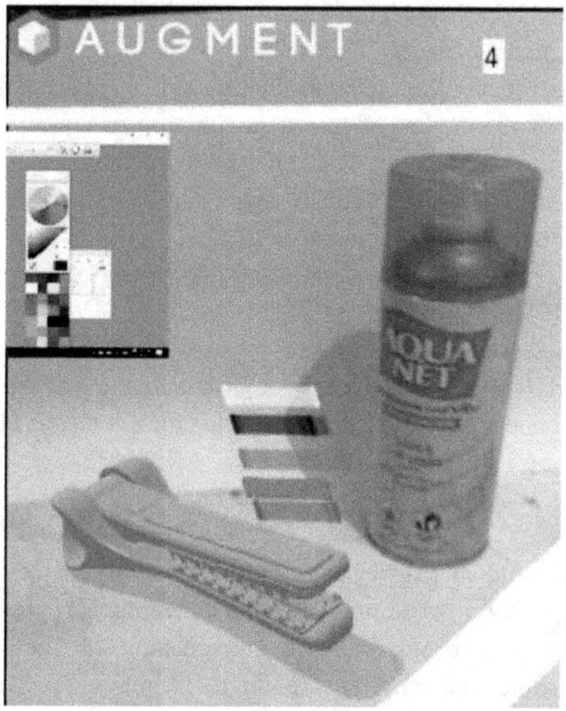

Figure 5.

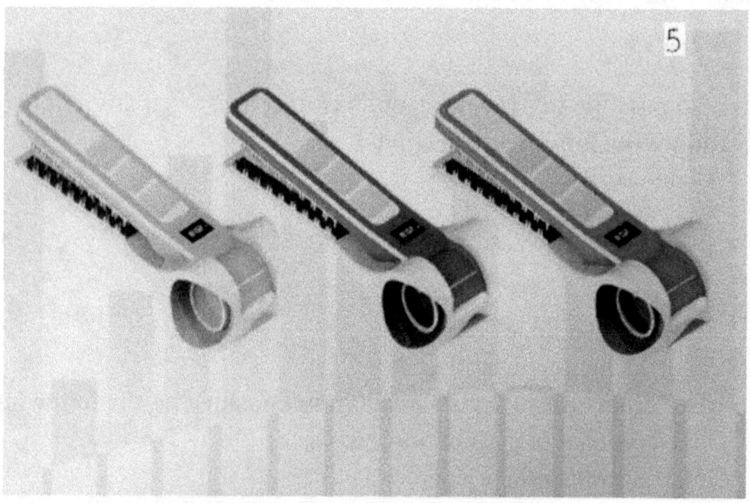

Figure 6.

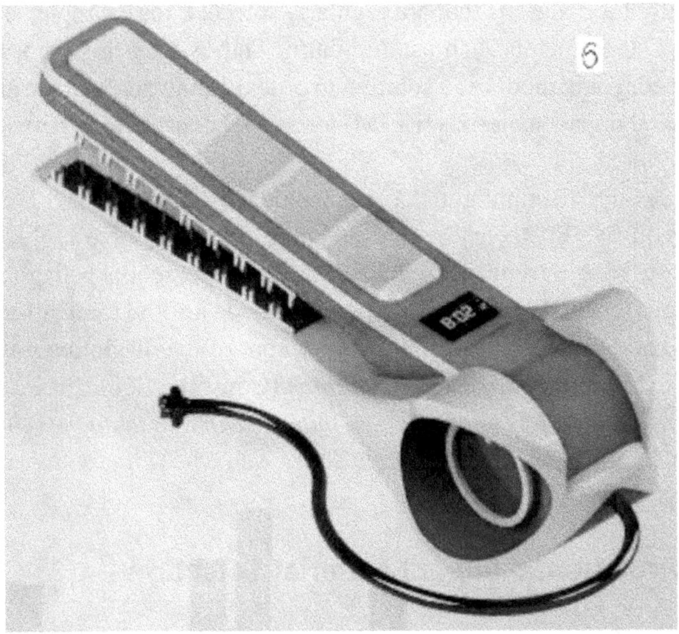

In those design terms, it can be considered as a circular process where evaluation promotes feedback before the act of conceptualizing objects. Information obtained when evaluating helps as a tool to weigh and verify working methods used for its development. Therefore, design's evaluation and process become cyclical, while enriching future design concepts (virtual proposals that fulfill requirements assigned by the designers themselves), which will necessarily have some subjectivity, and their references are in teacher's experience (Córdoba et al., 2002). Therefore, evaluation based on AR describing and validating established requirements in real contexts but from a three-dimensional design, will drastically reduce subjectivity levels in a teacher evaluation.

SOLUTIONS AND RECOMMENDATIONS

3D models evaluation through AR must provide the student with extraordinary knowledge, besides considering it a transcendental and evolutionary exercise in teaching-learning activities. Therefore, designer needs constant update in relation to the ICTs, which will facilitate solving recurrent problems that arise in his academic path, also selecting materials precisely is a requirement that must be solved every time there is a design proposal. Meanwhile, 3D concepts proposals usually happen automatically for materials that are regularly selected, for example; stainless steel, plastics and some metals such as aluminum. That is why this work proposes the following pedagogic model as a solution in order to analyze, evaluate and select low environmental impact materials (LEIM) for any 3D concept aimed to be industrially developed.

It is necessary to highlight that such model is supported with the cognitive structural modifiability theory by Reuven Feuerstein. In order to apply such model, it is necessary to have a strongly convinced teacher with essential pedagogy principles, considering: a) capacity to inject the student with desire and motivation to do things differently and b) understand from the very core of the discipline how essential it is to use LEIM and new selection processes (Consoli, 2008). Piaget says that *the main goal in education is to create men that are capable to do new things, not just repeating what other generations have done; men who are creative, inventive and discoverers.*

Low Environmental Impact Material Selection

It is always a challenge for a designer to evaluate materials selection, not just for conventional design projects, but those where using new technologies is implemented. Nevertheless, a teacher's personality plays a primary role and this could even be the base for satisfactory results in teaching new design methods. A great number of desired attributes in personality and conduct principles to develop low environmental impact design concepts based on new technologies are: a) understanding the advantages of using ICTs effectively, b) combination of tolerance, affection and ecological thinking, c) relentless defense of sustainability theories, d) setting the example by developing ecological projects, e) assigning work and encouraging an environmental responsibility before the profession, f) promote creating habits, values and responsibilities that build a better environment (Jerez & Tarride 2000).

Due to the above, the professor must assume the following didactic functions that are directly linked to developing Industrial Design 3D concepts in AR and contents in subjects taught.

1. Functioning as guiding or hodegetics. Guiding means adaptation, graduation and accessibility to inform clearly how, when and where to look for the most pertinent information on LEIM to be applied through AR.
2. Professor must be a promoter of a change and can turn to academic space authorities, cultural diffusion places and having periodical reviews of students' change of attitude.

3. To transfer precise knowledge of educational program contents in Industrial Design, as well as to expose new technological tendencies for education.
4. Decisive action is an excellent strategy to incorporate ICTs in selecting LEIM, as here is a risk of falling into sterile memorization of knowledge.

Due to the multidisciplinary characteristics of Industrial Design, the following table is presented, which will allow the designer to evaluate the correlation there is between curriculum subjects and selection of LEIM in 3D concepts, working from activities to possible implementation of AR.

As a result, the aim is to optimize performance index in a design process, from the material selection point of view and according to restrictions given by functioning, as well as geometrical configuration of it. In order to make this phase more efficient, the proposal is to develop databases that have the main properties of materials; however, it is necessary to have a constant communication and information system so as to obtain more specific properties of some materials. Given the importance of optimizing a design process, we provide the following scheme for Industrial Design teachers.

FUTURE RESEARCH DIRECTIONS

This present research opens up the possibility to focus on processes required to apply different materials to the design projects. For example, teaching techniques

Table 2. Learning Units of the curriculum of the Degree in Industrial Design and their relationship with (LEIM) to apply RA.

<table>
<tr><th>Learning Units/ Industrial Design</th><th>Learning Style</th><th>Classroom Techniques</th></tr>
<tr><td rowspan="4">Material resistance
Materials and processes
Woodworking
Polymer Practices
Metalworking
Ceramics and Glass Practices
Textile Practices</td><td>Visual Activities</td><td>• Videos
• Field Trips
• Simulators
• Exhibitions
• (Towards AR)</td></tr>
<tr><td>Hearing Activities</td><td>• Readings
• Discussions</td></tr>
<tr><td>Manual activities</td><td>• Materials Laboratory
• Practices
• Field investigations.
• (Towards AR)</td></tr>
<tr><td>Reflection</td><td>• Readings
• Scientific Writings</td></tr>
</table>

Table 3. The components that are part of a cyclic Educational strategy for (LEIM). For Industrial Design studio programs

T = Teacher	S = Student	C = Knowledge about LEIM and AR	M =Methodology.	D=Design
• Motivational / daring • Sociable / network weaver. • Sensitive / caring for others. • Emotionally stable	• Innovative / proactive. • Responsible / goals achieved. • Sensitive and respectful towards others. • Reflective. • Critical. • Open to global needs. • Honest with him and others. • Committed to knowledge. • Attitude (enthusiastic) • Open to the evolution of education systems.	• Energy evaluation of its manufacture. • Low energy consumption throughout its life cycle. • (Stone materials such as earth, gravel or sand). • Renewable and abundant resources, (wood). • Impact on ecosystems • Bauxite that comes from the rainforests. • Emissions they generate. Chlorofluorocarbons (CFC). • Behavior as waste. • Extraction: Consideration for the transformation of the medium.	• Systematized • Relevant. • Combination • Adapted to the current context.	• Minimum of components. • Solar energy. • Combination of natural materials. • Natural color • Less material, less energy. • Search for social guarantees. • 100% cyclical projects.

for wood work using AR. Each method requires specific technical abilities, which could be transferred to students in a fast and efficient manner. Cutting, measuring, gluing, assembling or proposing new ways to transform material can be favorable for making an Industrial Designer more professional. It is important to highlight that working with any material will always be an essential part of design projects and even more if one can save on the material used to carry out with learning exercises.

CONCLUSION

This work clearly establishes how important it is to implement new teaching-learning techniques, emerging technologies and ability for educators to get adapted to disciplines such as Industrial Design, on the basis of an unstoppable manner to receive information through the ICTs. In those terms, the work clearly establishes how relevant proactive and open participation is for changes in teachers, even more if they work with areas focused to creativity. In turn, evaluation is highlighted as a teaching strategy for fast and meaningful learning, not just for the student, but also for the whole university community that is part of professionalizing industrial designers. To sum up, modifying, innovating and implementing new technologies in evaluation schemes can promote new criteria for structuring complete academic programs or study plans.

REFERENCES

Abreu, M. O. (2013). *Design and preparation of evaluation guides*. University Autonomous of the State of Mexico.

Ayer, S. K., Messner, J. I., & Anumba, C. J. (2016). Augmented Reality Gaming in Sustainable Design Education. *Journal of Architectural Engineering*, *22*(1), 04015012. doi:10.1061/(ASCE)AE.1943-5568.0000195

Azuma, R., Baillot, Y., Behringer, R., Feiner, S., Julier, S., & MacIntyre, B. (2001). Recent advances in augmented reality. *IEEE Computer Graphics and Applications*, *21*(6), 34–47. doi:10.1109/38.963459

Berlyne, D. E. (1970). Novelty, Complexity, and Hedonic Value. *Perception & Psychophysics*, *8*(November), 279–286. doi:10.3758/BF03212593

Bhamra, T., & Lofthouse, V. (2007). *Design for sustainability: a practical approach*. Gower Publishing, Ltd.

Billinghurst, M. (2002). Augmented reality in education. *New Horizons for Learning*, 12.

Bloch, P. H., Brunel, F. F., & Arnold, T. J. (2003). Individual differences in the centrality of visual product aesthetics: Concept and measurement. *The Journal of Consumer Research*, *29*(4), 551–565. doi:10.1086/346250

Bottani, E., & Rizzi, A. (2006). Strategic management of logistics service: A fuzzy QFD approach. *International Journal of Production Economics*, *103*(2), 585–599. doi:10.1016/j.ijpe.2005.11.006

Burton, S., Armstrong, J., & Wall, B. (2017). *Sustainable performance in architecture*. Retrieved July 2, 2017, from http://www.lsiarchitects.co.uk

Chang, J. J., & Carroll, J. D. (1972). *How to use PREFMAP and PREFMAP-2: Programs which relate preference data to multidimensional scaling solutions* (Unpublished manuscript). Bell Telephone Labs.

Cizek, G. J. (1997). Learning, achievement, and assessment: Constructs at a crossroads. Handbook of classroom assessment: Learning, adjustment, and achievement, 1-32.

Consoli, M. E. V. (2008). Reuven Feuerstein's Theory of Cognitive Structural Modifiability. *Educational Investigation, 12*(22), 203-221.

Córdoba, C., González, J., Nasser, J., Ortíz, J., & Zamora, A. (2002). *Design evaluation.* Lithoimpresora S.A de C.V.

Cox, D., & Cox, A. D. (2002). Beyond first impressions: The effects of repeated exposure on consumer liking of visually complex and simple product designs. *Journal of the Academy of Marketing Science, 30*(2), 119–130. doi:10.1177/03079459994371

Cuendet, S., Bonnard, Q., Do-Lenh, S., & Dillenbourg, P. (2013). Designing augmented reality for the classroom. *Computers & Education, 68*, 557–569. doi:10.1016/j.compedu.2013.02.015

De Boer, S. J. (1990). Systematic decisions in methodical engineering design. *Scriftenreihe WDK*, 17.

Dentsoras, A. J. (2008). Representation of Design Concepts and Concept Evaluation Criteria through Design Parameters and Performance Variables. *DS 57: Proceedings of AEDS 2008 Workshop.*

Dillenbourg, P., Zufferey, G., Alavi, H., Jermann, P., Do-Lenh, S., Bonnard, Q., & Kaplan, F. (2011). Classroom orchestration: The third circle of usability. *CSCL2011 Proceedings, 1*, 510-517.

Eysenck, H. J. (1941). A critical and experimental study of colour preferences. *The American Journal of Psychology, 54*(3), 385–394. doi:10.2307/1417683

Friedrich, W., Jahn, D., & Schmidt, L. (2002, September). ARVIKA-Augmented Reality for Development, Production and Service. In ISMAR (Vol. 2002, pp. 3-4). Academic Press.

Garnica, E., & Calderon, J. A. F. (2015). Augmented Reality and Education. *Journal Engineering, Mathematics and Information Sciences, 2*(3).

Gordon, P. C., & Holyoak, K. J. (1983). Implicit Learning and Generalization of the 'Mere Exposure' Effect. *Journal of Personality and Social Psychology, 45*(September), 492–500. doi:10.1037/0022-3514.45.3.492

Grossman, R. P., & Wisenblit, J. Z. (1999). What We Know About Consumers' Color Choices. *Journal of Marketing Practice, 5*(3), 78–88. doi:10.1108/EUM0000000004565

Herrera Batista, L. M. Á. (2002). The sources of learning in virtual educational environments. *Reencuentro*, (35).

Hoegg, J., Alba, J. W., & Dahl, D. W. (2010). The good, the bad, and the ugly: Influence of aesthetics on product feature judgments. *Journal of Consumer Psychology*, *20*(4), 419–430. doi:10.1016/j.jcps.2010.07.002

Holbrook, M. B. (1995). An Empirical Approach to Representing Patterns of Consumer Tastes, Nostalgia, and Hierarchy in the Market for Cultural Products. *Empirical Studies of the Arts*, *13*(1), 55–71. doi:10.2190/RJA4-H8TK-F30Q-0U3F

Holbrook, M. B., & Zirlin, R. B. (1985). Artistic creation, artworks, and aesthetic appreciation: Some philosophical contributions to nonprofit marketing. *Advances in Nonprofit Marketing, 1*(1), 1-54.

Hsu, W., & Woon, I. M. Y. (1998). Current research in the conceptual design of mechanical products. *Computer Aided Design*, *30*(5), 377–389. doi:10.1016/S0010-4485(97)00101-2

Huang, G. Q. (2002). Web-based support for collaborative product design review. *Computers in Industry*, *48*(1), 71–88. doi:10.1016/S0166-3615(02)00011-8

Hutchins, E. (1995). How a cockpit remembers its speeds. *Cognitive Science*, *19*(3), 265–288. doi:10.120715516709cog1903_1

Jarod, K. (2007). *Use of shape preference information in product design*. Guidelines for a Decision Support Method Adapted to NPD Processes.

Jerez, S., & Tarride, M. (2000). Reflections on the need for paradigmatic change in education. *The Journal of Educational Thought*, 27.

Kumar, M., & Garg, N. (2010). Aesthetic principles and cognitive emotion appraisals: How much of the beauty lies in the eye of the beholder? *Journal of Consumer Psychology*, *20*(4), 485–494. doi:10.1016/j.jcps.2010.06.015

Liu, H. T. (2011). Product design and selection using fuzzy QFD and fuzzy MCDM approaches. *Applied Mathematical Modelling*, *35*(1), 482–496. doi:10.1016/j.apm.2010.07.014

Lockamy, A., & Khurana, A. (1995). Quality function deployment: Total quality management for new product design. *International Journal of Quality & Reliability Management*, *12*(6), 73–84. doi:10.1108/02656719510089939

Loken, B., & Ward, J. (1990). Alternative Approaches to Understanding the Determinants of Typicality. *The Journal of Consumer Research, 17*(September), 111–126. doi:10.1086/208542

Lombardo, S. (1991). Event and Decay of the Aesthetic Experience. *Empirical Stutdies of the Arts, 9*(2), 123-141.

Martindale, C., & Moore, K. (1988). Priming, prototypicality, and preference. *Journal of Experimental Psychology. Human Perception and Performance, 14*(4), 661–670. doi:10.1037/0096-1523.14.4.661

Mazo, I. (1998). Five disciplines for intelligent organization. *Human Capital, 11*(111), 26-30.

Netmedia.mx. (2017). *The Future of the Automotive Industry Augmented Reality.* Retrieved March, 24, 2017, from https://www.netmedia.mx/analisis/el-futuro-de-la-industria-automotriz realidad-aumentada/

Papanek, V., & Fuller, R. B. (1972). *Design for the real world.* London: Thames and Hudson.

Rodriguez Morales, G. (1988). *Industrial design manual.* Gustavo.

Roozenburg, N. F. M., & Eekels, J. (1996). *Product Design: Fundamentals and Methods.* Chichester, UK: John Wiley and Sons, Ltd.

Rosch, E. (1975). Cognitive Representations of Semantic Categories. *Journal of Experimental Psychology, 104*(September), 192–233.

Sampaio, D., & Almeida, P. (2016). Pedagogical Strategies for the Integration of Augmented Reality in ICT Teaching and Learning Processes. *Procedia Computer Science, 100*, 894–899. doi:10.1016/j.procs.2016.09.240

Silvera, D. H., Josephs, R. A., & Giesler, R. B. (2002). Bigger is better: The influence of physical size on aesthetic preference judgments. *Journal of Behavioral Decision Making, 15*(3), 189–202. doi:10.1002/bdm.410

Turner, H. L. (2010). *Quantification of product color preference in a utility function.* Masters Theses. 4780.

Ullman, D. G. (1992). *The mechanical design process* (Vol. 2). New York: McGraw-Hill.

Ullmer, B., & Ishii, H. (2000). Emerging frameworks for tangible user interfaces. *IBM Systems Journal, 39*(3-4), 915-931.

UNESCO. (1998). *Virtual environment of learning.* Retrieved January 11, 2017, from http://unesdoc.unesco.org/images/0022/002277/227729e.pdf

Uva, A. E., Cristiano, S., Fiorentino, M., & Monno, G. (2010). Distributed design review using tangible augmented technical drawings. *Computer Aided Design, 42*(5), 364–372. doi:10.1016/j.cad.2008.10.015

Uva, A. E., Fiorentino, M., & Monno, G. (2011). Augmented reality integration in product development. *Proceedings of the International conference on Innovative Methods in Product Design*, 73-79.

Veryzer, R. W. Jr, & Hutchinson, J. W. (1998). The influence of unity and prototypicality on aesthetic responses to new product designs. *The Journal of Consumer Research, 24*(4), 374–394. doi:10.1086/209516

Yang, X., Zhang, J., & Peracchio, L. A. (2010). Understanding the impact of self-concept on the stylistic properties of images. *Journal of Consumer Psychology, 20*(4), 508–520. doi:10.1016/j.jcps.2010.06.012

KEY TERMS AND DEFINITIONS

3D Model: Concept developed in three-dimensions from computer-aided design.

Ergonomic: Object to comply with requirements regarding appropriate and comfortable interactions with users.

Evaluation for the Design: Give value to an object made from the design requirements.

Formal Coherence: Balance, presenting an object, whereas its structure and function.

Industrial Design: Creative activity that focuses on solving problems of form, aesthetics, function, and manufacturing of an object that will be made, considering environmental, economic, political, and cultural factors to increase the quality of life of persons.

Visual Balance: Balance between function, form, color, and texture of an object.

Visual Perception: People's ability to select, sort, and rework visual sensory data.

Related References

To continue our tradition of advancing research in the field of education, we have compiled a list of recommended IGI Global readings. These references will provide additional information and guidance to further enrich your knowledge and assist you with your own research and future publications.

Abrami, P. C., Savage, R. S., Deleveaux, G., Wade, A., Meyer, E., & LeBel, C. (2010). The learning toolkit: The design, development, testing and dissemination of evidence-based educational software. In P. Zemliansky & D. Wilcox (Eds.), *Design and implementation of educational games: Theoretical and practical perspectives* (pp. 168–188). Hershey, PA: IGI Global. doi:10.4018/978-1-61520-781-7.ch012

Ackfeldt, A., & Malhotra, N. (2012). Do managerial strategies influence service behaviours? Insights from a qualitative study. In R. Eid (Ed.), *Successful customer relationship management programs and technologies: Issues and trends* (pp. 174–187). Hershey, PA: IGI Global. doi:10.4018/978-1-4666-0288-5.ch013

Adi, A., & Scotte, C. G. (2013). Barriers to emerging technology and social media integration in higher education: Three case studies. In M. Pătruţ & B. Pătruţ (Eds.), *Social media in higher education: Teaching in web 2.0* (pp. 334–354). Hershey, PA: IGI Global. doi:10.4018/978-1-4666-2970-7.ch017

Aldana-Vargas, M. F., Gras-Martí, A., Montoya, J., & Osorio, L. A. (2013). Pedagogical counseling program development through an adapted community of inquiry framework. In Z. Akyol & D. Garrison (Eds.), *Educational communities of inquiry: Theoretical framework, research and practice* (pp. 350–373). Hershey, PA: IGI Global. doi:10.4018/978-1-4666-2110-7.ch017

Alegre, O. M., & Villar, L. M. (2011). Faculty professional learning: An examination of online development and assessment environments. In G. Vincenti & J. Braman (Eds.), *Teaching through multi-user virtual environments: Applying dynamic elements to the modern classroom* (pp. 66–93). Hershey, PA: IGI Global. doi:10.4018/978-1-61692-822-3.ch006

Alegre, O. M., & Villar, L. M. (2012). Faculty professional learning: An examination of online development and assessment environments. In *Organizational learning and knowledge: Concepts, methodologies, tools and applications* (pp. 305–331). Hershey, PA: IGI Global. doi:10.4018/978-1-60960-783-8.ch119

Alegre-Rosa, O. M., & Villar-Angulo, L. M. (2010). Training of teachers in virtual scenario: An excellence model for quality assurance in formative programmes. In S. Mukerji & P. Tripathi (Eds.), *Cases on transnational learning and technologically enabled environments* (pp. 190–213). Hershey, PA: IGI Global. doi:10.4018/978-1-61520-749-7.ch011

Andegherghis, S. (2012). Technology and traditional teaching. In I. Chen & D. McPheeters (Eds.), *Cases on educational technology integration in urban schools* (pp. 74–79). Hershey, PA: IGI Global. doi:10.4018/978-1-61350-492-5.ch019

Anderson, K. H., & Muirhead, W. (2013). Blending storytelling with technology in the professional development of police officers. In H. Yang & S. Wang (Eds.), *Cases on formal and informal e-learning environments: Opportunities and practices* (pp. 143–165). Hershey, PA: IGI Global. doi:10.4018/978-1-4666-1930-2.ch008

Anderson, S., & Oyarzun, B. (2013). Multi-modal professional development for faculty. In J. Keengwe & L. Kyei-Blankson (Eds.), *Virtual mentoring for teachers: Online professional development practices* (pp. 43–65). Hershey, PA: IGI Global. doi:10.4018/978-1-4666-1963-0.ch003

Annetta, L. A., Holmes, S., & Cheng, M. (2012). Measuring student perceptions: Designing an evidenced centered activity model for a serious educational game development software. In R. Ferdig & S. de Freitas (Eds.), *Interdisciplinary advancements in gaming, simulations and virtual environments: Emerging trends* (pp. 165–182). Hershey, PA: IGI Global. doi:10.4018/978-1-4666-0029-4.ch011

Austin, R., & Anderson, J. (2006). Re-schooling and information communication technology: A case study of Ireland. In L. Tan Wee Hin & R. Subramaniam (Eds.), *Handbook of research on literacy in technology at the K-12 level* (pp. 176–194). Hershey, PA: IGI Global. doi:10.4018/978-1-59140-494-1.ch010

Ayling, D., Owen, H., & Flagg, E. (2014). From basic participation to transformation: Immersive virtual professional development. In S. Leone (Ed.), *Synergic integration of formal and informal e-learning environments for adult lifelong learners* (pp. 47–74). Hershey, PA: IGI Global. doi:10.4018/978-1-4666-4655-1.ch003

Ayoola, K. A. (2010). An appraisal of a computer-based continuing professional development (CPD) Course for Nigerian English teachers and teacher-trainers. In R. Taiwo (Ed.), *Handbook of research on discourse behavior and digital communication: Language structures and social interaction* (pp. 642–650). Hershey, PA: IGI Global. doi:10.4018/978-1-61520-773-2.ch041

Baia, P. (2011). The trend of commitment: Pedagogical quality and adoption. In S. D'Agustino (Ed.), *Adaptation, resistance and access to instructional technologies: Assessing future trends in education* (pp. 273–315). Hershey, PA: IGI Global. doi:10.4018/978-1-61692-854-4.ch017

Banas, J. R., & Velez-Solic, A. (2013). Designing effective online instructor training and professional development. In J. Keengwe & L. Kyei-Blankson (Eds.), *Virtual mentoring for teachers: Online professional development practices* (pp. 1–25). Hershey, PA: IGI Global. doi:10.4018/978-1-4666-1963-0.ch001

Banks, W. P., & Van Sickle, T. (2011). Digital partnerships for professional development: Rethinking university–public school collaborations. In M. Bowdon & R. Carpenter (Eds.), *Higher education, emerging technologies, and community partnerships: Concepts, models and practices* (pp. 153–163). Hershey, PA: IGI Global. doi:10.4018/978-1-60960-623-7.ch014

Barbour, M. K., Siko, J., Gross, E., & Waddell, K. (2013). Virtually unprepared: Examining the preparation of K-12 online teachers. In R. Hartshorne, T. Heafner, & T. Petty (Eds.), *Teacher education programs and online learning tools: Innovations in teacher preparation* (pp. 60–81). Hershey, PA: IGI Global. doi:10.4018/978-1-4666-1906-7.ch004

Bartlett, J. E. II, & Bartlett, M. E. (2009). Innovative strategies for preparing and developing career and technical education leaders. In V. Wang (Ed.), *Handbook of research on e-learning applications for career and technical education: Technologies for vocational training* (pp. 248–261). Hershey, PA: IGI Global. doi:10.4018/978-1-60566-739-3.ch020

Baylen, D. M., & Glacken, J. (2007). Promoting lifelong learning online: A case study of a professional development experience. In Y. Inoue (Ed.), *Online education for lifelong learning* (pp. 229–252). Hershey, PA: IGI Global. doi:10.4018/978-1-59904-319-7.ch011

Beedle, J., & Wang, S. (2013). Roles of a technology leader. In S. Wang & T. Hartsell (Eds.), *Technology integration and foundations for effective leadership* (pp. 228–241). Hershey, PA: IGI Global. doi:10.4018/978-1-4666-2656-0.ch013

Begg, M., Dewhurst, D., & Ross, M. (2010). Game informed virtual patients: Catalysts for online learning communities and professional development of medical teachers. In J. Lindberg & A. Olofsson (Eds.), *Online learning communities and teacher professional development: Methods for improved education delivery* (pp. 190–208). Hershey, PA: IGI Global. doi:10.4018/978-1-60566-780-5.ch011

Begg, M., Dewhurst, D., & Ross, M. (2010). Game informed virtual patients: Catalysts for online learning communities and professional development of medical teachers. In R. Luppicini & A. Haghi (Eds.), *Cases on digital technologies in higher education: Issues and challenges* (pp. 304–322). Hershey, PA: IGI Global. doi:10.4018/978-1-61520-869-2.ch020

Benton, C. J., White, O. L., & Stratton, S. K. (2014). Collaboration not competition: International education expanding perspectives on learning and workforce articulation. In V. Wang (Ed.), *International education and the next-generation workforce: Competition in the global economy* (pp. 64–82). Hershey, PA: IGI Global. doi:10.4018/978-1-4666-4498-4.ch004

Benus, M. J., Yarker, M. B., Hand, B. M., & Norton-Meier, L. A. (2013). Analysis of discourse practices in elementary science classrooms using argument-based inquiry during whole-class dialogue. In M. Khine & I. Saleh (Eds.), *Approaches and strategies in next generation science learning* (pp. 224–245). Hershey, PA: IGI Global. doi:10.4018/978-1-4666-2809-0.ch012

Betts, K., Kramer, R., & Gaines, L. L. (2013). Online faculty and adjuncts: Strategies for meeting current and future demands of online education through online human touch training and support. In M. Raisinghani (Ed.), *Curriculum, learning, and teaching advancements in online education* (pp. 94–112). Hershey, PA: IGI Global. doi:10.4018/978-1-4666-2949-3.ch007

Biesinger, K. D., & Crippen, K. J. (2010). Designing and delivering technology integration to engage students. In J. Yamamoto, J. Leight, S. Winterton, & C. Penny (Eds.), *Technology leadership in teacher education: Integrated solutions and experiences* (pp. 298–313). Hershey, PA: IGI Global. doi:10.4018/978-1-61520-899-9.ch016

Bledsoe, C., & Pilgrim, J. (2013). Three instructional models to integrate technology and build 21st century literacy skills. In J. Whittingham, S. Huffman, W. Rickman, & C. Wiedmaier (Eds.), *Technological tools for the literacy classroom* (pp. 243–262). Hershey, PA: IGI Global. doi:10.4018/978-1-4666-3974-4.ch014

Bloom, L., & Dole, S. (2014). Virtual school of the smokies. In S. Mukerji & P. Tripathi (Eds.), *Handbook of research on transnational higher education* (pp. 674–689). Hershey, PA: IGI Global. doi:10.4018/978-1-4666-4458-8.ch034

Bober, M. J. (2005). Ensuring quality in technology-focused professional development. In C. Howard, J. Boettcher, L. Justice, K. Schenk, P. Rogers, & G. Berg (Eds.), *Encyclopedia of distance learning* (pp. 845–852). Hershey, PA: IGI Global. doi:10.4018/978-1-59140-555-9.ch121

Bober, M. J. (2009). Ensuring quality in technology-focused professional development. In P. Rogers, G. Berg, J. Boettcher, C. Howard, L. Justice, & K. Schenk (Eds.), *Encyclopedia of distance learning* (2nd ed.; pp. 924–931). Hershey, PA: IGI Global. doi:10.4018/978-1-60566-198-8.ch129

Boling, E. C., & Beatty, J. (2012). Overcoming the tensions and challenges of technology integration: How can we best support our teachers? In R. Ronau, C. Rakes, & M. Niess (Eds.), *Educational technology, teacher knowledge, and classroom impact: A research handbook on frameworks and approaches* (pp. 136–156). Hershey, PA: IGI Global. doi:10.4018/978-1-60960-750-0.ch006

Bovard, B., Bussmann, S., Parra, J., & Gonzales, C. (2010). Transitioning to e-learning: Teaching the teachers. In *Web-based education: Concepts, methodologies, tools and applications* (pp. 259–276). Hershey, PA: IGI Global. doi:10.4018/978-1-61520-963-7.ch019

Bowskill, N. (2009). Informal learning projects and world wide voluntary co-mentoring. In P. Rogers, G. Berg, J. Boettcher, C. Howard, L. Justice, & K. Schenk (Eds.), *Encyclopedia of distance learning* (2nd ed.; pp. 1169–1177). Hershey, PA: IGI Global. doi:10.4018/978-1-60566-198-8.ch167

Bowskill, N., & McConnell, D. (2010). Collaborative reflection in globally distributed inter-cultural course teams. In G. Berg (Ed.), *Cases on online tutoring, mentoring, and educational services: Practices and applications* (pp. 172–184). Hershey, PA: IGI Global. doi:10.4018/978-1-60566-876-5.ch014

Bradley, J. B., Rachal, J., & Harper, L. (2013). Online professional development for adults: Utilizing andragogical methods in research and practice. In V. Bryan & V. Wang (Eds.), *Technology use and research approaches for community education and professional development* (pp. 171–193). Hershey, PA: IGI Global. doi:10.4018/978-1-4666-2955-4.ch011

Braun, P. (2013). Clever health: A study on the adoption and impact of an ehealth initiative in rural Australia. In M. Cruz-Cunha, I. Miranda, & P. Gonçalves (Eds.), *Handbook of research on ICTs and management systems for improving efficiency in healthcare and social care* (pp. 69–87). Hershey, PA: IGI Global. doi:10.4018/978-1-4666-3990-4.ch004

Breen, P. (2014). An intramuscular approach to teacher development in international collaborative higher education. In S. Mukerji & P. Tripathi (Eds.), *Handbook of research on transnational higher education* (pp. 368–390). Hershey, PA: IGI Global. doi:10.4018/978-1-4666-4458-8.ch019

Brown, C. A., & Neal, R. E. (2013). Definition and history of online professional development. In J. Keengwe & L. Kyei-Blankson (Eds.), *Virtual mentoring for teachers: Online professional development practices* (pp. 182–203). Hershey, PA: IGI Global. doi:10.4018/978-1-4666-1963-0.ch010

Brown, C. W., & Peters, K. A. (2013). STEM academic enrichment and professional development programs for K-12 urban students and teachers. In R. Lansiquot (Ed.), *Cases on interdisciplinary research trends in science, technology, engineering, and mathematics: Studies on urban classrooms* (pp. 19–56). Hershey, PA: IGI Global. doi:10.4018/978-1-4666-2214-2.ch002

Burgess, M. (2013). Using second life to support student teachers' socio-reflective practice: A mixed-method analysis. In R. Lansiquot (Ed.), *Cases on interdisciplinary research trends in science, technology, engineering, and mathematics: Studies on urban classrooms* (pp. 107–127). Hershey, PA: IGI Global. doi:10.4018/978-1-4666-2214-2.ch006

Burner, K. J. (2012). Web 2.0, the individual, and the organization: Privacy, confidentiality, and compliance. In V. Dennen & J. Myers (Eds.), *Virtual professional development and informal learning via social networks* (pp. 25–38). Hershey, PA: IGI Global. doi:10.4018/978-1-4666-1815-2.ch002

Buzzetto-More, N. (2010). Applications of second life. In H. Song & T. Kidd (Eds.), *Handbook of research on human performance and instructional technology* (pp. 149–162). Hershey, PA: IGI Global. doi:10.4018/978-1-60566-782-9.ch009

Bynog, M. (2013). Development of a technology plan. In S. Wang & T. Hartsell (Eds.), *Technology integration and foundations for effective leadership* (pp. 88–101). Hershey, PA: IGI Global. doi:10.4018/978-1-4666-2656-0.ch006

Calway, B. A., & Murphy, G. A. (2011). A work-integrated learning philosophy and the educational imperatives. In P. Keleher, A. Patil, & R. Harreveld (Eds.), *Work-integrated learning in engineering, built environment and technology: Diversity of practice in practice* (pp. 1–24). Hershey, PA: IGI Global. doi:10.4018/978-1-60960-547-6.ch001

Carlén, U., & Lindström, B. (2012). Informed design of educational activities in online learning communities. In A. Olofsson & J. Lindberg (Eds.), *Informed design of educational technologies in higher education: Enhanced learning and teaching* (pp. 118–134). Hershey, PA: IGI Global. doi:10.4018/978-1-61350-080-4.ch007

Cassidy, A., Sipos, Y., & Nyrose, S. (2014). Supporting sustainability education and leadership: Strategies for students, faculty, and the planet. In S. Mukerji & P. Tripathi (Eds.), *Handbook of research on transnational higher education* (pp. 207–231). Hershey, PA: IGI Global. doi:10.4018/978-1-4666-4458-8.ch012

Cavanagh, T. B. (2011). Leveraging online university education to improve K-12 science education: The ScienceMaster case study. In M. Bowdon & R. Carpenter (Eds.), *Higher education, emerging technologies, and community partnerships: Concepts, models and practices* (pp. 221–233). Hershey, PA: IGI Global. doi:10.4018/978-1-60960-623-7.ch020

Chapman, D. L. (2013). Overview of technology plans. In S. Wang & T. Hartsell (Eds.), *Technology integration and foundations for effective leadership* (pp. 71–87). Hershey, PA: IGI Global. doi:10.4018/978-1-4666-2656-0.ch005

Chapman, D. L., Bynog, M., & Yocom, H. (2013). Assessment, evaluation, and revision of a technology plan. In S. Wang & T. Hartsell (Eds.), *Technology integration and foundations for effective leadership* (pp. 124–150). Hershey, PA: IGI Global. doi:10.4018/978-1-4666-2656-0.ch008

Chylinski, R., & Hanewald, R. (2009). Creating supportive environments for CALL teacher autonomy. In R. de Cássia Veiga Marriott & P. Lupion Torres (Eds.), *Handbook of research on e-learning methodologies for language acquisition* (pp. 387–408). Hershey, PA: IGI Global. doi:10.4018/978-1-59904-994-6.ch024

Chylinski, R., & Hanewald, R. (2011). Creating supportive environments for CALL teacher autonomy. In *Instructional design: Concepts, methodologies, tools and applications* (pp. 840–860). Hershey, PA: IGI Global. doi:10.4018/978-1-60960-503-2.ch403

Clouse, N. K., Williams, S. R., & Evans, R. D. (2011). Developing an online mentoring program for beginning teachers. In S. D'Agustino (Ed.), *Adaptation, resistance and access to instructional technologies: Assessing future trends in education* (pp. 410–428). Hershey, PA: IGI Global. doi:10.4018/978-1-61692-854-4.ch024

Colomo-Palacios, R., Tovar-Caro, E., García-Crespo, Á., & Gómez-Berbís, J. M. (2012). Identifying technical competences of IT professionals: The case of software engineers. In R. Colomo-Palacios (Ed.), *Professional advancements and management trends in the IT sector* (pp. 1–14). Hershey, PA: IGI Global. doi:10.4018/978-1-4666-0924-2.ch001

Corbeil, M. E., & Corbeil, J. R. (2012). Creating ongoing online support communities through social networks to promote professional learning. In V. Dennen & J. Myers (Eds.), *Virtual professional development and informal learning via social networks* (pp. 114–133). Hershey, PA: IGI Global. doi:10.4018/978-1-4666-1815-2.ch007

Corbitt, B., Holt, D., & Segrave, S. (2008). Strategic design for web-based teaching and learning: Making corporate technology systems work for the learning organization. In L. Tomei (Ed.), *Online and distance learning: Concepts, methodologies, tools, and applications* (pp. 897–904). Hershey, PA: IGI Global. doi:10.4018/978-1-59904-935-9.ch075

Corbitt, B., Holt, D. M., & Segrave, S. (2008). Strategic design for web-based teaching and learning: Making corporate technology system work for the learning organization. In L. Esnault (Ed.), *Web-based education and pedagogical technologies: Solutions for learning applications* (pp. 280–302). Hershey, PA: IGI Global. doi:10.4018/978-1-59904-525-2.ch016

Coutinho, C. P. (2010). Challenges for teacher education in the learning society: Case studies of promising practice. In H. Yang & S. Yuen (Eds.), *Handbook of research on practices and outcomes in e-learning: Issues and trends* (pp. 385–401). Hershey, PA: IGI Global. doi:10.4018/978-1-60566-788-1.ch023

Cowie, B., Jones, A., & Harlow, A. (2011). Technological infrastructure and implementation environments: The case of laptops for New Zealand teachers. In S. D'Agustino (Ed.), *Adaptation, resistance and access to instructional technologies: Assessing future trends in education* (pp. 40–52). Hershey, PA: IGI Global. doi:10.4018/978-1-61692-854-4.ch003

Crichton, S. (2007). A great wall of difference: Musings on instructional design in contemporary China. In M. Keppell (Ed.), *Instructional design: Case studies in communities of practice* (pp. 91–105). Hershey, PA: IGI Global. doi:10.4018/978-1-59904-322-7.ch005

Croasdaile, S. (2009). Inter-organizational e-collaboration in education. In N. Kock (Ed.), *E-collaboration: Concepts, methodologies, tools, and applications* (pp. 1157–1170). Hershey, PA: IGI Global. doi:10.4018/978-1-60566-652-5.ch086

Croasdaile, S. (2009). Inter-organizational e-collaboration in education. In J. Salmons & L. Wilson (Eds.), *Handbook of research on electronic collaboration and organizational synergy* (pp. 16–29). Hershey, PA: IGI Global. doi:10.4018/978-1-60566-106-3.ch002

Csoma, K. (2010). EPICT: Transnational teacher development through blended learning. In S. Mukerji & P. Tripathi (Eds.), *Cases on technological adaptability and transnational learning: Issues and challenges* (pp. 147–161). Hershey, PA: IGI Global. doi:10.4018/978-1-61520-779-4.ch008

Cunningham, C. A., & Harrison, K. (2011). The affordances of second life for education. In G. Vincenti & J. Braman (Eds.), *Teaching through multi-user virtual environments: Applying dynamic elements to the modern classroom* (pp. 94–119). Hershey, PA: IGI Global. doi:10.4018/978-1-61692-822-3.ch007

Curwood, J. S. (2014). From collaboration to transformation: Practitioner research for school librarians and classroom teachers. In K. Kennedy & L. Green (Eds.), *Collaborative models for librarian and teacher partnerships* (pp. 1–11). Hershey, PA: IGI Global. doi:10.4018/978-1-4666-4361-1.ch001

Cuthell, J. P. (2010). Thinking things through: Collaborative online professional development. In J. Lindberg & A. Olofsson (Eds.), *Online learning communities and teacher professional development: Methods for improved education delivery* (pp. 154–167). Hershey, PA: IGI Global. doi:10.4018/978-1-60566-780-5.ch009

D'Agustino, S., & King, K. P. (2011). Access and advancement: Teacher transformation and student empowerment through technology mentoring. In S. D'Agustino (Ed.), *Adaptation, resistance and access to instructional technologies: Assessing future trends in education* (pp. 362–380). Hershey, PA: IGI Global. doi:10.4018/978-1-61692-854-4.ch021

Dana, N. F., Krell, D., & Wolkenhauer, R. (2013). Taking action research in teacher education online: Exploring the possibilities. In R. Hartshorne, T. Heafner, & T. Petty (Eds.), *Teacher education programs and online learning tools: Innovations in teacher preparation* (pp. 357–374). Hershey, PA: IGI Global. doi:10.4018/978-1-4666-1906-7.ch019

Dawson, K., Cavanaugh, C., & Ritzhaupt, A. D. (2013). ARTI: An online tool to support teacher action research for technology integration. In R. Hartshorne, T. Heafner, & T. Petty (Eds.), *Teacher education programs and online learning tools: Innovations in teacher preparation* (pp. 375–391). Hershey, PA: IGI Global. doi:10.4018/978-1-4666-1906-7.ch020

De Simone, C., Marquis, T., & Groen, J. (2013). Optimizing conditions for learning and teaching in K-20 education. In V. Wang (Ed.), *Handbook of research on teaching and learning in K-20 education* (pp. 535–552). Hershey, PA: IGI Global. doi:10.4018/978-1-4666-4249-2.ch031

Dennen, V. P., & Jiang, W. (2012). Twitter-based knowledge sharing in professional networks: The organization perspective. In V. Dennen & J. Myers (Eds.), *Virtual professional development and informal learning via social networks* (pp. 241–255). Hershey, PA: IGI Global. doi:10.4018/978-1-4666-1815-2.ch014

Dexter, S. (2002). eTIPS - Educational technology integration and implementation principles. In P. Rogers (Ed.), Designing instruction for technology-enhanced learning (pp. 56-70). Hershey, PA: IGI Global. doi:10.4018/978-1-930708-28-0.ch003

Dickerson, J., Winslow, J., & Lee, C. Y. (2013). Teacher training and technology: Current uses and future trends. In V. Wang (Ed.), *Handbook of research on technologies for improving the 21st century workforce: Tools for lifelong learning* (pp. 243–256). Hershey, PA: IGI Global. doi:10.4018/978-1-4666-2181-7.ch016

DiMarco, J. (2006). Cases and interviews. In J. DiMarco (Ed.), *Web portfolio design and applications* (pp. 222–276). Hershey, PA: IGI Global. doi:10.4018/978-1-59140-854-3.ch012

Doherty, I. (2013). Achieving excellence in teaching: A case study in embedding professional development for teaching within a research-intensive university. In D. Salter (Ed.), *Cases on quality teaching practices in higher education* (pp. 280–290). Hershey, PA: IGI Global. doi:10.4018/978-1-4666-3661-3.ch017

Donnelly, R. (2009). Transformative potential of constructivist blended problem-based learning in higher education. In C. Payne (Ed.), *Information technology and constructivism in higher education: Progressive learning frameworks* (pp. 182–202). Hershey, PA: IGI Global. doi:10.4018/978-1-60566-654-9.ch012

Donnelly, R. (2010). The nature of complex blends: Transformative problem-based learning and technology in Irish higher education. In Y. Inoue (Ed.), *Cases on online and blended learning technologies in higher education: Concepts and practices* (pp. 1–22). Hershey, PA: IGI Global. doi:10.4018/978-1-60566-880-2.ch001

Donnelly, R., & O'Farrell, C. (2006). Constructivist e-learning for staff engaged in coninuous professional development. In J. O'Donoghue (Ed.), *Technology supported learning and teaching: A staff perspective* (pp. 160–175). Hershey, PA: IGI Global. doi:10.4018/978-1-59140-962-5.ch010

Downing, K. F., & Holtz, J. K. (2008). Virtual school science. In K. Downing & J. Holtz (Eds.), *Online science learning: Best practices and technologies* (pp. 30–48). Hershey, PA: IGI Global. doi:10.4018/978-1-59904-986-1.ch003

Ehmann Powers, C., & Hewett, B. L. (2008). Building online training programs for virtual workplaces. In P. Zemliansky & K. St.Amant (Eds.), *Handbook of research on virtual workplaces and the new nature of business practices* (pp. 257–271). Hershey, PA: IGI Global. doi:10.4018/978-1-59904-893-2.ch019

Ellis, J. B., West, T. D., Grimaldi, A., & Root, G. (2013). Ernst & Young leadership and professional development center: Accounting designed for leaders. In R. Carpenter (Ed.), *Cases on higher education spaces: Innovation, collaboration, and technology* (pp. 330–355). Hershey, PA: IGI Global. doi:10.4018/978-1-4666-2673-7.ch017

Falco, J. (2008). Leading the art of the conference: Revolutionizing schooling through interactive videoconferencing. In D. Newman, J. Falco, S. Silverman, & P. Barbanell (Eds.), *Videoconferencing technology in K-12 instruction: Best practices and trends* (pp. 133–143). Hershey, PA: IGI Global. doi:10.4018/978-1-59904-331-9.ch010

Farmer, L. (2009). Fostering online communities of practice in career and technical education. In V. Wang (Ed.), *Handbook of research on e-learning applications for career and technical education: Technologies for vocational training* (pp. 192–203). Hershey, PA: IGI Global. doi:10.4018/978-1-60566-739-3.ch015

Farmer, L. (2010). Lights, camera, action! Via teacher librarian video conferencing. In S. Rummler & K. Ng (Eds.), *Collaborative technologies and applications for interactive information design: Emerging trends in user experiences* (pp. 179–188). Hershey, PA: IGI Global. doi:10.4018/978-1-60566-727-0.ch013

Farmer, L. S. (2012). Curriculum development for online learners. In V. Wang, L. Farmer, J. Parker, & P. Golubski (Eds.), *Pedagogical and andragogical teaching and learning with information communication technologies* (pp. 88–104). Hershey, PA: IGI Global. doi:10.4018/978-1-60960-791-3.ch007

Farmer, L. S. (2013). Assessment processes for online professional development. In J. Keengwe & L. Kyei-Blankson (Eds.), *Virtual mentoring for teachers: Online professional development practices* (pp. 161–180). Hershey, PA: IGI Global. doi:10.4018/978-1-4666-1963-0.ch009

Farmer, L. S. (2014). The roles of professional organizations in school library education. In V. Wang (Ed.), *International education and the next-generation workforce: Competition in the global economy* (pp. 170–193). Hershey, PA: IGI Global. doi:10.4018/978-1-4666-4498-4.ch010

Fok, A. W., & Ip, H. H. (2009). An agent-based framework for personalized learning in continuous professional development. In M. Syed (Ed.), *Strategic applications of distance learning technologies* (pp. 96–110). Hershey, PA: IGI Global. doi:10.4018/978-1-59904-480-4.ch007

Fragaki, M., & Lionarakis, A. (2011). Education for liberation: A transformative polymorphic model for ICT integration in education. In G. Kurubacak & T. Yuzer (Eds.), *Handbook of research on transformative online education and liberation: Models for social equality* (pp. 198–231). Hershey, PA: IGI Global. doi:10.4018/978-1-60960-046-4.ch011

Fuller, J. S., & Bachenheimer, B. A. (2013). Using an observation cycle for helping teachers integrate technology. In A. Ritzhaupt & S. Kumar (Eds.), *Cases on educational technology implementation for facilitating learning* (pp. 69–84). Hershey, PA: IGI Global. doi:10.4018/978-1-4666-3676-7.ch004

Gairin-Sallán, J., & Rodriguez-Gómez, D. (2010). Teacher professional development through knowledge management in educational organisations. In J. Lindberg & A. Olofsson (Eds.), *Online learning communities and teacher professional development: Methods for improved education delivery* (pp. 134–153). Hershey, PA: IGI Global. doi:10.4018/978-1-60566-780-5.ch008

Gairín-Sallán, J., & Rodríguez-Gómez, D. (2012). Teacher professional development through knowledge management in educational organisations. In *Organizational learning and knowledge: Concepts, methodologies, tools and applications* (pp. 1297–1315). Hershey, PA: IGI Global. doi:10.4018/978-1-60960-783-8.ch404

García, K., & Suzuki, R. (2008). The blended learning classroom: An online teacher training program. In M. Lytras, D. Gasevic, P. Ordóñez de Pablos, & W. Huang (Eds.), *Technology enhanced learning: Best practices* (pp. 57–80). Hershey, PA: IGI Global. doi:10.4018/978-1-59904-600-6.ch003

Gerbic, P., & Stacey, E. (2009). Conclusion. In E. Stacey & P. Gerbic (Eds.), *Effective blended learning practices: Evidence-based perspectives in ICT-facilitated education* (pp. 298–311). Hershey, PA: IGI Global. doi:10.4018/978-1-60566-296-1.ch016

Gibbons, A. N. (2010). Reflections concerning technology: A case for the philosophy of technology in early childhood teacher education and professional development programs. In S. Blake & S. Izumi-Taylor (Eds.), *Technology for early childhood education and socialization: Developmental applications and methodologies* (pp. 1–19). Hershey, PA: IGI Global. doi:10.4018/978-1-60566-784-3.ch001

Gonzales, C., Bussmann, S., Bovard, B., & Parra, J. (2007). Transitioning to e-learning: Teaching the teachers. In R. Sharma & S. Mishra (Eds.), *Cases on global e-learning practices: Successes and pitfalls* (pp. 52–72). Hershey, PA: IGI Global. doi:10.4018/978-1-59904-340-1.ch005

Gormley, P., Bruen, C., & Concannon, F. (2010). Sustainability through staff engagement: Applying a community of practice model to web 2.0 academic development programmes. In R. Donnelly, J. Harvey, & K. O'Rourke (Eds.), *Critical design and effective tools for e-learning in higher education: Theory into practice* (pp. 326–345). Hershey, PA: IGI Global. doi:10.4018/978-1-61520-879-1.ch020

Grandgenett, N., Ostler, E., Topp, N., & Goeman, R. (2012). Robotics and problem-based learning in STEM formal educational environments. In B. Barker, G. Nugent, N. Grandgenett, & V. Adamchuk (Eds.), *Robots in K-12 education: A new technology for learning* (pp. 94–119). Hershey, PA: IGI Global. doi:10.4018/978-1-4666-0182-6.ch005

Grant, M. R. (2010). Train the trainer: A competency-based model for teaching in virtual environments. In W. Ritke-Jones (Ed.), *Virtual environments for corporate education: Employee learning and solutions* (pp. 124–146). Hershey, PA: IGI Global. doi:10.4018/978-1-61520-619-3.ch008

Griffin, P., Care, E., Robertson, P., Crigan, J., Awwal, N., & Pavlovic, M. (2013). Assessment and learning partnerships in an online environment. In E. McKay (Ed.), *ePedagogy in online learning: New developments in web mediated human computer interaction* (pp. 39–54). Hershey, PA: IGI Global. doi:10.4018/978-1-4666-3649-1.ch003

Griswold, W. (2013). Transformative learning and educational technology integration in a post-totalitarian context: Professional development among school teachers in rural Siberia, Russia. In E. Jean Francois (Ed.), *Transcultural blended learning and teaching in postsecondary education* (pp. 128–144). Hershey, PA: IGI Global. doi:10.4018/978-1-4666-2014-8.ch008

Gruich, M. R. (2013). Defining professional development for technology. In S. Wang & T. Hartsell (Eds.), *Technology integration and foundations for effective leadership* (pp. 152–170). Hershey, PA: IGI Global. doi:10.4018/978-1-4666-2656-0.ch009

Guidry, K. R., & Pasquini, L. (2013). Twitter chat as an informal learning tool: A case study using #sachat. In H. Yang & S. Wang (Eds.), *Cases on formal and informal e-learning environments: Opportunities and practices* (pp. 356–377). Hershey, PA: IGI Global. doi:10.4018/978-1-4666-1930-2.ch019

Gunn, C., & Blake, A. (2009). Blending technology into an academic practice qualification for university teachers. In E. Stacey & P. Gerbic (Eds.), *Effective blended learning practices: Evidence-based perspectives in ICT-facilitated education* (pp. 259–279). Hershey, PA: IGI Global. doi:10.4018/978-1-60566-296-1.ch014

Hanewald, R. (2013). Professional development with and for emerging technologies: A case study with Asian languages and cultural studies teachers in Australia. In J. Keengwe (Ed.), *Pedagogical applications and social effects of mobile technology integration* (pp. 175–192). Hershey, PA: IGI Global. doi:10.4018/978-1-4666-2985-1.ch010

Hansen, C. C. (2012). ABCs and PCs: Effective professional development in early childhood education. In I. Chen & D. McPheeters (Eds.), *Cases on educational technology integration in urban schools* (pp. 230–235). Hershey, PA: IGI Global. doi:10.4018/978-1-61350-492-5.ch032

Hao, S. (2012). Turn on your mobile devices: Potential and considerations of informal mobile learning. In V. Dennen & J. Myers (Eds.), *Virtual professional development and informal learning via social networks* (pp. 39–58). Hershey, PA: IGI Global. doi:10.4018/978-1-4666-1815-2.ch003

Harteis, C. (2010). Contributions of e-collaborative knowledge construction to professional learning and expertise. In B. Ertl (Ed.), *E-collaborative knowledge construction: Learning from computer-supported and virtual environments* (pp. 91–108). Hershey, PA: IGI Global. doi:10.4018/978-1-61520-729-9.ch005

Hartsell, T., Herron, S. S., Fang, H., & Rathod, A. (2011). Improving teachers' self-confidence in learning technology skills and math education through professional development. In *Instructional design: Concepts, methodologies, tools and applications* (pp. 1487–1503). Hershey, PA: IGI Global. doi:10.4018/978-1-60960-503-2.ch609

Hartsell, T., Herron, S. S., Fang, H., & Rathod, A. (2012). Improving teachers' self-confidence in learning technology skills and math education through professional development. In L. Tomei (Ed.), *Advancing education with information communication technologies: Facilitating new trends* (pp. 150–164). Hershey, PA: IGI Global. doi:10.4018/978-1-61350-468-0.ch013

Hartsell, T., & Wang, S. (2013). Introduction to technology integration and leadership. In S. Wang & T. Hartsell (Eds.), *Technology integration and foundations for effective leadership* (pp. 1–17). Hershey, PA: IGI Global. doi:10.4018/978-1-4666-2656-0.ch001

Hauge, T. E., & Norenes, S. O. (2010). VideoPaper as a bridging tool in teacher professional development. In J. Lindberg & A. Olofsson (Eds.), *Online learning communities and teacher professional development: Methods for improved education delivery* (pp. 209–228). Hershey, PA: IGI Global. doi:10.4018/978-1-60566-780-5.ch012

Haythornthwaite, C., & De Laat, M. (2012). Social network informed design for learning with educational technology. In A. Olofsson & J. Lindberg (Eds.), *Informed design of educational technologies in higher education: Enhanced learning and teaching* (pp. 352–374). Hershey, PA: IGI Global. doi:10.4018/978-1-61350-080-4.ch018

Heinrichs, L., Fellander-Tsai, L., & Davies, D. (2013). Clinical virtual worlds: The wider implications for professional development in healthcare. In K. Bredl & W. Bösche (Eds.), *Serious games and virtual worlds in education, professional development, and healthcare* (pp. 221–240). Hershey, PA: IGI Global. doi:10.4018/978-1-4666-3673-6.ch014

Helleve, I. (2010). Theoretical foundations of teachers' professional development. In J. Lindberg & A. Olofsson (Eds.), *Online learning communities and teacher professional development: Methods for improved education delivery* (pp. 1–19). Hershey, PA: IGI Global. doi:10.4018/978-1-60566-780-5.ch001

Hemphill, L. S., & McCaw, D. S. (2009). Moodling professional development training that worked. In L. Tan Wee Hin & R. Subramaniam (Eds.), *Handbook of research on new media literacy at the K-12 level: Issues and challenges* (pp. 808–822). Hershey, PA: IGI Global. doi:10.4018/978-1-60566-120-9.ch050

Hensley, M. K. (2010). Teaching new librarians how to teach: A model for building a peer learning program. In E. Pankl, D. Theiss-White, & M. Bushing (Eds.), *Recruitment, development, and retention of information professionals: Trends in human resources and knowledge management* (pp. 179–190). Hershey, PA: IGI Global. doi:10.4018/978-1-61520-601-8.ch010

Hernández-Gantes, V. M. (2011). Helping faculty design online courses in higher education. In V. Wang (Ed.), *Encyclopedia of information communication technologies and adult education integration* (pp. 779–794). Hershey, PA: IGI Global. doi:10.4018/978-1-61692-906-0.ch047

Herrington, J., & Oliver, R. (2006). Professional development for the online teacher: An authentic approach. In T. Herrington & J. Herrington (Eds.), *Authentic learning environments in higher education* (pp. 283–295). Hershey, PA: IGI Global. doi:10.4018/978-1-59140-594-8.ch020

Hicks, T. (2013). Adding the "digital layer": Examining one teacher's growth as a digital writer through an NWP summer institute and beyond. In K. Pytash & R. Ferdig (Eds.), *Exploring technology for writing and writing instruction* (pp. 345–357). Hershey, PA: IGI Global. doi:10.4018/978-1-4666-4341-3.ch020

Hinson, J. M., & Bordelon Sellers, R. (2004). Professional development recommendations for online courses. In C. Cavanaugh (Ed.), *Development and management of virtual schools: Issues and trends* (pp. 135–157). Hershey, PA: IGI Global. doi:10.4018/978-1-59140-154-4.ch007

Hirtle, J., & Smith, S. (2010). When virtual communities click: Transforming teacher practice, transforming teachers. In H. Yang & S. Yuen (Eds.), *Handbook of research on practices and outcomes in e-learning: Issues and trends* (pp. 182–196). Hershey, PA: IGI Global. doi:10.4018/978-1-60566-788-1.ch011

Holland, I. E. (2007). Evolution of the Milwaukee public schools portal. In A. Tatnall (Ed.), *Encyclopedia of portal technologies and applications* (pp. 397–401). Hershey, PA: IGI Global. doi:10.4018/978-1-59140-989-2.ch067

Holt, J., Unruh, L., & Dougherty, A. M. (2011). Enhancing a rural school-university teacher education partnership through an e-mentoring program for beginning teachers. In M. Bowdon & R. Carpenter (Eds.), *Higher education, emerging technologies, and community partnerships: Concepts, models and practices* (pp. 212–220). Hershey, PA: IGI Global. doi:10.4018/978-1-60960-623-7.ch019

Hood, D. W., & Huang, W. D. (2013). Professional development with graduate teaching assistants (TAs) teaching online. In J. Keengwe & L. Kyei-Blankson (Eds.), *Virtual mentoring for teachers: Online professional development practices* (pp. 26–42). Hershey, PA: IGI Global. doi:10.4018/978-1-4666-1963-0.ch002

Hu, X. C., & Meyen, E. L. (2013). A comparison of student and instructor preferences for design and pedagogy features in postsecondary online courses. In M. Raisinghani (Ed.), *Curriculum, learning, and teaching advancements in online education* (pp. 213–229). Hershey, PA: IGI Global. doi:10.4018/978-1-4666-2949-3.ch015

Hucks, D., & Ragan, M. (2013). Technology expanding horizons in teacher education: Transformative learning experiences. In J. Keengwe (Ed.), *Research perspectives and best practices in educational technology integration* (pp. 61–79). Hershey, PA: IGI Global. doi:10.4018/978-1-4666-2988-2.ch004

Hui, D., & Russell, D. L. (2009). Understanding the effectiveness of collaborative activity in online professional development with innovative educators through intersubjectivity. In L. Tomei (Ed.), *Information communication technologies for enhanced education and learning: Advanced applications and developments* (pp. 283–302). Hershey, PA: IGI Global. doi:10.4018/978-1-60566-150-6.ch020

Hulme, M., & Hughes, J. (2006). Patchwork e-dialogues in the professional development of new teachers. In J. O'Donoghue (Ed.), *Technology supported learning and teaching: A staff perspective* (pp. 210–223). Hershey, PA: IGI Global. doi:10.4018/978-1-59140-962-5.ch013

Hunt, L., & Sankey, M. (2013). Getting the context right for quality teaching and learning. In D. Salter (Ed.), *Cases on quality teaching practices in higher education* (pp. 261–279). Hershey, PA: IGI Global. doi:10.4018/978-1-4666-3661-3.ch016

Hur, J. W., Brush, T., & Bonk, C. (2012). An analysis of teacher knowledge and emotional sharing in a teacher blog community. In V. Dennen & J. Myers (Eds.), *Virtual professional development and informal learning via social networks* (pp. 219–239). Hershey, PA: IGI Global. doi:10.4018/978-1-4666-1815-2.ch013

Hurst, A. (2012). Reflections on personal experiences of staff training and continuing professional development for academic staff in the development of high quality support for disabled students in higher education. In D. Moore, A. Gorra, M. Adams, J. Reaney, & H. Smith (Eds.), *Disabled students in education: Technology, transition, and inclusivity* (pp. 288–304). Hershey, PA: IGI Global. doi:10.4018/978-1-61350-183-2.ch015

Hyatt, K. J. (2011). Technology: A reflective tool for professional development. In L. Tomei (Ed.), *Online courses and ICT in education: Emerging practices and applications* (pp. 134–142). Hershey, PA: IGI Global. doi:10.4018/978-1-60960-150-8.ch011

Jackson, T. (2012). Ways to mentor methods' faculty integration of technologies in their courses. In D. Polly, C. Mims, & K. Persichitte (Eds.), *Developing technology-rich teacher education programs: Key issues* (pp. 519–534). Hershey, PA: IGI Global. doi:10.4018/978-1-4666-0014-0.ch033

Jamieson-Proctor, R., & Finger, G. (2009). Measuring and evaluating ICT use: Developing an instrument for measuring student ICT use. In L. Tan Wee Hin & R. Subramaniam (Eds.), *Handbook of research on new media literacy at the K-12 level: Issues and challenges* (pp. 326–339). Hershey, PA: IGI Global. doi:10.4018/978-1-60566-120-9.ch021

Jarvis, D. H. (2012). Teaching mathematics teachers online: Strategies for navigating the intersection of andragogy, technology, and reform-based mathematics education. In A. Juan, M. Huertas, S. Trenholm, & C. Steegmann (Eds.), *Teaching mathematics online: Emergent technologies and methodologies* (pp. 187–199). Hershey, PA: IGI Global. doi:10.4018/978-1-60960-875-0.ch009

Jimoyiannis, A., Gravani, M., & Karagiorgi, Y. (2012). Teacher professional development through virtual campuses: Conceptions of a 'new' model. In H. Yang & S. Yuen (Eds.), *Handbook of research on practices and outcomes in virtual worlds and environments* (pp. 327–347). Hershey, PA: IGI Global. doi:10.4018/978-1-60960-762-3.ch017

Johnson, E. S., & Pitcock, J. (2008). Preparing online instructors: Beyond using the technology. In K. Orvis & A. Lassiter (Eds.), *Computer-supported collaborative learning: Best practices and principles for instructors* (pp. 89–113). Hershey, PA: IGI Global. doi:10.4018/978-1-59904-753-9.ch005

Johnson, K., & Tashiro, J. (2010). Interprofessional care and health care complexity: Factors shaping human resources effectiveness in health information management. In S. Kabene (Ed.), *Human resources in healthcare, health informatics and healthcare systems* (pp. 250–280). Hershey, PA: IGI Global. doi:10.4018/978-1-61520-885-2.ch015

Johnson, K., & Tashiro, J. (2013). Interprofessional care and health care complexity: Factors shaping human resources effectiveness in health information management. In *User-driven healthcare: Concepts, methodologies, tools, and applications* (pp. 1273–1302). Hershey, PA: IGI Global. doi:10.4018/978-1-4666-2770-3.ch064

Johnson, M. L. (2014). Moving from theory to practice: Integrating personal learning networks into a graduate-level student development theory course. In S. Leone (Ed.), *Synergic integration of formal and informal e-learning environments for adult lifelong learners* (pp. 165–177). Hershey, PA: IGI Global. doi:10.4018/978-1-4666-4655-1.ch008

Johnson, V. (2009). Understanding dynamic change and creation of learning organizations. In P. Rogers, G. Berg, J. Boettcher, C. Howard, L. Justice, & K. Schenk (Eds.), *Encyclopedia of distance learning* (2nd ed.; pp. 2187–2191). Hershey, PA: IGI Global. doi:10.4018/978-1-60566-198-8.ch323

Jones, M. G., & Harris, L. (2012). Using student choice to promote technology integration: The buffet model. In D. Polly, C. Mims, & K. Persichitte (Eds.), *Developing technology-rich teacher education programs: Key issues* (pp. 192–204). Hershey, PA: IGI Global. doi:10.4018/978-1-4666-0014-0.ch013

Joyes, G., Fisher, T., Firth, R., & Coyle, D. (2014). The nature of a successful online professional doctorate. In K. Sullivan, P. Czigler, & J. Sullivan Hellgren (Eds.), *Cases on professional distance education degree programs and practices: Successes, challenges, and issues* (pp. 296–330). Hershey, PA: IGI Global. doi:10.4018/978-1-4666-4486-1.ch011

Kelly, D. (2009). Modeling best practices in web-based academic development. In R. Donnelly & F. McSweeney (Eds.), *Applied e-learning and e-teaching in higher education* (pp. 35–55). Hershey, PA: IGI Global. doi:10.4018/978-1-59904-814-7.ch003

Kelly, D. K. (2010). Modeling best practices in web-based academic development. In A. Tatnall (Ed.), *Web technologies: Concepts, methodologies, tools, and applications* (pp. 1578–1595). Hershey, PA: IGI Global. doi:10.4018/978-1-60566-982-3.ch085

Kelly, R. (2014). Administration: Making a connection with the library's strongest advocate. In K. Kennedy & L. Green (Eds.), *Collaborative models for librarian and teacher partnerships* (pp. 175–184). Hershey, PA: IGI Global. doi:10.4018/978-1-4666-4361-1.ch015

Kennedy-Clark, S., & Thompson, K. (2013). A MUVEing success: Design strategies for professional development in the use of multi-user virtual environments and educational games in science education. In S. D'Agustino (Ed.), *Immersive environments, augmented realities, and virtual worlds: Assessing future trends in education* (pp. 16–41). Hershey, PA: IGI Global. doi:10.4018/978-1-4666-2670-6.ch002

Kent, A. M. (2013). Teacher leadership: Learning and leading. In J. Lewis, A. Green, & D. Surry (Eds.), *Technology as a tool for diversity leadership: Implementation and future implications* (pp. 230–242). Hershey, PA: IGI Global. doi:10.4018/978-1-4666-2668-3.ch018

Keppell, M. J. (2007). Instructional designers on the borderline: Brokering across communities of practice. In M. Keppell (Ed.), *Instructional design: Case studies in communities of practice* (pp. 68–89). Hershey, PA: IGI Global. doi:10.4018/978-1-59904-322-7.ch004

Kidd, T. T., & Keengwe, J. (2012). Technology integration and urban schools: Implications for instructional practices. In L. Tomei (Ed.), *Advancing education with information communication technologies: Facilitating new trends* (pp. 244–256). Hershey, PA: IGI Global. doi:10.4018/978-1-61350-468-0.ch020

King, K. P. (2008). The transformation model. In C. Van Slyke (Ed.), *Information communication technologies: Concepts, methodologies, tools, and applications* (pp. 1102–1108). Hershey, PA: IGI Global. doi:10.4018/978-1-59904-949-6.ch073

King, K. P. (2012). Impact of podcasts as professional learning: Teacher created, student created, and professional development podcasts. In S. Chhabra (Ed.), *ICTs for advancing rural communities and human development: Addressing the digital divide* (pp. 237–250). Hershey, PA: IGI Global. doi:10.4018/978-1-4666-0047-8.ch016

Kitchenham, A. (2011). Blending professional development for rural educators an exploratory study. In D. Parsons (Ed.), *Combining e-learning and m-learning: New applications of blended educational resources* (pp. 225–238). Hershey, PA: IGI Global. doi:10.4018/978-1-60960-481-3.ch014

Klieger, A., & Oster-Levinz, A. (2010). How online tasks promote teachers' expertise within the technological pedagogical content knowledge (TPACK). In T. Yuzer & G. Kurubacak (Eds.), *Transformative learning and online education: Aesthetics, dimensions and concepts* (pp. 219–235). Hershey, PA: IGI Global. doi:10.4018/978-1-61520-985-9.ch015

Koh, S., Lee, S., Yen, D. C., & Havelka, D. (2005). Information technology professional career development: A progression of skills. In M. Hunter & F. Tan (Eds.), *Advanced topics in global information management* (Vol. 4, pp. 142–157). Hershey, PA: IGI Global. doi:10.4018/978-1-59140-468-2.ch009

Kopcha, T., & Valentine, K. D. (2013). A framework for developing robust online professional development materials to support teacher practice under the common core. In D. Polly (Ed.), *Common core mathematics standards and implementing digital technologies* (pp. 319–331). Hershey, PA: IGI Global. doi:10.4018/978-1-4666-4086-3.ch021

Koumpis, A. (2010). Culture of services. In A. Koumpis (Ed.), *Service science for socio-economical and information systems advancement: Holistic methodologies* (pp. 312–347). Hershey, PA: IGI Global. doi:10.4018/978-1-60566-683-9.ch010

Kyei-Blankson, L., & Keengwe, J. (2013). Faculty-faculty interactions in online learning environments. In L. Tomei (Ed.), *Learning tools and teaching approaches through ICT advancements* (pp. 127–135). Hershey, PA: IGI Global. doi:10.4018/978-1-4666-2017-9.ch012

Larson, L., & Vanmetre, S. (2010). Learning together with the interactive white board. In N. Lambropoulos & M. Romero (Eds.), *Educational social software for context-aware learning: Collaborative methods and human interaction* (pp. 69–78). Hershey, PA: IGI Global. doi:10.4018/978-1-60566-826-0.ch005

Laurillard, D., & Masterman, E. (2010). TPD as online collaborative learning for innovation in teaching. In J. Lindberg & A. Olofsson (Eds.), *Online learning communities and teacher professional development: Methods for improved education delivery* (pp. 230–246). Hershey, PA: IGI Global. doi:10.4018/978-1-60566-780-5.ch013

Lawrence, J., Burton, L., Summers, J., Noble, K., & Gibbings, P. D. (2013). An associate dean's community of practice: Rising to the leadership challenges of engaging distance students using blended models of learning and teaching. In J. Willems, B. Tynan, & R. James (Eds.), *Global challenges and perspectives in blended and distance learning* (pp. 212–222). Hershey, PA: IGI Global. doi:10.4018/978-1-4666-3978-2.ch017

Lee, D. M. (2004). Organizational entry and transition from academic study: Examining a critical step in the professional development of young IS workers. In M. Igbaria & C. Shayo (Eds.), *Strategies for managing IS/IT personnel* (pp. 113–142). Hershey, PA: IGI Global. doi:10.4018/978-1-59140-128-5.ch006

Leh, A. S., & Grafton, L. (2009). Promoting new media literacy in a school district. In L. Tan Wee Hin & R. Subramaniam (Eds.), *Handbook of research on new media literacy at the K-12 level: Issues and challenges* (pp. 607–619). Hershey, PA: IGI Global. doi:10.4018/978-1-60566-120-9.ch038

Lehew, A. J., & Polly, D. (2013). The use of digital resources to support elementary school teachers' implementation of the common core state standards. In D. Polly (Ed.), *Common core mathematics standards and implementing digital technologies* (pp. 332–338). Hershey, PA: IGI Global. doi:10.4018/978-1-4666-4086-3.ch022

Leng, J., & Sharrock, W. (2010). Collaborative practices in computer-aided academic research. In I. Portela & M. Cruz-Cunha (Eds.), *Information communication technology law, protection and access rights: Global approaches and issues* (pp. 249–270). Hershey, PA: IGI Global. doi:10.4018/978-1-61520-975-0.ch016

Ley, K., & Gannon-Cook, R. (2010). Marketing a blended university program: An action research case study. In S. Mukerji & P. Tripathi (Eds.), *Cases on technology enhanced learning through collaborative opportunities* (pp. 73–90). Hershey, PA: IGI Global. doi:10.4018/978-1-61520-751-0.ch005

Linton, J., & Stegall, D. (2013). Common core standards for mathematical practice and TPACK: An integrated approach to instruction. In D. Polly (Ed.), *Common core mathematics standards and implementing digital technologies* (pp. 234–249). Hershey, PA: IGI Global. doi:10.4018/978-1-4666-4086-3.ch016

Lithgow, C. M., Wolf, J. L., & Berge, Z. L. (2011). Virtual worlds: Corporate early adopters pave the way. In S. Hai-Jew (Ed.), *Virtual immersive and 3D learning spaces: Emerging technologies and trends* (pp. 25–43). Hershey, PA: IGI Global. doi:10.4018/978-1-61692-825-4.ch002

Lloyd, M., & Duncan-Howell, J. (2010). Changing the metaphor: The potential of online communities in teacher professional development. In J. Lindberg & A. Olofsson (Eds.), *Online learning communities and teacher professional development: Methods for improved education delivery* (pp. 60–76). Hershey, PA: IGI Global. doi:10.4018/978-1-60566-780-5.ch004

Lockyer, L., Patterson, J., Rowland, G., & Hearne, D. (2007). ActiveHealth: Enhancing the community of physical and health educators through online technologies. In M. Keppell (Ed.), *Instructional design: Case studies in communities of practice* (pp. 331–348). Hershey, PA: IGI Global. doi:10.4018/978-1-59904-322-7.ch017

Loose, C. (2013). Teachers as researchers and instructional leaders. In V. Wang (Ed.), *Handbook of research on teaching and learning in K-20 education* (pp. 710–725). Hershey, PA: IGI Global. doi:10.4018/978-1-4666-4249-2.ch041

Luetkehans, L. M., & Hunt, R. D. (2014). School librarians as significant other: Using online professional learning communities for the development of pre-service teachers. In K. Kennedy & L. Green (Eds.), *Collaborative models for librarian and teacher partnerships* (pp. 56–66). Hershey, PA: IGI Global. doi:10.4018/978-1-4666-4361-1.ch006

Lyublinskaya, I., & Tournaki, N. (2012). The effects of teacher content authoring on TPACK and on student achievement in algebra: Research on instruction with the TI-Nspire™ handheld. In R. Ronau, C. Rakes, & M. Niess (Eds.), *Educational technology, teacher knowledge, and classroom impact: A research handbook on frameworks and approaches* (pp. 295–322). Hershey, PA: IGI Global. doi:10.4018/978-1-60960-750-0.ch013

Mackey, J. (2009). Virtual learning and real communities: Online professional development for teachers. In E. Stacey & P. Gerbic (Eds.), *Effective blended learning practices: Evidence-based perspectives in ICT-facilitated education* (pp. 163–181). Hershey, PA: IGI Global. doi:10.4018/978-1-60566-296-1.ch009

Mackey, J., & Mills, A. (2003). An examination of ICT planning maturity in schools: A stage theory perspective. In T. McGill (Ed.), *Current issues in IT education* (pp. 376–395). Hershey, PA: IGI Global. doi:10.4018/978-1-93177-753-7.ch030

Manathunga, C., & Donnelly, R. (2009). Opening online academic development programmes to international perspectives and dialogue. In R. Donnelly & F. McSweeney (Eds.), *Applied e-learning and e-teaching in higher education* (pp. 85–109). Hershey, PA: IGI Global. doi:10.4018/978-1-59904-814-7.ch005

Marinho, R. (2010). Faculty development in instructional technology in the context of learning styles and institutional barriers. In S. Mukerji & P. Tripathi (Eds.), *Cases on interactive technology environments and transnational collaboration: Concerns and perspectives* (pp. 1–38). Hershey, PA: IGI Global. doi:10.4018/978-1-61520-909-5.ch001

Mark, C. L. (2013). Evaluating and funding the professional development program. In S. Wang & T. Hartsell (Eds.), *Technology integration and foundations for effective leadership* (pp. 206–226). Hershey, PA: IGI Global. doi:10.4018/978-1-4666-2656-0.ch012

Marshall, J. C. (2013). Measuring and facilitating highly effective inquiry-based teaching and learning in science classrooms. In M. Khine & I. Saleh (Eds.), *Approaches and strategies in next generation science learning* (pp. 290–306). Hershey, PA: IGI Global. doi:10.4018/978-1-4666-2809-0.ch015

Marshall, K. (2008). E-portfolios in teacher education. In G. Putnik & M. Cruz-Cunha (Eds.), *Encyclopedia of networked and virtual organizations* (pp. 516–523). Hershey, PA: IGI Global. doi:10.4018/978-1-59904-885-7.ch068

Martin, M. (2008). Integrating videoconferencing into the classroom: A perspective from Northern Ireland. In D. Newman, J. Falco, S. Silverman, & P. Barbanell (Eds.), *Videoconferencing technology in K-12 instruction: Best practices and trends* (pp. 253–268). Hershey, PA: IGI Global. doi:10.4018/978-1-59904-331-9.ch019

Maurer, M. J. (2012). Telementoring and virtual professional development: A theoretical perspective from science on the roles of self-efficacy, teacher learning, and professional learning communities. In *Organizational learning and knowledge: Concepts, methodologies, tools and applications* (pp. 1158–1176). Hershey, PA: IGI Global. doi:10.4018/978-1-60960-783-8.ch319

McAnuff-Gumbs, M., & Verbeck, K. (2013). Toward a model of multi-level professional learning communities to guide the training and practice of literacy coaches. In H. Yang & S. Wang (Eds.), *Cases on online learning communities and beyond: Investigations and applications* (pp. 361–402). Hershey, PA: IGI Global. doi:10.4018/978-1-4666-1936-4.ch019

McCarthy, J. (2012). Connected: Online mentoring in Facebook for final year digital media students. In A. Okada, T. Connolly, & P. Scott (Eds.), *Collaborative learning 2.0: Open educational resources* (pp. 204–221). Hershey, PA: IGI Global. doi:10.4018/978-1-4666-0300-4.ch011

McConnell, D. (2005). Networked collaborative e-learning. In E. Li & T. Du (Eds.), *Advances in electronic business* (Vol. 1, pp. 222–257). Hershey, PA: IGI Global. doi:10.4018/978-1-59140-381-4.ch008

McCormack, V. (2010). Utilizing VoiceThread to increase teacher candidates' reflection and global implications for usage. In J. Yamamoto, J. Kush, R. Lombard, & C. Hertzog (Eds.), *Technology implementation and teacher education: Reflective models* (pp. 108–123). Hershey, PA: IGI Global. doi:10.4018/978-1-61520-897-5.ch007

McGrath, E., Lowes, S., McKay, M., Sayres, J., & Lin, P. (2012). Robots underwater! Learning science, engineering and 21st century skills: The evolution of curricula, professional development and research in formal and informal contexts. In B. Barker, G. Nugent, N. Grandgenett, & V. Adamchuk (Eds.), *Robots in K-12 education: A new technology for learning* (pp. 141–167). Hershey, PA: IGI Global. doi:10.4018/978-1-4666-0182-6.ch007

McGuigan, A. (2012). Blogospheric learning in a continuing professional development context. In A. Okada, T. Connolly, & P. Scott (Eds.), *Collaborative learning 2.0: Open educational resources* (pp. 222–237). Hershey, PA: IGI Global. doi:10.4018/978-1-4666-0300-4.ch012

McIntosh, S. (2005). Expanding the classroom: Using online discussion forums in college and professional development courses. In K. St.Amant & P. Zemliansky (Eds.), *Internet-based workplace communications: Industry and academic applications* (pp. 68–87). Hershey, PA: IGI Global. doi:10.4018/978-1-59140-521-4.ch004

McNair, V., & Marshall, K. (2006). How eportfolios support development in early teacher education. In A. Jafari & C. Kaufman (Eds.), *Handbook of research on eportfolios* (pp. 474–485). Hershey, PA: IGI Global. doi:10.4018/978-1-59140-890-1.ch042

McNair, V., & Marshall, K. (2008). How eportfolios support development in early teacher education. In L. Tomei (Ed.), *Online and distance learning: Concepts, methodologies, tools, and applications* (pp. 2130–2137). Hershey, PA: IGI Global. doi:10.4018/978-1-59904-935-9.ch172

McPherson, M., Baptista Nunes, M., Sandars, J., & Kell, C. (2008). Technology and continuing professional education: The reality beyond the hype. In T. Kidd & I. Chen (Eds.), *Social information technology: Connecting society and cultural issues* (pp. 296–312). Hershey, PA: IGI Global. doi:10.4018/978-1-59904-774-4.ch019

Medina, A. L., Tobin, M. T., Pilonieta, P., Chiappone, L. L., & Blanton, W. E. (2012). Application of computer, digital, and telecommunications technologies to the clinical preparation of teachers. In D. Polly, C. Mims, & K. Persichitte (Eds.), *Developing technology-rich teacher education programs: Key issues* (pp. 480–498). Hershey, PA: IGI Global. doi:10.4018/978-1-4666-0014-0.ch031

Meletiou-Mavrotheris, M. (2012). Online communities of practice as vehicles for teacher professional development. In A. Juan, M. Huertas, S. Trenholm, & C. Steegmann (Eds.), *Teaching mathematics online: Emergent technologies and methodologies* (pp. 142–166). Hershey, PA: IGI Global. doi:10.4018/978-1-60960-875-0.ch007

Meltzer, S. T. (2013). The impact of new technologies on professional development. In V. Bryan & V. Wang (Eds.), *Technology use and research approaches for community education and professional development* (pp. 40–52). Hershey, PA: IGI Global. doi:10.4018/978-1-4666-2955-4.ch003

Milman, N. B., Hillarious, M., O'Neill, V., & Walker, B. (2013). Going 11 with laptop computers in an independent, co-educational middle and high school. In J. Keengwe (Ed.), *Pedagogical applications and social effects of mobile technology integration* (pp. 156–174). Hershey, PA: IGI Global. doi:10.4018/978-1-4666-2985-1.ch009

Moon, B. (2012). Teaching teachers: The biggest educational challenge in sub-Saharan Africa. In R. Hogan (Ed.), *Transnational distance learning and building new markets for universities* (pp. 198–209). Hershey, PA: IGI Global. doi:10.4018/978-1-4666-0206-9.ch012

Mørch, A. I., & Andersen, R. (2012). Mutual development: The software engineering context of end-user development. In A. Dwivedi & S. Clarke (Eds.), *End-user computing, development, and software engineering: New challenges* (pp. 103–125). Hershey, PA: IGI Global. doi:10.4018/978-1-4666-0140-6.ch005

Morrow, D., & Bagnall, R. G. (2010). Hybridizing online learning with external interactivity. In F. Wang, J. Fong, & R. Kwan (Eds.), *Handbook of research on hybrid learning models: Advanced tools, technologies, and applications* (pp. 24–41). Hershey, PA: IGI Global. doi:10.4018/978-1-60566-380-7.ch002

Mountain, L. A. (2008). Videoconferencing: An alternative to traditional professional development in the K-12 setting. In D. Newman, J. Falco, S. Silverman, & P. Barbanell (Eds.), *Videoconferencing technology in K-12 instruction: Best practices and trends* (pp. 213–225). Hershey, PA: IGI Global. doi:10.4018/978-1-59904-331-9.ch016

Mouzakis, C., & Bourletidis, C. (2010). A blended learning course for teachers' ongoing professional development in Greece. In J. Yamamoto, J. Kush, R. Lombard, & C. Hertzog (Eds.), *Technology implementation and teacher education: Reflective models* (pp. 1–24). Hershey, PA: IGI Global. doi:10.4018/978-1-61520-897-5.ch001

Mouzakis, C., Tsaknakis, H., & Tziortzioti, C. (2012). Theoretical rationale for designing a blended learning teachers' professional development program. In P. Anastasiades (Ed.), *Blended learning environments for adults: Evaluations and frameworks* (pp. 274–289). Hershey, PA: IGI Global. doi:10.4018/978-1-4666-0939-6.ch014

Murphy, M. G., & Calway, P. B. (2011). Continuing professional development: Work and learning integration for professionals. In P. Keleher, A. Patil, & R. Harreveld (Eds.), *Work-integrated learning in engineering, built environment and technology: Diversity of practice in practice* (pp. 25–51). Hershey, PA: IGI Global. doi:10.4018/978-1-60960-547-6.ch002

Mustapha, W. Z. (2012). The art and science of designing and developing an online English language training module for adult learners. In N. Alias & S. Hashim (Eds.), *Instructional technology research, design and development: Lessons from the field* (pp. 270–286). Hershey, PA: IGI Global. doi:10.4018/978-1-61350-198-6.ch017

Mutohar, A., & Hughes, J. E. (2013). Toward web 2.0 integration in indonesian education: Challenges and planning strategies. In N. Azab (Ed.), *Cases on web 2.0 in developing countries: Studies on implementation, application, and use* (pp. 198–221). Hershey, PA: IGI Global. doi:10.4018/978-1-4666-2515-0.ch008

Newman, D. L., Clure, G., Deyoe, M. M., & Connor, K. A. (2013). Using technology in a studio approach to learning: Results of a five year study of an innovative mobile teaching tool. In J. Keengwe (Ed.), *Pedagogical applications and social effects of mobile technology integration* (pp. 114–132). Hershey, PA: IGI Global. doi:10.4018/978-1-4666-2985-1.ch007

Newman, D. L., Coyle, V. C., & McKenna, L. A. (2013). Changing the face of ELA classrooms: A case study of TPACK professional development. In J. Keengwe (Ed.), *Research perspectives and best practices in educational technology integration* (pp. 270–287). Hershey, PA: IGI Global. doi:10.4018/978-1-4666-2988-2.ch014

Ng, A. W., & Ho, F. (2014). Dynamics of knowledge renewal for professional accountancy under globalization. In P. Ordóñez de Pablos & R. Tennyson (Eds.), *Strategic approaches for human capital management and development in a turbulent economy* (pp. 264–278). Hershey, PA: IGI Global. doi:10.4018/978-1-4666-4530-1.ch017

Ng, F. F. (2005). Knowledge management in higher education and professional development in the construction industry. In A. Kazi (Ed.), *Knowledge management in the construction industry: A socio-technical perspective* (pp. 150–165). Hershey, PA: IGI Global. doi:10.4018/978-1-59140-360-9.ch009

Ng, F. F. (2008). Knowledge management in higher education and professional development in the construction industry. In M. Jennex (Ed.), *Knowledge management: Concepts, methodologies, tools, and applications* (pp. 2355–2368). Hershey, PA: IGI Global. doi:10.4018/978-1-59904-933-5.ch195

Nguyen, V., & Szymanski, M. (2013). A state of the art cart: Visual arts and technology integration in teacher education. In J. Keengwe (Ed.), *Research perspectives and best practices in educational technology integration* (pp. 80–104). Hershey, PA: IGI Global. doi:10.4018/978-1-4666-2988-2.ch005

Niemitz, M., Slough, S., St. John, K., Leckie, R. M., Peart, L., & Klaus, A. (2010). Integrating K-12 hybrid online learning activities in teacher education programs: Reflections from the school of rock expedition. In J. Yamamoto, J. Kush, R. Lombard, & C. Hertzog (Eds.), *Technology implementation and teacher education: Reflective models* (pp. 25–43). Hershey, PA: IGI Global. doi:10.4018/978-1-61520-897-5.ch002

Norris, D. M. (2005). Driving systemic change with e-learning. In C. Howard, J. Boettcher, L. Justice, K. Schenk, P. Rogers, & G. Berg (Eds.), *Encyclopedia of distance learning* (pp. 687–695). Hershey, PA: IGI Global. doi:10.4018/978-1-59140-555-9.ch100

Northrup, P. T., & Harrison, W. T. Jr. (2011). Using learning objects for rapid deployment to mobile learning devices for the U.S. coast guard. In *Instructional design: Concepts, methodologies, tools and applications* (pp. 527–540). Hershey, PA: IGI Global. doi:10.4018/978-1-60960-503-2.ch303

Northrup, P. T., Rasmussen, K. L., & Dawson, D. B. (2004). Designing and reusing learning objects to streamline WBI development. In A. Armstrong (Ed.), *Instructional design in the real world: A view from the trenches* (pp. 184–200). Hershey, PA: IGI Global. doi:10.4018/978-1-59140-150-6.ch011

Northrup, P. T., Rasmussen, K. L., & Dawson, D. B. (2008). Designing and reusing learning objects to streamline WBI development. In S. Clarke (Ed.), *End-user computing: Concepts, methodologies, tools, and applications* (pp. 1–1). Hershey, PA: IGI Global. doi:10.4018/978-1-59904-945-8.ch037

Oigara, J. N. (2013). Integrating technology in teacher education programs. In J. Keengwe (Ed.), *Research perspectives and best practices in educational technology integration* (pp. 28–43). Hershey, PA: IGI Global. doi:10.4018/978-1-4666-2988-2.ch002

Orrill, C. H., & Polly, D. (2012). Technology integration in mathematics: A model for integrating technology through content development. In D. Polly, C. Mims, & K. Persichitte (Eds.), *Developing technology-rich teacher education programs: Key issues* (pp. 337–356). Hershey, PA: IGI Global. doi:10.4018/978-1-4666-0014-0.ch022

Ostashewski, N., & Reid, D. (2013). The networked learning framework: A model for networked professional learning utilizing social networking sites. In J. Keengwe & L. Kyei-Blankson (Eds.), *Virtual mentoring for teachers: Online professional development practices* (pp. 66–83). Hershey, PA: IGI Global. doi:10.4018/978-1-4666-1963-0.ch004

Ostashewski, N., & Reid, D. (2013). The iPad in the classroom: Three implementation cases highlighting pedagogical activities, integration issues, and teacher professional development strategies. In J. Keengwe (Ed.), *Pedagogical applications and social effects of mobile technology integration* (pp. 25–41). Hershey, PA: IGI Global. doi:10.4018/978-1-4666-2985-1.ch002

Pachler, N., Daly, C., & Turvey, A. (2010). Teacher professional development practices: The case of the haringey transformation teachers programme. In J. Lindberg & A. Olofsson (Eds.), *Online learning communities and teacher professional development: Methods for improved education delivery* (pp. 77–95). Hershey, PA: IGI Global. doi:10.4018/978-1-60566-780-5.ch005

Parker, D. (2013). Implementing the professional development program. In S. Wang & T. Hartsell (Eds.), *Technology integration and foundations for effective leadership* (pp. 190–205). Hershey, PA: IGI Global. doi:10.4018/978-1-4666-2656-0.ch011

Payne, A. (2013). Designing a professional development program. In S. Wang & T. Hartsell (Eds.), *Technology integration and foundations for effective leadership* (pp. 171–189). Hershey, PA: IGI Global. doi:10.4018/978-1-4666-2656-0.ch010

Peacock, S., & Dunlop, G. M. (2006). Developing e-learning provision for healthcare professionals' continuing professional development. In J. O'Donoghue (Ed.), *Technology supported learning and teaching: A staff perspective* (pp. 106–124). Hershey, PA: IGI Global. doi:10.4018/978-1-59140-962-5.ch007

Piecka, D. C., Ruberg, L., Ruckman, C., & Fullwood, D. (2012). NASATalk as a discovery learning space: Self-discovery learning opportunities. In S. Hai-Jew (Ed.), *Constructing self-discovery learning spaces online: Scaffolding and decision making technologies* (pp. 49–71). Hershey, PA: IGI Global. doi:10.4018/978-1-61350-320-1.ch004

Pilkington, R. (2010). Building practitioner skills in personalised elearning: Messages for professional development. In J. O'Donoghue (Ed.), *Technology-supported environments for personalized learning: Methods and case studies* (pp. 167–184). Hershey, PA: IGI Global. doi:10.4018/978-1-60566-884-0.ch010

Polly, D. (2011). Preparing teachers to integrate technology effectively: The case of higher-order thinking skills (HOTS). In S. D'Agustino (Ed.), *Adaptation, resistance and access to instructional technologies: Assessing future trends in education* (pp. 395–409). Hershey, PA: IGI Global. doi:10.4018/978-1-61692-854-4.ch023

Polly, D. (2013). Designing and teaching an online elementary mathematics methods course: Promises, barriers, and implications. In R. Hartshorne, T. Heafner, & T. Petty (Eds.), *Teacher education programs and online learning tools: Innovations in teacher preparation* (pp. 335–356). Hershey, PA: IGI Global. doi:10.4018/978-1-4666-1906-7.ch018

Polly, D., Grant, M. M., & Gikas, J. (2011). Supporting technology integration in higher education: The role of professional development. In D. Surry, R. Gray Jr, & J. Stefurak (Eds.), *Technology integration in higher education: Social and organizational aspects* (pp. 58–71). Hershey, PA: IGI Global. doi:10.4018/978-1-60960-147-8.ch005

Polly, D., Mims, C., & McCombs, B. (2012). Designing district-wide technology-rich professional development. In I. Chen & D. McPheeters (Eds.), *Cases on educational technology integration in urban schools* (pp. 236–243). Hershey, PA: IGI Global. doi:10.4018/978-1-61350-492-5.ch033

Powell, E. (2009). Facilitating reflective teaching: Video-stimulated reflective dialogues as a professional development process. In V. Wang (Ed.), *Handbook of research on e-learning applications for career and technical education: Technologies for vocational training* (pp. 100–111). Hershey, PA: IGI Global. doi:10.4018/978-1-60566-739-3.ch008

Prisk, J., & Lee, K. (2012). How to utilize an online community of practice (CoP) to enhance innovation in teaching and learning. In V. Wang (Ed.), *Encyclopedia of e-leadership, counseling and training* (pp. 532–544). Hershey, PA: IGI Global. doi:10.4018/978-1-61350-068-2.ch039

Prpic, J. K., & Moore, G. (2012). E-portfolios as a quantitative and qualitative means of demonstrating learning outcomes and competencies in engineering. In K. Yusof, N. Azli, A. Kosnin, S. Yusof, & Y. Yusof (Eds.), *Outcome-based science, technology, engineering, and mathematics education: Innovative practices* (pp. 124–154). Hershey, PA: IGI Global. doi:10.4018/978-1-4666-1809-1.ch007

Pullman, N., & Streff, K. (2009). Creating a security education, training, and awareness program. In M. Gupta & R. Sharman (Eds.), *Handbook of research on social and organizational liabilities in information security* (pp. 325–345). Hershey, PA: IGI Global. doi:10.4018/978-1-60566-132-2.ch020

Quinton, S. (2007). Delivering online expertise, online. In M. Keppell (Ed.), *Instructional design: Case studies in communities of practice* (pp. 193–214). Hershey, PA: IGI Global. doi:10.4018/978-1-59904-322-7.ch010

Reali, A. M., Tancredi, R. M., & Mizukami, M. D. (2012). Online mentoring as a tool for professional development and change of novice and experienced teachers: A Brazilian experience. In V. Dennen & J. Myers (Eds.), *Virtual professional development and informal learning via social networks* (pp. 203–218). Hershey, PA: IGI Global. doi:10.4018/978-1-4666-1815-2.ch012

Redmon, R. J. Jr. (2009). E-mail reflection groups as collaborative action research. In J. Salmons & L. Wilson (Eds.), *Handbook of research on electronic collaboration and organizational synergy* (pp. 349–361). Hershey, PA: IGI Global. doi:10.4018/978-1-60566-106-3.ch023

Rice, M. L., & Bain, C. (2013). Planning and implementation of a 21st century classroom project. In A. Benson, J. Moore, & S. Williams van Rooij (Eds.), *Cases on educational technology planning, design, and implementation: A project management perspective* (pp. 76–92). Hershey, PA: IGI Global. doi:10.4018/978-1-4666-4237-9.ch005

Richardson, S. L., Barnes, S. L., & Torain, D. S. (2012). Using technology to support algebra teaching and assessment: A teacher development case study. In I. Chen & D. McPheeters (Eds.), *Cases on educational technology integration in urban schools* (pp. 224–229). Hershey, PA: IGI Global. doi:10.4018/978-1-61350-492-5.ch031

Rieber, L. P., Francom, G. M., & Jensen, L. J. (2011). Feeling like a first year teacher: Toward becoming a successful online instructor. In D. Surry, R. Gray Jr, & J. Stefurak (Eds.), *Technology integration in higher education: Social and organizational aspects* (pp. 42–57). Hershey, PA: IGI Global. doi:10.4018/978-1-60960-147-8.ch004

Ring, G., & Foti, S. (2006). Using eportfolios to facilitate professional development among pre-service teachers. In A. Jafari & C. Kaufman (Eds.), *Handbook of research on eportfolios* (pp. 340–357). Hershey, PA: IGI Global. doi:10.4018/978-1-59140-890-1.ch031

Riverin, S. (2009). Blended learning and professional development in the K-12 sector. In E. Stacey & P. Gerbic (Eds.), *Effective blended learning practices: Evidence-based perspectives in ICT-facilitated education* (pp. 182–202). Hershey, PA: IGI Global. doi:10.4018/978-1-60566-296-1.ch010

Robertshaw, M. B., Leary, H., Walker, A., Bloxham, K., & Recker, M. (2009). Reciprocal mentoring "in the wild": A retrospective, comparative case study of ICT teacher professional development. In E. Stacey & P. Gerbic (Eds.), *Effective blended learning practices: evidence-based perspectives in ICT-facilitated education* (pp. 280–297). Hershey, PA: IGI Global. doi:10.4018/978-1-60566-296-1.ch015

Robertson, L., & Hardman, W. (2013). More than changing classrooms: Professors' transitions to synchronous e-teaching. In P. Ordóñez de Pablos & R. Tennyson (Eds.), *Strategic role of tertiary education and technologies for sustainable competitive advantage* (pp. 156–175). Hershey, PA: IGI Global. doi:10.4018/978-1-4666-4233-1.ch007

Rockland, R., Kimmel, H., Carpinelli, J., Hirsch, L. S., & Burr-Alexander, L. (2012). Medical robotics in K-12 education. In B. Barker, G. Nugent, N. Grandgenett, & V. Adamchuk (Eds.), *Robots in K-12 education: A new technology for learning* (pp. 120–140). Hershey, PA: IGI Global. doi:10.4018/978-1-4666-0182-6.ch006

Rockland, R., Kimmel, H., Carpinelli, J., Hirsch, L. S., & Burr-Alexander, L. (2014). Medical robotics in K-12 education. In Robotics: Concepts, methodologies, tools, and applications (pp. 1096-1115). Hershey, PA: IGI Global. doi:10.4018/978-1-4666-4607-0.ch053

Rodesiler, L., & Tripp, L. (2012). It's all about personal connections: Pre-service English teachers' experiences engaging in networked learning. In V. Dennen & J. Myers (Eds.), *Virtual professional development and informal learning via social networks* (pp. 185–202). Hershey, PA: IGI Global. doi:10.4018/978-1-4666-1815-2.ch011

Ronau, R. N., & Rakes, C. R. (2012). A comprehensive framework for teacher knowledge (CFTK): Complexity of individual aspects and their interactions. In R. Ronau, C. Rakes, & M. Niess (Eds.), *Educational technology, teacher knowledge, and classroom impact: A research handbook on frameworks and approaches* (pp. 59–102). Hershey, PA: IGI Global. doi:10.4018/978-1-60960-750-0.ch004

Rosen, Y., & Rimor, R. (2013). Teaching and assessing problem solving in online collaborative environment. In R. Hartshorne, T. Heafner, & T. Petty (Eds.), *Teacher education programs and online learning tools: Innovations in teacher preparation* (pp. 82–97). Hershey, PA: IGI Global. doi:10.4018/978-1-4666-1906-7.ch005

Ruberg, L., Calinger, M., & Howard, B. C. (2010). Evaluating educational technologies: Historical milestones. In L. Tomei (Ed.), *ICTs for modern educational and instructional advancement: New approaches to teaching* (pp. 285–297). Hershey, PA: IGI Global. doi:10.4018/978-1-60566-936-6.ch024

Russell, D. L. (2007). The mediated action of educational reform: An inquiry into collaboative online professional development. In R. Sharma & S. Mishra (Eds.), *Cases on global e-learning practices: Successes and pitfalls* (pp. 108–122). Hershey, PA: IGI Global. doi:10.4018/978-1-59904-340-1.ch009

Sáenz, J., Aramburu, N., & Rivera, O. (2010). Exploring the links between structural capital, knowledge sharing, innovation capability and business competitiveness: An empirical study. In D. Harorimana (Ed.), *Cultural implications of knowledge sharing, management and transfer: Identifying competitive advantage* (pp. 321–354). Hershey, PA: IGI Global. doi:10.4018/978-1-60566-790-4.ch015

Sales, G. C. (2009). Preparing teachers to teach online. In P. Rogers, G. Berg, J. Boettcher, C. Howard, L. Justice, & K. Schenk (Eds.), *Encyclopedia of distance learning* (2nd ed.; pp. 1665–1672). Hershey, PA: IGI Global. doi:10.4018/978-1-60566-198-8.ch244

Sales, G. C. (2011). Preparing teachers to teach online. In *Instructional design: Concepts, methodologies, tools and applications* (pp. 8–17). Hershey, PA: IGI Global. doi:10.4018/978-1-60960-503-2.ch102

Sampson, D. G., & Kallonis, P. (2012). 3D virtual classroom simulations for supporting school teachers' continuing professional development. In J. Jia (Ed.), *Educational stages and interactive learning: From kindergarten to workplace training* (pp. 427–450). Hershey, PA: IGI Global. doi:10.4018/978-1-4666-0137-6.ch023

Sari, E., & Lim, C. P. (2012). Online learning community: building the professional capacity of Indonesian teachers. In J. Jia (Ed.), *Educational stages and interactive learning: From kindergarten to workplace training* (pp. 451–467). Hershey, PA: IGI Global. doi:10.4018/978-1-4666-0137-6.ch024

Scheckler, R. (2010). Case studies from the inquiry learning forum: Stories reaching beyond the edges. In J. Lindberg & A. Olofsson (Eds.), *Online learning communities and teacher professional development: Methods for improved education delivery* (pp. 42–59). Hershey, PA: IGI Global. doi:10.4018/978-1-60566-780-5.ch003

Schifter, C. (2008). "Making teachers better": A brief history of professional development for teachers. In C. Schifter (Ed.), *Infusing technology into the classroom: Continuous practice improvement* (pp. 41–57). Hershey, PA: IGI Global. doi:10.4018/978-1-59904-765-2.ch003

Schifter, C. (2008). Effecting change in the classroom through professional development. In C. Schifter (Ed.), *Infusing technology into the classroom: Continuous practice improvement* (pp. 259–274). Hershey, PA: IGI Global. doi:10.4018/978-1-59904-765-2.ch014

Schifter, C. (2008). Continuous practice improvement. In C. Schifter (Ed.), *Infusing technology into the classroom: Continuous practice improvement* (pp. 58–86). Hershey, PA: IGI Global. doi:10.4018/978-1-59904-765-2.ch004

Schifter, C. (2008). Finger painting to digital painting: First grade. In C. Schifter (Ed.), *Infusing technology into the classroom: Continuous practice improvement* (pp. 109–126). Hershey, PA: IGI Global. doi:10.4018/978-1-59904-765-2.ch006

Schrader, P., Strudler, N., Asay, L., Graves, T., Pennell, S. L., & Stewart, S. (2012). The pathway to Nevada's future: A case of statewide technology integration and professional development. In I. Chen & D. McPheeters (Eds.), *Cases on educational technology integration in urban schools* (pp. 204–223). Hershey, PA: IGI Global. doi:10.4018/978-1-61350-492-5.ch030

Scott, D. E., & Scott, S. (2010). Innovations in the use of technology and teacher professional development. In J. Lindberg & A. Olofsson (Eds.), *Online learning communities and teacher professional development: Methods for improved education delivery* (pp. 169–189). Hershey, PA: IGI Global. doi:10.4018/978-1-60566-780-5.ch010

Scott, D. E., & Scott, S. (2012). Multi-faceted professional development models designed to enhance teaching and learning within universities. In A. Olofsson & J. Lindberg (Eds.), *Informed design of educational technologies in higher education: Enhanced learning and teaching* (pp. 412–435). Hershey, PA: IGI Global. doi:10.4018/978-1-61350-080-4.ch021

Scott, S. (2010). The theory and practice divide in relation to teacher professional development. In J. Lindberg & A. Olofsson (Eds.), *Online learning communities and teacher professional development: Methods for improved education delivery* (pp. 20–40). Hershey, PA: IGI Global. doi:10.4018/978-1-60566-780-5.ch002

Semich, G. W., & Gibbons, B. (2011). The professional development school: A building block for training public school faculty on new technologies. In L. Tomei (Ed.), *Online courses and ICT in education: Emerging practices and applications* (pp. 99–108). Hershey, PA: IGI Global. doi:10.4018/978-1-60960-150-8.ch008

Shambaugh, N. (2013). A professional development school technology integration and research plan. In A. Ritzhaupt & S. Kumar (Eds.), *Cases on educational technology implementation for facilitating learning* (pp. 45–68). Hershey, PA: IGI Global. doi:10.4018/978-1-4666-3676-7.ch003

Sherman, G., & Byers, A. (2011). Electronic portfolios in the professional development of educators. In S. D'Agustino (Ed.), *Adaptation, resistance and access to instructional technologies: Assessing future trends in education* (pp. 429–444). Hershey, PA: IGI Global. doi:10.4018/978-1-61692-854-4.ch025

Simelane, S. (2010). Professional development programme in the use of educational technology to implement technology-enhanced courses successfully. In S. Mukerji & P. Tripathi (Eds.), *Cases on technology enhanced learning through collaborative opportunities* (pp. 91–110). Hershey, PA: IGI Global. doi:10.4018/978-1-61520-751-0.ch006

Skibba, K. (2013). Adult learning influence on faculty learning cycle: Individual and shared reflections while learning to teach online lead to pedagogical transformations. In J. Keengwe & L. Kyei-Blankson (Eds.), *Virtual mentoring for teachers: Online professional development practices* (pp. 263–291). Hershey, PA: IGI Global. doi:10.4018/978-1-4666-1963-0.ch014

Skinner, L. B., Witte, M. M., & Witte, J. E. (2010). Challenges and opportunities in career and technical education. In V. Wang (Ed.), *Definitive readings in the history, philosophy, theories and practice of career and technical education* (pp. 197–215). Hershey, PA: IGI Global. doi:10.4018/978-1-61520-747-3.ch012

Slabon, W. A., & Richards, R. L. (2012). Story-based professional development: Using a conflict management wiki. In V. Dennen & J. Myers (Eds.), *Virtual professional development and informal learning via social networks* (pp. 256–275). Hershey, PA: IGI Global. doi:10.4018/978-1-4666-1815-2.ch015

Spaulding, D. T. (2008). Virtual field trips: Advantages and disadvantages for educators and recommendation for professional development. In D. Newman, J. Falco, S. Silverman, & P. Barbanell (Eds.), *Videoconferencing technology in K-12 instruction: Best practices and trends* (pp. 191–199). Hershey, PA: IGI Global. doi:10.4018/978-1-59904-331-9.ch014

Speaker, R. B., Levitt, G., & Grubaugh, S. (2013). Professional development in a virtual world. In J. Keengwe & L. Kyei-Blankson (Eds.), *Virtual mentoring for teachers: Online professional development practices* (pp. 122–148). Hershey, PA: IGI Global. doi:10.4018/978-1-4666-1963-0.ch007

Stacey, E., & Gerbic, P. (2009). Introduction to blended learning practices. In E. Stacey & P. Gerbic (Eds.), *Effective blended learning practices: Evidence-based perspectives in ICT-facilitated education* (pp. 1–19). Hershey, PA: IGI Global. doi:10.4018/978-1-60566-296-1.ch001

Stanfill, D. (2012). Standards-based educational technology professional development. In V. Wang (Ed.), *Encyclopedia of e-leadership, counseling and training* (pp. 819–834). Hershey, PA: IGI Global. doi:10.4018/978-1-61350-068-2.ch060

Steel, C., & Andrews, T. (2012). Re-imagining teaching for technology-enriched learning spaces: An academic development model. In M. Keppell, K. Souter, & M. Riddle (Eds.), *Physical and virtual learning spaces in higher education: Concepts for the modern learning environment* (pp. 242–265). Hershey, PA: IGI Global. doi:10.4018/978-1-60960-114-0.ch015

Stewart, C., Horarik, S., & Wolodko, K. (2013). Maximising technology usage in research synthesis of higher education professional development research. In J. Willems, B. Tynan, & R. James (Eds.), *Global challenges and perspectives in blended and distance learning* (pp. 1–16). Hershey, PA: IGI Global. doi:10.4018/978-1-4666-3978-2.ch001

Stieha, V., & Raider-Roth, M. (2012). Disrupting relationships: A catalyst for growth. In J. Faulkner (Ed.), *Disrupting pedagogies in the knowledge society: Countering conservative norms with creative approaches* (pp. 16–31). Hershey, PA: IGI Global. doi:10.4018/978-1-61350-495-6.ch002

Stockero, S. L. (2010). Serving rural teachers using synchronous online professional development. In J. Yamamoto, J. Leight, S. Winterton, & C. Penny (Eds.), *Technology leadership in teacher education: Integrated solutions and experiences* (pp. 111–124). Hershey, PA: IGI Global. doi:10.4018/978-1-61520-899-9.ch007

Stylianou-Georgiou, A., Vrasidas, C., Christodoulou, N., Zembylas, M., & Landone, E. (2006). Technologies challenging literacy: Hypertext, community building, reflection, and critical literacy. In L. Tan Wee Hin & R. Subramaniam (Eds.), *Handbook of research on literacy in technology at the K-12 level* (pp. 21–33). Hershey, PA: IGI Global. doi:10.4018/978-1-59140-494-1.ch002

Szecsy, E. M. (2011). Building knowledge without borders: Using ICT to develop a binational education research community. In G. Kurubacak & T. Yuzer (Eds.), *Handbook of research on transformative online education and liberation: Models for social equality* (pp. 67–85). Hershey, PA: IGI Global. doi:10.4018/978-1-60960-046-4.ch004

Tawfik, A. A., Reiseck, C., & Richter, R. (2013). Project management methods for the implementation of an online faculty development course. In A. Benson, J. Moore, & S. Williams van Rooij (Eds.), *Cases on educational technology planning, design, and implementation: A project management perspective* (pp. 153–167). Hershey, PA: IGI Global. doi:10.4018/978-1-4666-4237-9.ch009

Taylor, D. B., Hartshorne, R., Eneman, S., Wilkins, P., & Polly, D. (2012). Lessons learned from the implementation of a technology-focused professional learning community. In D. Polly, C. Mims, & K. Persichitte (Eds.), *Developing technology-rich teacher education programs: Key issues* (pp. 535–550). Hershey, PA: IGI Global. doi:10.4018/978-1-4666-0014-0.ch034

Tedford, D. (2010). Perspectives on the influences of social capital upon internet usage of rural Guatemalan teachers. In S. Mukerji & P. Tripathi (Eds.), *Cases on technological adaptability and transnational learning: Issues and challenges* (pp. 218–243). Hershey, PA: IGI Global. doi:10.4018/978-1-61520-779-4.ch012

Terantino, J. M. (2012). An activity theoretical approach to examining virtual professional development and informal learning via social networks. In V. Dennen & J. Myers (Eds.), *Virtual professional development and informal learning via social networks* (pp. 60–74). Hershey, PA: IGI Global. doi:10.4018/978-1-4666-1815-2.ch004

Thompson, T. L., & Kanuka, H. (2009). Establishing communities of practice for effective and sustainable professional development for blended learning. In E. Stacey & P. Gerbic (Eds.), *Effective blended learning practices: Evidence-based perspectives in ICT-facilitated education* (pp. 144–162). Hershey, PA: IGI Global. doi:10.4018/978-1-60566-296-1.ch008

Thornton, J. (2010). Framing pedagogy, diminishing technology: Teachers experience of online learning software. In H. Song & T. Kidd (Eds.), *Handbook of research on human performance and instructional technology* (pp. 263–283). Hershey, PA: IGI Global. doi:10.4018/978-1-60566-782-9.ch016

Thornton, K., & Yoong, P. (2010). The application of blended action learning to leadership development: A case study. In P. Yoong (Ed.), *Leadership in the digital enterprise: Issues and challenges* (pp. 163–180). Hershey, PA: IGI Global. doi:10.4018/978-1-60566-958-8.ch012

Ting, A., & Jones, P. D. (2010). Using free source eportfolios to empower ESL teachers in collaborative peer reflection. In J. Yamamoto, J. Kush, R. Lombard, & C. Hertzog (Eds.), *Technology implementation and teacher education: Reflective models* (pp. 93–107). Hershey, PA: IGI Global. doi:10.4018/978-1-61520-897-5.ch006

Tomei, L. A. (2008). The KARPE model revisited – An updated investigation for differentiating teaching and learning with technology in higher education. In L. Tomei (Ed.), *Adapting information and communication technologies for effective education* (pp. 30–40). Hershey, PA: IGI Global. doi:10.4018/978-1-59904-922-9.ch003

Torrisi-Steele, G. (2005). Toward effective use of multimedia technologies in education. In S. Mishra & R. Sharma (Eds.), *Interactive multimedia in education and training* (pp. 25–46). Hershey, PA: IGI Global. doi:10.4018/978-1-59140-393-7.ch002

Torrisi-Steele, G. (2008). Toward effective use of multimedia technologies in education. In M. Syed (Ed.), *Multimedia technologies: Concepts, methodologies, tools, and applications* (pp. 1651–1667). Hershey, PA: IGI Global. doi:10.4018/978-1-59904-953-3.ch118

Trujillo, K. M., Wiburg, K., Savic, M., & McKee, K. (2013). Teachers learn how to effectively integrate mobile technology by teaching students using math snacks animations and games. In J. Keengwe (Ed.), *Pedagogical applications and social effects of mobile technology integration* (pp. 98–113). Hershey, PA: IGI Global. doi:10.4018/978-1-4666-2985-1.ch006

Tynan, B., & Barnes, C. (2010). Web 2.0 and professional development of academic staff. In M. Lee & C. McLoughlin (Eds.), *Web 2.0-based e-learning: Applying social informatics for tertiary teaching* (pp. 365–379). Hershey, PA: IGI Global. doi:10.4018/978-1-60566-294-7.ch019

Tynan, B., & Barnes, C. (2012). Web 2.0 and professional development of academic staff. In *Virtual learning environments: Concepts, methodologies, tools and applications* (pp. 94–108). Hershey, PA: IGI Global. doi:10.4018/978-1-4666-0011-9.ch107

Uehara, D. L. (2007). Research in the Pacific: Utilizing technology to inform and improve teacher practice. In Y. Inoue (Ed.), *Technology and diversity in higher education: New challenges* (pp. 213–232). Hershey, PA: IGI Global. doi:10.4018/978-1-59904-316-6.ch011

Velez-Solic, A., & Banas, J. R. (2013). Professional development for online educators: Problems, predictions, and best practices. In J. Keengwe & L. Kyei-Blankson (Eds.), *Virtual mentoring for teachers: Online professional development practices* (pp. 204–226). Hershey, PA: IGI Global. doi:10.4018/978-1-4666-1963-0.ch011

Venkatesh, V., Bures, E., Davidson, A., Wade, C. A., Lysenko, L., & Abrami, P. C. (2013). Electronic portfolio encouraging active and reflective learning: A case study in improving academic self-regulation through innovative use of educational technologies. In A. Ritzhaupt & S. Kumar (Eds.), *Cases on educational technology implementation for facilitating learning* (pp. 341–376). Hershey, PA: IGI Global. doi:10.4018/978-1-4666-3676-7.ch019

Watson, C. E., Zaldivar, M., & Summers, T. (2010). ePortfolios for learning, assessment, and professional development. In R. Donnelly, J. Harvey, & K. O'Rourke (Eds.), Critical design and effective tools for e-learning in higher education: Theory into practice (pp. 157-175). Hershey, PA: IGI Global. doi:10.4018/978-1-61520-879-1.ch010

Whitehouse, P., McCloskey, E., & Ketelhut, D. J. (2010). Online pedagogy design and development: New models for 21st century online teacher professional development. In J. Lindberg & A. Olofsson (Eds.), *Online learning communities and teacher professional development: Methods for improved education delivery* (pp. 247–262). Hershey, PA: IGI Global. doi:10.4018/978-1-60566-780-5.ch014

Williams, I. M., & Olaniran, B. A. (2012). Professional development through web 2.0 collaborative applications. In V. Dennen & J. Myers (Eds.), *Virtual professional development and informal learning via social networks* (pp. 1–24). Hershey, PA: IGI Global. doi:10.4018/978-1-4666-1815-2.ch001

Wilson, A., & Christie, D. (2010). Realising the potential of virtual environments: A challenge for Scottish teachers. In J. Lindberg & A. Olofsson (Eds.), *Online learning communities and teacher professional development: Methods for improved education delivery* (pp. 96–113). Hershey, PA: IGI Global. doi:10.4018/978-1-60566-780-5.ch006

Wilson, G. (2009). Case studies of ICT-enhanced blended learning and implications for professional development. In E. Stacey & P. Gerbic (Eds.), *Effective blended learning practices: Evidence-based perspectives in ICT-facilitated education* (pp. 239–258). Hershey, PA: IGI Global. doi:10.4018/978-1-60566-296-1.ch013

Witt, L. A., & Burke, L. A. (2003). Using cognitive ability and personality to select information technology professionals. In M. Mahmood (Ed.), *Advanced topics in end user computing* (Vol. 2, pp. 1–17). Hershey, PA: IGI Global. doi:10.4018/978-1-59140-065-3.ch001

Wynne, C. W. (2014). Cultivating leaders from within: Transforming workers into leaders. In S. Mukerji & P. Tripathi (Eds.), *Handbook of research on transnational higher education* (pp. 42–58). Hershey, PA: IGI Global. doi:10.4018/978-1-4666-4458-8.ch003

Yakavenka, H. (2012). Developing professional competencies through international peer learning communities. In V. Dennen & J. Myers (Eds.), *Virtual professional development and informal learning via social networks* (pp. 134–154). Hershey, PA: IGI Global. doi:10.4018/978-1-4666-1815-2.ch008

Yamamoto, J., Linaberger, M., & Forbes, L. S. (2005). Mentoring and technology integration for teachers. In D. Carbonara (Ed.), *Technology literacy applications in learning environments* (pp. 161–170). Hershey, PA: IGI Global. doi:10.4018/978-1-59140-479-8.ch012

Yukawa, J. (2011). Telementoring and project-based learning: An integrated model for 21st century skills. In D. Scigliano (Ed.), *Telementoring in the K-12 classroom: Online communication technologies for learning* (pp. 31–56). Hershey, PA: IGI Global. doi:10.4018/978-1-61520-861-6.ch003

Zellermayer, M., Mor, N., & Heilweil, I. (2009). The intersection of theory, tools and tasks in a postgraduate learning environment. In C. Payne (Ed.), *Information technology and constructivism in higher education: Progressive learning frameworks* (pp. 319–333). Hershey, PA: IGI Global. doi:10.4018/978-1-60566-654-9.ch021

Zuidema, L. A. (2008). Parawork. In P. Zemliansky & K. St.Amant (Eds.), *Handbook of research on virtual workplaces and the new nature of business practices* (pp. 81–97). Hershey, PA: IGI Global. doi:10.4018/978-1-59904-893-2.ch007

Zygouris-Coe, V. I. (2013). A model for online instructor training, support, and professional development. In J. Keengwe & L. Kyei-Blankson (Eds.), *Virtual mentoring for teachers: Online professional development practices* (pp. 97–121). Hershey, PA: IGI Global. doi:10.4018/978-1-4666-1963-0.ch006

Zygouris-Coe, V. I., & Swan, B. (2010). Challenges of online teacher professional development communities: A statewide case study in the United States. In J. Lindberg & A. Olofsson (Eds.), *Online learning communities and teacher professional development: Methods for improved education delivery* (pp. 114–133). Hershey, PA: IGI Global. doi:10.4018/978-1-60566-780-5.ch007

Compilation of References

Abadin, D. D. S. C., & Ángela, V. C. (2010). Increasing and Alternative Communication. CEAPAT.

Abdoli-Sejzi, A. (2015). Augmented reality and virtual learning environment. *Journal of Applied Sciences Research, 11*(8), 1–5.

Abreu, M. O. (2013). *Design and preparation of evaluation guides*. University Autonomous of the State of Mexico.

ACCESIBLE. (n.d.). *Home page of the ACCESSIBLE project*. Retrieved July 20, 2007, from http://www.accessible-eu.org/

Agrebi, S., & Jallais, J. (2015). Explain the intention to use smartphones for mobile shopping. *Journal of Retailing and Consumer Services, 22*, 16–23. doi:10.1016/j.jretconser.2014.09.003

Akkoyunlu, B. (1996). The influence of computer literacy competencies and existing curriculum programs on student achievement and attitudes. *Hacettepe University Education Faculty Journal, 12*(12), 127–134.

Al-Azawi, R., Ayesh, A., & Al-Obaidy, M. (2014). Towards agent-based agile approach for game development methodology. *Proceeding of the 2014 World Congress on Computer Applications and Information Systems* (WCCAIS). 10.1109/WCCAIS.2014.6916626

Alcedo & Chacón. (2011). *El Enfoque Lúdico como Estrategia Metodológica para Promover el Aprendizaje del Inglés en Niños de Educación Primaria*. SABER. Revista Multidisciplinaria del Consejo de Investigación de la Universidad de Oriente.

Aldrich, H. E. (2007). *Organizations and Environments*. Stanford University Press.

Alexander, P. A., Graham, S., & Harris, K. R. (1998). A perspective on strategy research: Progress and prospects. *Educational Psychology Review, 10*(2), 129–154. doi:10.1023/A:1022185502996

Alkhamisi, A. O., & Monowar, M. M. (2013). Rise of Augmented Reality: Current and Future Application Areas. *International Journal of Internet and Distributed Systems, 1*(04), 25–34. doi:10.4236/ijids.2013.14005

American Psychiatric Association. (2013). *Diagnostic and statistical manual of mental disorders* (5th ed.). Washington, DC: Author.

Anderton, K. (2016, November 14). *Augmented reality, the future, and Pokémon Go*. Retrieved from https://www.forbes.com/sites/kevinanderton/2016/11/14/augmented-reality-the-future-and-pokemon-go-infographic/#72acaa6b7e98

Andreas, W. (1999, May 22). Wake up call. *The Scotsman*, 1-2.

Andrei, E. (2017, June). Technology in teaching English language learners: The case of three middle school teachers. *TESOL Journal*, *8*(2), 409–431. doi:10.1002/tesj.280

Anjana, A. (1997, January 27). Accidents and the human factor. *The Times*, 17.

Aslan, S., & Balci, O. (2015). GAMED: Digital Educational Game Development Methodology. *Simulation*, *91*(4), 307–319. doi:10.1177/0037549715572673

Ayer, S. K., Messner, J. I., & Anumba, C. J. (2016). Augmented Reality Gaming in Sustainable Design Education. *Journal of Architectural Engineering*, *22*(1), 04015012. doi:10.1061/(ASCE)AE.1943-5568.0000195

Azuma, R. (2015). Location-Based Mixed and Augmented Reality Storytelling. In Fundamentals of Wearable Computers and Augmented Reality (pp. 259-276). Academic Press. doi:10.1201/b18703-15

Azuma, R. T. (1997). A Survey of Augmented Reality. *Presence (Cambridge, Mass.)*, *6*(4), 355–385. doi:10.1162/pres.1997.6.4.355

Azuma, R., Baillot, Y., Behringer, R., Feiner, S., Julier, S., & MacIntyre, B. (2001). Recent advances in augmented reality. *IEEE Comput Graph*, *21*(6), 34–47. doi:10.1109/38.963459

Bacca, J., Baldiris, S., Fabregat, R., & Graf, S., & Kinshuk. (2014). Augmented Reality Trends in Education: A Systematic Review of Research and Applications. *Journal of Educational Technology & Society*, *17*(4), 133–149.

Bacca, J., Baldiris, S., Fabregat, R., & Graf, S., & Kinshuk. (2014). Augmented reality trends in education: A systematic review of research applications. *Journal of Educational Technology & Society*, *17*(4), 133–149.

Bailey, K. (2008). *Methods of social research*. Simon and Schuster.

Bardovi-Harlig, K. (2013). Developing L2 pragmatics. *Language Learning*, *63*(1), 68–86. doi:10.1111/j.1467-9922.2012.00738.x

Barsom, E., Graafland, M., & Schijven, M. (2016). Systematic review on the effectiveness of augmented reality applications in medical training. *Surgical Endoscopy*, *30*(10), 4174–4183. doi:10.100700464-016-4800-6 PMID:26905573

Beard, A. N., Thompson, P., Santos-Reyes, J., & Goodwin, J. (2005). *Risk assessment and safety management module*. Edinburgh, UK: H-W University.

Beaudin, J., Intille, S., Tapia, E. M., Rockinson, R., & Morris, M. (2007). *Context-sensitive microlearning of a foreign language vocabulary on a mobile device*. Retrieved from http://web.media.mit.edu/~intille/papers-files/BeaudinIntilleETAL07.pdf

Bello, R. M. A., Mora, L. M. A., Alberto, P. F., Sánchez, P. C. R., & Carmona, F. M. E. (2016), CompHi: History of Computers with Augmented Reality. *Revista Revista CiBIyT, 11*(31), 17-20.

Bell, R., Maeng, J., & Binns, I. (2013). Learning in context: Technology integration in a teacher preparation program informed by situated learning theory. *Journal of Research in Science Education, 50*(3), 348–379.

Benda, P., Ulman, M., & Smejkalová, M. (2015). Augmented reality as a working aid for intellectually disabled persons for work in horticulture. *Ecological Informatics, 7*(4), 31–37.

Benton, L., Johnson, H., Ashwin, E., Brosnan, M., & Grawemeyer, B. (2012). Developing IDEAS: supporting children with autism within a participatory design team. In *CHI '12 Proceedings of the SIGCHI Conference on Human Factors in Computing Systems*. Association for Computing Machinery (ACM). 10.1145/2207676.2208650

Berlyne, D. E. (1970). Novelty, Complexity, and Hedonic Value. *Perception & Psychophysics, 8*(November), 279–286. doi:10.3758/BF03212593

Bertalanffy, I. Von. (1981). A systems view of man: collected essays. Boulder, Co: Westview Press.

Bhamra, T., & Lofthouse, V. (2007). *Design for sustainability: a practical approach*. Gower Publishing, Ltd.

Billinghurst, M. (2002). Augmented reality in education. *New Horizons for Learning, 12*.

Billinghurst, M., Kato, H., & Poupyrev, I. (2001). The MagicBook-moving seamlessly between reality and virtuality. *IEEE Computer Graphics and Applications, 21*(3), 6–8.

Billinghurst, M., Kato, H., & Poupyrev, I. (2008). Tangible augmented reality. In *Proceedings of the Conference and Exhibition on Computer Graphics & Interactive Techniques in Asia* (pp. 1-11). ACM.

Bishop, B. (2012). Analysis of reference transactions to inform library applications (apps). *Library & Information Science Research, 34*(4), 265–270. doi:10.1016/j.lisr.2012.06.001

Black, D. (1989, March 20). The human element at the core of disaster. *The Independent*.

Bloch, P. H., Brunel, F. F., & Arnold, T. J. (2003). Individual differences in the centrality of visual product aesthetics: Concept and measurement. *The Journal of Consumer Research, 29*(4), 551–565. doi:10.1086/346250

Boehm, B. W. (1988). A Spiral Model of Software Development and Enhancement. *Computer, 21*(5), 61–72. doi:10.1109/2.59

Bottani, E., & Rizzi, A. (2006). Strategic management of logistics service: A fuzzy QFD approach. *International Journal of Production Economics, 103*(2), 585–599. doi:10.1016/j.ijpe.2005.11.006

Bower, M., Howe, C., McCredie, N., Robinson, A., & Grover, D. (2014). Augmented reality in education-cases, places, and potentials. *Educational Media International, 51*(1), 1–15. doi:10.1080/09523987.2014.889400

Bowman, D., Kruijff, E., LaVoila, J., & Poupyrev, I. (2005). *3D User Interfaces: Theory and Practice*. Addison-Wesley.

Bravo, E., Santana, M., & Rodon, J. (2015). Information systems and performance: The role of technology, the task and the individual. *Journal Behaviour and Information Technology., 1*(3), 247–260. doi:10.1080/0144929X.2014.934287

Brinkman, B., & Brinkman, S. (2013). AR in the library: A pilot study of multi-target acquisition usability. *2013 IEEE international symposium on mixed and augmented reality*, 241-242.

Brown, S. M., & Bebko, J. M. (2012). Generalization, overselectivity, and discrimination in the autism phenotype: A review. *Research in Autism Spectrum Disorders, 6*(2), 733–740. doi:10.1016/j.rasd.2011.10.012

Bujak, K., Radu, I., Catrambone, R., MacIntyre, B., Zheng, R., & Golubski, G. (2013). A psychological perspective on augmented reality in the mathematics classroom. *Computers & Education, 68*, 536–544. doi:10.1016/j.compedu.2013.02.017

Bulearca, M. y Tamarjan, D. (2010). Augmented Reality: A sustainable marketing tool? *Global Business and Management Research: An International Journal, 2* (2-3), 237-252.

Burton, S., Armstrong, J., & Wall, B. (2017). *Sustainable performance in architecture*. Retrieved July 2, 2017, from http://www.lsiarchitects.co.uk

Bybee, R. W. (2010). What is STEM education? *Science, 329*(5995), 996–996. doi:10.1126cience.1194998 PMID:20798284

Cabero, J., & Barroso, J. (2016). The educational possibilities of augmented reality. *New Approaches in Educational Research, 5*(1), 44–50.

Carmigniani, J., & Furht, B. (2011). Augmented reality: An overview. In B. Furht (Ed.), *Handbook of augmented reality* (pp. 3–46). New York, NY: Springer. doi:10.1007/978-1-4614-0064-6_1

Carreón, G. (2002). *Manual de Bibliotecas*. Madrid: Fundación Germán Sánchez Ruipérez.

Carro, R. M., Breda, A. M., Castillo, G., & Bajuelos, A. L. (2002). A Methodology for Developing Adaptive Educational-Game Environments. In *Proceedings of AH 2002: Adaptive Hypermedia and Adaptive Web-Based Systems*, Malaga, Spain: Springer. 10.1007/3-540-47952-X_11

Carter, R. (2013). *Defining characteristics of an integrated STEM curriculum in K-12 education* (PhD Thesis). University of Arkansas.

Casas, X., Herrera, G., Coma, I., & Fernández, M. (2012). *A kinect-based augmented reality system for individuals with autism spectrum disorders. Grapp/ivapp, 440- 446. Center for Disease Control*. Atlanta, GA: CDC. Retrieved from https://www.cdc.gov/ncbddd/autism/data.html

Caudell, T. P., & Mizell, D. W. (1992). Augmented reality: an application of heads-up display technology to manual manufacturing processes. *Proceedings of the Twenty-Fifth Hawaii International Conference on System Sciences*, 659-669. 10.1109/HICSS.1992.183317

Chang, J. J., & Carroll, J. D. (1972). *How to use PREFMAP and PREFMAP-2: Programs which relate preference data to multidimensional scaling solutions* (Unpublished manuscript). Bell Telephone Labs.

Chang, K.-E., Chang, C.-T., Hou, H.-T., Sung, Y.-T., Chao, H.-L., & Lee, C.-M. (2014). Development and behavioral pattern analysis of a mobile guide system with augmented reality for painting appreciation instruction in an art museum. *Computers & Education*, *71*, 185–197. doi:10.1016/j.compedu.2013.09.022

Checkland, P. B. (1995). *Systems Thinking, System Practice*. John Wiley and Sons.

Checkland, P. B. (2013). *Systems Thinking, Systems Practice*. Wiley.

Checkland, P. B., & Scholes, J. (1999). *Soft Systems Methodology in Action*. Chichester, UK: Wiley.

Chen, J. (2014). *Proceedings from EUROCALL Conference: CALL design principles and practices*. Groningen, Netherlands: Academic Press.

Chen, C.-M., & Tsai, Y.-N. (2012). Interactive augmented reality system for enhancing library instruction in elementary schools. *Computers & Education*, *59*(2), 638–652. doi:10.1016/j.compedu.2012.03.001

Cheng, K. H., & Tsai, C. C. (2013). Affordances of augmented reality in science learning: Suggestions for future research. *Journal of Science Education and Technology*, *22*(4), 449–462. doi:10.100710956-012-9405-9

Chen, M., Yu, S., & Chiang, F. K. (2017). A dynamic ubiquitous learning resource model with context and its effects on ubiquitous learning. *Interactive Learning Environments*, *25*(1), 127–141. doi:10.1080/10494820.2016.1143846

Chen, Z., & Soldner, M. (2014). *Stem Attrition: College Students' Paths into and out of Stem Fields*. U.S. Department of Education.

Chien, C. H., Chen, C. H., & Jeng, T. S. (2010). An interactive augmented reality system for learning anatomy structure. In T. Athanasios (Ed.), *Proceedings of the International MultiConference of Engineers and Computer Scientists* (pp. 370-375). Hong Kong, China: International Association of Engineers.

Child, J. (1997). Strategic Choice in the Analysis of Action, Structure, Organizations and Environment: Retrospect and Prospect. *Organization Studies*, *18*(1), 43–76. doi:10.1177/017084069701800104

Chiu, J. L., DeJaegher, C. J., & Chao, J. (2015). The effects of augmented virtual science laboratories on middle school-students' understanding of gas properties. *Computers & Education*, *85*, 59–73. doi:10.1016/j.compedu.2015.02.007

Choudari, A., Joshi, S., Bembalkar, A., Marathe, N. y Sankpal, L.J. (2013). Book tracking application in android for library using GPS. *International Journal of Innovative Research in Computer and Communication Engineering, 1*(1), 30-34.

Christie, P., Newson, E., Newson, J., & Prevezner, W. (1992). An interactive approach to language and communication for non-speaking children. In Child and Adolescent Therapy: A Handbook. Milton Keynes, UKs: Open University Press.

Chu, H. C., Hwang, G. J., Tsai, C. C., & Tseng, J. C. R. (2010). A two-tier test approach to developing location-aware mobile learning system for natural science course. *Computers & Education, 55*(4), 1618–1627. doi:10.1016/j.compedu.2010.07.004

Cizek, G. J. (1997). Learning, achievement, and assessment: Constructs at a crossroads. Handbook of classroom assessment: Learning, adjustment, and achievement, 1-32.

Clarke, R. V. (Ed.). (1997). *Situational Crime Prevention: successful case studies* (2nd ed.). Harrow and Heston.

Clarke, R. V., & Eck, J. (2003). *Becoming a Problem-Solving Crime Analyst: In 55 Small Steps.* London: Jill Dando Institute of Crime Science.

Clements, P., Bachmann, F., Bass, L., Garlan, D., Ivers, J., Little, R., ... Stafford, J. (2010). *Documentación de las arquitecturas de software: Views and Beyond, segunda edición.* Boston: Addison-Wesley.

Cloud4All. (n.d.). *Home page of the Cloud4All project.* Retrieved July 20, 2007, from http://www.cloud4all.info

Cognition and Technology Group at Vanderbilt. (1990). Anchored instruction and its relationship to situated cognition. *Educational Researcher, 19*(6), 2–10. doi:10.3102/0013189X019006002

Cognition and Technology Group at Vanderbilt. (1997). *The jasper project: Lessons in curriculum, instruction, assessment, and professional development.* Mahwah, NJ: Lawrence Erlbaum Associates Publishers.

Cohen, H., Amerine-Dickens, M., & Smith, T. (2006). Early intensive behavioral treatment: Replication of the UCLA Model in a community setting. *Developmental and Behavioral Pediatrics, 27*(Supplement 2), 145–155. doi:10.1097/00004703-200604002-00013 PMID:16685181

Cohen, L. E., & Felson, M. (1979). Social change and crime rate trends: A routine activity approach. *American Sociological Review, 44*(4), 588–608. doi:10.2307/2094589

Coleman, J. (2013). Data Flow Sequences: A Revision of Data Flow Diagrams for Modelling Applications using XML. *International Journal of Advanced Computer Science and Applications, 4*(5), 28–31.

Consoli, M. E. V. (2008). Reuven Feuerstein's Theory of Cognitive Structural Modifiability. *Educational Investigation, 12*(22), 203-221.

Córdoba, C., González, J., Nasser, J., Ortíz, J., & Zamora, A. (2002). *Design evaluation.* Lithoimpresora S.A de C.V.

Cornford, T., & Shaikh, M. (2013). *Introduction to information Systems. Undergraduate study in Economics, Management, Finance and the Social Sciences*. University of London.

Cornish, D., & Clarke, R. V. (1998). Understanding Crime Displacement: An application of Rational Choice Theory. In *Criminology Theory Reader*. New York: New York University Press.

Coştu, S. (2009). *Teacher experiences from a learning environment based on contextual teaching and learning in mathematics teaching* (Unpublished Master Thesis). KTÜ, Institute of Science, Trabzon.

Cox, D., & Cox, A. D. (2002). Beyond first impressions: The effects of repeated exposure on consumer liking of visually complex and simple product designs. *Journal of the Academy of Marketing Science*, *30*(2), 119–130. doi:10.1177/03079459994371

Creswell, J. W. (2012). *Qualitative Inquiry and Research Design: Choosing Among Five Approaches*. SAGE Publications.

Crystal, D. (Ed.). (1997). *The Cambridge encyclopedia of language* (2nd ed.). New York: Cambridge University Press.

Cuendet, S., Bonnard, Q., Do-Lenh, S., & Dillenbourg, P. (2013). Designing augmented reality for the classroom. *Computers & Education*, *68*, 557–569. doi:10.1016/j.compedu.2013.02.015

Cuxart, F. (2000). Autism, Descriptive and therapeutic aspects. Málaga. *Ediciones Aljibe S.*

Davis, D., & Berland, M. (2013). Supporting English learners with participatory augmented reality simulations. *On the Horizon*, *21*(4), 294–303. doi:10.1108/OTH-01-2012-0001

De Boer, S. J. (1990). Systematic decisions in methodical engineering design. *Scriftenreihe WDK*, 17.

De Crescenzio, F., Fantini, M., Persiani, F., Stefano, L., Azzari, P., & Salti, S. (2011). Augmented reality for aircraft maintenance training and operations support. *IEEE Computer Graphics and Applications*, *31*(1), 96–101. doi:10.1109/MCG.2011.4 PMID:24807975

De Pablos, H., Agius, J., Romero, S., & Salgado, S. (2012). *Organización y transformación de los sistemas de información en la empresa*. ESIC Editorial.

De Sousa, T., Kelvin, L., Dias, C., & De Carvalho, C. G. (2017). A Formal Semantics for Use Case Diagram Via Event-B. *Journal of Software*, *12*(3), 189–200. doi:10.17706/jsw.12.3.189-200

Dede, C. (2009). Immersive interfaces for engagement and learning. *Science*, *323*(5910), 66–69. doi:10.1126cience.1167311 PMID:19119219

Den Brok, W. L. J. E., & Sterkenburg, P. S. (2014). Self-controlled technologies to support skill attainment in persons with an autism spectrum disorder and/or an intellectual disability: a systematic literature review. *Disability and Rehabilitation Assitive Technology*, 1-10.

Dentsoras, A. J. (2008). Representation of Design Concepts and Concept Evaluation Criteria through Design Parameters and Performance Variables. *DS 57: Proceedings of AEDS 2008 Workshop.*

Di Serio, Á., Ibáñez, M. B., & Kloos, C. D. (2013). Impact of an augmented reality system on students' motivation for a visual art course. *Computers & Education, 68*, 586–596. doi:10.1016/j.compedu.2012.03.002

Diegmann, P., Schmidt-Kraepelin, M., van den Eynden, S., & Basten, D. (2015). *Proceedings from the 12th International Conference on Wirtschaftsinformatik.* Osnabrück, Germany: Academic Press.

Dijkman, R., & Joosten, S. (2002). *Deriving use case diagrams from business process models.* Technical Report 02-08. CTIT.

Dillenbourg, P., Zufferey, G., Alavi, H., Jermann, P., Do-Lenh, S., Bonnard, Q., & Kaplan, F. (2011). Classroom orchestration: The third circle of usability. *CSCL2011 Proceedings, 1*, 510-517.

Dini, G., & Mura, D. (2015). Application of augmented reality techniques in through-life engineering services. *Procedia CIRP, 38*, 14–23. doi:10.1016/j.procir.2015.07.044

Dita, F. A. (2016). A foreign language learning application using mobile augmented reality. *Informações Econômicas, 20*(4), 76–87. doi:10.12948/issn14531305/20.4.2016.07

DOE. (2008). *Department of Energy (DOE).* Washington, DC: Guideline Root Cause Analysis Guidance Document, Nuclear Energy and Office of Nuclear Safety Policy and Standards.

Dong, Y., & Yu, D. (2005). Estimation of failure probability of oil and gas transmission pipelines by fuzzy fault tree analysis. *Journal of Loss Prevention in the Process Industries, 18*(2), 83–88. doi:10.1016/j.jlp.2004.12.003

Dönmez Usta, N. (2011). *Developing, implementing and evaluating cai materials related to? radioactivity? topic based on constructivist learning theory* (Unpublished Master Thesis). KTÜ, Institute of Educational Sciences, Trabzon.

Dori, Y., & Belcher, J. (2005). Learning electromagnetism with visualization and active learning. In J. Gilbert (Ed.), *Models and Modeling in Science Education* (Vol. 1, pp. 187–216). Dordrecht, The Netherlands: Springer. doi:10.1007/1-4020-3613-2_11

Druin, A. (1999). Cooperative inquiry: developing new technologies for children with children. In *Proc. CHI*. ACM Press. 10.1145/302979.303166

Dunleavy, M., & Dede, C. (2014). Augmented reality teaching and learning. In M. Spector, M. Merrill, & J. Bishop (Eds.), *Handbook of Research on Educational Communications and Technology* (pp. 735–745). Heidelberg, Germany: Spring Publishing. doi:10.1007/978-1-4614-3185-5_59

Dunleavy, M., Dede, C., & Mitchell, R. (2009). Affordances and limitations of immersive participatory augmented reality simulations for teaching and learning. *Journal of Science Education and Technology, 18*(1), 7–22. doi:10.100710956-008-9119-1

Dunston, P. S., & Wang, X. (2005). Mixed Reality-Based Visualization Interfaces for Architecture, Engineering, and Construction Industry. *Journal of Construction Engineering and Management*, *131*(12), 1301–1309. doi:10.1061/(ASCE)0733-9364(2005)131:12(1301)

Durga, K., Gopika, V., Sanyasi-Rao, V. V. S., Kushwaha, H. S., Verma, A. K., & Srividya, A. (2009). Dynamic fault tree analysis using Monte Carlo simulation in probabilistic safety assessment. *Reliability Engineering & System Safety*, *94*(4), 872–883. doi:10.1016/j.ress.2008.09.007

EDUCAUSE Learning Initiative. (2005). *7 things you should know about augmented reality. Advancing learning through It innovation*. Retrieved from http://www.educause.edu/ir/library/pdf/ELI7007.pdf

Elena. (2016). *A propósito D. Autism. The importance of the family in the intervention*. Colegio Oficial de la psicología de Castilla- La Mancha.

Ellis, R. (2003). *Task-based language learning and teaching*. Oxford, UK: Oxford University Press.

Embrey, D. (1991, October). Bringing organizational factors to the fore of human error management. *Nuclear Engineering International*, 50–52.

Emery, F. E. (Ed.). (1981). *Systems Thinking* (Vols. 1–2). Harmondsworth, UK: Penguin.

Ericsson. (2017). *4K and Augmented Reality*. Retrieved from https://www.ericsson.com/mx/en/networked-society/live-sports-experience/4k-and-augmented-reality

Esposito, N. (2005). A Short and Simple Definition of What a Video Game Is. *Proceedings of DiGRA 2005 Conference: Changing Views - Worlds in Play*.

Estapa, A. y Nadolny, L. (2015). The Effect of an Augmented Reality Enhanced Mathematics Lesson on Student Achievement and Motivation. *Journal of STEM Education: Innovations and Research*, *16*(3), 40-48.

Eysenck, H. J. (1941). A critical and experimental study of colour preferences. *The American Journal of Psychology*, *54*(3), 385–394. doi:10.2307/1417683

FastCV-sdk Documentation. (2017). Retrieved from https://developer.qualcomm.com/software/fastcv-sdk

Felson, M., & Clarke, R. V. (1998). Opportunity Makes the Thief: practical theory for crime prevention. Police Research Series, Paper 98.

Ferrer-Torregrosa, J., Jiménez-Rodríguez, M., Torralba-Estelles, J., Garzón-Farinós, F., Pérez-Bermejo, M., & Fernández-Ehrling, N. (2016). Distance learning ects and flipped classroom in the anatomy learning: Comparative study of the use of augmented reality, video and notes. *BMC Medical Education*, *16*(223), 1–9. PMID:27581521

Figueiredo, M. (2015). Teaching Mathematics with Augmented Reality. *Proceedings of 12th International Conference on Technology in Mathematics Teaching*, 183.

Flood, R. L. (2001). *The relationship of "Systems Thinking" to Action Research. In Handbook of Action Research-Participative Inquiry & Practice*. Sage.

Fombona Cadavieco. (2012). *Pascual Sevillano María Ángeles, Madeira Ferreira, Galindo Dolores*. Augmented Reality in Museums, Social Museum.

Forrester, J. W. (1961). *Industrial Dynamics*. MIT Press.

Foster, P., & Cunniff, S. (2016). *Augmented Reality in the Classroom* (Honors Thesis). Loyola Marymount University.

Frasca, G. (2001). *Videogames of the Oppressed: Videogames as a Means for Critical Thinking and Debate*. Institute of Technology.

Friedrich, W., Jahn, D., & Schmidt, L. (2002, September). ARVIKA-Augmented Reality for Development, Production and Service. In ISMAR (Vol. 2002, pp. 3-4). Academic Press.

Fuboa, S., Kepinga, L., & Xiaominga, X. (2016). Railway accidents analysis based on the improved algorithm of the maximal information coefficient. *Intelligent Data Analysis*, *20*(3), 597–613. doi:10.3233/IDA-160822

Garbarino, S., Guglielmi, O., Sanna, A., Mancardi, G. L., & Magnavita, N. (2016). Risk of Occupational Accidents in Workers with Obstructive Sleep Apnea: Systematic Review and Meta-analysis. *Sleep*, *39*(6), 1211–1218. doi:10.5665leep.5834 PMID:26951401

García Eligio de la Puente. (2004). Psychology in care for people with disabilities. Psychology in Care, (23), 355-362.

García Flores &Mora Lumbreras Marva. (2015). Midori: Video Game for the Learning of children with Autism in the Area of Language and Communication. In *Emerging Technologies in Education, Memory of the National Encounter of Computer Science*. Sociedad Mexicana de Ciencias de la Computación.

Garnica, E., & Calderon, J. A. F. (2015). Augmented Reality and Education. *Journal Engineering, Mathematics and Information Sciences*, *2*(3).

Gersten, R., Fuchs, L. S., Compton, D., Coyne, M., Greenwood, C., & Innocenti, M. S. (2005). Quality indicators for group experimental and quasi-experimental research in special education. *Exceptional Children*, *71*(2), 149–164. doi:10.1177/001440290507100202

Ghasemi, A., & Javidan, R. (2014). A New Model as English Tutorial Assistant based on Augmented Reality. *Journal of Educational and Management Studies*, *4*(3), 695–701.

Giap, N., Yin, O., Hong, L., & And Ee, T. (2016). An Augmented Reality System for Biology Science Education in Malaysia. *International Journal of Innovative Computing*, *6*(2), 8–13.

Giglioli, I., Pallavicini, F., & Pedroli, E. (2015). Augmented reality: A brand new challenge for the assessment and treatment of psychological disorders. *Computational and Mathematical Methods in Medicine*, *2015*, 1–12. doi:10.1155/2015/862942 PMID:26339283

Giraldi, G. A., Silva, R., & Oliveira, J. C. (2003). *Introduction to Virtual Reality.* LNCC Research Report #06/2003, National Laboratory for Scientific Computation. Retrieved July 20, 2007, from http://gpii.net/

Godwin-Jones, R. (2008). Mobile computing trends: Lighter, faster, smarter. *Language Learning & Technology*, *15*(2), 3–9.

Godwin-Jones, R. (2011). Mobile apps for language learning. *Language Learning & Technology*, *12*(3), 3–9.

Godwin-Jones, R. (2014). Games in language learning: Opportunities and challenges. *Language Learning & Technology*, *18*(2), 9–19.

Godwin-Jones, R. (2016). Augmented reality and language learning: From annotated vocabulary to place-based mobile games. *Language Learning & Technology*, *20*(3), 9–19.

González, C., Vallejo, D., Albusac, J. A., & Castro, J. J. (2011). *Augmented Reality: A Practical Approach with ARToolKit and Blender*. Bubok Publishing S. L.

Gordon, P. C., & Holyoak, K. J. (1983). Implicit Learning and Generalization of the 'Mere Exposure' Effect. *Journal of Personality and Social Psychology*, *45*(September), 492–500. doi:10.1037/0022-3514.45.3.492

Gorm, P., Plat, N., & Toetenel, H. (1994). A Formal Semantics of Data Flow Diagrams. *Formal Aspects of Computing*, *6*(6), 586–606. doi:10.1007/BF03259387

Grabowski, M., & Roberts, K. H. (1996). Human and organizational error in large scale systems. *IEEE Trans Systems man Cybernet Part A. Systems Humans*, *26*(1), 2–16. doi:10.1109/3468.477856

Greenfield, P. M. (2009). Technology and informal education: What is taught, what is learned. *Science*, *323*(5910), 69–71. doi:10.1126cience.1167190 PMID:19119220

Griffiths, A. (2001). Implementing task-based instruction to facilitate language learning: Moving away from theory. *TEFLIN Journal*, *3*(1), 49–59.

Griffiths, M. D. (2002b). The educational benefits of videogames. *Education for Health*, *20*(3), 47–51.

Grossman, R. P., & Wisenblit, J. Z. (1999). What We Know About Consumers' Color Choices. *Journal of Marketing Practice*, *5*(3), 78–88. doi:10.1108/EUM0000000004565

Gutiérrez, M. (2014). Augmented Reality Environments in Learning, Communicational and Professional Contexts in Higher Education. *Digital Education Review*, *26*, 22–35.

Hanna, L., Neapolitan, D., & Risden, K. (2004). Evaluating computer game concepts with children. *Proceedings of the 2004 conference on Interaction design and children: building a community*, 49-56. 10.1145/1017833.1017840

Hanson, K., & Shelton, B. E. (2008). Design and Development of Virtual Reality: Analysis of Challenges Faced by Educators. *Journal of Educational Technology & Society*, *11*(1), 118–131.

Heidi, E. (2017). *Kinds of accident in Great Britain, 2016*. Health and Safety Executive.

Herrera Batista, L. M. Á. (2002). The sources of learning in virtual educational environments. *Reencuentro*, (35).

Herrera, G., Alcantud, F., Jordan, R., Blanquer, A., Labajo, G., & de Pablo, C. (2008). Development of symbolic play through the use of virtual reality tools in children with autistic spectrum disorders: Two case studies. *Autism, 12*(2), 7–21. doi:10.1177/1362361307086657 PMID:18308764

Herrera, G., Casas, X., Sevilla, J., Rosa, L., Pardo, C., Plaza, J., & Le Groux, S. (2012). Pictogram room: Natural interaction technologies to aid in the development of children with autism. *Annuary of Clinical and Health Psychology, 8*, 39–44.

Heyes, C. (2001). Causes and Consequences of Imitation. *Trends in Cognitive Sciences, 5*(6), 253–261. doi:10.1016/S1364-6613(00)01661-2 PMID:11390296

Hoegg, J., Alba, J. W., & Dahl, D. W. (2010). The good, the bad, and the ugly: Influence of aesthetics on product feature judgments. *Journal of Consumer Psychology, 20*(4), 419–430. doi:10.1016/j.jcps.2010.07.002

Holbrook, M. B., & Zirlin, R. B. (1985). Artistic creation, artworks, and aesthetic appreciation: Some philosophical contributions to nonprofit marketing. *Advances in Nonprofit Marketing, 1*(1), 1-54.

Holbrook, M. B. (1995). An Empirical Approach to Representing Patterns of Consumer Tastes, Nostalgia, and Hierarchy in the Market for Cultural Products. *Empirical Studies of the Arts, 13*(1), 55–71. doi:10.2190/RJA4-H8TK-F30Q-0U3F

Holden, C. L., & Sykes, J. M. (2011). Leveraging Mobile Games for Place-Based Language Learning. *International Journal of Game-Based Learning, 1*(2), 1–18. doi:10.4018/ijgbl.2011040101

Holden, C., & Sykes, J. (2013). Place-based mobile games for pragmatic learning. In N. Taguchi & J. Sykes (Eds.), *Technology in interlanguage pragmatics research and teaching* (pp. 1–15). Philadelphia, PA: John Benjamins. doi:10.1075/lllt.36.09hol

Honkamaa, P., Jäppinen, J., & Woodward, C. (2007). *A Lightweight Approach for Augmented Reality on Camera Phones using 2D Images to Simulate in 3D*. VTT Technical Research Centre of Finland.

Honkamaa, P., Jäppinen, J., & Woodward, C. (2007). *A lightweight approach for augmented reality on camera phones using 2D images to simulate in 3D*. VTT Technical Research Centre of Finland. doi:10.1145/1329469.1329490

Hoopingarner, D. (2009). Best practices in technology and language learning. *Language and Linguistics Compass, 3*(1), 222–235. doi:10.1111/j.1749-818X.2008.00123.x

Horner, R. H., Carr, E. G., Halle, J., McGee, G., Odom, S., & Wolery, M. (2005). The use of single-subject research to identify evidence-based practice in special education. *Exceptional Children, 71*(2), 165–179. doi:10.1177/001440290507100203

Ho, S. C., Hsieh, S. W., Sun, P. C., & Chen, C. M. (2017). To activate English learning: Listen and speak in real life context with AR featured u-learning system. *Journal of Educational Technology & Society*, *20*(2), 176–187.

Hsu, W., & Woon, I. M. Y. (1998). Current research in the conceptual design of mechanical products. *Computer Aided Design*, *30*(5), 377–389. doi:10.1016/S0010-4485(97)00101-2

Huang, G. Q. (2002). Web-based support for collaborative product design review. *Computers in Industry*, *48*(1), 71–88. doi:10.1016/S0166-3615(02)00011-8

Hughes, R. (2014). *Augmented reality: Developments, technologies, and applications*. Hauppauge, NY: Nova Publishers.

Hugues, O., Fuchs, P., & Nannipieri, O. (2011). New augmented reality taxonomy: technologies and features of augmented environment. In B. Furth (Ed.), *Handbook of augmented reality* (pp. 47–63). New York: Springer. doi:10.1007/978-1-4614-0064-6_2

Hung, P. H., Hwang, G. J., Lin, Y. F., Wu, T. H., & Su, I. H. (2013). Seamless connection between learning and assessment - applying progressive learning tasks in mobile ecology inquiry. *Journal of Educational Technology & Society*, *16*(1), 194–205.

Hutchins, E. (1995). How a cockpit remembers its speeds. *Cognitive Science*, *19*(3), 265–288. doi:10.120715516709cog1903_1

Ibáñez, M. B., Di Serio, A., Villarán, D., & Delgado-Kloos, C. (2016). *The Acceptance of Learning Augmented Reality Environments: A Case Study.* 16th International Conference on Advanced Learning Technologies (ICALT), Austin, TX. 10.1109/ICALT.2016.124

Ibáñez, M. B., Di Serio, Á., Villarán, D., & Delgado Kloos, C. (2014). Experimenting with electromagnetism using augmented reality: Impact on flow student experience and educational effectiveness. *Computers & Education*, *71*, 1–13. doi:10.1016/j.compedu.2013.09.004

Ibanez, M., Kloos, C., Leony, D., Rueda, J., & Maroto, D. (2011). Learning a foreign language in a mixed-reality environment. *IEEE Internet Computing*, *15*(6), 44–47. doi:10.1109/MIC.2011.78

Ibrahim, R., & Jaafar, A. (2009). Educational games (EG) design framework: combination of game design, pedagogy and content modeling. *Proceedings of the International Conference on Electrical Engineering and Informatics*, 1, 293-298. 10.1109/ICEEI.2009.5254771

Izak. (2017). *The special need ware, the proud creator of Autismate365 and TeachMate365.* Retrieved from autismate.com

Izkara, J. L., Perez, J., Basogain, X., & Borro, D. (2009). Mobile augmented reality, an advanced tool for the construction sector. *Proc. 24th CIB W78 Conference*, 453-460.

Jarod, K. (2007). *Use of shape preference information in product design.* Guidelines for a Decision Support Method Adapted to NPD Processes.

Javornik, A. (2016, April 16). What marketers need to understand about augmented reality. *Harvard Business Review*. Retrieved from https://hbr.org/2016/04/what-marketers-need-to-understand-about-augmented-reality

Jensen, H. J. (1998). *Self organizad criticality. Cambridge Lecture Notes in Physics*. Cambridge University Press. doi:10.1017/CBO9780511622717

Jerez, S., & Tarride, M. (2000). Reflections on the need for paradigmatic change in education. *The Journal of Educational Thought*, 27.

John, I., & Muthig, D. (2002). Tailoring Use Cases for Product Line Modeling. *Proceedings REPL 02. International Workshop on Requirements Engineering for Product Lines*.

Johnson, L., Levine, A., Smith, R., & Stone, S. (2010). Simple augmented reality. The 2010 Horizon Report, 21-24. Austin, TX: The New Media Consortium.

Johnson, L., Adams Becker, S., Estrada, V., & Martín, S. (2013). *Technology Outlook for STEM+ Education 2013-2018: An NMC Horizon Project Sector Analysis*. New Media Consortium.

Johnson, L., Smith, R., Willis, H., Levine, A., & Haywood, K. (2011). *The 2011 Horizon Report*. Austin, TX: The New Media Consortium.

Johnson, W. (2010). Serious use of a serious game for language learning. *International Journal of Artificial Intelligence in Education*, *20*, 175–195.

Johnson, W. G. (1980). *MORT Safety Assurance Systems*. New York: Marcel Dekker.

Kamarainen, A., Metcalf, S., Grotzer, T., Browne, A., Mazzuca, D., Tutwiler, S., & Dede, C. (2013). EcoMOBILE: Integrating augmented reality and probeware with environmental education field trips. *Computers & Education*, *68*, 545–556. doi:10.1016/j.compedu.2013.02.018

Karal, H., & Abdüsselam, M. S. (2015). Augmented Reality. In B. Akkoyunlu, A. İşman, & H.F. Odabaşı (Eds.), Education technology readings 2015 (pp. 149-171). Ankara: Pegem Akademi.

Kaufmann, H. (2002). Construct 3D: An augmented reality application for mathematics and geometry education. *Proc. 10th ACM international Conference on Multimedia*, 656-657.

Kauker, F., Kaminski, T., Karcher, M., Dowdall, M., Brown, J., Hosseini, A., & Strand, P. (2016). Model analysis of worst place scenarios for nuclear accidents in the northern marine environment. *Environmental Modelling & Software*, *77*, 13–18. doi:10.1016/j.envsoft.2015.11.021

Khan, F., Rathnayaka, S., & Ahmed, S. (2015). Methods and models in process safety and risk management: Past, present and future. *Process Safety and Environmental Protection*, *98*, 116–147. doi:10.1016/j.psep.2015.07.005

Khot, N., Mudur, K., Thorat, O., & Doulatramani, Y. (2017). A Management Information System on Cloud. *International Research Journal of Engineering and Technology*, *4*(4), 372–380.

Kientz, J. A., Hayes, G. R., Westeyn, T. L., Starner, T., & Abowd, G. D. (2007). Pervasive computing and autism: Assisting caregivers of children with special needs. *IEEE Pervasive Comp. Magazine*, *6*(1), 28–35. doi:10.1109/MPRV.2007.18

Kim, D. H. (1993). *Systems Archetypes: Diagnosing systemic issues and designing high leverage interventions.* Pegasus Communications. USA.

Kipper, G., & Rampolla, J. (2012). *Augmented reality: An emerging technologies guide to AR.* Academic Press.

Kipper, G., & Rampolla, J. (2013). *Augmented Reality: An Emerging Technologies Guide to AR* (1st ed.). Amsterdam: Elsevier. doi:10.1016/B978-1-59-749733-6.00001-2

Kirner, T. G., Reis, F. M. V., & Kirner, C. (2012). Development of an interactive book with Augmented Reality for teaching and learning geometric shapes. *Information Systems and Technologies*, 1-6.

Kirner, T.G., Reis, F.M.V., & Kirner, C. (2012). Development of an interactive book with Augmented Reality for teaching and learning geometric shapes. *Information Systems and Technologies (CISTI)*, 1-6.

Klopfer, E., & Squire, K. (2008). Environmental detectives - The development of an augmented reality platform for environmental simulations. *Educational Technology Research and Development*, *56*(2), 203–228. doi:10.100711423-007-9037-6

Kolb, D. A. (1984). *Experiential learning: Experience as the source of learning and development.* Englewood Cliffs, NJ: Prentice Hall.

Kounavis, C., Kasimati, A., & Zamani, E. (2012). Enhancing the tourism experience through mobile augmented reality: Challenges and prospects. *International Journal of Engineering Business Management*, *4*, 1–6. doi:10.5772/51644

KPMG International. (2016). How augmented and virtual reality are changing the insurance landscape: Seizing the opportunity. Amstelveen, The Netherlands: Author.

Krevelen, D. W., & Poelman, F. (2010). A Survey of Augmented Reality Technologies, Applications and Limitations. *The International Journal of Virtual Reality*, *9*(2), 1–20.

Kruchten, P. B. (1995). The 4+1 View Model of architecture. *IEEE Software*, *12*(6), 42–50.

Kucuk, S., Yilmaz, R., & Goktas, Y. (2014). Augmented reality for learning English: Achievement, attitude, and cognitive load levels of students. *Education in Science*, *39*(176), 393–404.

Kumar, M., & Garg, N. (2010). Aesthetic principles and cognitive emotion appraisals: How much of the beauty lies in the eye of the beholder? *Journal of Consumer Psychology*, *20*(4), 485–494. doi:10.1016/j.jcps.2010.06.015

Kunii, O., Akagi, M., & Kita, E. (1995). Health consequences and medical and public health response to the Great Hanshin Awaji Earth-quake in Japan: A case study in disaster planning. *Medicine and Global Survival*, *2*, 32–45.

Kurubacak, G., & Altinpulluk, H. (2017). *Mobile Technologies and Augmented Reality in Open Education*. IGI Global. doi:10.4018/978-1-5225-2110-5

Lara, B. L. (2004). *Augmented reality: A technology waiting for users. Revista Digital Universitaria*. UNAM.

Laudon, J., & Kenneth, C. (2006). *Sistemas de información gerencial- Administración de la empresa digital*. Pearson Educación-Prentice Hall.

Laudon, K., & Laudon, P. (2014). *Management Information Systems Managing the Digital Firm*. Pearson Education Limited.

Lave, J., & Wenger, E. (1991). *Situated learning: Legitimate peripheral participation*. Cambridge, MA: Cambridge University Press. doi:10.1017/CBO9780511815355

Leblanc, F., Champagne, B. J., Augestad, K. M., Neary, P. C., Senagore, A. J., Ellis, C. N., & Delaney, C. P. (2010). A Comparison of Human Cadaver and Augmented Reality Simulator Models for Straight Laparoscopic Colorectal Skills Acquisition Training. *Journal of the American College of Surgeons*, *211*(2), 250–255. doi:10.1016/j.jamcollsurg.2010.04.002 PMID:20670864

Lee, K. (2012). Augmented reality in education and training. *TechTrends*, *56*(1), 13–21. doi:10.100711528-012-0559-3

Lee, O. (2005). Science education with English language learners: Synthesis and research agenda. *Review of Educational Research*, *75*(4), 491–530. doi:10.3102/00346543075004491

Leigh, A., & Read, T. (1998). *Brit Pop II: problem-oriented Policing in Practice*. Home Office.

Leo, K. (1943). Autistic disturbances of affective contact. *Pathology*.

Lindaman, D., & Nolan, D. (2015). Mobile-assisted language learning: Application development projects within reach for language teachers. *International Association for Language Learning Technology Journal*, *45*(1), 1–22.

Liu, T.-Y., Tan, T.-H., & Chu, Y.-L. (2007). *2D Barcode and Augmented Reality Supported English Learning System*. 6th IEEE/ACIS International Conference on Computer and Information Science (ICIS 2007), Melbourne, Australia.

Liu, H. T. (2011). Product design and selection using fuzzy QFD and fuzzy MCDM approaches. *Applied Mathematical Modelling*, *35*(1), 482–496. doi:10.1016/j.apm.2010.07.014

Liu, P. E., & Tsai, M. (2013). Using augmented-reality-based mobile learning material in EFL English composition: An exploratory case study. *British Journal of Educational Technology*, *44*(1), E1–E4. doi:10.1111/j.1467-8535.2012.01302.x

Liu, P. L. (2016). Mobile English vocabulary learning based on concept-mapping strategy. *Language Learning & Technology*, *20*(1), 128–140. Retrieved from http://llt.msu.edu/issues/october2016/liu.pdf

Liu, T. Y. (2009). A context-aware ubiquitous learning environment for language listening and speaking. *Journal of Computer Assisted Learning*, *25*(6), 515–527. doi:10.1111/j.1365-2729.2009.00329.x

Lockamy, A., & Khurana, A. (1995). Quality function deployment: Total quality management for new product design. *International Journal of Quality & Reliability Management*, *12*(6), 73–84. doi:10.1108/02656719510089939

Loken, B., & Ward, J. (1990). Alternative Approaches to Understanding the Determinants of Typicality. *The Journal of Consumer Research*, *17*(September), 111–126. doi:10.1086/208542

Lombardo, S. (1991). Event and Decay of the Aesthetic Experience. *Empirical Stutdies of the Arts, 9*(2), 123-141.

Lorah, E. R., Parnell, A., Whitby, P. S., & Hantula, D. (2014). A systematic review of tablet computers and portable media players as speech generating devices for individuals with autism spectrum disorder. *Journal of Autism and Developmental Disorders*, 1–13. PMID:25413144

Luria, A. (1977). *Evolutionary Introduction to Psychology*. Barcelona: Fontanella.

Lu, S., & Liu, Y. (2015). Integrating augmented reality technology to enhance children's learning in marine education. *Environmental Education Research*, *21*(4), 525–541. doi:10.1080/13504622.2014.911247

Macey, M. (2014). *ALA releases 2014 State of America's Libraries Report*. Journal American Library Asotiation.

Mademtzi, M. (2016). *The use of a kinect-based technology within the school environment to enhance sensory-motor skills of children with autism* (Doctoral dissertation). University of Birmingham.

Mahadzir, N., & Phung, L. (2013). The use of augmented reality pop-up book to increase motivation in English language learning for national primary school. *Journal of Research & Method in Education*, *1*(1), 26–38.

Maribel, C. M., & Mora, L. M. A. (2017). Augmented Reality Focused on Arachnophobia. *Revista Iztatl Computación, 6*(11), 32-39.

Marisol, H. H., & Mora, L. M. A. (2016). Veterinary Medicine through Augmented Reality. *Revista Iztatl Computación, 5*(10), 49-56.

Markeless, A. (2013). Augmented Reality Tracking for Enhancing the User Interaction during Virtual Rehabilitation. *XV Symposium on Virtual and Augmented Reality.*

Martín Gutiérrez, J., & Meneses Fernández, M. D. (2014). Augmented Reality Environments for Learning, Communication and Professional Contexts in Higher Education. *Digital Education Review*, *26*, 22–34.

Martindale, C., & Moore, K. (1988). Priming, prototypicality, and preference. *Journal of Experimental Psychology. Human Perception and Performance*, *14*(4), 661–670. doi:10.1037/0096-1523.14.4.661

Martín-Gutiérrez, J., Navarro, R. E., & Acosta, M. M. (2011). Mixed reality for development of spatial skills of first-year engineering students. In *IEEE 2011 Frontiers in Education Conference*. IEEE.

Martin, J., & Siehl, C. (1990). Organizational culture and counterculture: an uneasy symbiosis. In B. D. Sypher (Ed.), *Case studies in organizational communication. Gilford Press.*

Marva-Angélica, M.-L., Sergio, M.-G., & Carolina-Rocío, S.-P. (2017). *Augmented Reality Applied in the Museum of Memory of Tlaxcala. In Software Engineering: Methods, Modeling, and Teaching* (Vol. 4). Editorial Universidad de Medellín, Pontificia Universidad Católica del Perú, and Universidad Nacional de Colombia.

Matsumoto, Y., Sakamoto, K., Nomura, S., Hirotomi, T., Shiwaku, K., & Hirakawa, M. (2009). Activity Replay System of Life Review Therapy Using Mixed Reality Technology. *Proceedings of the International MultiConference of Engineers and Computer Scientists*, 1-6.

Mayer, R. (2009). *Multimedia Learning* (2nd ed.). Cambridge, UK: Cambridge University Press. doi:10.1017/CBO9780511811678

Mazo, I. (1998). Five disciplines for intelligent organization. *Human Capital, 11*(111), 26-30.

McLellan, H. (1996). Situated learning: Multiple perspectives. In H. McLellan (Ed.), *Situation learning perspectives* (pp. 5–17). Educational Technology Publications.

McMahon, D., Cihak, D., Wright, R., & Bell, S. (2015). Augmented reality for teaching science vocabulary to postsecondary eduation students with intellectual disabilities and autism. *Journal of Research in Education*, *48*(1), 38–56.

McMahon, D., Cihak, D., Wright, R., & Bell, S. (2015). Augmented reality for teaching science vocabulary to postsecondary education students with intellectual disabilities and autism. *Journal of Research in Education*, *48*(1), 38–56.

Mekni, M., & Lemieux, A. (2014). Augmented reality: Applications, challen- ges and future trends. *Applied Computational Science Proceedings of the 13th International Conference on Applied Computer and Applied Computational Science (ACACOS 14)*, 23– 25.

Mesibov, G. B., & Howley, M. (2003). *Accessing the Curriculum for Pupils with Autistic Spectrum Disorders*. London: David Fulton Publishers.

Metaio. (2017). Retrieved from http://www.metaio.com

Milgram, P., Takemura, H., & Utsumi, F. K. (1994). Augmented reality: a class of displays on the reality–virtuality continuum. Proceedings of telemanipulator and telepresence technologies, 2351, 282-292.

Ming-Hung, S., Hsue-Cheng, Ch., & Jing-Rong, Ch. (2006). Using intuitionistic fuzzy sets for fault-tree analysis on printed circuit board assembly. *Microelectronics and Reliability*, *46*(12), 2139–2148. doi:10.1016/j.microrel.2006.01.007

Mintzberg, H. (2001). *Diseño de organizaciones eficientes*. New York: Penguin University Books.

Miranda Bojórquez, E., Vergara Villegas, O. O., Cruz Sánchez, V. G., García-Alcaraz, J. L., & Favela Vara, J. (2016). Study on Mobile Augmented Reality Adoption for Mayo Language Learning. *Mobile Information Systems, 2016.*

Mitchell, P., Parsons, S., & Leonard, A. (2007). Using virtual environments for teaching social understanding to adolescents with autistic spectrum disorders. *Journal of Autism and Developmental Disorders*, *37*(3), 589–600. doi:10.100710803-006-0189-8 PMID:16900403

Monda, B., Das, B., & Banerjee, P. (2014). Formal Specification of UML Use Case Diagram - A CASL based approach. *International Journal of Computer Science and Information Technologies*, *5*(3), 2713–2717.

Mónica, T. (2013). Innovative technologies for Autism. *First International Conference: The Autism Spectrum. A Different Perspective.*

Mullen, T. (2011). *Prototyping Augmented Reality*. Indianapolis, IN: John Wiley & Sons.

Müller, D., Bruns, F. W., Erbe, H. H., Robben, B., & Yoo, Y. H. (2007). Mixed Reality Learning Spaces for Collaborative Experimentation: A Challenge for Engineering Education and Training. *International Journal of Online Engineering*, *3*(4), 27–41.

Müller, D., & Ferreira, J. M. (2004, December). MERVEL: A Mixed Reality Learning Environment for Vocational Training Mechatronics. *Proceedings of International Conference on Technology-Enhanced Learning.*

Mutiara, G. A., Hapsari, G. I., & Handayani, R. (2014). Design and Implementation Learning Media of a Computer Hardware Introduction as a Teaching Tool Based-on Augmented Reality Technology. *Contemporary Engineering Sciences*, *7*(13), 611–616. doi:10.12988/ces.2014.4667

Netmedia.mx. (2017). *The Future of the Automotive Industry Augmented Reality.* Retrieved March, 24, 2017, from https://www.netmedia.mx/analisis/el-futuro-de-la-industria-automotriz realidad-aumentada/

Nicolson, D., Chalk, C., Robert, W., Funnell, J., & Daniel, S. (2006). Can virtual reality improve anatomy education? A randomised controlled study of a computer-generated three-dimensional anatomical ear model. *Medical Education*, *40*(11), 1081–1087. doi:10.1111/j.1365-2929.2006.02611.x PMID:17054617

Nunan, D. (1992). *Research Methods in Language Learning*. Cambridge, UK: Cambridge University Press.

Odom, S. L., Boyd, B. A., Hall, L. J., & Hume, K. (2010). Evaluation of comprehensive treatment models for individuals with autism spectrum disorders. *Journal of Autism and Developmental Disorders, 40*(4), 425–436. doi:10.100710803-009-0825-1 PMID:19633939

Orgill, M. (2007). Situated cognition. In G. M. Bodner & M. Orgill (Eds.), *Theoretical frameworks for research in chemistry/science education* (pp. 187–203). Upper Saddle River, NJ: Prentice Hall.

Orlosky, J., Kiyokawa, K., & Takemura, H. (2017). Virtual and Augmented Reality on the 5G Highway. *Journal of Information Processing, 25*(0), 133–141. doi:10.2197/ipsjjip.25.133

Orman, E. K., Price, H. E., & Russell, C. R. (2017). Feasibility of Using an Augmented Immersive Virtual Reality Learning Environment to Enhance Music Conducting Skills. *Journal of Music Teacher Education, 27*(1), 24–35. doi:10.1177/1057083717697962

Oscar, G. (2017). *New Apple patents show interest in augmented reality, C / net in Spanish.* Retrieved from https://www.cnet.com/es/noticias/apple-realidad-aumentada-patentes/

Papanek, V., & Fuller, R. B. (1972). *Design for the real world.* London: Thames and Hudson.

Paterson, N., Naliuka, K., Jensen, S., Carrigy, T., Haahr, M., & Conway, F. (2010). Design, implementation and evaluation of audio for a location aware augmented reality game. In *Proceedings from the 3rd International Conference on Fun and Games*. New York, NY: ACM. 10.1145/1823818.1823835

Patton, M. Q. (2014). *Qualitative research and evaluation methods.* Ankara: Pegem Akademi.

Pavio, A., & Begg, I. (1981). *Psychology of language*. Prentice-Hall.

Pavlik, J., & Bridges, F. (2013). The emergence of augmented reality (AR) as a storytelling medium in journalism. *Journalism & Communication Monographs, 15*(1), 4–59. doi:10.1177/1522637912470819

Peniche, A., Diaz, C., Helmuth, T., & Paramo, G. (2012). *Proceedings from the WSEAS International Conference on Computer Engineering and Applications*. WSEAS.

Pennycook, A. (2017). *La política cultural del inglés como lengua internacional*. Taylor and Francis.

Perez-Fuster, P. (2017). *Enhancing skills in individuals with Autism Spectrum Disorders through technology-mediated interventions* (Doctoral dissertation). University of Valencia.

Pérez-López, D., & Contero, M. (2013). Delivering educational multimedia contents through an augmented reality application: A case study on its impact on knowledge acquisition and retention. *TOJET: The Turkish Online Journal of Educational Technology, 12*(4).

Perez-Lopez, D., & Contero, M. (2013). Delivering educational multimedia contents through an augmented reality application: A case study on its impact on knowledge acquisition and retention. *TOJET: The Turkish Online Journal of Educational Technology, 12*(4), 19–28.

Perrow, C. (1984). *Normal accidents: living with high risk technologies*. New York: Basic Books.

Peterson, M. (2010). Computerized games and simulations in computer-assisted language learning: A meta-analysis of research. *Simulation & Gaming*, *41*(1), 72–93. doi:10.1177/1046878109355684

Pictogram Room. (n.d.). Retrieved July 20, 2007, from http://www.pictogramas.org

Portalés, C., Gimeno, J., Casas, S., Olanda, R., & Giner, F. (2016). *Interacting with augmented reality mirrors. In Handbook of Research on Human-Computer Interfaces* (pp. 216–244). Developments, and Applications. doi:10.4018/978-1-5225-0435-1.ch009

Presman, R. (2010). *Ingenieria del Software*. McGraw-Hill.

Pressman, R. (2002). Ingeniería de software, un enfoque práctico. McGraw Hill.

Prosperity4All. (n.d.). *Home page of the Prosperity4All project*. Retrieved July 20, 2007, from http://www.prosperity4all.eu/

Rabbi, I. & Ullah, S. (2013). A survey on augmented reality challenges and tracking. *Acta Graphica znanstveni časopis za tiskarstvo i grafičke komunikacije, 24*(1-2), 29-46.

Rabbi, I., & Ullah, S. (2013). A survey on augmented reality challenges and tracking. *Acta Graphica znanstveni časopis za tiskarstvo i grafičke komunikacije, 24*(1-2), 29-46.

Ramzali, N., Lavasani, M. R. M., & And Ghodousi, J. (2015). Safety barriers analysis of offshore drilling system by employing Fuzzy Event Tree Analysis. *Safety Science*, *78*, 49–59. doi:10.1016/j.ssci.2015.04.004

Raynor, M. E. (1998). That vision thing: Do we need it? *Long Range Planning*, *31*(3), 368–376. doi:10.1016/S0024-6301(98)80004-6

Read, T., & Nick, T. (1998). *Not Rocket Science? Problem-solving and Crime Reduction*. Home Office.

Reenskaug, T., & Coplien, J. (2009). The DCI Architecture: A New Vision of Object-Oriented Programming. *Artima Developer Best Practices in Enterprise Software Development*.

Reichow, B. (2011). Development, procedures, and application of the evaluative method for determining evidence-based practices in autism. In B. Reichow, P. Doehring, D. V. Cicchetti, & F. R. Volkmar (Eds.), *Evidence-based practices and treatments for children with autism* (pp. 25–39). New York, NY: Springer. doi:10.1007/978-1-4419-6975-0_2

Reyes, R. G., Olmos, P. S., & Hernández, H. M. (2016). Private Label Sales through Catalogs with Augmented Reality. In Handbook of Research on Strategic Retailing of Private Label Products in a Recovering Economy. IGI Global.

Rice, R. (2011, Jan 20). *The Augmented Reality Hype Cycle*. Retrieved January 20, 2011, from url: http://www.sprxmobile.com/the-augmented-reality-hype-cycle

Rice, A. L. (2013). *The Enterprise and Its Environment: A System Theory of Management Organization*. London: Psychology Press.

Riddle, R. S., Wasser, D. E., & McCarthy, M. (2017). Touching The Human Neuron: User-Centric Augmented Reality Viewing and Interaction of in-vivo Cellular Confocal Laser Scanning Microscopy (CLSM) Utilizing High Resolution zStack Data Sets for Applications in Medical Education and Clinical Medicine Using GLASS and Motion Tracking Technology. *The Journal of Biocommunication*, *41*(1), 22–31. doi:10.5210/jbc.v41i1.7563

Riobó Iglesias, J., Aznar Relancio, S., Gracia Bandrés, M. A., & Romero San Martín, D. (2015). *TecsMedia: Análisis de tendencias: Realidad Aumentada y Realidad Virtual. División de Tecnologías Multimedia del Instituto Tecnológico de Aragón*. ITAINNOVA.

Rodríguez Escalona Mirelle. (2017). *Autism*. Retrieved from http://www.academia.edu/14904027/A_UTISMO

Rodriguez Morales, G. (1988). *Industrial design manual*. Gustavo.

Rodríguez, C. (2017). Animation studies in Colombia: Acrobatics in the Timeline. Pontificia Universidad Javeriana.

Roesner, F., Kohno, T., & Molnar, D. (2013). Security and privacy for augmented reality. *Communications of the AMC,* 1-10.

Rogers, S. J., & Dawson, G. (2010). *Early start Denver model for young children with autism: Promoting language, learning, and engagement*. New York, NY: Guilford Press.

Rogers, W. P. (1986). *Report of the presidential commission on the space shuttle challenger accident*. Washington, DC: US Government Printing Office.

Rollo, M., Bucher, T., Smith, S., & Collins, C. (2017). ServAR: An augmented reality guide to the serving of food. *International Journal of Behavioral Nutrition*, *14*(65), 1–10. PMID:28499433

Roozenburg, N. F. M., & Eekels, J. (1996). *Product Design: Fundamentals and Methods*. Chichester, UK: John Wiley and Sons, Ltd.

Rosch, E. (1975). Cognitive Representations of Semantic Categories. *Journal of Experimental Psychology*, *104*(September), 192–233.

Sampaio, D., & Almeida, P. (2016). Pedagogical Strategies for the Integration of Augmented Reality in ICT Teaching and Learning Processes. *Procedia Computer Science*, *100*, 894–899. doi:10.1016/j.procs.2016.09.240

Samsung. (2017). *The Look at Me Project*. Retrieved from http://pages.samsung.com/ca/whoeyeam/English/

Sánchez, J. L. G., Zea, N. P., & Gutiérrez, F. L. (2009). From Usability to Playability: Introduction to Player-Centred Video Game Development Process. *Proc. of 1st Int. Conf. HCD 2009.*

Savioja, P., Järvinen, P., Karhela, T., Siltanen, P., & Woodward, C. (2007). *Developing an Augmented Reality Tool for Modern Maintenance Work.* Paper presented in 12th International Conference on Human- Computer Interaction, Beijing, China.

Schall, G., Wagner, D., Reitmayr, G., Taichmann, E., Wieser, M., Schmalstieg, D., & Hoffmann-Wellenhof B. (2008). Global pose estimation using multi-sensor fusion for outdoors augmented reality. *Proc. 8th IEEE International Symposium on Mixed and Augmented Reality (ISMAR 2008)*, 153-162.

Schall, G., Mendez, E., & Schmalstieg, D. (2008). Virtual redlining for civil engineering in real environments. *Proc. The 7th IEEE International Symposium on Mixed and Augmented Reality (ISMAR 2008)*, 95-98. 10.1109/ISMAR.2008.4637332

Schmitz, B., Specht, M., & Klemke, R. (2012). An analysis of the educational potential of augmented reality games for learning. *Proceedings of the 11th world conference on mobile and contextual learning*, 140-147.

Schoijet, M. (1993). Accidentes tecnológicos. *Ciencias*, *30*, 55–60.

Scott, C. E. (2009). *A comparative case study of the characteristics of science, technology, engineering, and mathematics (STEM) focused high schools* (PhD Thesis). George Mason University.

Seedhouse, P., Preston, A., Oliver, P., Jackson, D., Heslop, P., Balaam, M., ... Kipling, M. (2014). The European Digital Kitchen Project. *Bellaterra Journal of Teaching & Learning Language and Literature*, *7*(1), 1–16.

Sengupta, P., & Wilensky, U. (2009). Learning electricity with NIELS: Thinking with electrons and thinking in levels. *International Journal of Computers for Mathematical Learning*, *14*(1), 21–50. doi:10.100710758-009-9144-z

Senn, J. A. (2001). Analysis and design of information systems. McGraw Hill.

She, J. H., Wu, C., Wang, H., & Chen, S. (2009). Design of an e-learning system for technical Chinese courses using cognitive theory of multimedia learning. *Electronics and Communications in Japan*, *92*(8), 393–400. doi:10.1002/ecj.10204

Shelton, B. E., & Hedley, N. R. (2002). Using augmented reality for teaching earth-sun relationships to undergraduate geography students. Augmented Reality Toolkit. In *Proceedings of The First IEEE International Workshop* (pp. 8-21). IEEE. 10.1109/ART.2002.1106948

Shelton, B. E., & Hedley, N. R. (2004). Exploring a cognitive basis for learning spatial relationships with augmented reality. Technology, Instruction. *Cognition and Learning*, *1*(4), 323.

Sherman, W., & Craig, A. (2003). *Understanding Virtual Reality: Interface, Applications and Design.* Morgan Kaufmann Publishers.

Shin, D. H., & Dunston, P. S. (2008). Identification of application areas for augmented reality in industrial construction based on technological suitability. *Automation in Construction*, *17*(7), 882–894. doi:10.1016/j.autcon.2008.02.012

Shirazi, A., & Behzadan, A. H. (2015). Content Delivery Using Augmented Reality to Enhance Students' Performance in a Building Design and Assembly Project. *Advances in Engineering Education*, *4*(3), 1–24.

Silvera, D. H., Josephs, R. A., & Giesler, R. B. (2002). Bigger is better: The influence of physical size on aesthetic preference judgments. *Journal of Behavioral Decision Making*, *15*(3), 189–202. doi:10.1002/bdm.410

Skehan, P. (1998). *A cognitive approach to language learning*. Oxford, UK: Oxford University Press.

Slimani, A., Sbert, M., Boada, I., Elouaai, F., & Bouhorma, M. (2016). Improving Serious Game Design Through a Descriptive Classification: A comparation of Methodologies. *Journal of Theoretical and Applied Information Technology*, *92*(1), 130-143.

Slussareff, M., & Boháčková, P. (2016). Students as game designers vs. 'just' players: Comparison of two different approaches to location-based games implementation into school curricula. *Digital Education Review*, *29*, 284–297.

Smith, K. (2011). Universal life: The use of virtual worlds among people with disabilities. *Universal Access in the Information Society*, *11*(4), 387–398. doi:10.100710209-011-0254-8

Solak, E., & Cakir, R. (2016). Investigating the role of augmented reality technology in the language classroom. *Croatian Journal of Education*, *18*(4), 1067–1085.

Soomerauer, P., & Muller, O. (2014). Augmented reality in informal learning environments: A field experiment in a mathematics exhibition. *Computers & Education*, *79*, 59–68. doi:10.1016/j.compedu.2014.07.013

Stair, R., & Reynolds, G. (2008). *Fundamentals of information systems*. Course Technology Press.

Steele, J., Hedberg, J., Fitzgerald, R., Munnerley, D., Bacon, M., & Wilson, A. (2012). Confronting an augmented reality. *Research in Learning Technology*, *20*(1), 39–48.

Steven, M. (2017). Virtual Reality. Cambridge University Press.

Strickland, D., Marcus, L. M., Mesibov, G. B., & Hogan, K. (1996). Brief report: Two case studies using virtual reality as a learning tool for autistic children. *Journal of Autism and Developmental Disorders*, *26*(6), 651–659. doi:10.1007/BF02172354 PMID:8986851

Stringhini, M. (2011). *High Level Computer Vision using OpenCV*. Sao Paulo, Brazil: Faculdade de Computacao e Informatica, Universidade Presbiteriana Mackenzie.

Sutherland, C., Hashtrudi-Zaad, K., Sellens, R., Abolmaesumi, P., & Mousavi, P. (2013). An augmented reality haptic training simulator for spinal needle procedures. *IEEE Transactions on Biomedical Engineering*, *60*(11), 3009–3018. doi:10.1109/TBME.2012.2236091 PMID:23269747

Takacs, G., Chandrasekhar, V., Tsai, S. S., Chen, D. M., Grzeszczuk, R., & Girod, B. (2010). Unified real-time tracking and recognition with rotation-invariant fast features. *Proc. The Twenty-Third IEEE Conference on Computer Vision and Pattern Recognition*, 934-941. 10.1109/CVPR.2010.5540116

Tang, A., Owen, C., Biocca, F., & Mou, W. (2003). Proceedings from CHI '03*: The Conference on Human Factors in Computing Systems*. Fort Lauderdale, FL: ACM.

Tanner, P., Karas, C., & Schofield, D. (2014). Augmenting a Child's Reality: Using Educational Tablet Technology. *Journal of Information Technology Education: Innovations in Practice*, *13*, 45-55.

Techakosit, S., & Wannapiroon, P. (2015). Connectivism learning environment in augmented reality science laboratory to enhance scientific literacy. *Procedia: Social and Behavioral Sciences*, *174*, 2108–2115. doi:10.1016/j.sbspro.2015.02.009

Temkin, B., Acosta, E., Malvankar, A., & Vaidyanath, S. (2006). An Interactive Three-Dimensional Virtual Body Structures System for Anatomical Training Over the Internet. *Clinical Anatomy (New York, N.Y.)*, *19*(3), 267–274. doi:10.1002/ca.20230 PMID:16506202

Thomas, I., Int Panis, L., & Vandenbulcke, G. (2017). On the location of reported and unreported cycling accidents: A spatial network analysis for Brussels. *Cybergeo, European Journal of Geography*, *818*, 1-22.

Thomas, B., Close, B., Donoghue, J., Squires, J., De Bondi, P., & Piekarski, W. (2002). First Person Indoor/Outdoor Augmented Reality Application: ARQuake. *Personal and Ubiquitous Computing*, *6*(1), 75–86. doi:10.1007007790200007

Townsley, M., & Pease, K. (2001). *What makes a good SARA?* Merseyside Police.

Troughton-Smith. (2016). *Grace - Image exchange for people with verbal disabilities*. Academic Press.

Tsai, M., Liu, P., & Yau, N. (2013). Using electronic maps and augmented reality-based training materials as escape guidelines for nuclear accidents: An explorative case study in Taiwan. *British Journal of Educational Technology*, *44*(1), 18–21. doi:10.1111/j.1467-8535.2012.01325.x

Turna, Ö., Bolat, M., & Keskin, S. (2012, June). Interdisciplinary Approach: Music, Physics, Mathematics Example. *Proceedings of X. National Science and Mathematics Education Congress*.

Turner, H. L. (2010). *Quantification of product color preference in a utility function*. Masters Theses. 4780.

Turnipseed, D. (1994). The Relationship Between the Social Environment of Organizations and the Climate for Innovation and Creativity. *Creativity and Innovation Management*, *3*(3), 184–195. doi:10.1111/j.1467-8691.1994.tb00172.x

Tuscany. (2017). *Tuscany+, Application Aggregation AppAgg*. Retrieved from https://appagg.com/ios/travel/tuscany-849156.html

Uchiyama, H., & Marchand, E. (2012). Object detection and pose tracking for augmented reality: recent approaches. *18th Korea-Japan Joint Workshop on Frontiers of Computer Vision (FCV)*.

Ullman, D. G. (1992). *The mechanical design process* (Vol. 2). New York: McGraw-Hill.

Ullmer, B., & Ishii, H. (2000). Emerging frameworks for tangible user interfaces. *IBM Systems Journal*, *39*(3-4), 915-931.

UML. (2005). *To OMG's Unified Modeling Language*. Retrieved from http://www.uml.org/what-is-uml.htm

UNESCO. (1998). *Virtual environment of learning*. Retrieved January 11, 2017, from http://unesdoc.unesco.org/images/0022/002277/227729e.pdf

US. (1997). *Facilitator's Guide – The Mechanics of Problem Solving: Train-the-trainers. The Community Policing Consortium, supported by the US Department of Justice*. Office of Community Oriented Policing Services.

US-Chemical Safety & Hazard Investigation Board. (2007). *Investigation report-refinery explosion and fire*. Author.

Uva, A. E., Fiorentino, M., & Monno, G. (2011). Augmented reality integration in product development. *Proceedings of the International conference on Innovative Methods in Product Design*, 73-79.

Uva, A. E., Cristiano, S., Fiorentino, M., & Monno, G. (2010). Distributed design review using tangible augmented technical drawings. *Computer Aided Design*, *42*(5), 364–372. doi:10.1016/j.cad.2008.10.015

Vacchetti, L., Lepetit, V., & Fua, P. (2004). Combining Edge and Texture Information for Real-Time Accurate 3D Camera Tracking. *Proceedings of the Third IEEE and ACM International Symposium on Mixed and Augmented Reality*, 48-57. 10.1109/ISMAR.2004.24

Valle, R. (2014). *Teaching with augmented reality is here*. Retrieved from http://edtechreview.in/trends-insights/insights/1503-teaching-with-augmented-reality-it-s-here

Vallino, J. R. (1998). *Interactive augmented reality* (Doctoral dissertation). University of Rochester.

Van Vuuren, W. (2000). *Organizational Failure: An Exploratory Study in the Steel Industry and the Medical Domain* (PhD Thesis). Institute for Business Engineering and Technology Application, The Netherlands.

Vanvuchelen, M., Roeyers, H., & Weerdt, W. (2007). Nature of motor imitation problems in school-aged boys with autism: A motor or a cognitive problem? En Autism: An International. *Journal of Research Practice*, *11*(3), 225–240. PMID:17478576

Vassigh, S., Elias, A., Ortega, F. R., Davis, D., Gallardo, G., Alhaffar, H., . . . Rishe, N. D. (2016). *Integrating Building Information Modeling with Augmented Reality for Interdisciplinary Learning*. International Symposium on Mixed and Augmented Reality (ISMAR-Adjunct), Mérida, Mexico. 10.1109/ISMAR-Adjunct.2016.0089

Vate-U-Lan, P. (2012). Una realidad aumentada 3D Pop-Up Book: El desarrollo de un proyecto multimedia para la enseñanza del idioma inglés. *2012 IEEE Conferencia Internacional sobre Multimedia y Expo*.

Vázquez, R. S., & Salinas Alguacil, L. N. (2013). Arquitectura organizacional para soluciones empresariales de software. *Revista Cubana de Ciencias Informáticas, 7*(3), 1-13. Retrieved from http://scielo.sld.cu/scielo.php?script=sci_arttext&pid=S2227-18992013000300001&lng=es&tlng=es

Veryzer, R. W. Jr, & Hutchinson, J. W. (1998). The influence of unity and prototypicality on aesthetic responses to new product designs. *The Journal of Consumer Research*, *24*(4), 374–394. doi:10.1086/209516

Vesely, W. E., Goldberg, F., Roberts, N. H., & Haasl, D. F. (1981). *Fault Tree Handbook.* Washington, DC: D.C. Nuclear Regulatory Commission.

Von Bertalanffy, K. L. (1969). General system theory: Foundations, development, applications (rev. ed.). New York: George Braziller.

Vuforia Documentation Qualcomm. (2017). Retrieved from https://www.qualcomm.com/products/vuforia

VUMS. (n.d.). *Home page of the VUMS project*. Retrieved July 20, 2007, from http://vums.it.gr/

Wadle, M. (2016). *Update: Fire at the North Harbor in Ludwigshafen. News Release*. BASF.

Wagner, D., & Barakonyi, I. (2003, October). Augmented reality kanji learning. In *Proceedings of the 2nd IEEE/ACM International Symposium on Mixed and Augmented Reality* (p. 335). IEEE Computer Society. 10.1109/ISMAR.2003.1240747

Walsh, A. (2011). Blurring the boundaries between our physical and electronic libraries: Location aware technologies; QR codes and RFID tags. *The Electronic Library*, *29*(4), 429–437. doi:10.1108/02640471111156713

Wang, X., & Dunston, P.S. (2007). Design, Strategies, and Issues Towards an Augmented Reality-Based Construction Training Platform. *Journal of information technology in construction (ITcon), 12*, 363-380.

Wang, H. Y., Liu, G. Z., & Hwang, G. J. (2017). Integrating socio-cultural contexts and location-based systems for ubiquitous language learning in museums: A state of the art review of 2009-2014. *British Journal of Educational Technology, 48*(2), 653–671. doi:10.1111/bjet.12424

Wang, L. S., Kim, M. J., Love, P. E. D., & Kang, S. C. (2013). Augmented Reality in built environment: Classification and implications for future research. *Automation in Construction, 32*, 1–13. doi:10.1016/j.autcon.2012.11.021

Wang, Y. F., Petrina, S., & Feng, F. (2017). VILLAGE-Virtual immersive language learning and gaming environment: Immersion and presence. *British Journal of Educational Technology, 48*(20), 431–450. doi:10.1111/bjet.12388

Wass, S. V., & Porayska-Pomsta, K. (2013). The uses of cognitive training technologies in the treatment of autism spectrum disorders. *Autism, 18*(3), 1–21. PMID:24129912

Webel, S., Bockholt, U., Engelke, T., Gavish, N., Olbrich, M., & Preusche, C. (2013). An augmented reality training platform for assembly and maintenance skills. *Robotics and Autonomous Systems, 61*(4), 398–403. doi:10.1016/j.robot.2012.09.013

Weidenhausen, J., Knoepfle, Ch., & Stricker, D. (2003). Lessons learned on the way to industrial augmented reality applications, a retrospective on ARVIKA. *Computers & Graphics, 27*(6), 887–891. doi:10.1016/j.cag.2003.09.001

Weiser, M., Gold, R., & Brown, J. S. (1999). The origins of ubiquitous computing research at PARC in the late 1980's. *IBM Systems Journal, 38*(4), 693–696. doi:10.1147j.384.0693

West, D. (2012). *Digital schools*. Washington, DC: Brookings Institution Press.

Wimpory, D., Chadwick, P., & Nash, S. (1995). Musical interaction therapy for children with autism: An evaluation case study with a two year follow up. *Journal of Autism and Developmental Disorders, 25*(5), 541–552. doi:10.1007/BF02178299 PMID:8567598

Winkler, T., Herczeg, M., & Kritzenberger, H. (2002). Mixed reality environments as collaborative and constructive learning spaces for elementary school children. In *EdMedia: World Conference on Educational Media and Technology* (pp. 1034-1039). Association for the Advancement of Computing in Education (AACE).

Winn, W., Windschitl, M., Fruland, R., & Lee, Y. (2002). When does immersion in a virtual environment help students construct understanding. *Proceedings of International Conference of the Learning Sciences*, 497-503.

Wong, C., Odom, S. L., Hume, K. A., Cox, A. W., & Schultz, T. R. (2015, July). Evidence-Based Practices for Children, Youth, and Young Adults with Autism Spectrum Disorder: A Comprehensive Review. *Journal of Autism and Developmental Disorders, 45*(7), 1951–1966. doi:10.100710803-014-2351-z PMID:25578338

Woods, E., Billinghurst, M., Looser, J., Aldridge, G., Brown, D., Garrie, B., & Nelles, C. (2004, June). Augmenting the science centre and museum experience. *Proceedings of the 2nd international conference on Computer graphics and interactive techniques in Australasia and South East Asia*, 230-236. 10.1145/988834.988873

Woodward, C., Lahti, J., Rönkkö, J., Honkamaa, P., Hakkarainen, M., Jäppinen, J., ... Hyväkkä, J. (2007). Virtual and augmented reality in the Digitalo building project. *International Journal of Design Sciences and Technology*, *14*(1), 23–40.

WTC. (2017). *Technology For Smart Education.* Retrieved from www.webteamcorp.com

Wu, H., Lee, S., Chang, H., & Liang, J. (2013). Current status, opportunities and challenges of augmented reality in education. *Computers & Education*, *62*, 41–49. doi:10.1016/j.compedu.2012.10.024

Yang, M., & Liao, W. (2014). Computer-assisted culture learning in an online augmented reality environment based on free-hand gesture interaction. *Transactions on Learning Technologies*, *7*(2), 107–117. doi:10.1109/TLT.2014.2307297

Yang, X., Zhang, J., & Peracchio, L. A. (2010). Understanding the impact of self-concept on the stylistic properties of images. *Journal of Consumer Psychology*, *20*(4), 508–520. doi:10.1016/j.jcps.2010.06.012

Yang, Y. F. (2011). Engaging students in an online situation learning language environment. *Computer Assisted Language Learning*, *24*(2), 181–198. doi:10.1080/09588221.2010.538700

Yonglei, T., & Chenho, K. (2003). Formal definition and verification of data flow diagrams. *Journal of Systems and Software*, *16*, 29–36.

Yoon, S., Steinmeier, C., Wang, J., & Tucker, S. (2011). Learning science through knowledge-building and augmented reality in museums. In *Proceedings of CSCL2011* (*Vol. 1*, pp. 9-16). Academic Press.

Yu, D., Jin, J. S., Luo, S., & Lai, W. (2010). A useful visualization technique: a literature review for augmented reality and its application, limitation and future direction. In M. L. Huang, Q. V. Nguyen, & K. Zhang (Eds.), *Visual information communication* (pp. 311–337). New York: Springer.

Yuen, S., Yaoyuneyong, G., & Johnson, E. (2011). Augmented reality: An overview and five directions for AR in education. *Journal of Educational Technology Development and Exchange*, *4*(2), 119–140.

Zagoranski, S., & Divjak, S. (2003). Use of augmented reality in education. *EUROCON Computer as a Tool The IEEE Region*, *8*(2), 339–342. doi:10.1109/EURCON.2003.1248213

Zak, E. (2014). Do You Believe in Magic? Exploring the Conceptualization of Augmented Reality and its Implications for the User in the Field of Library and Information Science. *Information Technology and Libraries*, *33*(4), 23–50. doi:10.6017/ital.v33i4.5638

Zendjebil, I., Ababsa, F.-E., Didier, J.-Y., Vairon, J., & Frauciel, L. (2008). Outdoor Augmented Reality: State of the Art and Issues. *10th ACM/IEEE Virtual Reality International Conference (VRIC 2008)*, 177-187.

Zhou, F., Duh, H. B. L., & Billinghurst, M. (2008). Trends in augmented reality tracking, interaction and display: a review of ten years of ISMAR. *7th IEEE and ACM international symposium on mixed and augmented reality (ISMAR 2008).*

Zhu, E., Hadadgar, A., Masiello, I., & Zary, N. (2014). Augmented reality in healthcare education: An integrative review. *PeerJ*, *2*(469), 2–17. PMID:25071992

Zoellner, M. (2009). An Augmented Reality Presentation System for Remote Cultural Heritage Sites. In *Proceedings of the 10th International Symposium on Virtual Reality, Archaeology and Cultural Heritage.* University of Malta.

Zyda, M. (2005). *From visual simulation to virtual reality to games.* IEEE Computer Society.

About the Contributors

Mustafa Serkan Abdusselam is an assistant professor at Giresun University. His research focuses on the use of Augmented Reality in learning and education.

Sanluis-Ramírez Ariel, Computer Engineer certified in PSP (Personal Software Process) specialized in web development Full Stack. Co-author of Aura: Application in Augmented Reality for the learning of children with autism. The areas in which they are developed professionally are Databases, Development of hybrid applications, development of embedded systems and research in the improvement of the UX.

Sergio Casas-Yrurzum has a master's degree in Computer Engineering and also a bachelor's degree in Telecommunications Engineering - Telematics Specialty. He received the Spanish National Award on University Studies in 2008. He received his PhD in Computational Mathematics at the University of Valencia in 2014. He works as a senior researcher in the Robotics Institute (IRTIC) of the University of Valencia, where he is also a part-time professor at the School of Engineering (ETSE). His expertise is in the simulation field with special focus on Virtual Reality, Augmented Reality and motion cueing.

Gerardo Herrera is the responsible of the Autism & IT Group at the IRTIC Technological Institute of the University of Valencia (Spain). He has published a number of papers on IT for people at risk of exclusion, including in high impact scientific journals such as ACM-Tochi, Presence Journal (MIT Press) and Autism (AIJRP from Sage Publications). He is currently the project coordinator of two EU Erasmus+ project (strategic partnerships in the field of education): SMART-ASD (2015-2017): "Enhancing Communication And Learning With Tablets, Smartphones And Smartwatches In Students With Autism Spectrum Disorders And/Or Learning Difficulties" and AMUSE (2016-2018): Autism in Mainstream Units in Schools across Europe: Identification and dissemination of best practice.

Marva Angélica Mora Lumbreras is Professor of the Degree in Computer Engineering and Postgraduate in Computing and Electronics at the Autonomous University of Tlaxcala (UAT), obtained a doctorate in Computer Science by the University of the Americas with Magna mention Cum Laude, had a Master's degree in Science with a specialization in Computer Systems by the University of the Americas, Puebla with Cum Laude and a Bachelor's degree in Computer Engineering from the Autonomous University of Tlaxcala. She is a PROMEP Profile since 2002, as well as Editor of the Iztatl Computación Magazine of the UAT. Dr. Marva has published articles indexed and refereed nationally and internationally in the areas of Virtual Reality and Augmented Reality. In addition to authoring books such as "Advances in Distributed and Intelligent Systems", "Algorithm a Competency-Based Approach" published in 2013, "Big Data, Virtual Educational Technology" published in 2015 and "IT Technologies" published in 2016, works edited by UAT. In July of 2017 published the book Virtual History of Quetzalcoatl with the Editorial Academic Spanish EAE.

Méndez-Trejo María de Lourdes, Computer Engineer, PSP certified (Personal Software Process), Co-Author of Aura Augmented Reality Application for the learning of children with autism. The areas in which she develops professionally are: in Database, Webmaster and administrator of courses Institutional Moodle of FCByT. Interests, in the development of innovative applications that help the education and be part of technological and research projects.

Raymundo Ocaña studied his degree in the Autonomous University of the State of Mexico within the educational program of Industrial Design, obtaining his title in 1993 with the project "Cranial Subjection System for necropsies", which was endorsed by the Director of the Service DF Medical Examiner. In 1998 he concluded the Specialty in "Strategic Design of Industrial Products" also within the UAEM. In December 2004, he obtained a Master's Degree in Education from the Universidad Franco Mexicana, and in 2011 he earned a PhD in Education from the Universidad Abierta de Tlaxcala. In the area of teaching, he has been a full-time professor in the UAEM's industrial design education program since 1993, obtaining recognition in the year 2005 as Profesor Perfil PROMEP. He has participated as a member of the Curricular Committee of the Faculty of Architecture and Design and Member of the Institutional Network of Curricular Innovation. Likewise, he has held the positions of Academic Coordinator of the degree in Industrial Design (1996-2005), responsible for the Institutional Tutoring Program (ProInsTA 2002-2003) and Assistant Academic Director (2005 to 2013). In 2015 he published the book "The sketch, basic tool of design" and, at the beginning of 2016, he joined the Committee of Architecture, Design and Urbanism of the CIEES (Interinstitutional Committees for the Evaluation of Higher Education) as an Evaluation Fellow. Finally, on November 30 of that year, he is appointed by the H. University Council of the UAEM as Director of the University Center UAEM Zumpango for the period 2016-2020.

Samuel Olmos Peña was born in Mexico City. He obtained his both PhD in Systems Engineering and a Master of Science in Systems Engineering in the National Polytechnic Institute. In both graduation exams he graduated with honors. He received the award as the best student of generation in the PhD and Master studies. His expertise area is about risk analysis/accidents, public safety and natural disasters. From 2012, he is an academic staff member at the Autonomous University of the State of Mexico in Computer Engineering Department. He is a researcher fellow of the research group "Safety accidents, Risk and Reliability Analysis" (SARACS; www.saracs.com.mx) and at the Mexican Researchers System.

Cristina Portalés Ricart (PhD in Geodesy and Cartography, 2008) is senior researcher at the Institute of Robotics and Information and Communication Technologies at Universitat de València (Spain), where she previouslyhad been a Juan de la Cierva post-doc fellow. She formerly graduated with a double degree: Engineer in Geodesy and Cartography from the Universidad Politécnica de Valencia (Spain) and MSc in Surveying and Geoinformation from Technische Universität Wien (Austria). Afterwards she was a PhD research fellow at the Mixed Reality Laboratory of the University of Nottingham (UK, 2005) and at the Interaction and Entertainment Research Centre of the Nanyang University of Singapore (Singapore, 2006). She was the first woman to receive the best paper EH Thompson Award, given by the Remote Sensing and Photogrammetry Society (2010). From 2011-2012 she worked at AIDO (technological institute of Optics, Colour and Imaging), being primarily involved in the technical management of the FP7 project SYDDARTA. She is the author of more than 50 scientific publications including international conferences, high impact journals, books and book chapters. Her current research interests are focused on geometric calibration, image processing, 3D reconstruction, multispectral imaging, HCI and augmented reality.

Omar Sánchez is Doctor of Science in Education Professor of the University Autonomous of the State of Mexico. Coordinator of research and studies advanced of the University Center UAEM Valley of Chalco (2017). Coordinator of the internal network of international cooperation RICI of the University Centre of UAEM Valley of Chalco (2016). Coordinator of the Office of open knowledge of the University Centre of UAEM Valley of Chalco. (2016). Officer level magazine legacy Faculty of architecture and design Uaemex (2013).

Javier Sevilla is graduated in Computer Science from the Valencia Polytechnic University (Spain) in 1995. He worked at iSOCO, S.A where he researched the semantic web visualisation area, and participated in many international projects. He has managed many national and international IT projects related to disability. He is co-founder of the ADAPTA Foundation and researcher in the Autism & IT Group at the IRTIC Technological Institute of the University of Valencia (Spain). In these organizations, he is leading IT projects that apply the technology to improve the quality of life of people with autism.

Aubrey Statti is an affiliate faculty member for the Doctorate of Educational Psychology and Technology program at The Chicago School of Professional Psychology. She also serves as a contributing faculty member to Liberty University and Walden University. She holds an EdD in Educational Leadership and a MA in Professional Counseling. Dr. Statti's research interests include educational technology, digital literacy, rural education, and augmented reality.

Kelly Torres is the Department Chair for the Educational Psychology and Technology program at The Chicago School of Professional Psychology. Torres holds a Ph.D. in Learning and Cognition, a M.S. in Curriculum and Instruction, and a K-12 Florida teaching certificate. Her areas of research focuses on students' levels of engagement in online learning environments and learners' perceptions of their language learning experiences.

Ebru Turan Guntepe is a research assistant at Giresun University. Her research focuses on information and communication technologies, technologies integration, design of technologies-supported learning environments, and game-based learning environments.

Lucia Vera is graduated in Computer Science from the University of Valencia (Spain) in 1999. She received an extraordinary prize by the University of Valencia for the best academic record of the Computer Engineering promotion in 1999. Also she has an Executive Master in Project Management by the University of Valencia. She works as a senior researcher in the Robotics Institute (IRTIC) of the University of Valencia. Her expertise is in virtual characters and in the development of applications for simulation, training or learning mainly in the areas of Virtual and Augmented Reality.

Index

F

G

H

I

L

M

N

O

P

R

S

T

U

V

W

www.ingramcontent.com/pod-product-compliance
Lightning Source LLC
LaVergne TN
LVHW061550290926
849162LV00004B/960